Colonization and Domestic Service

This groundbreaking book brings together two key themes that have not been addressed together previously in any sustained way: domestic service and colonization. Colonization offers a rich and exciting new paradigm for analyzing the phenomenon of domestic labor by non-family workers, paid and otherwise. Colonization is used here in its broadest sense, to refer to the expropriation and exploitation of land and resources by one group over another, and encompassing imperial/extraction and settler modes of colonization, internal colonization, and present-day neocolonialism. Contributors from diverse fields and disciplines share new and stimulating insights on the various connections between domestic employment and the processes of colonization, both past and present, in a range of original essays dealing with Indonesian, Canadian Aboriginal, Australian Aboriginal, Pacific Islander, African, Jamaican, Indian, Chinese, Anglo-Indian, Sri Lankan, and 'white' domestic servants.

Victoria K. Haskins is an Associate Professor of History at the University of Newcastle, Australia.

Claire Lowrie is a Lecturer in History at the University of Wollongong, Australia.

Routledge International Studies of Women and Place

Series Editors: Janet Henshall Momsen and Janice Monk, University of California, Davis and University of Arizona, USA

1 **Gender, Migration and Domestic Service**
   Edited by Janet Henshall Momsen

2 **Gender Politics in the Asia-Pacific Region**
   Edited by Brenda S. A. Yeoh, Peggy Teo and Shirlena Huang

3 **Geographies of Women's Health**
   Place, Diversity and Difference
   Edited by Isabel Dyck, Nancy Davis Lewis and Sara McLafferty

4 **Gender, Migration and the Dual Career Household**
   Irene Hardill

5 **Female Sex Trafficking in Asia**
   The Resilience of Patriarchy in a Changing World
   Vidyamali Samarasinghe

6 **Gender and Landscape**
   Renegotiating the Moral Landscape
   Edited by Lorraine Dowler, Josephine Carubia and Bonj Szczygiel

7 **Maternities**
   Gender, Bodies and Spaces
   Robyn Longhurst

8 **Gender and Family among Transnational Professionals**
   Edited by Anne Coles and Anne-Meike Fechter

9 **Gender and Agrarian Reforms**
   Susie Jacobs

10 **Gender and Rurality**
   Lia Bryant and Barbara Pini

11 **Feminist Advocacy and Gender Equity in the Anglophone Caribbean**
   Envisioning a Politics of Coalition
   Michelle V. Rowley

12 **Women, Religion and Space in China**
   Islamic Mosques & Daoist Temples, Catholic Convents & Chinese Virgins
   Maria Jaschok and Shui Jingjun

13 **Gender and Wildfire**
   Landscapes of Uncertainty
   Christine Eriksen

14 **Colonization and Domestic Service**
   Historical and Contemporary Perspectives
   Edited by Victoria K. Haskins and Claire Lowrie

Also available in this series:

Full Circles
Geographies of Women over the Life Course
Edited by Cindi Katz and Janice Monk

'Viva'
Women and Popular Protest in Latin America
Edited by Sarah A Radcliffe and Sallie Westwood

Different Places, Different Voices
Gender and Development in Africa, Asia and Latin America
Edited by Janet Momsen and Vivian Kinnaird

Servicing the Middle Classes
Class, Gender and Waged Domestic Labour in Contemporary Britain
Nicky Gregson and Michelle Lowe

Women's Voices from the Rainforest
Janet Gabriel Townsend

Gender, Work and Space
Susan Hanson and Geraldine Pratt

Women and the Israeli Occupation
Edited by Tamar Mayer

Feminism / Postmodernism / Development
Edited by Marianne H. Marchand and Jane L. Parpart

Women of the European Union
The Politics of Work and Daily Life
Edited by Maria Dolors Garcia Ramon and Janice Monk

Who Will Mind the Baby?
Geographies of Childcare and Working Mothers
Edited by Kim England

Feminist Political Ecology
Global Issues and Local Experience
Edited by Dianne Rocheleau, Barbara Thomas-Slayter, and Esther Wangari

Women Divided
Gender, Religion and Politics in Northern Ireland
Rosemary Sales

Women's Lifeworlds
Women's Narratives on Shaping their Realities
Edited by Edith Sizoo

Gender, Planning and Human Rights
Edited by Tovi Fenster

Gender, Ethnicity and Place
Women and Identity in Guyana
Linda Peake and D. Alissa Trotz

Colonization and Domestic Service

Historical and Contemporary Perspectives

Edited by Victoria K. Haskins
and Claire Lowrie

NEW YORK AND LONDON

First published 2015
by Routledge
711 Third Avenue, New York, NY 10017

and by Routledge
2 Park Square, Milton Park, Abingdon, Oxon OX14 4RN

*Routledge is an imprint of the Taylor & Francis Group,
an informa business*

© 2015 Taylor & Francis

The right of the editor to be identified as the author of the editorial material, and of the authors for their individual chapters, has been asserted in accordance with sections 77 and 78 of the Copyright, Designs and Patents Act 1988.

All rights reserved. No part of this book may be reprinted or reproduced or utilized in any form or by any electronic, mechanical, or other means, now known or hereafter invented, including photocopying and recording, or in any information storage or retrieval system, without permission in writing from the publishers.

Trademark notice: Product or corporate names may be trademarks or registered trademarks, and are used only for identification and explanation without intent to infringe.

Library of Congress Cataloging-in-Publication Data

Colonization and domestic service : historical and contemporary perspectives / edited by Victoria K. Haskins and Claire Lowrie.
    pages cm. — (Routledge international studies of women and place ; 14)
    Includes bibliographical references and index.
 1. Household employees—History. 2. Women household employees—History. 3. Colonization—Social aspects. I. Haskins, Victoria K. (Victoria Katharine), 1967– editor of compilation. II. Lowrie, Claire, editor of compilation.
    HD8039.D5C65   2014
    331.7'6164091712—dc23   2014035537

ISBN: 978-1-138-01389-6 (hbk)
ISBN: 978-1-315-77228-8 (ebk)

Typeset in Sabon
by Apex CoVantage, LLC

All royalties from the sale of this book go to the
National Domestic Workers' Alliance.

Printed and bound in the United States of America by Publishers Graphics, LLC on sustainably sourced paper.

Contents

Figures   xi
Table   xiii
Acknowledgments   xv

Introduction: Decolonizing Domestic Service: Introducing
a New Agenda   1
VICTORIA K. HASKINS AND CLAIRE LOWRIE

1. An Historical Perspective: Colonial Continuities in
   the Global Geography of Domestic Service   19
   B. W. HIGMAN

PART I
Anxieties and Intimacies   41
VICTORIA K. HASKINS AND CLAIRE LOWRIE

2. Domesti-City: Colonial Anxieties and Postcolonial
   Fantasies in the Figure of the Maid   45
   SHIREEN ALLY

3. Settling In, From Within: Anglo-Indian 'Lady Helps'
   in 1920s New Zealand   63
   JANE MCCABE

4. 'Ah Look Afta De Child Like Is Mine': Discourses of
   Mothering in Jamaican Domestic Service, 1920–1970   79
   MICHELE A. JOHNSON

5. 'Always a Good Demand': Aboriginal Child Domestic Servants
   in Nineteenth- and Early Twentieth-Century Australia   97
   SHIRLEENE ROBINSON

6. Maids' Talk: Linguistic Containment and Mobility
   of Sri Lankan Housemaids in Lebanon   113
   FIDA BIZRI

7. Foreign Domestic Workers in Singapore: Historical and
   Contemporary Reflections on the Colonial Politics of Intimacy   131
   MARIA PLATT

PART II
Domination and Resistance   149
VICTORIA K. HASKINS AND CLAIRE LOWRIE

8. 'Strictly Legal Means': Assault, Abuse and the Limits of
   Acceptable Behavior in the Servant–Employer Relationship
   in Metropole and Colony 1850–1890   153
   FAE DUSSART

9. Imperial Legacies and Neoliberal Realities: Domestic
   Worker Organizing in Postcolonial New York City   172
   ALANA LEE GLASER

10. Tactics of Survival: Images of Aboriginal Women
    and Domestic Service   182
    MICHAEL AIRD

11. 'I Would Like the Girls at Home': Domestic Labor and the
    Age of Discharge at Canadian Indian Residential Schools   191
    MARY JANE LOGAN MCCALLUM

12. White Mistresses and Chinese 'Houseboys': Domestic Politics in
    Singapore and Darwin from the 1910s to the 1930s   210
    CLAIRE LOWRIE

PART III
Legacies and Dreams   235
VICTORIA K. HASKINS AND CLAIRE LOWRIE

13. Baby Halder's *A Life Less Ordinary*: A Transition from
    India's Colonial Past?   239
    SWAPNA M. BANERJEE

14. From Our Own Backyard? Understanding UK Au Pair
    Policy as Colonial Legacy and Neocolonial Dream   256
    ROSIE COX

15. Taking Colonialism Home: Cook Island 'Housegirls'
    in New Zealand, 1939–1948   273
    CHARLOTTE MACDONALD

16. British Caribbean Women Migrants and Domestic Service in
    Latin America, 1850–1950: Race, Gender and Colonial Legacies   289
    NICOLA FOOTE

17. Contemporary Balinese Cruise Ship Workers, Passengers and
    Employers: Colonial Patterns of Domestic Service   309
    PAMELA NILAN, LUH PUTU ARTINI AND STEVEN THREADGOLD

18. A Contemporary Perspective: 'Picking the Fruit from the Tree':
    From Colonial Legacy to Global Protections in Transnational
    Domestic Worker Activism   328
    JENNIFER N. FISH

    Conclusion: Agency, Representation, and Subalternity: Some
    Concluding Thoughts   348
    VICTORIA K. HASKINS AND CLAIRE LOWRIE

    Contributors   351
    Index   355

Figures

2.1 Queen Sophie in Newtown, Johannesburg, August 2010. Photo by Shireen Ally. 46

3.1 A group of Kalimpong emigrants with the Didsbury Family at the Didsbury residence, Wellington, in July 1937. Gammie Family Archives. 75

10.1 Sophie Mumming from Woorabinda, Fortitude Valley, c.1906. Photo by Roland Ruddle. neg68943, courtesy John Oxley Library, State Library of Queensland. 182

10.2 Katie Williams, Beaudesert, 1924. Photo by Peter Hyllisted. Courtesy Doris Yuke collection. 182

10.3 Katie, Lilly, & Clara Williams, c.1920. Photo by Peter Hyllisted. Courtesy Doris Yuke collection. 183

10.4 Evelyn Monkland at Barambah Aboriginal Settlement, c.1925. Photo from the Betty McKenzie collection. © Image courtesy of Queensland Museum. EH433. 184

10.5 Emma Sommerset with her daughters Eva and Doris and her employers' son, Brisbane, 1915–1920. Courtesy Doris Yuke collection. 185

10.6 Emma Sommerset with her daughters Eva and Doris and her employers' son, Brisbane, 1915–1920. Courtesy Doris Yuke collection. 185

10.7 Emma Sommerset with her daughters Eva and Doris, Brisbane, c.1914. Courtesy Doris Yuke collection. 185

10.8 Agnes Bell and members of the Daylight family, Cherbourg, 1940s. Courtesy Ted Williams. 186

10.9 Agnes Williams, Tamrookum, 1991. Photo by Michael Aird. 186

10.10 Dina Johnson with Nell and Bert Cameron, Moray Downs, 1905. Courtesy Bill Cameron. 187

10.11 Nell Cameron, Sydney, 1930s. Courtesy Bill Cameron. 187

xii *Figures*

10.12 Nell Cameron on verandah of the Bellevue Hotel, Brisbane, 1942. Courtesy Bill Cameron. 188
10.13 Nell Cameron being escorted to the opera by her employers' son, Brisbane, c.1949. Courtesy Bill Cameron. 188
10.14 Grace Jones, Teneriffe, 1992. Photo by Sharyn Rosewarne. Courtesy Queensland Newspapers. 189
12.1 Burns Philp Steamship Line between Singapore and Darwin. *Picturesque Travel*, Burns Philp and Company, no. 6, 1925. From the collections of the National Library of Australia. 213
12.2 'Chinese Man Servant with His European Master,' Singapore, 1908. Courtesy of the National Archives of Singapore. 215
12.3 'Chinese Staff Employed by Dr Gilruth. Ah Chow (Seated), Ah Bong (Table Boy), Ah How (Dobie) and House Boy,' Darwin, c.1912–1919. Gilruth Collection, Northern Territory Library. 216

Table

1.1　Domestic Workers by Former Colony/Metropole Type, c.2010.　23

Acknowledgments

This edited collection began life as a research symposium held in Newcastle, New South Wales, Australia, in July 2012, supported by the Faculty of Education and Arts and the Deputy Vice-Chancellor for Research at the University of Newcastle, Australia. The editors would like to acknowledge and thank all those wonderful scholars who took part then, as participants, chairs, or actively engaged audience members. We would especially like to thank our three keynote presenters, Mary Romero, Barry Higman, and Swapna Banerjee, whose inspirational words set the tone for both the event and the book to come. The active and collegial engagement of all of those who attended, many of whom had travelled great distances to attend at personal expense, and who had made their drafts available for pre-circulation, made the symposium the outstanding success it was. We wish to acknowledge too, the hard work and sheer competence of Kristy Rocavert and Camilla Fisher 'behind the scenes' to make it happen. We would also like to especially acknowledge and thank our colleague and co-convenor Pam Nilan for her involvement in the symposium, and in the development of this edited collection.

The process of putting together the complete manuscript has incurred many debts, firstly to our contributors who so graciously and professionally abided our lengthy rounds of submissions and revisions. We are deeply grateful to the many committed scholars that gave their time and energies to peer-reviewing the various chapters for us, ensuring that a multidisciplinary work like this could speak to a range of audiences and thus be truly interdisciplinary as well, and to those who gave advice in finding expert readers or for the direction of our collection overall: they include Al-Tamimi Huda, Marg Allen, Tracey Banivanua Mar, Eileen Boris, Bridget Brereton, Barbara Brookes, Chilla Bulbeck, Antoinette Burton, Kit Candlin, Adrian Carton, Indrani Chatterjee, Nupur Chaudhuri, Jacklyn Cock, Ann Curthoys, Ana Dragojlovic, Becky Elmhirst, Antoinette Fauve-Chamoux, Michael Fisher, Marie Francois, Mark Frost, Heather Goodall, Paula Hamilton, Pen Hetherington, Alison Holland, Liz Hutchinson, Margaret Jolly, Ray Jureidini, Amanda Kaladelfos, Doreen Lee, Helma Lutz, Julia Martinez, Doreen Mattingley, Janet Momsen, Tamara Mose Brown, Soumyen Mukherjee, Premilla

Nadasen, Unn Gyda Næss, Sebastian Nordhoff, Fiona Paisley, Katie Pickles, Lynette Russell, Raffaella Sarti, Carolyn Steedman, Frances Steel, Nicole Tarulevicz, Sarah Thomason, Myrna Tonkinson, Lara Vapnek, Angela Wanhalla, and Carol Williams. We also acknowledge the anonymous readers for Routledge, for their thoughtful and constructive suggestions in our shaping of this collection.

Our editor Max Novick at Routledge has been always available to offer friendly and helpful advice and assistance through the process. We are also very grateful indeed to Janet Henshall Momsen and Janice Monk for their interest in our collection, and their generous offer to publish it as part of their own Routledge series. And we would like to thank Emma L. Hamilton and Emma Warren for their painstaking care as editorial assistants in helping us to prepare the final manuscript.

Finally, we wish to acknowledge and pay our deepest respects to domestic workers past and present, whose labors have been so often overlooked, yet so powerfully shape the world we all live in.

Introduction
Decolonizing Domestic Service: Introducing a New Agenda

Victoria K. Haskins and Claire Lowrie

What is the relationship between domestic service and colonization, historically and into the present? How does domestic service connect and intersect with the experiences of dispossession, displacement and expropriation, and the social and cultural upheavals that such processes generate? This collection of essays represents a concerted effort to map out the ongoing significance of colonization for shaping the patterns of domestic service. It is an undertaking that seems timely now. We have witnessed a resurgence in domestic labor on a global scale in recent years, only growing in strength and intensity, that has produced an explosion of literature reflecting on domestic work. The triumvirate of race, class and gender categories of analysis has fundamentally reoriented perspectives within multiple disciplines in the last three or four decades. Scholars now routinely acknowledge and address the significance of the lives of women, working people and people of color (domestic workers often belonging to all three categories), as well as recognizing the importance of structural relations these categories entail, in themselves and in combination. Add to this the vibrant dynamic of postcolonial or 'new imperial' studies, attending to the domestic and the intimate as sites of power in colonial, postcolonial and neocolonial projects, and we have all the ingredients for a new way of approaching domestic service.

For the purposes of creating this collection, we use the term 'domestic service' to refer to the work of an individual for another individual or family, in carrying out personal household tasks such as cleaning, cooking, childcare and carework in general. Whether paid or unpaid, voluntary or coerced, such work is regarded as distinct from that carried out by family members or friends for each other, because it is not a social or kinship obligation incumbent on the worker, nor a favor or kindness performed by them, but constitutes a definite 'service.' The fact that, in either context, such work has real economic value and impact does not change this distinction. While the terms 'service' and, especially, 'servant' are vexed and much out of favor today, for the sake of definition (and, when it comes to the historical period, to avoid being anachronistic) the term 'service' is more useful for articulating the focus of our attention. However, wherever possible and appropriate, those terms bearing less negative connotations, 'domestic work' and 'domestic workers,' are used in preference.

Our definition of colonization is broad (see Higman's opening chapter in this volume for a discussion of the different forms of colonization). However, we use it in the materialist and traditional sense, rather than the metaphorical, to refer to the expropriation and exploitation of land and/or resources by one group over another (or multiple other groups); and to encompass imperial and extraction modes of colonization and settler colonialism, internal colonization and slavery extracting resources from groups within. Also included in this definition are present-day forms of colonialism, including neocolonialism under systems of liberal globalization and international corporate capitalism, or what Anne McClintock (1995: 13) has deftly described as 'imperialism-without-colonies.'

This collection seeks to bring these two themes, domestic service and colonization, into a shared frame of analysis. By integrating diverse disciplinary perspectives in the process and blending transnational and local as well as historical and contemporary case studies, we aim to show the significance of the relationship between domestic service and colonization for the broader field of scholarship in both areas. Teasing out this relationship is more than just an academic exercise, however. In recent years, the scholarly theory and practice of 'decolonization,' emerging out of the field of Indigenous studies, primarily, as well as feminist postcolonial scholarship, has had a transformative impact on the way scholars see their accountability to their subjects and those people they write about (key works include Tuhiwai Smith 1999 and Mohanty 2003). Such an approach not only requires a self-reflexivity on the part of the researcher and an awareness of their subject position and location vis-à-vis those they research, but a commitment to centering the methods, theories, outlooks and agendas of the colonized. In this sense, decolonizing scholarship (and activism) goes beyond just reacting to and opposing colonial power, to generate positive and constructive new directions that are based upon local, if often interconnected, sources of culture and identity (Sium et al. 2012; Zavala 2013).[1] It would seem politically productive to bring to bear decolonizing research strategies on questions of domestic service both historical and contemporary, and this collection of essays represents a first tentative, interdisciplinary step in that direction.

To embark on any kind of decolonizing approach to domestic service, we must understand how domestic service and colonization are entwined. From an assortment of historical and contemporary studies, it is possible to distil an historical outline of domestic work in colonization, and likewise to trace something of a genealogy of scholarly insights into the subject. The following sections provide an overview of this history and scholarship, before elaborating on the essays in this collection and the insights they have to offer to a project of decolonizing domestic service.

DOMESTIC SERVICE AND COLONIZATION: AN HISTORICAL OUTLINE

The use of Native/Indigenous and imported labor, both slaves and indentured workers, as domestic servants appears as a constant in colonization from antiquity. In the modern period, one of the earliest historical references to colonial domestic labor is found in the anecdotes of a seventeenth-century traveler in the Caribbean, Richard Ligon. Ligon recounted a planter making a trade with his neighbor, of a pig in exchange for a English female servant: "tis an ordinary thing there, to sell their servants to one another for the time they have to serve; and in exchange, receive any commodities that are in the Island' (Ligon 1998: 59). He described his flirtations with the beautiful African slave mistresses of the planters there, and the use of Carib Indian men as footmen and the women as house slaves (Ligon 1998: 16–17, 54). As European colonization expanded into the Americas, Asia, the Pacific and Africa during the eighteenth and nineteenth centuries, colonizers drew on a combination of European and pre-existing traditions of household service (where such existed) to meet their requirements for domestic labor. In addition to enslaved local men, women and children, domestic workers were kidnapped and traded or otherwise recruited from other colonial territories to work as servants, alongside (sometimes) working-class Europeans brought out from the metropole. A retinue of household servants, often of multiple racial and cultural backgrounds and typically predominantly male, came to be not merely a status symbol for colonial Europeans, but metonymic for the entire imperial project. As colonial regimes became entrenched they also constructed various systems to 'reform' mixed-race and poor white children and women that helped supply local demands for domestic labor while dealing with the emergence of these problematic, indefinable populations. Settler colonies, which often deployed genocidal practices to clear the land of Indigenous peoples, likewise developed welfare and child rescue schemes that trained destitute settler girls as well as captive Indigenous and mixed-race girls and young women for service, while drawing upon their founding metropole for further importations of potential domestic workers recruited from the poor and indigent (Stoler 2001; Haskins 2007). (For examples of the types of 'civilizing' imperatives guiding the training of Indigenous girls for service in this volume see McCabe; McCallum; Robinson.) As these white settler colonies secured independence from their founding colonizer countries to greater or lesser degrees, beginning with the United States of America in the late eighteenth century and continuing throughout the nineteenth century, they further developed distinctive patterns of domestic service, drawing upon a combination of immigrant labor—both external and internal, in the case of African-American people migrating from the South after the Civil War—and 'rescued' labor of poor and Indigenous children and women.

From the end of the Second World War and accelerating into the 1960s, the era of decolonization saw marked changes in the patterns of domestic service, even as the occupation itself persisted. In the many former colonies, new national elites and an emergent middle-class wanting assistance in the home began employing domestic workers who shared the same ethnicity as themselves (see for example Johnson in this volume); or, increasingly, mobilized pre-existing and new international networks to bring in workers from other countries, typically also former colonies, as guest or migrant workers, who did not hold the same rights as other residents (on guest or migrant workers in this volume see Bizri; Cox; Foote; Glaser; Macdonald; Platt). In those countries where decolonization had followed a Marxist socialist model and domestic service was officially decried as 'private' and uncollectivized employment, such as Cuba and China, the occupation nonetheless continued (albeit much reduced in numbers and visibility) and by the end of the twentieth century had returned in full force even at these sites (Keremitsis 1992: 105; Smith and Padula 1996: 39–40; Fleites-Lear 2003: 296; Yan 2008: 19, 33–34). Formerly colonized countries including Indonesia, Sri Lanka and the Philippines have today become major sending-countries of migrant workers bound for employment in other nations, many of which are former colonies or colonial dependencies themselves (for examples in this volume see Bizri; Platt). At the same time, the former colonizer nations of Britain and western Europe, along with the United States, have also eagerly drawn upon a renewed supply of foreign workers to meet the increasing demand for domestic work, as legal and social barriers to middle-class women's employment across the occupational spectrum broke down in these countries. Today, in contrast to the colonial period, the occupation is predominantly female, although there has been something of a 're-masculinization' of domestic service in certain places (Ray 2000: 693–94; Sarti and Scrinzi 2010; Kilkey et al. 2013: 31–33). But with this re-appearance of domestic service have come frankly more disturbing reiterations of the kinds of power imbalances and excesses seen in the colonial period (including, not least, the trafficking of slaves and bonded workers). This dramatic and unpredicted revival of domestic service and its attendant problems has become something of a conundrum to historians and scholars of contemporary domestic work alike.

AN OVERVIEW OF THE SCHOLARSHIP

If incorporating colonizing (or de-colonizing) perspectives and analysis may help us to understand the nature of this revival of domestic service today, it is important to recognize that for many years, colonization did not figure in studies of domestic service at all. Throughout most of the twentieth century, beginning from the early work of American historian-cum-sociologist Lucy Maynard Salmon (1897), the occupation was considered a pre-industrial, feudal hangover destined for obsolescence in the modern world (Tinsman 1992). Although Salmon had mentioned the existence of Native American domestic servants in the early colonial period, albeit incidentally (1897: 49–51), the European and American scholarship that eventually followed in the second half of the twentieth century tended not to refer to colonized domestic workers at all, let alone to consider the broader context of colonization as any other than a side-aspect of domestic service histories (Davidoff 1974; Horn 1975; McBride 1974 and 1976; Branca 1975; Katzman 1978; Dudden 1983; Fairchilds 1984). Those who did refer, fleetingly, to colonization assumed that it too was on the way out. Emily Nett, for instance, characterized the servant as the 'genetic carrier' of an outdated colonial heritage even as she predicted the ultimate demise of the occupation in Latin America (1966: 444).

An early and rather idiosyncratic exception to the tendency to ignore the colonized domestic worker was the 1954 essay by J. Jean Hecht on *Continental and Colonial Servants in Eighteenth Century England*. A forerunner to his (1956) book-length argument about domestic servants' role as cultural transmitters of bourgeois values in England in the 1700s, Hecht's historical essay traversed the English elite's penchant for employing 'exotic' servants from Europe and from the colonies of the West Indies, America and the Indian subcontinent. In Hecht's view, servants imported from colonized climes were a fashionable luxury because of the prestige they offered in an age of Enlightenment and in the context of emergent theories of race: such servants 'made it possible to study one of the less civilized races at first hand' and were certain to attract attention for their "owners"' (Hecht 1954: 36). Hecht then drew explicit comparisons with this history and the then-present of his readers, the 1950s, arguing that with the disappearance of a 'supply of native domestics' (by which he meant English workers), employers were 'making strenuous efforts to bring replacements to England from abroad' (Hecht 1954: 55). Ironically, Hecht did not take into account the postwar decolonizing movements of his time that might have given another aspect to what he was observing around him as he wrote. Nor did Hecht remark upon the history of employing colonized peoples as domestic workers in their own countries or other colonies, which might have enriched his interpretation of the servant as a mediator of employers' cultural values downwards.

During the 1980s and early 1990s seminal works by sociologists, particularly Judith Rollins (1985) on Black American domestic workers and Mary Romero (1992) on Chicana domestic workers in the United States, and Jacklyn Cock's 1980 study of domestic service in South Africa under apartheid, fundamentally challenged the influential notion (McBride 1974: 63) that domestic service was essentially a transitional, 'life-stage' occupation for women undergoing processes of modernization. These writers, who emphasized the racial hierarchies and divisions that were reproduced and indeed intensified through domestic work, showed that for women of color at least, domestic work was not an avenue for social mobility but rather an ultra-exploitative occupational prison in which they, and their daughters, were confined. Issues of class and class relations had been embedded in the key historical works, especially those by Fairchilds (1984) and Davidoff (1974), the latter relating the historic exclusion of servants, as dependents, from full citizenship to the exclusion of women, thus powerfully drawing gender into the analysis. But it was these new sociological works that insisted that 'race' was a central category of analysis when looking at domestic service: indeed, that domestic service could be seen as 'the racial division of reproductive labor' (Glenn 1992: 6).

The occasional deployment of the internal colonialism model to explain the position of women domestic workers of color in the United States has never really gained traction (for instance, see Glenn 1985: 88–91; Chang 2000: 101–102, 107–10; see also Stoler 2001: 844–45 for discussion of the attempts to deploy this model in the US more generally). However, early regional studies of domestic service in colonial contexts suggested that integrating colonization into the analysis could complicate existing theories of domestic service. Elsa M. Chaney and Mary Garcia Castro compiled *Muchachas No More*, a groundbreaking interdisciplinary collection on domestic workers in Latin America and the Caribbean in 1989. The opening chapter by Elizabeth Kuznesof noted that the advent of domestic service in the Americas coincided with the beginning of Spanish colonization, and asserted that the racial and class divisions that were part and parcel of colonization resulted in the transformation of what had been, in traditional Spanish society, a 'respectable, transitional, educational, frequently affectionate, life-stage relationship of subordination to a family head, into a dead-end, low-status, nonregulated and often hostile condition of exploitation' (Kuznesof 1989: 17, 32).

In the same year that *Muchachas* was released, anthropologist Karen Tranberg Hansen published her comprehensive study of domestic work in Zambia (formerly Rhodesia) from 1900 to the then-present, the mid-1980s, declaring bluntly that 'the upward mobility thesis . . . has been useless' (1989: 20) in analyzing the occupation here, both in the colonial period and even after Independence. In the latter period black Zambians made up the largest single group of employers, but colonialist social practices that reproduced structures of inequality had persisted (225, 249). Describing domestic service as a 'fixture' of colonial society (29), Hansen argued that the twentieth-century Zambian experience highlighted how domestic service was no 'archaic remnant of feudal practices' but a labor process that could take many different forms, and was indeed increasing in advanced capitalist economies, including the US (*xii–xiii*). Hanson also focused directly on gender and sexuality, pointing out that colonial domestic service was shaped as a 'male institution' (83) and that Ester Boserup's theory that domestic service inevitably feminized with growth and modernization simply did not hold for many developing countries (259). Hansen's attention to the masculine nature of colonial domestic service has been underscored by other studies addressing the question of male domestic labor, in Africa in particular, but also in the Asia-Pacific region (van Onselen 1982: 1–73; Schmidt 1992: 155–79; Bujra 2000; Dickson-Waiko 2007; Martinez and Lowrie 2009; Martinez and Lowrie 2012; Lowrie 2013; see also Lowrie in this volume). Hansen further described not only how 'class condescension and racism' had combined in colonial servant-keeping practices (54) but also how domestic service had fulfilled a critical function in maintaining colonial rule:

> In domestic service, Africans were to become domesticated. To socialize Africans for subordinate roles in white households in the new political and economic order, colonial employers instituted a hierarchical labor process that accentuated the difference between themselves and their workers.
>
> (Hansen 1989: 30)

Hansen's work would intersect with a growing body of literature addressing the role of white women in colonization that pointed towards the significance of the home and household work for the construction and maintenance of the power relations that underpinned colonial rule (Knapman 1986; Chaudhuri and Strobel 1992; Ware 1992; for a recent historiographical overview, see Camiscioli 2013). With the emergence of the 'new imperial history' informed by postcolonial theory in the 1990s, domestic work, and domesticity more generally, came to be seen as critical to understanding the mechanisms of colonial power. Literary scholar Anne McClintock (1995) emphasized the deep imbrication of domesticity in imperialism, exploring a feminized and racialized 'cult of domesticity' that emerged in the Victorian era as a direct product of the imperial project. Historian Elsbeth Locher-Scholten (1998), looking at colonial domestic service relationships in the Dutch East Indies (present-day Indonesia), argued that the experience of nearness and dependence had in fact stimulated the colonialist ideology and practice of distance (144), and that the complex, contradictory way that native domestic servants were both included and excluded from the family relation is what made domestic service such a compelling trope for colonial relations more generally (152). Historical anthropologist Ann Laura Stoler further elaborated upon the inescapable tensions inherent in the colonial home, particularly in an essay she wrote with Karen Strassler on memory and Javanese domestic workers in the Dutch East Indies (Stoler and Strassler 2002). For Stoler, domestic work was not only of fundamental importance for the shaping of the boundaries between colonizer and colonized, but a 'dense transfer point of power' in the Foucauldian sense and a site for colonial governance (Stoler 2001: 831). In her emphasis on the colonial state's determination to control and manage emotional attachments within domestic service, Stoler's work has been transformative in generating something of an 'affective turn' in the scholarship on domestic work and colonialism.

The impact of such ethnographic and cultural approaches and methods has also gone some way to shifting the weighty Eurocentric bias in the scholarship. Locher-Scholten noted that domestic service was 'hardly a Western invention in Java' and that the colonizers had adapted themselves to pre-existing Indigenous hierarchies in which elaborate systems of domestic servitude played a key role (1998: 134). This awareness that domestic service has alternative and local histories informed the work of Swapna Banerjee on colonial Bengal. Tracing a genealogy of domestic service back far beyond the British period to the beginnings of recorded history on the subcontinent, Banerjee observed that here, unlike Hansen's Zambia, domestic service was not simply a colonial institution (2004: 34). At the same time she noted how the emergence of a Bengali middle-class in the colonial period was dependent on servant labor. Thus the cultural production of a distinctive 'cult of domesticity' in Bengal was based on locally constructed hierarchies of difference between mistresses and servants. Banerjee noted too the significance of the feminization of Indian domestic service (see also Banerjee's chapter in this volume). Attention to the formation and construction of class and other identities in present-day domestic service was central to Kathleen M. Adams and Sara Dickey's (2000) edited collection of anthropological essays on domestic service in a wide range of South and Southeast Asian settings, in which the surrounding society emerged as a key factor in shaping domestic service relations.

Despite the historical use of Indigenous labor in domestic service there is relatively little scholarship on the subject, past or present. This oversight seems to derive from the belief that Indigenous peoples, being originally hunter-gathers and subsistence agriculturalists or pastoralists with no traditions of domestic service at all, were not only averse to such work but were able to refuse it (for instance, see Roy 2000: 102).[2] In Latin American studies of domestic service, the participation of Indian people is often subsumed under broader categories such as the peasant or the *mestizo* domestic workers, with little attention given to their unique position as colonized Indigenous peoples (for some historiographical exceptions, see Burkett 1978; van Deusen 2012). However, studies in Australia where Indigenous peoples have a long history of working in the households of their colonizers, often under duress, highlight the importance of this arena for shaping settler colonial relations and histories.

In Australia, Aboriginal and Torres Strait Islander peoples only ever represented a tiny minority in the ranks of domestic workers and as a result, attention in more generalist studies has been directed instead to white and immigrant workers (Baxter 2005; Higman 2002, 2003; Hamilton 1985; Kingston 1975). However, Aboriginal histories from the 1970s began to address a history of enforced female Aboriginal domestic labor, that increasingly came to public awareness in Australia at the end of the twentieth century as part of the contested history of Aboriginal child removal (see, for example, Tucker 1977; Huggins 1987/88; Walden 1995; Read 1999; Haebich 2000; Hetherington 2002; Haskins 2005a; Robinson 2008; see also Robinson, and Aird in this volume). Victoria Haskins has elaborated how Aboriginal domestic service, as a 'contact zone' (Pratt 1993: 6–7) of Australian colonization, came to be a site of sustained government state intervention (Haskins 2001, 2009, 2012a); and she has recently extended a similar analysis to Native American domestic service history (Haskins 2012b). In some parts of northern Australia, as in Papua New Guinea, a colonial pattern of male Indigenous domestic employment also emerged (Martinez and Lowrie 2009; Dickson-Waiko 2007). Other studies of Indigenous domestic service, in Australia and elsewhere, have looked at the ways in which a gendered cultural control as well as labor exploitation was imposed upon, and resisted by Indigenous people, through domestic work relations, or have looked specifically at the role and impact of white women as employers in Indigenous domestic service (Knapman 1986; Tonkinson 1988; Bulbeck 1991; Huggins 1992; Sabbioni 1993; Haskins 2005b; Rodman et al. 2007; Jacobs 2007 and 2009: 329–69).

A late twentieth-century resurgence of domestic service in the form of global transnational migrations of domestic workers generated an explosion of incredibly rich scholarship in the social sciences (to mention a few of the major works: Momsen 1999; Anderson 2000; Chang 2000; Parreñas 2001; Hondagneu-Sotelo 2001; Ehrenreich and Hochschild 2002; Fauve-Chamoux 2004; Huang et al. 2005; Zimmerman et al. 2006; Cox 2006; Lutz 2008). These works, and other focused studies, centered on specific groups of migrant domestic workers or individual receiving nations, trace international transfers of labor and transnational links and dependencies, as well as the mechanisms by which nation-states (primarily the receiving countries) seek to control and manage this potentially destabilizing and politically sensitive movement (Cheng 2003: 168–69). Some writers attend directly to the colonial and postcolonial entanglements of this experience (Constable 1997; Chin 1998; Fish 2006; Ally 2009; Lan 2006), but there has been no comprehensive, focused analysis of how colonization, in particular, has shaped and continues to shape the revival we see today. There is, however, an emerging and buoyant scholarly interest in integrating postcolonial theoretical paradigms in the analysis of present-day transnational encounters in domestic work (for example, see Marchetti 2010; Klocker 2013; Chia 2013). There is no doubt that increasingly, both scholars and activists in the area of domestic work will be looking closely at theories of (post/neo)colonialism and colonization for the possibilities these can offer to understanding the present situation, at the same time as scholars of colonialism and colonization seek to grasp the significance of domestic service for such projects. It is in response to such multi-faceted and wide-ranging interest that this collection emerges.

COLONIZATION AND DOMESTIC SERVICE: AN INTERDISCIPLINARY CONVERSATION

In 2011, the editors of this collection, Victoria Haskins and Claire Lowrie, together with our colleague Pamela Nilan, invited proposals for an interdisciplinary edited collection of original research papers on the topic of colonization and domestic service. Selected papers were to be pre-circulated in draft form and workshopped in a research symposium to be held in Newcastle, on the east coast of Australia, in July 2012.

As it turned out we received many more proposals than we had expected, more than double the amount we could manage even in a two-day forum—a reflection of the importance of the subject and the interest that there is in it. There were some surprising gaps, it must be said. No papers were offered on African-American domestic service history (despite the debates sparked by the recent film, *The Help* [2011]); none, even more surprising, given the tradition in the literature, on Latin America, and only one dealing with the Middle East. However, those submitted did represent a significant range of disciplines, including sociology, geography, anthropology, Indigenous and women's studies, and history, and covered a diverse array of topics and regions.

In our selection of papers, we were guided by our aim of generating productive interdisciplinary conversations within the workshop. After an extensive process of peer-review and revisions—especially necessary because the interdisciplinary intent of the project meant that all essays required assessment from experts both within and outside their own discipline—many of the papers originally presented at the symposium appear here in revised form. In addition, several new papers were commissioned in place of papers that were withdrawn. Our final collection includes contributions from historians, sociologists and anthropologists, not to mention a geographer, a curator, and a linguist: the conversation here has, indeed, been genuinely interdisciplinary and collaborative.

The essays in this collection all reflect in different ways upon the relationship between colonization and domestic service, approaching the subject from diverse perspectives and methodologies. But several distinct (though entwined) broad themes emerged: the intimacies and anxieties that surround domestic service in colonizing contexts; the structures of domination and strategies of resistance which emerge in such contexts; and the legacies and contemporary reiterations of colonization in domestic service. These themes form the three sections of this collection: Part I. Anxieties and Intimacies; Part II. Domination and Resistance; and Part III. Legacies and Dreams.

In Part I, six essays highlight the complexities and emotional intensity of the intimacies and anxieties that underpin domestic service in colonial and postcolonial contexts. The following section, on domination and resistance, focuses upon the individual and collective forms of domestic worker resistance in the past and into the present, drawing out the connections between resistance to colonization, and the colonizing context in which resistance to abuse is enacted. In the third thematic part, the chapters revolve around the complex overlaying of past and present forms (or imagined forms) of colonial domestic service relationships. In nearly all cases, the individual essays reflect upon all of these themes and each could conceivably have been allotted to any section. We based our grouping of them on how they best intersect and engage with each other, to enrich our understanding of the complexities of the relationship between colonization and domestic service. An explanation of each of the three themes and how the chapters relate to them is provided by an introductory discussion at the beginning of each section.

Our decision to organize the collection along thematic lines is intended to highlight the commonalities in the domestic service encounter in different historical periods, sociopolitical contexts and geographic regions. We might have just as easily organized the chapters according to the type of colonial system under discussion, the time period, or by geography. The Asia-Pacific region features heavily in this collection, including chapters on nineteenth and early twentieth-century Australia (Aird; Lowrie; Robinson), twentieth-century New Zealand (Macdonald; McCabe), contemporary Indonesia (Nilan, Artini and Threadgold) and Singapore, both historically and today (Lowrie; Platt). The Caribbean features in several chapters, including Michelle Johnson's chapter on domestic work in twentieth-century Jamaica; Alana Lee Glaser on Caribbean, West African and Latina migrant workers in contemporary New York City; and Nicola Foote's study on British Caribbean workers in Latin America between 1850 and 1950. Domestic work in India in the contemporary and colonial period features in two chapters (Banerjee; Dussart) while Fida Bizri's chapter on Sri Lankan domestic workers in Lebanon deals with women from South Asia and the Horn of Africa working in the Middle East from the late twentieth century to the present. North America is the region under consideration in two chapters (McCallum on early twentieth-century Canada; Glaser on New York), Central America in another (Foote), and Southern Africa, specifically contemporary, post-apartheid South Africa, is the setting for Shireen Ally's chapter. Europe features in the chapters by Rosie Cox (on contemporary Britain and Eastern European workers) and Fae Dussart (on late nineteenth-century Britain).

In terms of the types of colonial systems that are represented in the volume, a number of chapters deal with white settler colonial nations, including South Africa, Australia, New Zealand, Canada and the United States as mentioned above. Others deal with what B. W. Higman, in this volume, terms 'Occupation Colonies,' including India, Sri Lanka, Singapore and Indonesia; then others with 'Settlement Colonies' (covering present-day Latin American and Caribbean nations); and one (Bizri) looking at a former French Mandate. It can be seen that domestic service in colonies and former colonies of the British empire is thus very strongly represented in this collection, in addition to the two chapters addressing domestic service within Britain itself (Dussart; Cox).

A wide variety of domestic workers and domestic service contexts, historical and contemporary, are covered in this volume. Chapters on Indigenous child servants working in Australian settler homes (Robinson; Aird) can be found alongside those that focus on today's Foreign Domestic Workers working in various postcolonial cities (Platt; Glaser; Bizri). The diverse spectrum of domestic service situations which are explored in this collection range from local housekeeper/nannies employed in Afro-Jamaican households (Johnson) to young Balinese men and women serving white working-class tourists on the high seas. The domestic workers featured in this volume include Bulgarian and Romanian au pairs working in today's English homes (Cox); Chinese 'houseboys' working for Anglo employers in colonial Singapore and Darwin (Lowrie); West Indian women workers in US expatriate homes in the Panama Canal Zone (Foote); and a West Bengali peasant woman finding her voice working in the cities of Delhi and Calcutta (Banerjee). Such myriad domestic service contexts and experiences highlight the complexities of the relationship between colonization and domestic service, historically and into the present.

As 'book ends' to both contain and showcase this immense diversity and scope within the themes, the opening chapter by B. W. Higman and the closing chapter by Jennifer N. Fish are global in their purview. Higman, an economic historian, grapples with the question of whether historical colonization has explanatory power in accounting for the patterns and extent of domestic labor as an occupation today in over a hundred different nations of the world. Were a correlation between the existence of a colonial past and the appearance of a significant domestic work sector today to be found, he suggests, it might indicate that domestic service today is indeed a legacy of colonization, or, less directly, a product of social, political and economic structures left behind by colonialism. Higman does find points of correlation, most notable being that those present-day states deriving from former imperial and colonial projects (whether as former colonies *or* as colonizer countries themselves) have altogether roughly double the numbers of domestic workers per capita than states without colonial histories. Yet sweeping generalizations are unsafe and within the larger picture there are many complicating factors and distinctions. For instance, within that group of states with vested colonial pasts, settler colonial nations have notably fewer domestic workers today compared to others, especially compared with former plantation colonies, where historically, forced labor was drawn upon to exploit the resources of the colonized country. Where continuities do exist, Higman argues that these need to be read not as inert legacies of the past that simply extend into the present, but as having been (re)produced out of present-day economic inequalities, which are in turn contingent upon historical specificities. Readers will find Higman's essay especially useful as an introduction to the definitions and varieties of both systems of colonization and kinds of domestic work situations that are addressed in this volume.

Sociologist Jennifer N. Fish's concluding chapter considers the struggle by domestic worker groups around the world today to have their rights as workers enshrined in international law and paid domestic labor recognized as a vital sector of the global economy. In 2011, as a result of their efforts, the International Labour Organization (a specialist UN body with its origins in the 1919 Versailles Peace Conference) established a convention setting out the first ever global standards for paid work in private homes, the Domestic Workers Convention. Signatory countries agree to take measures to ensure fair and decent working conditions and to prevent abuse and child labor exploitation in domestic employment: at this point in time (March 2014) ten ILO member states have now ratified the convention, with the European Commission, the executive body of the European Union, recently authorizing EU member states to ratify it. As Fish shows, the activists drew upon the transnational connections created within a new global economy of domestic work to organize and act collectively. She examines how contemporary transnational activists deliberately utilized and drew upon the historical imagery of colonized and enslaved domestic service, to underscore their demand for recognition, respect and standards of 'decent work' established through legal and official institutions, in a postcolonial global economy. A scholar-activist, Fish provides a finely drawn and nuanced analysis of contemporary transnational domestic worker activism that points towards a better future for domestic workers who have found their voice in solidarity.

In presenting this collection we do not argue that colonization is the only significant factor in understanding domestic service, nor even always the most important; nor do we contend that domestic service is the central mode of relations in analyzing colonization (although it may well be just that, in certain specific given circumstances). What we do assert, however, is the importance of a new agenda for re-conceptualizing both colonization and domestic service, as each critically and crucially informs and shapes the other.

NOTES

1. For the debate about how Indigenous agendas align with anti-racist and anti-(neo)colonial agendas in a global economy, see Lawrence and Dua (2005); Sharma and Wright (2008–09).
2. I use Indigenous here in the contemporary sense, to refer to those who trace their descent and cultural lineage from the original or first people/nations of any particular place or region, and who remain distinct from all other groups in that sense, within the larger social collective and nation.

REFERENCES

Adams, Kathleen M., and Sara Dickey. 2000. *Home and Hegemony: Domestic Service and Identity Politics in South and Southeast Asia*. Ann Arbor: University of Michigan Press.
Ally, Shireen. 2009. *From Servants to Workers: South African Domestic Workers and the Democratic State*. Ithaca: Cornell University Press.
Anderson, Bridget. 2000. *Doing the Dirty Work? The Global Politics of Domestic Labour*. London: Zed Books.
Banerjee, Swapna M. 2004. *Men, Women, and Domestics: Articulating Middle-Class Identity in Colonial Bengal*. Oxford: Oxford University Press.
Baxter, Janeen. 2005. 'Male Breadwinners and White Australians: The Role of Employment and Immigration Policies in Shaping Domestic Labour Patterns in Australia.' In *Asian Women as Transnational Domestic Workers*, edited by Shirleena Huang, Brenda S. A. Yeoh and Noor Abdul Rahman, 380–94. Singapore: Marshall Cavendish Academic.
Branca, Patricia. 1975. 'A New Perspective on Women's Work: A Comparative Typology.' *Journal of Social History* 9(2): 129–53.
Bujra, Janet. 2000. *Serving Class: Masculinity and the Feminisation of Domestic Service in Tanzania*. Edinburgh: Edinburgh University Press.
Bulbeck, Chilla. 1991. 'New Histories of the Memsahib and Missus: The Case of Papua New Guinea.' *Journal of Women's History* 3(2): 82–105.
Burkett, Elinor C. 1978. 'Indian Women and White Society: The Case of 16th Century Peru.' In *Latin American Women: Historical Perspectives*, edited by Asunción Laurin, 101–28. Washpool: Greenwood Press.
Camiscioli, Elisa. 2013. 'Women, Gender, Intimacy, and Empire.' *Journal of Women's History* 25(4): 138–48.
Chaney, Elsa M., and Mary Garcia Castro, eds. 1989. *Muchachas No More: Household Workers in Latin America and the Caribbean*. Philadelphia: Temple University Press.
Chang, Grace. 2000. *Disposable Domestics: Immigrant Domestic Workers in the Global Economy*. Boston: South End Press.
Chaudhuri, Nupur, and Margaret Strobel, eds. 1992. *Western Women and Imperialism: Complicity and Resistance*. Bloomington: Indianapolis Indiana University Press.
Cheng, Shu-Ju Ada. 2003. 'Rethinking the Globalization of Domestic Service: Foreign Domestic, State Control, and the Politics of Identity in Taiwan.' *Gender and Society* 17(2): 166–86.
Chia, Galvin. 2013. 'Focussing the Familiar? Locating the Foreign Domestic Worker in Postcolonial Hong Kong Discourse.' In *Cross-sections: The Bruce Hall Academic Journal*, edited by Bianca Hennessy, Eric Shek and Eliza Thompson, 1–18. Canberra: ANU eView.
Chin, Christine B. N. 1998. *In Service and In Servitude: Foreign Female Domestic Workers and the Malaysian 'Modernity' Project*. New York: Columbia University Press.
Cock, Jacklyn. 1980. *Maids and Madams: A Study in the Politics of Exploitation*. Johannesburg: Ravan Press.
Constable, Nicole. 1997. *Maid to Order in Hong Kong: Stories of Filipina Workers*. Ithaca: Cornell University Press.
Cox, Rosie. 2006. *The Servant Problem: Domestic Employment in a Global Economy*. London: I. B. Taurus.
Davidoff, Leonore. 1974. 'Mastered for Life: Servant and Wife in Victorian and Edwardian England.' *Journal of Social History* 7(4): 406–28.

Dickson-Waiko, Anne. 2007. 'Colonial Enclaves and Domestic Spaces in British New Guinea.' In *Britishness Abroad: Transnational Movements and Imperial Cultures*, edited by Kate Darian-Smith, Patricia Grimshaw and Stuart Macintyre, 205–30. Melbourne: Melbourne University Press.

Dudden, Faye E. 1983. *Serving Women: Household Service in Nineteenth-Century America*. Connecticut: Wesleyan University Press.

Ehrenreich, Barbara, and Arlie Russell Hochschild, eds. 2002. *Global Woman: Nannies, Maids, and Sex Workers in the New Economy*. New York: Metropolitan Books.

Fairchilds, Cissie. 1984. *Domestic Enemies: Servants & Their Masters in Old Regime France*. Baltimore: John Hopkins University Press.

Fauve-Chamoux, Antoinette, ed. 2004. *Domestic Service and the Formation of European Identity: Understanding the Globalization of Domestic Work, 16th–21st Centuries*. Bern: Peter Lang.

Fleites-Lear, Marisela. 2003. 'Women, Family, and the Cuban Revolution.' In *Cuban Communism 1959–2003*, edited by Irving Louis Horowitz and Jaime Suchlicki, 276–302. New Brunswick: Transaction Publishers.

Fish, Jennifer Natalie. 2006. *Domestic Democracy: At Home in South Africa*. New York: Routledge.

Glenn, Evelyn Nakano. 1985. 'Racial Ethnic Women's Labor: The Intersection of Race, Gender and Class Oppression.' *Review of Radical Political Economics* 17(3): 86–108.

Glenn, Evelyn Nakano. 1992. 'From Servitude to Service Work: Historical Continuities in the Racial Division of Paid Reproductive Labor.' *Signs* 18(1): 1–43.

Haebich, Anna. 2000. *Broken Circles: Fragmenting Indigenous Families 1800–2000*. Fremantle: Fremantle Arts Centre Press.

Hamilton, Paula. 1985. *'No Irish Need Apply': Aspects of the Employer–Employee Relationship in Australian Domestic Service 1860–1900*. London: Working Papers in Australian Studies.

Hansen, Karen Tranberg. 1989. *Distant Companions: Servants and Employers in Zambia, 1900–1985*. Ithaca: Cornell University Press.

Haskins, Victoria. 2001. 'On the Doorstep: Aboriginal Domestic Service as a "Contact Zone."' *Australian Feminist Studies* 16: 13–25.

Haskins, Victoria. 2005a. *My One Bright Spot*. Basingstoke: Palgrave.

Haskins, Victoria. 2005b. 'A Devotion I Hope I May Fully Repay: Joan Kingsley-Strack.' In *Uncommon Ground: White Women and Aboriginal History*, edited by Anna Cole, Victoria Haskins and Fiona Paisley, 57–79. Canberra: Aboriginal Studies Press.

Haskins, Victoria. 2007. 'Domestic Service and Frontier Feminism: The Call for a Woman Visitor to "Half-Caste" Girls and Women in Domestic Service, Adelaide, 1925–1928.' *Frontiers: A Journal of Women Studies* 28(1–2): 124–64.

Haskins, Victoria. 2009. 'From the Centre to the City: Modernity, Mobility and Mixed-Descent Aboriginal Domestic Workers from Central Australia.' *Women's History Review* 18(1): 155–75.

Haskins, Victoria. 2012a. "'Plenty European Ladies Told Me You Should Give Me Fair Place Same as Everybody': Gender, Race and Aboriginal Domestic Service.' In *Women's Activism: Global Perspectives from the 1890s to the present*, edited by Margaret Allen, Francisca de Haan, Krassimira Daskalova and June Purvis, 153–67. London: Routledge.

Haskins, Victoria. 2012b. *Matrons and Maids: Regulating Indian Domestic Service in Tucson, 1914–1934*. Tucson: University of Arizona Press.

Hecht, J. Jean. 1954. *Continental and Colonial Servants in Eighteenth Century England*. Northampton: Smith College Studies in History, vol. XL.

Hecht, J. Jean. 1956. *The Domestic Servant Class in Eighteenth Century England*. London: Routledge & Kegan Paul.
Hetherington, Penelope. 2002. *Settlers, Servants and Slaves: Aboriginal and European Children in Nineteenth-Century Western Australia*. Crawley: University of Western Australia Press.
Higman, B. W. 2002. *Domestic Service in Australia*. Melbourne: Melbourne University Press.
Higman, B. W. 2003. 'Testing the Boundaries of White Australia: Domestic Servants and Immigration Policy, 1901–45.' *Immigrants & Minorities* 22(1): 1–21.
Hondagneu-Sotelo, Pierrette. 2001. *Domestica: Immigrant Workers Cleaning and Caring in the Shadows of Affluence*. Berkeley: University of California Press.
Horn, Pamela. 1975. *The Rise and Fall of the Victorian Servant*. New York and Dublin: Gill & MacMillan and St Martins Press.
Huang, Shirleena, Brenda S. A. Yeoh, and Noor Abdul Rahman, eds. 2005. *Asian Women as Transnational Domestic Workers*. Singapore: Marshall Cavendish Academic.
Huggins, Jackie. 1987/88. "Firing On in the Mind': Aboriginal Women Domestic Servants in the Inter-War Years.' *Hecate* 13(2): 5–23.
Huggins, Jackie. 1992. 'Wedmedi—If Only You Knew.' In *Sister Girl*, compiled by Jackie Huggins [1998], 25–36. St Lucia: University of Queensland Press.
Jacobs, Margaret D. 2007. 'Working on the Domestic Frontier: American Indian Domestic Servants in White Women's Households in the San Francisco Bay Area, 1920–1940.' *Frontiers: A Journal of Women Studies* 28(1–2): 165–99.
Jacobs, Margaret D. 2009. *White Mother to a Dark Race: Settler Colonialism, Maternalism, and the Removal of Indigenous Children in the American West and Australia, 1880–1940*. Lincoln: University of Nebraska Press.
Katzman, David. 1978. *Seven Days a Week: Women and Domestic Service in Industrializing America*. New York: Oxford University Press.
Keremitsis, Dawn. 1992. 'Women in the Workplace.' In *Cuba: A Different America*, edited by Wilbur R. Chaffee and Gary Prevost, 102–15. Lanham: Rowman & Littlefield.
Kilkey, Majella, Diane Perrons and Ania Plomien. 2013. *Gender, Migration and Domestic Work: Masculinities, Male Labour and Fathering in the UK and USA*. Basingstoke: Palgrave Macmillan.
Kingston, Beverley. 1975. *My Wife, My Daughter and Poor Mary Ann: Women and Work in Australia*. Melbourne: Nelson.
Klocker, Natascha. 2013. 'Struggling with Child Domestic Work: What Can a Postcolonial Perspective Offer?' *Children's Geographies*. DOI: 10.1080/14733285.2013.827870. Accessed January 1, 2014.
Knapman, Claudia. 1986. *White Women in Fiji 1835–1930: The Ruin of Empire?* Sydney: Allen & Unwin.
Kuznesof, Elizabeth. 1989. 'A History of Domestic Service in Spanish America, 1492–1980.' In *Muchachas No More: Household Workers in Latin America and the Caribbean*, edited by Elsa M. Chaney and Mary Garcia Castro, 17–35. Philadelphia: Temple University Press.
Lan, Pei-Chia. 2006. *Global Cinderellas: Migrant Domestics and Newly Rich Employers in Taiwan*. Durham: Duke University Press.
Lawrence, Bonita, and Enakshi Dua. 2005. 'Decolonizing Antiracism.' *Social Justice* 32(4): 120–43.
Ligon, Richard. 1998. *A True & Exact History Of the Island of Barbadoes Illustrated with a Map of the Island, as also the Principal Trees and Plants there, Set forth in their Due Proportions and Shapes, drawn out by their several and respective Scales*. London: Frank Cass [reprint of 1970 facsimile of 1657 edition].

Locher-Scholten, Elsbeth. 1998. 'So Close and Yet So Far: The Ambivalence of Dutch Colonial Rhetoric on Javanese Servants in Indonesia, 1900–1942.' In *Domesticating the Empire: Race, Gender, and Family Life in French and Dutch Colonialism*, 2nd ed., edited by Julia Clancy-Smith and Frances Gouda, 131–53. Charlottesville: University Press of Virginia.
Lowrie, Claire. 2013. 'White "Men" and Their Chinese "Boys": Sexuality, Masculinity and Colonial Power in Singapore and Darwin, 1880s–1930s.' *History Australia* 10(13): 35–57.
Lutz, Helma, ed. 2008. *Migration and Domestic Work: A European Perspective on a Global Theme*. Surrey: Ashgate.
Marchetti, Sabrina. 2010. 'Paid Domestic Labour and Postcoloniality: Narratives of Eritrean and Afro-Surinamese Migrant Women.' Unpublished PhD thesis, Utrecht University, Netherlands.
Martinez, Julia, and Claire Lowrie. 2009. 'Colonial Constructions of Masculinity: Transforming Aboriginal Men into "Houseboys."' *Gender and History* 21(2): 305–23.
Martinez, Julia, and Claire Lowrie. 2012. 'The Transcolonial Influences on Everyday American Imperialism: The Politics of Chinese Domestic Servants in the Philippines.' *Pacific Historical Review* 81(4): 511–36.
McBride, Theresa M. 1974. 'Social Mobility for the Lower Classes: Domestic Servants in France.' *Journal of Social History* 8(1): 63–78.
McBride, Theresa M. 1976. *The Domestic Revolution: The Modernisation of Household Service in England and France 1820–1920*. London: Croom Helm.
McClintock, Anne. 1995. *Imperial Leather: Race, Gender and Sexuality in the Colonial Contest*. London: Routledge.
Mohanty, Chandra Talpade. 2003. *Feminism without Borders: Decolonizing Theory, Practicing Solidarity*. Durham: Duke University Press.
Momsen, Janet Henshall, ed. 1999. *Gender, Migration and Domestic Service*. London: Routledge.
Nett, Emily M. 1966. 'The Servant Class in a Developing Country: Ecuador.' *Journal of Inter-American Studies* 8(3): 437–52.
Parreñas, Rhacel Salazar. 2001. *Servants of Globalization: Women, Migration and Domestic Work*. Stanford: Stanford University Press.
Pratt, Mary Louise. 1993. *Imperial Eyes: Travel Writing and Transculturation*. New York: Routledge.
Ray, Raka. 2000. 'Masculinity, Femininity, and Servitude: Domestic Workers in Calcutta in the Late Twentieth Century.' *Feminist Studies* 26(3): 691–718.
Read, Peter. 1999. *A Rape of the Soul So Profound*. Sydney: Allen & Unwin.
Robinson, Shirleene. 2008. *Something like Slavery? Queensland's Aboriginal Child Workers, 1842–1945*. Melbourne: Australian Scholarly Publishing.
Rodman, Margaret, Daniela Kraemer, Lissant Bolton and Jean Tarisesei, eds. 2007. *House-Girls Remember: Domestic Workers in Vanuatu*. Honolulu: University of Hawai'i Press.
Rollins, Judith. 1985. *Between Women: Domestics and Their Employers*. Philadelphia: Temple University Press.
Romero, Mary. 1992. *Maid in the U.S.A*. New York: Routledge.
Roy, Raja Devasish. 2000. 'Occupations and Economy in Transition: A Case Study of the Chittagong Hill Tracts.' In *Traditional Occupations of Indigenous and Tribal Peoples: Emerging Trends*, edited by Virginia Thomas, 73–123. France: International Labour Organization.
Sabbioni, Jennifer. 1993. '"I Hate Working For White People."' *Hecate* 19(2): 7–29.
Salmon, Lucy Maynard. 1897. *Domestic Service*. New York: Arno Press [reprint in 1972].

Sarti, Raffaella, and Francesca Scrinzi. 2010. 'Introduction to the Special Issue: Men in a Woman's Job, Male Domestic Workers, International Migration and the Globalization of Care.' *Men and Masculinities* 13(1): 4–15.
Schmidt, Elizabeth. 1992. *Peasants, Traders, and Wives: Shona Women in the History of Zimbabwe, 1870–1939*. Portsmouth: Heinemann.
Sharma, Nandita, and Cynthia Wright. 2008–2009. 'Decolonizing Resistance, Challenging Colonial States.' *Social Justice* 35(3): 120–38.
Sium, Aman, Chandni Desai and Eric Ritskes. 2012. 'Towards the "Tangible Unknown": Decolonization and the Indigenous future.' *Decolonization: Indigeneity, Education & Society* 1(1): i–xiii.
Smith, Lois M., and Alfred Padula. 1996. *Sex and Revolution: Women in Socialist Cuba*. Oxford: Oxford University Press.
Stoler, Ann Laura. 2001. 'Tense and Tender Ties: The Politics of Comparison in North American History and (Post) Colonial Studies.' *Journal of American History* 88(3): 829–65.
Stoler, Ann Laura, and Karen Strassler. 2002. 'Memory-Work in Java: A Cautionary Tale.' In *Carnal Knowledge and Imperial Power: Race and the Intimate in Colonial Rule*, edited by Ann Laura Stoler, 162–203. Berkeley: University of California Press.
Tinsman, Heidi. 1992. 'The Indispensible Services of Sisters: Considering Domestic Service in the United States and Latin American Studies.' *Journal of Women's History* 4(1): 37–59.
Tonkinson, Myrna, 1988. 'Sisterhood or Aboriginal Servitude? Black Women and White Women on the Australian Frontier,' *Aboriginal History* 12(1): 27–39.
Tucker, Margaret. 1977. *If Everyone Cared: Autobiography of Margaret Tucker*. Sydney: Ure Smith.
Tuhiwai Smith, Linda. 1999. *Decolonizing Methodologies: Research and Indigenous Peoples*. London: Zed Books.
van Deusen, Nancy. 2012. 'The Intimacies of Bondage: Female Indigenous Servants and Slaves and Their Spanish Masters, 1492–1555.' *Journal of Women's History* 24(1): 13–43.
van Onselen, Charles. 1982. *Studies in the Social and Economic History of the Witwatersrand 1886–1914. Vol. 2. New Nineveh*. Johannesburg: Raven Press.
Walden, Inara. 1995. "That Was Slavery Days': Aboriginal Domestic Servants in New South Wales in the Twentieth Century.' *Labour History* 69: 196–207.
Ware, Vron. 1992. *Beyond the Pale: White Women, Racism and History*. London: Verso.
Yan Hairong. 2008. *New Masters, New Servants: Migration, Development, and Women Workers in China*. Durham: Duke University Press.
Zavala, Miguel. 2013. 'What Do We Mean by Decolonizing Research Strategies? Lessons from Decolonizing, Indigenous Research Projects in New Zealand and Latin America.' *Decolonization: Indigeneity, Education & Society* 2(1): 55–71.
Zimmerman, Mary K., Jacquelyn S. Litt and Christine E. Bose, eds. 2006. *Global Dimensions of Gender and Carework*. Stanford: Stanford University Press.

1 An Historical Perspective
Colonial Continuities in the Global Geography of Domestic Service

B. W. Higman

The decline and fall of the great formal empires of the modern world, in the aftermath of the Second World War, occurred in tandem with a decline in the importance of domestic service. In the West, the dominant site of imperial metropolitan societies, it was predicted that domestic service might completely disappear as a significant occupation. Such predictions were most common around 1960, when decolonization was at its height (Coser 1973–74: 39). Like many bold predictions, the demise of domestic service was exaggerated. It took new forms and flourished in new environments, just as the supposed end of empire saw transformation into neocolonial and postcolonial forms. The outcome was a new map of global patterns of domestic service, overlaying the new map of global political geography.

However new these two maps might appear, both contain elements from the past, marking the persistence of political boundaries and of social barriers. In particular, it can be asked how far contemporary patterns of domestic service incorporate continuities from colonization that derive from deeply rooted hierarchies of wealth and inequality, and how far these patterns depend on recent social and economic change unrelated to the processes of formal colonization that dominated earlier periods. Existing theories of servant growth make little mention of the process of colonization but focus instead on macroeconomic engines of change, notably inequality, technological change, urbanization, modernization and stages of economic development (Boserup 1970: 103–104; Branca 1975: 130; McBride 1976: 116; Katzman 1978: *vii*; Cowan 1983). In thinking about associations between colonization and domestic service, a central question to be asked is whether colonization commands the explanatory power sufficient to make it worthy of addition to these theories of servant growth. The question can be asked both of the contemporary world and of periods in the past.

It is worth observing that colonies and domestic servants share some fundamental characteristics. Most obviously, they both come into being through dependence on an existing agent, whether state or household. Without denying agency to colonists or servants, it is the continuing authority of a metropole or master that commands settlement (in colonization) or the employment relation (in domestic service). This applies to all servants, whether found in colonies or elsewhere. Everywhere, servants were part of a larger hierarchy of authority and status that brought together public and domestic spheres. Being a servant in a colony introduced an additional layer of command, the servant-employing colonist being in turn subject to the authority of colonial/imperial power.

Constructing a comprehensive picture of colonization and domestic service in the great sweep of world history is beyond the capacity of this chapter. Systematic data do however exist for a substantial slice of the contemporary world and analysis of these data enables a testing of associations between colonization and domestic service in two major ways. In the first place, it can be asked whether being incorporated into a colonial empire—either as metropole or colony—translates into the existence of a large (or small) domestic service sector in the present. This relationship can be understood either as a continuity bequeathed by the colonial domestic service sector or as an independent product of the structural heritage of colonialism. Further, it can be asked whether the contemporary experience of domestic service differs significantly between states according to the specific types of colonization they experienced.

Several complications surround the specification of these questions. There are problems of definition and problems of data. There are also problems deriving from the relative and changing significance of intervening factors and experience. Many recent scholars have found these problems intractable and preferred approaches that illustrate the human—often individual—experience of people within particular colonial societies, seen through the lens of qualitative cultural history, together with postcolonial and reflexive analysis. Similarly, contemporary labor economists sometimes exclude personal services from their studies because of problems of identification and data sources, and the persistent difficulty of regulating the sector (Bailly, Devetter and Horn 2013: 303).

The approach taken in this chapter is more representative of older studies of domestic service—particularly those undertaken from the 1940s to the 1970s—which followed the path of economic history and depended heavily on quantitative evidence (Stigler 1947). These methods are the central pillars of my own earlier studies of the history of domestic service, in Jamaica (Higman 1989) and Australia (Higman 2002). While acknowledging the difficulties associated with the approach, and recognizing the valuable contributions that have been made by alternative strategies, I maintain the view that attempting to understand the changing global pattern of servant growth in its quantitative dimensions is an important objective. In order to proceed along this path it is necessary first to say something about the ways colonies and servants have been defined and classified.

CLASSIFYING COLONIES

Colonization is understood as both metaphor and mechanism. Although the metaphorical usage can reveal much about the mechanism, my analysis in this chapter is concerned principally with the process and with the lives of those peoples who formally identified their own contemporary territories as *colonies*. Today, very few places are described as colonies, whatever their constitutional status (Aldrich and Connell 1998: 2–9). On the other hand, postcolonial critiques of the notion of 'nation' are underpinned by the argument that all modern nation-states are indeed products of the process of colonization, whatever their place in the classification and hierarchy of the formal colonial world. Further, the process of 'colonization' continued (and continues) long after declarations of formal independence (Burton 2003: 1; Ghosh and Kennedy 2006; Stoler 2006: 35–36). Thus formulations in which metropole and colony are separate entities, with influence and power moving in only one direction, have been overtaken by concepts of multilateral webs in which the colonized play an equally significant role in shaping the colonizer (Stoler 2002: 136). This complex web of colonial–national interactions applies not only to the era of formal colonization but equally to the experience of the past fifty years.

Beginning in the nineteenth century, attempts were often made by imperial political economists to classify colonies into specific types (Merivale 1861: *xii*; Rawson 1884: 565; Lucas 1887: 1–3). Recent history writing often strongly reflects these early formulations. Wolfgang Reinhard (2011: 3–4), for example, finds three types sufficient: (1) trading posts and military bases; (2) colonies of settlement, which entailed the removal or decimation of Indigenous peoples and the establishment of immigrant populations; and (3) colonies of rule, in which colonizers extracted wealth from existing societies, often with the collaboration of local elites. A more nuanced typology is acknowledged by Bouda Etemad. Firstly, a 'mixed' type (represented by Mexico and Peru) where 'white colonists, numerically a minority but nevertheless in substantial numbers, formed an urban upper-class that lived on the income produced by commercial exchanges and the large landed properties cultivated by subjugated indigenous farmers.' Colonies of this type were long-lasting and remained dominant until the middle of the eighteenth century; and new examples were later established in Algeria, Southern Rhodesia, Kenya and Angola. Secondly, says Etemad, colonies of 'occupation' existed where small colonizing contingents managed large Indigenous populations. The modern version of this type is the 'dependency.' Thirdly, 'plantation' colonies were developed by the Portuguese, based on sugar and slavery. Fourthly, there were colonies founded on coastal trading posts and fortified military bases. Fifthly, Etemad identifies the 'settlement colony,' a type absent from the Spanish empire but developed by the English and French in North America and the Dutch at the Cape. Here Etemad restricts 'settlement colonies' to the thirteen colonies of North America, Canada, South Africa, Australia and New Zealand—an attenuated version of older more comprehensive classifications of 'settlement' (Etemad 2007: 136–38).

Although classification is less of a preoccupation in the postcolonial world, it is intriguing that a new type—the 'settler colony'—has recently become common currency. This term was rare before 1960 but has grown in popularity and usage. The more complete term *white settler colony* has grown at the same rate, but remains uncommon. On the other hand, *black settler colony* is almost completely absent from the literature. Theoreticians of 'settler colonialism,' notably James Belich (2009: 26) and Lorenzo Veracini (2010: 6), accept that 'settlers' are not necessarily Europeans, but the vast weight of the literature is devoted to their experience. At the same time, not every example of white European colonization has been acknowledged as a settler colony—notably, Ireland is rarely discussed. The term *settler colony* seems to have emerged not from historical analysis of places formerly known as *settlement colonies* or *colonies of settlement* but from rhetoric surrounding the Algerian War, ignited in 1954. It was this bloody conflict that created the image of a unified settler community rooted in struggle and exile—the world of Albert Camus's *L'Etranger*—set in the context of a literal *décolonisation* that meant the removal of the (European) *colon* (settler) from the land (Kraft 1961; Shepard 2006: 55–56; Churchill 2010: 101–102). English-language interpretations then gave *decolonization* a wider meaning—the end of empire—and identified Algeria as a *settler colony*. Gradually, historians began to attach the term *settler colony* to (some) older colonial units and, by the 1970s, they were comfortable with the idea of *settler society*. Settler colonies have been the location of many historical studies of domestic service (including some of the chapters in this volume; see Aird; Ally; Macdonald; McCabe; McCallum; and Robinson).

The analysis in this chapter recognizes four colonial types, and distinguishes these from the colonial powers (the imperial metropoles or colonizing states) and those places that were not colonized in the modern imperial era. The four types used are:

(1) settler colonies (in which imperial populations occupy and exploit lands taken from Indigenous peoples);
(2) settlement colonies (in which colonists depend on forced migrant labor to exploit lands taken from Indigenous peoples);
(3) mandates and protectorates (in which local rulers retain sovereignty, within the domain of an imperial state); and
(4) occupied colonies (in which limited forms of imperial suzerainty follow military conquest).

The allocation of states to each of these specific categories is set out in Table 1.1. Some states are candidates for allocation to more than one of the categories. The United States, for example, might be either a settler colony or a colonial power; here it has been located with the settler colonies, but tests are made to determine the outcome if the allocation is reversed. States are identified as colonies only if they had a substantial colonial history. Ethiopia, for example, suffered short-lived attempts at colonization but is not here included with the colonies. Large countries, such as the United States, contain within them significant regional blocs. Here, the principal units of analysis are the state and the world-region.

Table 1.1 Domestic Workers by Former Colony/Metropole Type, c.2010

	Domestic Workers per Thousand Population	Percentage Female	Total Number (in Thousands)
Settler Colonies			
Algeria	1	46	35
Australia	1	60	10
New Zealand	1	90	4
Canada	2	96	73
United States	2	93	700
Israel	7	91	46
Zimbabwe	14	62	183
South Africa	25	84	1 125
Settlement Colonies			
Gabon	1	100	1
Haiti	2	84	19
Sierra Leone	2	50	8
Ireland	3	90	10
Puerto Rico	5	67	18
Fiji	8	83	6
Aruba	11	100	1
Netherlands Antilles	11	100	2
Vanuatu	11	50	2
Botswana	15	72	25
Ecuador	16	78	210
Mauritius	16	89	19
Peru	16	95	424
Mexico	18	91	1 852
Chile	20	91	311
Philippines	21	85	1 729
Nicaragua	22	81	118
Dominican Republic	25	97	214
New Caledonia	26	80	5
Panama	27	88	78
Costa Rica	29	93	119
Bermuda	32	50	2
Iceland	35	90	10
Uruguay	38	91	129

(*Continued*)

Table 1.1 (Continued)

	Domestic Workers per Thousand Population	Percentage Female	Total Number (in Thousands)
Brazil	40	94	6 731
Seychelles	64	60	5
Mandates and Protectorates			
Iraq	1	40	10
Jordan	2	93	10
Cambodia	3	60	35
Korea (South)	3	77	135
Papua New Guinea	3	63	16
Morocco	4	84	120
Korea (North)	7	97	150
Lesotho	13	84	27
Namibia	13	83	24
Tanzania	20	80	701
Lebanon	44	97	93
Samoa	53	67	3
Bahrain	109	83	75
Kuwait	109	80	246
Occupied Colonies			
Angola	1	43	7
Bulgaria	1	50	2
Egypt	1	29	52
Ghana	1	62	8
Serbia and Montenegro	1	71	7
Ukraine	1	54	26
Kazakhstan	2	75	24
Latvia	2	75	4
Pakistan	2	80	285
Kyrgyzstan	3	67	15
Sri Lanka	3	77	60
Vietnam	3	60	241
Bangladesh	4	80	500
India	4	50	4 200
Mongolia	5	50	12
Uganda	5	64	112

	Domestic Workers per Thousand Population	Percentage Female	Total Number (in Thousands)
Syria	6	96	100
Tunisia	6	71	51
Malaysia	11	89	253
Mali	11	82	104
Indonesia	13	50	2 600
Cyprus	24	100	17
Hong Kong	34	80	230
Singapore	49	71	170
Colonial Powers			
Hungary	1	67	6
Japan	1	98	37
Netherlands	1	90	12
Russian Federation	1	73	50
Denmark	2	91	10
United Kingdom	2	61	136
Germany	3	7	216
Belgium	4	90	42
Greece	6	93	69
Italy	8	89	460
Portugal	14	98	150
China	12	90	15 000
Spain	18	93	753
Sweden	25	90	227
France	27	92	1 600
Not Colonies			
Croatia	1	80	5
Czech Republic	1	92	5
Iran	1	74	19
Lithuania	1	75	4
Macedonia	1	100	1
Moldova	1	80	5
Norway	1	100	2
Poland	1	94	16
Romania	1	89	30
Slovakia	1	100	6
Slovenia	1	100	1

(*Continued*)

Table 1.1 (Continued)

	Domestic Workers per Thousand Population	Percentage Female	Total Number (in Thousands)
Tajikistan	1	34	3
Armenia	2	80	5
Austria	2	92	12
Finland	2	50	8
Georgia	2	91	11
Nepal	2	53	35
Yemen	2	40	24
Thailand	3	89	196
Turkey	3	64	182
Ethiopia	4	91	249
Estonia	6	100	8
Taiwan	8	73	185
Luxembourg	11	80	5
Switzerland	11	90	80
Andorra	16	100	1
Saudi Arabia	36	85	800
Qatar	82	60	73
United Arab Emirates	98	62	236

Sources: ILO databases at http://laborsta.ilo.org; ILO 2013: 117–30; United Nations Demographic Yearbooks; Schwenken and Heimeshoff 2011; Hu 2011: 1; Turner 2007.

DEFINING DOMESTIC SERVANTS

The problem of defining who is a servant or domestic worker is fraught with ambiguities and contradictions made even more challenging by change over time, and by cultural and linguistic variations. Indeed, Raffaella Sarti (2005: 340), concluding an extensive review of the terms in Western Europe since the sixteenth century, acknowledges that these problems can appear so overwhelming that scholars are sometimes discouraged from even attempting study of the subject. Whereas *service* and *servant* are ancient terms, *domestic worker* is recent. Formerly, *domestic work* was simply the set of class-dependent tasks performed by a housewife, together with her daughters and perhaps sons, and other people not considered members of the family. It was the latter who were distinguished from the others by being placed in the social rank of *servant*. Exceptions occurred, pointing to a shadow area between family and servant, household and kin group. This was not the only kind of service, so it was necessary to call these people *domestic* servants in order to separate them from farm servants and apprentices, as well as bond servants and indentured servants—and these could all overlap. These contextual and terminological inconsistencies contributed to the understanding of domestic service as a unique type of occupation, defined by its tasks and site as much as its employment relationship (Humfrey 2011: 7).

Tracing the history of these terms across time and cultures is a study in itself. Because the analysis in this chapter is focused on contemporary patterns and depends heavily on data collected by the International Labour Organization (ILO), the definition used is that employed by this agency. In 2011, the ILO's Convention Concerning Decent Work for Domestic Workers defined *domestic work* as 'work performed in or for a household or households' and *domestic worker* as 'any person engaged in domestic work within an employment relationship.' (For a detailed discussion of the passing of this Convention, see Fish, this volume.) It specifically excluded persons performing domestic work 'only occasionally or sporadically and not on an occupational basis' (ILO 2011). It makes no reference to *service* or *servants* and avoids the problems that arise when specific tasks are introduced (Simonovsky and Luebker 2011: 2). The ILO definition is also useful in that it omits the condition that the domestic worker should work in the household of a family other than his or her own. Further, the relationship can be formal or informal, legal or illegal. The worker must simply be 'within an employment relationship.' The definition makes no mention of residence or the amount of time spent in particular households. This enables it to incorporate the labor of commercial service enterprises that have bourgeoned over the past fifty years, especially in cleaning and personal care. The only condition is that the work be carried out in private households. The growth of this sector has been associated with dramatic changes in the character and social relations of domestic work but these are not matters of definition.

PATTERNS OF CONTEMPORARY DOMESTIC SERVICE

Using the ILO's definition of a domestic worker, and the ILO's statistics (purposely cautious and derived in turn from censuses and household labor surveys), together with a brave estimate for China, it is possible to find data for 116 states circa 2010.[1] Although these are only a little more than one half of the world's states they do account for 5.3 billion people and 46 million adult domestic workers. These data imply a total of about 70 million domestic workers globally, though the true total is probably nearer to 100 million, and perhaps 130 million if child domestic workers are included (Simonovsky and Luebker 2011: 6–7; ILO 2013: 22–23). Problems of definition and data collection mean that the numbers must always be considered with suspicion, and the sources are sometimes significantly contradictory, but the 116 states included in the sample used here are at least well distributed across the globe and across economies and societies, and they encompass three-quarters of the world's people. The contrasts between states are often dramatic and it is these broad patterns, rather than less certain subtle differences, that deserve notice and emphasis.

In the 116 states, the average proportion is nine domestic workers per thousand population (Table 1.1). The range of experience is however considerable. At the bottom, states as diverse as Bulgaria, Norway, Ghana and Australia have less than one domestic worker per thousand population. At the top, the oil states of Qatar (the world's richest state), Bahrain, the United Arab Emirates and Kuwait all have more than 80 per thousand population. It is striking that in 2010 three of these states led the world in the proportion of international migrants in their populations: Qatar 87 percent, UAE 70 percent and Kuwait 69 percent (Goldin, Cameron and Balarajan 2011: 131; Gabaccia 2012: 212). The much larger Saudi Arabia has many more domestic workers though a smaller proportion (36 per thousand), most of them women from Indonesia, Sri Lanka, the Philippines and Nepal, often kept in 'slavery-like conditions' and subject to sexual abuse (Brysk 2012: 79). Not all Middle East states have such large populations of servants, however, and as a whole the region comes second to Latin America and the Caribbean. This region stands out, with 28 domestic workers per thousand, more than double the proportion in the Middle East. The prominence of Latin America and the Caribbean is long-standing (Boserup 1970: 103) and, in spite of substantial migration of domestic workers out of the region, the numbers grew rapidly to double over the past two decades (for further discussion of the changing patterns of domestic service in Latin America and the Caribbean, see the chapters by Foote and Johnson in this volume; for the Middle East, specifically Lebanon, see Bizri's chapter). The other world-regions hover below the typical nine, with the exceptions of North America and Australasia and the Pacific with only two domestic workers per thousand. Only in Latin America and the Caribbean, along with the Middle East, do domestic workers account for more than 5 percent of total employment (ILO 2013: 24–26).

The experience of colonization differs across the 116 states: 72 are former colonies, 15 are former colonial powers, and 29 were neither colonized nor colonizing states. How are these different types of colonial experience associated with domestic service in the contemporary world? The smallest proportion of domestic workers is located in the states that were never formally colonized—though many of these territories endured periods of foreign domination—with an average five domestic workers per thousand population (typified by Ethiopia and Estonia). The colonized states come next (eight, typified by Fiji) but the largest proportion of domestic workers (ten per thousand) is to be found in the homelands of the colonizing powers (most of these active imperialists until recent times, typified by Portugal).[2] This contrast does not apply in every specific case, however. For example, Brazil has three times as many domestic workers per capita as does Portugal. Overall, the density of domestic workers is greater in the metropolitan/imperial countries than in the countries they colonized, but the difference is not great. The more important finding is that states derived from former colonies and former colonial powers have roughly twice as many domestic workers per capita as states that were not part of the formal imperial project.

An Historical Perspective 29

During the modern period of formal empires, contemporaries often focused on contrasts between the experiences of the different imperial powers. Historians accepted this approach as a mode of comparison, and it continues to be important, partly because of legacies of culture and language. Some colonies had complex histories, of course, being passed from one metropole to another; for the purposes of this study they are allocated to the longest-ruling power. In terms of domestic service, there are indeed some significant differences. The former colonies of the French and British (those included in the 116 states) have relatively small proportions of domestic workers today (three and five per thousand respectively). The former colonies of the Dutch are also close to average (13), but those of Spain have significantly more (19 domestic workers per thousand). Portugal's former colonies have the most of this group of European colonizers, with 38 per thousand, reflecting the experience of Brazil. These are striking contrasts but the major reason for them is that the imperial powers held different kinds of colonies, rather than having anything to do with national character, or relatively harsh or benign attitudes to colonized Indigenous peoples. There is no significant correlation between contemporary proportions of domestic workers and (total) length of formal colonization or the length of the period since formal independence.

More interesting are contrasts between the colonies, using the classification into four types set out above in Table 1.1. Of these four types of colonies, the one with the largest contemporary proportion of domestic workers is the second, the settlement colonies, with 16 domestic workers per thousand population. The so-called settler colonies have less than one-third as many or just five per thousand. The Mandates and Protectorates have nine and the occupied type five per thousand. If the settler and settlement colonies are bundled together, the rate is 12 per thousand, more than twice the rate in the colonial types touched more lightly by formal empire. Looked at this way, the finding that the colonial powers have the most domestic workers (compared to both colonized and never-colonized places) needs to be revised. Now, the settler and settlement colonies combined are found to have slightly more domestic workers than the colonial powers. However, this is not because of the contribution of the settler colonies, which indeed push the contrast in the other direction.

One possible explanation of this pattern can be sought in the different kinds of economies and societies found in the colonies. In the world today, domestic workers are most common in those states that were formerly 'slave societies' (where more than 30 percent of the total population was enslaved). These states now have 16 domestic workers per thousand population. This rate is more than twice that found in the more numerous states that had smaller proportions of enslaved people in their populations. Societies dominated by indentured labor systems fall between these extremes (ten per thousand), as do those founded on free labor (eight per thousand).

Where the plantation ruled, and sometimes continues to rule, the rate is 16 domestic workers per thousand population, but not far behind are former family-farm colonies (14), trading post colonies (15) and mining colonies (12 per thousand). Only the numerous colonies based on peasant agriculture (including those heavily taxed under colonialism), and the relatively rare pastoral economies, had a smaller number (five per thousand). These patterns relate closely to the finding that Latin America and the Caribbean has the most servants at a regional level.

Thus it was the settlement colonies founded on the plantation and slavery that came to produce the largest proportions of domestic workers in the contemporary world. But since slavery has been abolished for more than one hundred years in all of these states, what is the process creating this result? Modern 'slavery' continues and accounts for millions of people, and often is associated with domestic work, but these cases are not concentrated in the former sites of 'slave societies.' The plantation has faded in recent decades. In many parts of the world, however, the system contributed to what George Beckford called the 'persistent poverty' which marked many tropical regions down to the late twentieth century, transmitted through an 'institutional legacy' that determined the structure of modern economies and a 'social and psychological legacy' which infiltrated social structure and attitudes (Beckford 1972: 30–42; Best and Levitt 2009). It is a useful theory but it must be admitted that, although it works well for most of Latin America and the Caribbean (cf. Johnson and Foote, this volume), the concept of 'plantation economy' appears less powerful when applied to the wider world.

Rather than looking for continuities, it may be asked whether broader structural features can be identified which characterized periods of freedom as well as slavery. A strong contender is the pattern of inequality. In the contemporary world, we have seen, domestic workers are particularly common in Latin America and the Caribbean, one of the most unequal regions in income and wealth. Inequality in this region has increased dramatically since the 1970s. Although improving its status slightly over the past decade, Brazil has typically had both the most unequal distribution of wealth and the largest number of domestic workers to population within the region. Latin America and the Caribbean is also the region most comprehensively dominated by colonial systems of plantation agriculture and slavery, with Brazil the outstanding slave society. Scholars have often traced the concentration of wealth to initial factor endowments—soil and climate—or to colonial institutions, but many other factors intervened (Arroyo Abad 2013: 47–74).

The data for the 116 contemporary states taken together suggest that the number of domestic workers per thousand increases broadly in line with per capita GDP. On the other hand, data for the highest income-earners in a smaller sample of countries show that the more income is distributed unequally among the top one percent, the fewer the domestic workers

(Atkinson, Piketty and Saez 2010: 679). It appears that the super-rich of the contemporary world do not direct their expenditure to the building of retinues of servants, in the way their historical counterparts—particularly those of the ancient imperial world—sought to flaunt their wealth. The modern rich have more ways of displaying status and spending their incomes.

Most of today's employers of domestic workers have relatively modest, middling incomes, and most of these employers generally choose to afford just one worker or a fraction of a worker. This shift is not so much a product of changes in levels of inequality within societies but a result of technological change. Household technologies directed at the production of goods (food, drink, warmth, clothing, tools), which once employed large groups of servants, have been replaced by industrial processes, and these same processes offer a wider range of employment possibilities. Changes in technology are closely related to urbanization but in the 116 states there is only a weak correlation between the percentage of their populations living in cities and numbers of domestic workers.

Technological change has also greatly increased the affordability of long-distance travel, including the movement of domestic workers around the world. But this is a response to global rather than local inequalities. It is almost always characterized by migration (often on a temporary basis) rather than colonization, and it can operate to increase the domestic worker population in both the sending and the receiving state by creating a global care chain. For example, when women move from Lesotho or Zimbabwe to South Africa to work as domestics (or as farm workers) they often have to employ women at home to care for their families, at a lower rate (Samers 2010: 169–71; Schwenken and Heimeshoff 2011: 21). This serves as a mechanism for increasing inequality both nationally and internationally. South Africa has 25 domestic workers per thousand population, roughly twice as many as in Lesotho and Zimbabwe. (For South Africa today, see Ally, this volume.) But as a result of this externally generated unequal relationship, both Lesotho (13 domestic workers per thousand) and impoverished Zimbabwe (14) have above-average proportions.

GENDER AND RELIGION

Within these broad patterns lie demographic differences—particularly gender differences—often intimately connected with the specific occupations of servants. This is the aspect of domestic service that most concerned Ester Boserup in her classic work *Woman's Role in Economic Development*, published in 1970. She found that where domestic service accounted for the largest numbers (as in Latin America), there the majority of servants were women, whereas in places with smaller contingents of domestics (in 'Arab, African and Asian countries'), males were prominent (Boserup 1970: 104).

This pattern persists and is sometimes interpreted as a colonial legacy, in which male servants are attributed higher status and thereby give prestige to their employers (Schwenken and Heimeshoff 2011: 10; see also Lowrie; and Nilan, Artini and Threadgold, this volume).

In the 116 contemporary states, 85 percent of the domestic workers are female. As expected, Latin America and the Caribbean have the largest proportion of women in the sector, at 93 percent, but the same proportion is found in North America where the servant population is much smaller. The smallest percentages of women occur in Africa and the Australasia/Pacific region (79 and 76 percent respectively). Falling between these extremes are Europe, Asia and the Middle East (all of them around 82 percent). Thus it appears the association between small contingents of domestic servants and relatively large proportions of males working in the sector no longer holds as perfectly as Boserup observed. In part, this may be explained by changes in household technologies (which formerly created roles specifically filled by males, notably 'outdoor' tasks) and the movement of women into private sector employment (as for example in Saudi Arabia). It also results from the disruption of traditional patterns by the substantial modern long-distance migration of workers, particularly women, to the richer economies of East Asia, the Middle East and Europe, thus contributing to the 'feminization of migration' (Samers 2010: 101).

These relationships are further complicated by religion. It is striking that whereas predominantly Christian and Muslim states have the same proportions of domestic workers relative to population (13 per thousand), females comprise 90 percent in the Christian states but only 73 percent in the Muslim. Predominantly Buddhist and Hindu states have much smaller proportions of domestic workers (six and one per thousand respectively) and substantially larger percentages of males in the sector (23 and 49). States lacking a dominant religion have a larger proportion of domestic workers (15 per thousand), 89 percent of them females or much the same as in the Christian states. Thus the major exception to Boserup's finding that the fewer the domestics in a population the more likely they are to be male occurs in the Muslim states with their aberrantly large proportion of males.

What have these patterns got to do with colonization? In the first place, Boserup's assertion works well in terms of the basic distinction made between (former) colonies and other types of states in the contemporary 116 units studied here. The 'never colonized' group has the smallest proportion of domestic workers (five per thousand) and the smallest percentage female (80). At the other extreme, the (former) colonial powers have the largest proportions of domestic workers (ten per thousand), matched by the largest percentage female (88 percent).[3] This finding appears to support the argument that the contemporary pattern is distorted by long-distance migration of domestic workers, particularly in the case of Europe. The (former) colonies fall between the extremes (with eight domestic workers per thousand, 80 percent female). Boserup's model also fits the contrasts observed between the different types of colonies. Thus modern states derived from 'settlement' colonies have relatively large proportions of domestic workers and large percentages of women, compared to other types of colonies. Further, 'settler colony' states have below-average contingents of domestic workers, only 88 percent female, whereas the 'non-settler' colonial states have three times as many servants, 92 percent of them female.

It comes as no surprise to find that the states formerly dominated by slavery and the plantation, the places with the largest contingents of domestic workers, also have the largest proportions of females in the sector. In the former slave societies, 94 percent are female and in the (former) plantation colonies 92 percent. By contrast, in the states derived from 'free' and peasant traditions, the much smaller servant populations are less dominated by females (70 percent).

CONTINUITY AND CHANGE

Unfulfilled predictions of the end of domestic service, or of the end of empire, provide striking examples of the long-term power of underlying structures and the weight of persistent social forms. Thus, although the pattern of domestic service observed in the contemporary world may seem to reflect historical legacies bequeathed by colonization as well as the impact of recent dramatic change in the global economy, it is more useful to think of continuity and change as part of a single evolutionary process (Burke 1993: 158–60). Continuity is not mere inertia. This is true even in those many cases where continuity is unwanted and is the product of social and political oppression, as clearly illustrated by the persistence of slavery and servitude alongside modern regulated market versions of domestic work.

The most fundamental conclusion arising from the analysis attempted here is that domestic workers are more common in states derived from formal colonization than in territories not part of the empires of the modern era. This applies equally to the colonies and the colonizing metropoles. Of the colonies, those that were slave societies based on plantation agriculture have the largest contingents of domestic workers today. Settler colony states have the least. These findings match the broad geographical pattern. The world-region with the largest proportion of domestic workers—Latin America and the Caribbean—bears the marks of deep and comprehensive colonization, slavery and the plantation. These associations between colonization and domestic service are compelling. It must be asked however whether they are part of the heritage of colonization or indicative of continuity created by even deeper forces, such as inequality.

Whether the roots be historically deep or shallow, domestic service grows best in societies where a substantial middle class coexists with significant inequality, rather than where the concentration of wealth is extreme, or where true egalitarianism exists. Inequality has taken on new forms in our contemporary world. In addition to inequality between nation states, the past two or three decades have witnessed significant change within states. Global inequalities are as significant as local inequalities in determining the scale and scope of the domestic worker population. The cheapness and speed of international travel has facilitated this new feature but has also made it often a temporary rather than permanent migration, independent of the settlement of people that characterizes colonization. Rather than being located in low-income countries, the majority of the world's poor now live in middle-income countries, creating new conditions in the supply of and demand for domestic workers (Milkman, Reese and Roth 1998: 484–96; Sumner 2012: 865). Thus, modern migrants undertaking domestic work are not necessarily the poorest of the poor, and some travel to places where they hope to find something nearer to gender equality. Many are willing to accept low-skilled employment in hopes of regaining their upward mobility, or simply to enable remittances that may in turn be used to finance care-chains. Thus, for contemporary domestic worker migrants, the global map of movement is quite different to that for the substantial free and coerced streams of the modern colonial era.

Examples of domestic service that appear to be legacies of colonization exist alongside thriving sectors created by new wealth in states which have flourished in the absence of formal colonization. Although the inequalities associated with slavery and the plantation carry through into contemporary societies, as in Latin America and the Caribbean, it can also be argued that even in these situations levels of inequality have varied significantly over time, particularly the past fifty years, breaking the direct causative chain.

Similar problems of interpretation apply to China and the oil states of the Middle East. In China the retreat of socialism was followed by rapid urbanization and industrialization, founded on neoliberal economic principles and private enterprise, and accompanied by a massive resurgence of domestic service. By the 1990s domestic service was recognized as an official occupation and actively encouraged by the state. The low status of the 'domestic service worker' in contemporary China matches that of the bondservant and servant regimes of feudalism and capitalism but the regrowth of the sector is a response to new forms of inequality and economic development (Hu 2011: 10–12, 33–35). It is not simply a legacy. Much the same can be said of the contemporary Middle East where rapid economic growth and unequal wealth has created a very visible domestic service sector—once again marked by slavery-like conditions of work. In both China and the oil states of the Middle East domestic workers are mostly migrants, either internal or international, but their migration is closely regulated and temporary. It is a long stretch to relate the recent growth in domestic service in China or the Middle East to a history of colonization, in strong contrast with the experience of Latin America. Thus, although colonization has indeed created long lasting, persistent forms of domestic service, formal colonization is by no means essential to the existence of substantial populations of domestic workers in the contemporary world. Probably, the same can be said of the colonial and pre-colonial past.

ACKNOWLEDGMENTS

For valued comments on the original draft of this essay, I thank Ann McGrath, Laurence Brown, Victoria Haskins and Claire Lowrie, and three anonymous readers.

NOTES

1. An unspecified database derived from similar sources finds 117 countries and territories, with a total of 52.6 million domestic workers: Simonovsky and Luebker 2011: 5.
2. It is worth noting that the pattern is unchanged if the United States is moved from the colonies to the colonial powers. See chapters by Cox and Glaser, this volume, for domestic workers in Britain and the US today, and Dussart for a historical comparison.
3. Again, the pattern is unchanged if the United States is moved from the colonies to the colonial powers.

REFERENCES

Aldrich, Robert, and John Connell. 1998. *The Last Colonies*. Cambridge: Cambridge University Press.
Arroyo Abad, Leticia. 2013. 'Persistent Inequality? Trade, Factor Endowments, and Inequality in Republican Latin America.' *Journal of Economic History* 73(1) 38–78.
Atkinson, A. B., Thomas Piketty and Emmanuel Saez. 2010. 'Top Incomes in the Long Run of History.' In *Top Incomes: A Global Perspective*, edited by A. B. Atkinson and Thomas Piketty, 664–759. Oxford: Oxford University Press.
Bailly, Franck, François-Xavier Devetter and François Horn. 2013. 'Can Working and Employment Conditions in the Personal Services Sector Be Improved?' *Cambridge Journal of Economics* 37(2): 299–321.
Beckford, George L. 1972. *Persistent Poverty: Underdevelopment in Plantation Economies of the Third World*. New York: Oxford University Press.
Belich, James. 2009. *Replenishing the Earth: The Settler Revolution and the Rise of the Anglo-World, 1783–1939*. Oxford: Oxford University Press.
Best, Lloyd, and Kari Polanyi Levitt. 2009. *Essays on the Theory of Plantation Economy: A Historical and Institutional Approach to Caribbean Economic Development*. Mona: University of the West Indies Press.
Boserup, Ester. 1970. *Woman's Role in Economic Development*. New York: St. Martin's Press.
Branca, Patricia. 1975. 'A New Perspective on Women's Work: A Comparative Typology.' *Journal of Social History* 9(2): 129–53.

Brysk, Alison. 2012. 'Rethinking Trafficking: Human Rights and Private Wrongs.' In *From Human Trafficking to Human Rights: Reframing Contemporary Slavery*, edited by Alison Brysk and Austin Choi-Fitzpatrick, 73–85. Philadelphia: University of Pennsylvania Press.

Burke, Peter. 1993. *History and Social Theory*. Ithaca: Cornell University Press.

Burton, Antoinette. 2003. 'Introduction: On the Inadequacy and the Indispensability of the Nation.' In *After the Imperial Turn: Thinking with and through the Nation*, edited by Antoinette Burton, 1–23. Durham: Duke University Press.

Churchill, Christopher. 2010. 'Camus and the Theatre of Terror: Artaudian Dramaturgy and Settler Society in the Works of Albert Camus.' *Modern Intellectual History* 7(1): 93–121.

Coser, Lewis A. 1973–74. 'Servants: The Obsolescence of an Occupational Role.' *Social Forces* 52(1): 31–40.

Cowan, Ruth Schwartz. 1983. *More Work for Mother: The Ironies of Household Technology from the Open Hearth to the Microwave*. New York: Basic Books.

Etemad, Bouda. 2007. *Possessing the World: Taking the Measurements of Colonisation from the Eighteenth to the Twentieth Century*. New York: Berghahn Books.

Gabaccia, Donna R. 2012. *Foreign Relations: American Immigration in Global Perspective*. Princeton: Princeton University Press.

Ghosh, Durba, and Dane Kennedy. 2006. 'Introduction.' In *Decentring Empire: Britain, India and the Transcolonial World*, edited by Durba Ghosh and Dane Kennedy, 1–15. New Delhi: Orient Longman.

Goldin, Ian, Geoffrey Cameron and Meera Balarajan. 2011. *Exceptional People: How Migration Shaped Our World and Will Define Our Future*. Princeton: Princeton University Press.

Higman, B. W. 1989. 'Domestic Service in Jamaica since 1750.' In *Muchachas No More: Household Workers in Latin America and the Caribbean*, edited by Elsa M. Chaney and Mary Garcia Castro, 37–66. Philadelphia: Temple University Press.

Higman, B. W. 2002. *Domestic Service in Australia*. Melbourne: Melbourne University Press.

Hu, Xinying. 2011. *China's New Underclass: Paid Domestic Labour*. London: Routledge.

Humfrey, Paula. 2011. 'Introduction.' In *The Experience of Domestic Service for Women in Early Modern London*, edited by Paula Humfrey, 1–42. Farnham: Ashgate.

International Labour Office. 2011. Provisional Record 15A, *Text of the Convention Concerning Decent Work for Domestic Workers*. Geneva: ILO.

International Labour Office. 2013. *Domestic Workers across the World: Global and Regional Statistics and the Extent of Legal Protection*. Geneva: ILO.

Katzman, David M. 1978. *Seven Days a Week: Women and Domestic Service in Industrializing America*. New York: Oxford University Press.

Kraft, Joseph. 1961. 'Settler Politics in Algeria.' *Foreign Affairs* 39(4): 591–600.

Lucas, C. P. 1887. *Introduction to a Historical Geography of the British Colonies*. Oxford: Clarendon Press.

McBride, Theresa M. 1976. *The Domestic Revolution: The Modernization of Household Service in England France, 1820–1920*. London: Croom Helm.

Merivale, Herman. 1861. *Lectures on Colonization and Colonies*. London: Longman, Green, Longman, and Roberts.

Milkman, Ruth, Ellen Reese and Benita Roth. 1998. 'The Macrosociology of Paid Domestic Labor.' *Work and Occupations* 25(4): 483–510.

Rawson, Rawson W. 1884. 'British and Foreign Colonies.' *Journal of the Statistical Society of London* 47(4): 547–608.

Reinhard, Wolfgang. 2011. *A Short History of Colonialism*. Manchester: Manchester University Press.
Samers, Michael. 2010. *Migration*. London: Routledge.
Sarti, Raffaella. 2005. 'Who Are Servants? Defining Domestic Service in Western Europe (16th-21st Centuries).' In *Proceedings of the Servant Project*, 2, edited by Suzy Pasleau and Isabelle Schopp with Raffaella Sarti, 3–59. Liège: Éditions de l'Université de Liège.
Schwenken, Helen, and Lisa-Marie Heimeshoff, eds. 2011. *Domestic Workers Count: Global Data on an Often Invisible Sector*. Kassel: Kassel University Press.
Shepard, Todd. 2006. *The Invention of Decolonization: The Algerian War and the Remaking of France*. Ithaca: Cornell University Press.
Simonovsky, Yamila, and Malte Luebker. 2011. 'Global and Regional Estimates on Domestic Workers.' *Domestic Work Policy Brief 4*. Geneva: ILO.
Stigler, George J. 1947. *Domestic Servants in the United States 1900–1940*. Occasional Paper 24. New York: National Bureau of Economic Research.
Stoler, Ann Laura. 2002. *Carnal Knowledge and Imperial Power: Race and the Intimate in Colonial Rule*. Berkeley: University of California Press.
Stoler, Ann Laura. 2006. 'Tense and Tender Ties: The Politics of Comparison in North American History and (Post) Colonial Studies.' In *Haunted by Empire: Geographies of Intimacy in North American History*, edited by Ann Laura Stoler, 23–67. Durham: Duke University Press.
Sumner, Andy. 2012. 'Where Do the Poor Live?' *World Development* 40(5): 865–77.
Turner, Barry, ed. 2007. *The Statesman's Yearbook: The Politics, Cultures and Economies of the World, 2008*. Basingstoke: Palgrave Macmillan.
Veracini, Lorenzo. 2010. *Settler Colonialism: A Theoretical Overview*. Basingstoke: Palgrave Macmillan.

Part I
Anxieties and Intimacies

Anxieties and Intimacies

Victoria K. Haskins and Claire Lowrie

Domestic labor is acknowledged as profoundly intimate and emotional labor, and as such riven with contradictions (see Boris and Parreñas 2010; Gutiérrez-Rodríguez 2007 & 2010). Because of this peculiarly intimate nature, domestic service was a site of particularly profound significance for imperial and colonial projects. At this domain, colonizer families learned and rehearsed the boundaries of rule, their children's sensibilities cultivated so as to ensure their identification as the privileged colonizer and their distance from those subordinates entrusted with their care. It was also, inevitably, a site of ambivalences and anxieties, where racial classifications could be defied as well as defined, and relations between colonizer and colonized might confound as well as confirm the categories of rule (Stoler 2001: 852, 830–31). The five chapters in this section all address in different and unique ways the kind of intimacies and anxieties that played out in colonial domestic service in the past, and continue to churn unceasingly in present-day domestic work relationships.

It becomes clear from the essays in this section that there can be multiple meanings attached to the intimacy of domestic service. We might refer, in the first instance, directly to the nature of the work performed in domestic service: close, personal, and private; bodily, mundane. As Shireen Ally insists, in the opening chapter on efforts to 'modernize' domestic work relations in contemporary South Africa, domestic workers are simply *not* workers like any other, precisely because of the intimate nature of their work, which generates its own internal dialectic of intimacy and distancing between employers and workers. The intimacy of colonial domestic service might be envisaged as a form of space, a kind of microcosmic contact zone, as Shirleene Robinson frames it, where colonization is rendered close-up and personal. In the chapters by Jane McCabe and Fida Bizri, the intimacy of domestic service resides primarily in its location within the structures and walls of family life; and likewise for Michele Johnson on Jamaica, where she shows how discourses of familial relations and roles have informed the practice of domestic service before, during and after decolonization. Then the intimacies to which Maria Platt refers in her study of domestic workers in present-day Singapore are of a distinctly bodily and sexual nature: not those intimate relations between employer and servant, but the efforts by employers to intervene in and control their workers' private and personal relationships outside the home.

Such intimacies generate anxieties and unresolvable contradictions that again are myriad, as both employers, and the state, seek solutions to the destabilizing effects of intimacy in domestic service. Fida Bizri documents how Lebanese employers have developed discursive strategies including a form of pidgin (a time-honored response to servants in colonial contexts) to protect their personal space and position of power, even as the Sri Lankan women working there eagerly embrace the opportunities of geographic mobility that acquisition of such a language provides. The next chapter, Jane McCabe's study of Eurasian girls in New Zealand in the 1920s and 1930s, shows that transnational mobility for domestic service could be seen by colonial authorities as one solution to the pressing colonial problem of mixed-race girls and the need to protect imperial space. Concern about where the daughters of British tea-planters and Indian women were to fit in the colonial society of late British India (where, crucially, they may have been cared for by servants themselves) was dealt with by their removal altogether, to a British settler outpost far away in the Pacific. Yet the uncertainty of their representation here (were they to be 'lady-helps' rather than servants?) reveals the persistent awkwardness about these dark-skinned girls' location within colonial families and society generally. Shirleene Robinson's chapter provides an even more disturbing historical perspective on the kind of solution domestic service provided to the 'problem' of mixed-race girls. Despite the stated aim to reform and uplift mixed-descent Aboriginal girls in Australia through their placement in white homes, such employment, Robinson shows, operated only to replicate the excessive abuses of frontier colonization, producing and re-producing the racial structures of rule that kept Indigenous peoples subordinate and marginalized.

Anxieties around domestic workers' and their activities on their legislated day off in contemporary Singapore are of a different order, at least on the surface. As Maria Pratt shows in her essay, however, the determination by female employers to exercise strict moral control and surveillance over their workers—even in opposition to the strictures of the state—can be read similarly to the colonialist reformist, civilizing impulse, as being in actuality a way of demarcating difference and the employer's position of power. The intimate lives of the domestic workers become a site where hierarchies are constructed.

Yet workers themselves draw upon relations of intimacy—in terms of their relations with their employers—as a strategy to even up power imbalances where they can. In twentieth-century Jamaica, over a long period encompassing the transition from colonization to independence, where the barriers between them would seem to be unusually permeable, Michele Johnson finds employers and workers fiercely deploying and contesting the meanings of intimate mothering as a way of negotiating their own best possible outcomes and maximizing their power. Shireen Ally notes that the representation of the black female domestic worker in and of itself is a potent source of anxiety in post-apartheid South Africa, standing as it does for conflicting meanings of vulnerability and strength and the perpetuation of the past in the present. Here the domestic worker, and domestic work generally, as an historical signifier of the racist colonialist past is a 'problem' that the state seeks to resolve by imposing 'modern' contractual regulations upon it (perhaps in some ways like the Singaporean state, regulating days off for the Indonesian domestic workers). Yet the domestic workers themselves may well reject such efforts by the state to take control, preferring instead to maintain their own independence and agency, paradoxically, by their manipulation of emotional attachments and engagement of intimacies.

Thus, the paradoxical capacity of the intimate nature of domestic service to both challenge and buttress hierarchies of race and colonial domination persists today, and the imagination of a postcolonial world remains haunted by the 'secret power' of the domestic servant to make manifest the colonial politics of intimacy.

REFERENCES

Boris, Eileen, and Rhacel Salazar Parreñas. 2010. 'Introduction.' In *Intimate Labors: Cultures, Technologies, and the Politics of Care*, edited by Eileen Boris and Rhacel Salazar Parreñas, 1–12. Stanford: Stanford University Press.

Gutiérrez-Rodríguez, Encarnación. 2007. 'The "Hidden Side" of the New Economy: On Transnational Migration, Domestic Work, and Unprecedented Intimacy.' *Frontiers* 28(3): 60–83.

Gutiérrez-Rodríguez, Encarnación. 2010. *Migration, Domestic Work and Affect: A Decolonial Approach on Value and the Feminization of Labor*. New York: Routledge.

Stoler, Ann Laura. 2001. 'Tense and Tender Ties: The Politics of Comparison in North American History and (Post) Colonial Studies.' *Journal of American History* 88(3): 829–65.

2 Domesti-City
Colonial Anxieties and Postcolonial Fantasies in the Figure of the Maid[1]

Shireen Ally

A TALE OF TWO MAIDS 'QUEEN SOPHIE'

On a cold morning in August 2010, residents of Johannesburg in South Africa awoke to a strangely quiet city. The frenzied hype of the soccer world cup was over, and the familiar routines of the city were finding their rhythm again. But on that cold quiet morning, residents of the city were confronted by a dazzling sight. The city had been taken over by a maid. Sophie, the creation of Johannesburg-based artist Mary Sibande, made an appearance across the city skyline. Giant images from Sibande's exhibition 'Long Live the Dead Queen' draped all over the sides of buildings, on rooftops, along the highways.[2] A public art project that curated the city as a gallery.[3]

The images are visually arresting. Sibande's fiberglass likeness, painted over in deep black, is transformed into Queen Sophie, dressed in a maid's uniform re-imagined as a richly colorful and elaborately ornate Victorian costume. In morphing the servant's uniform into the master's dress, Sibande re-dresses/redresses the colonial relation of master and servant: Sophie is visually recognizable as a maid, but she is also in a dramatic movement beyond.[4] Her eyes always closed, she is in a daydream of aspiration, a flight of fantasy.

Queen Sophie, the maid-cum-madam mutates into a superhero, 'a black superwoman figure who escapes her subaltern condition through fantasy,' as a local commentator put it (Mabandu 2009). Colonial relations are confronted, good triumphs over evil, and social justice is restored by Sophie the superhero. 'In assuming the guise of this highly politicized character, Sibande is able to explore, ridicule, and subvert the structures' of a colonial past, as a well-known art critic opined (Corrigall 2009). Re-fashioning the servant, Sibande repurposes a site of colonial subjugation for a postcolonial public.

'I did not want to present yet another image of a victimized maid,' Mary Sibande told me.[5] It is this repudiation of victimhood in the figure of the maid that is symbolically significant. Now, if that summarizes one thread in

Figure 2.1 Queen Sophie in Newtown, Johannesburg, August 2010. Photo by Shireen Ally.

the image of the domestic in public culture, a remarkably dissimilar image is mapped in public law.

THE 'MOST VULNERABLE' WORKER

On a Sunday afternoon in a middle-class suburb of Johannesburg, the local town hall is packed with domestic workers, decked out in their Sunday best. It's an event organized by the City and local labor department to 'celebrate' domestic workers. A well-dressed official of the labor department takes to the stage in a tone of seriousness, and rehearses in a bland baritone: 'Domestic workers are the most vulnerable of all workers' (Ally 2009: 90).[6] 'My mother was a domestic worker,' then Minister of Labor Membathisi Mdladlana was fond of recounting, personalizing the trope, 'so I know their plight and they are amongst the most vulnerable of all workers' (Ally 2009: 87).

This was the state's dominant logic of political inclusion for domestics, and the basis on which domestic workers were codified politically in law

(Ally 2009). Workers heard this repeatedly from the various city and state officials they encountered at innumerable information workshops held around the city and the country, at the state-mandated Commission for Conciliation Mediation and Arbitration (CCMA), even from state-sponsored training providers.

The official continued: 'Domestic workers are the most vulnerable of all workers. This is why we have now included domestic workers in labor legislation. This is why we are celebrating domestic workers today.' There is a chorus of *hm hmms* amongst the crowd. I recounted this story a week later to Eunice Dhladhla, Deputy Secretary-General of the South African Domestic Service and Allied Workers Union (SADSAWU), as we drove through the hectic streets of the inner city in my little purple car.[7] She met the anecdote with silence. Then, '*Hmm* . . . I'd prefer that he says we salute domestic workers, like comrades in struggle,' she offers. 'I don't think I like the idea of "celebrating" women because they are exploited, and vulnerable' (Ally 2009: 133).

Eunice exposed a fault line along which the 'celebration' of these two figures of the maid pivot: the active, capacitated heroic figure of Sophie, on the one hand; and the anonymous, vulnerable maid, passive in victimhood, on the other. In this chapter, I use this fault line to decipher the psychic and affective work animating the anxieties of intimacy that inhere in these figurings of the maid. Those anxieties, I argue, are not only classed but raced, not just feudal but potently *colonial*. While the 'vulnerable worker' invokes domestic service as a type of class despotism to be resolved through the modernization of domestic service, Sophie casts domestic service as a distinctively colonial relation. Both suggest, and are confounded by, the servant as a figure deeply implicated in the ambiguities, ambivalences, and anxieties of *intimacy*.

Revisiting Ann Stoler's (1995; 2002) and Anne McClintock's (1995) seminal explorations of the interpenetrating relations between colonialism and domestic service as a species of sentiment, I argue that the anxieties of racialized (and, interdependently, sexualized) intimacy delineate the servant as a fulcrum figure of the colonial frontier, and that the fantastical restaging of the servant in the postcolonial city confronts colonialism as a relation of the present as much as the past, as intractable as it is enduring.

THE 'MAID' AS POLITICALLY OBSTINATE

Domestic service has endured a long history as an intractable political problem. For feminism, women's relegation to the private sphere of the home (and in particular to the dependency on men through unpaid housework that this presumed) was emblematic of women's gendered subordination (cf. Friedan 1963). Post-war feminisms thus agitated for women's entry into paid employment outside the home as a material and symbolic resistance against patriarchy. But, paid domestic work exposed the unfinished sexual revolution that this entailed. As some women went to work outside the home, other women replaced them. In paid domestic work, primarily middle-class white women used their race and class privilege to, literally, buy their way out of the gendered responsibility for domestic labor, which was in turn displaced onto poor women (and increasingly women of color, black and immigrant women) whose work, to this day, remains low in status and poorly paid (cf. Rollins 1985; Parreñas 2001). Gender inequality was therefore not only unresolved, but further intensified, and splintered by race and class (Davis 1981).

But it was not just that paid domestic service reflected social inequalities. Rather, as a critical feminist scholarship began to forcefully demonstrate, domestic work was crucial to the *production* of race and class distinction (cf. Sanjek and Colen 1990). By releasing their employers from the dirty work of cleaning their own toilets and wiping lunch from their children's faces, the men and women who employ domestic servants are not only released for full-time employment outside the home, it is argued, they are also crucially distanced from the contaminating effects on class status of proximity to dirt (Campkin and Cox 2008). As such they are freed to accumulate other forms of cultural capital to which accrue the respectabilities of raced and classed distinction.

The maid has thus always been discomforting for feminists. Employing a domestic worker was no longer just deciding how to get the floors scrubbed, or the laundry done. To employ a maid or a nanny was to collude with an institution that manufactured durable social hierarchies. Gabrielle Meagher (2002) was forced to ask 'is it wrong to pay for housework?' while Joan Tronto (2002) was compelled to address 'the nanny question' in feminism. A difficult personal choice for many socially conscious working men and women, the maid became an obstinate political predicament for feminists.

At least as early as the first modern treatise on the political dilemmas of domestic service, the maid has confounded feminist politics. In 1906, Lucy Salmon initiated serious scholarly reflections on the modern 'problem' of domestic service. 'The most serious obstacle in the way of any improvement in domestic service,' she argued, was 'the failure on the part of men and women everywhere to recognize that the occupation is governed by economic law, that it is bound up inextricably with every other phase of the labor question. . . . The initial step toward improvement must be the recognition of this fact,' she concluded (Salmon 1906: 97).

The problems around paying someone to clean one's house or care for one's children have, in the century since Salmon, converged on her original problematic: that of the work not being considered employment at all. As contemporary feminist Pierrette Hondagneu-Sotelo put it, 'Paid domestic work is not distinctive in being the worst job of all, but because it is somehow regarded as something other than employment' (2001: 9). Domestic work as the seeming extension of women's 'natural' roles, as the prerogative of kin rather than contract, and sited in the domain of leisure not work, all conspire to render it outside its appropriate recognition as employment like any other.

The political resolution has organized itself as a recognition of paid domestic work as no more and no less than employment like any other. A modern, formal, depersonalized form of employment with decent wages and decent working conditions, it is argued, should make paid domestic work not so problematic after all. Put another way, the political panacea suggests that if you dispense with feudal attitudes of domestic servitude, and replace them with a modern, formal, contractual, legally regulated form of employment, just like any other, then domestic work need not be so politically troublesome.

Indeed, this has become *the* politics for the sector.[8] So, in South Africa, where domestic work was marked under apartheid precisely by the failure to recognize so-called servants as workers (Cock 1980), by 2004, the democratic South African state had almost fully embraced exactly this modernizing solution as a political resolution to the problem of paid domestic work.

I have shown elsewhere how the state crafted what is still one of the world's most extensive and expansive efforts to recognize paid domestic work as a form of employment like any other (Ally 2009). Existing labor legislation was redrafted to include domestic workers, extended with a landmark national minimum wage, mandatory formal contracts of employment, state-legislated annual increases, compulsory pay slips, extensive leave, severance pay, formal registration, a government-sponsored pension fund, access to unemployment insurance benefits (a world first), and a national certificate and qualification in domestic work through government-sponsored training (another world first).

The South African democratic state thus inaugurated one of the world's most comprehensive efforts to modernize, formalize, and professionalize domestic work, and it did so by legally codifying the maid as 'the most vulnerable worker.' Yet, the domestic workers I spoke to did not look anything like these so-called 'vulnerable' workers.

I met Patricia Kubu in May 2004. Her employer had been trying for the better part of six months to get her to sign a formal contract, yet Patricia simply refused. 'I will not sign that contract!' she told me with determination, the vein over her right temple throbbing. 'But, if you have a contract, you will be legally protected,' I tried to convince her. 'No, no, no. I don't want to sign that contract,' she protested (Ally 2009: 94). When I met Linda Mkhonto, she recollected how she 'negotiated' Saturdays off when the new legislation came into effect:

> First, when the legislation came out, we didn't talk about the laws . . . I know I should only work eight to five for Monday to Friday, because

I know the laws from the union. So, I know I mustn't work Saturdays. So, on Saturday, I don't tell her anything, I just go to my room in the back and pull the blankets over my head. On Monday when I go to work, she says I must be better now, not sick. I don't say anything. Next week, Saturday, I pull the blankets over my head. Monday, she is wondering. But we don't say anything to one another. Next Saturday, I pull the blankets. Now, she tells me she called the CCMA, and I'm supposed to work on Saturday until twelve, one. But, I know my rights. I know I'm not supposed to work. So, next Saturday, I pull the blankets. That Monday, she says maybe I shouldn't work on Saturdays.

(2009: 94)

This was an extraordinary tale. As I have argued previously, a potent cocktail of informality, personalized dependence on employers, and the failure of recourse to state institutions summarized apartheid-era labor relations in domestic service (Ally 2009). The democratic state's contracts of employment, legislated rights, and access to state-based industrial relations institutions targeted exactly domestics' so-called vulnerabilities. Yet, Patricia Kubu refused to sign a contract that would regulate her work through statutory protection. Instead of contractually defining the limits of her working time, or taking her case to the CCMA, Linda Mkhonto chose to 'pull the blankets' over her head. Workers were refusing to sign contracts, refusing state-based registration, and choosing to informally negotiate the conditions of their work (2009: 95).

In 1906, Lucy Salmon not only argued that the solution to the political problem that was paid domestic work would be to recognize it as employment like any other. She argued that *the law* was the 'inexorable' mechanism for that recognition (Salmon 1906: 99). It is prescient that Salmon's politics centered on both recognizing domestic service as economic activity like any other, and faith in the inexorability of the law—more than any other technology—to orchestrate such recognition. Yet, here were domestic workers in South Africa refusing exactly the legal regulation of their work as employment that had been touted as the politically progressive solution to the problem of paid domestic work for more than a century. What on earth was going on?

THE LABOR OF INTIMACY, THE INTIMACY OF LABOR

First, it turns out that while the ineluctable politics for paid domestic work is to modernize and depersonalize it like any other, domestic workers may not be *simply* workers like any other. 'I make their beds every day. I wash their sheets every day. I wash their underwear every day. I answer their phone and take messages. I am there before they leave for work and argue. I am there when they come home and argue. I know everything about what's going on in their lives,' explained Patricia Kubu. Joyce Nhlapo, a worker with razor-sharp wit, summarized the inextricability of domestic workers from the intimate lives of their employers. 'I work *in* a family, not for a family,' she said (Ally 2009: 96).

Homes are not impersonal and inert spaces for the seamless application of depersonalizing mandates, as I have argued at length elsewhere (cf. Ally 2009). Instead, domestic workers' workplaces are the intimate spaces of family life, and their work there is deeply implicated in all the close personal contact; the emotions, experiences, and intimacy that is the fabric of families and households. Domestic workers' work within the emotion-laden spaces of family life makes their work intimate. Such abiding intimacies are deeply disquieting for employers, who attempt to manage the contaminating effects of familiarity through the cultivation of social and physical distance, often through degradation and dehumanization.

The 'dialectic of intimacy and distancing' this structures in domestic service is a unique species of relations in which closeness, familiarity, and intimacy coexist with distancing, estrangement, and dehumanization (Ally 2011). In her breathtaking analysis of domestic service, Alison Light (2008) explores Virginia Woolf's relationship with her long-time servant (and companion) Nellie Boxall, and shows that it was not the abuse Virginia directed at Nellie, nor the difficult working conditions and dismal remuneration, neither was it the dramatic instantiation of class distinction that defined the relationship between them. More than anything, 'it was the ferocity of the feelings involved' (*xiv*). 'After all those years of living together,' writes Light, 'they were like a husband and wife who ought to divorce, but can't; they were deeply, hopelessly, attached' (*xiv*). Light surmises: 'Service, in other words, has always been an emotional as well as economic territory' (3), and 'domestic service . . . a species of psychological and emotional slavery' (*xxi*).

These ambiguities of intimacy—of degradation *and* care—are among the more potent sources of the unique architecture of dependence and exploitation in domestic service. The ubiquitous ideological deployment by employers of the domestic as 'like one of the family' actively manipulates these familial ambiguities as a practice of intimate power. In the historical context of the failure of state oversight, though, South African domestic workers *also* used the exact same ambiguities of intimacy to navigate a path through the tense mixture of beneficiation and degradation in personal service. 'I got her interested in the Lotto [national lottery],' Josephine Kekana animatedly told me:

> She was not interested in it. She said, how you going to win? I told her, no, you see, if you do not play, how *you* going to win? It's so nice, because we walk to the garage together on Friday, we buy a little bit of something sweet, then we always sit that night, we watch together for the numbers. . . . That time, when she won with her numbers, you must

see how we were jumping together. We even hugged each other. She was so happy.... It's very important to have that kind of relationship with them. Otherwise, they exploit you even more.

(Ally 2009: 102)

Cultivating intimacy was a clear tactic for Josephine. As it was for another worker who related how sitting down over tea each morning with her employer listening to her problems was a way to ensure an extended Christmas vacation. South African domestic workers chronicled the most striking tales of the manipulation of affect and intimacy as a means to restructure class relations, as a technique of class combat, and as a practice of power. 'I tell her how much I need her and the job,' said Kedibone Maake. That way, 'she feels responsible for me. She won't just tell me to go' (Ally 2009: 106). In this careful nurturing of dependence as part of the ambiguities of intimacy, Kedibone extracted from her employer's potentiality for power an additional obligation for reciprocity and mutual obligation.

In the absence of state regulation, workers also exploited the intimacies of service to socially regulate their working conditions through what one worker called, 'silently talking back':

When I first started working for that woman, she went to work and I was busy cleaning. When I got to the bathroom, I see that she left the panties in the bath, because she was thinking that it was my job to wash her panties. That was how little they thought of us, to just leave the panties in the bath like that, not even to ask you. So, I decided I am not going to tell her I don't do this kind of dirty job. That day, I just lifted the panties, just on the tip like this, and I put it around the tap. Then I cleaned the bath. When she came home, she saw what I did with the panties. The next day, she leaves them in the bath again. So, I do the same thing also. I just put them on the, what you say, on the bath, and I clean the bath. Then next day she does the same thing, and I also do the same thing. She can see I'm not going to clean them, so she doesn't leave them any more in the bath then after that.

(Ally 2009: 107)

Despite the extensive investments of the state in honing a set of legal entitlements and apparatuses to codify the limits of a domestics' work, and to depersonalize the relations between 'maids' and 'madams,' workers continued to manage the limits of their work through covert communication, continued to groom personalized affect for its benefits, and deployed the intimacies of service as a creative practice.

This was why the state's efforts had been so stubbornly received. It had imagined that an abstract depersonalizing political technology would rectify the problem of personalization by legal fiat. Instead, it confronted workers ingeniously harnessing the ambiguities inherent in the intimacies of service, and who were thus recalcitrant about the state's efforts that presumed them to be inertly, uniformly, and simply subjected. This forces into contradiction the state's rendering of the worker as 'vulnerable'—incapacitated, passive, victimized, requiring the protection of a more capacitated actor—with workers' own rendering of themselves as capable, creative, and assertive. And so we find ourselves back at Queen Sophie versus the vulnerable worker.

The vulnerable worker implies, as does the history of the political problem represented by the maid, a distinction between the feudal and the modern; specifically, of the despotism of personalized intimacy against the equality of modern depersonalization. In Lucy Salmon's (1912) thesis, it was against the feudalism of personal service that she advocated for 'democracy in the household,' in which recognizing domestic work as employment activity like any other was to pull it from its feudal past into its modern future. The vulnerable worker is located in this enduring rhetorical field. In the protections offered through the modern techniques of statist law, it was the risk of being made vulnerable to the feudalism of personalized intimacy that was supposedly attenuated.

Queen Sophie invokes a very different kind of lordship. Her sartorial posture (the maid's uniform transforming into the Victorian mistress's costume) intentionally redirects service as an order not of feudalism, but of *colonialism*. To argue that the problem with domestic work is that it is simply not recognized as employment like any other is to efface a crucial vector of its anxiety: its location not only—or not simply—in feudal relations, but its genesis and location in distinctively *modern colonial histories*. To seek to disinfect domestic service from its intimacies through the legal codes of modern employment misapprehends that the intimacies which coordinate contemporary domestic service are in fact a colonial artifact, and a distinctively modern one at that. And so, where the politics of employment like any other ends is where Sophie begins, in the affective densities drafted at the edge of that most volatile species of the intimate: colonial relations of race.

THE AMBIVALENCES AND ANXIETIES OF (RACIALIZED) INTIMACY

> He was a slightly-built, middle-aged white man, probably about fifty-five years old, dressed in a checked shirt and gaudy yellow shorts. The broad Afrikaans accent with which he spoke English was barely audible from behind his hands. He was trying to speak through his sobs, which shook his entire body. . . . He was recounting an early memory.
>
> As a little boy on the farm in the Northern Transvaal where he grew up, he had loved his African nanny. He had loved to snuggle his head between her full breasts; he had loved the songs she sang to him in her language; he had loved the food she fed him. But as he grew up,

his friends had taunted him for his affection for her, as she was 'net 'n kaffirmeid' (just a nigger servant girl). He had learned to deny his love for his first friend in life, and to call her names to prove his indifference. Now he was articulating a deep sense of loss and waste, anger at a social system that had raised him on lies and damaged his humanity.

(Steyn 2001: *i–ii*)

Melissa Steyn's (2001) *Whiteness Just Isn't What It Used to Be* begins with the maid as psychic repository of the colonial encounter of whiteness with its 'other' in South Africa—a sensorium where intimacy and estrangement, love and humiliation, attachment and denigration, coexist. The kitchen is not only a place of the intimacy of labor, or the labor of intimacy. It designates a terrain of colonial contact, and is a site dense with the psychic and affective anxieties of racialized intimacy.

In early twentieth-century Natal, as Prinisha Badassy (2006) expertly unearths, the racialized domesticity of colonial life between white masters and their Indian indentured servants was characterized as much by cruelty as it was by the cultivation of care.[9] Masters inflicted physical and psychic violence on their servants, while some servants responded with violence of their own—raping and poisoning their masters, even bludgeoning them to death. Yet 'the proximity and intimacy within the colonial home in Natal allowed for the nurturing of close bonds between settler families and their servants,' Badassy reveals (2006: 106). Indeed, masters and servants co-directed mutual intimacies amidst mutual forms of violence, making colonial domesticity a contact zone of the ambivalences of raced intimacy as cruelty *and* compassion.

Ann Stoler (2002) stunningly dissects the intimacies of domestic service in the Dutch East Indies to expose exactly this coincidence, and the constitutive relationships between race and the intimate in colonial rule. In delineating the 'the affective grid of colonial politics' (2002: 7), the intimate is exposed as a relation of rule. Consistently, European masters and their native servants are primary protagonists in these 'intimate injuries of empire' (2002: 213). In textured detail, Stoler shows how nostalgic sentimentality for the servant in the childhood memories of settler colonists betrays the ambivalences of racial distinction forged in the intimacies of colonial servitude.

At the same time, Stoler's (1995) adroit quarrel with Foucault's (1988) *History of Sexuality* exposes the deep and intricate relations between raced and sexed intimacies in colonial service. Attending to the problem that Foucault's history of bourgeois and Victorian sexuality did not include a discussion of its imperial coordinates, Stoler shows how metropolitan selves were indeed constituted, in part, by the affects of empire. Stoler suggestively shows how, for example, the paranoia attending child masturbation in the colonies indexed the civilizational compass of Victorian morality in a racial frame, and how it was the figure of the native servant that coordinated these panics. In Java, hysteria over white infantile sexuality was trained on 'primitive' nannies' (presumed) sexual (mis)education of their young white charges, and Victorian bourgeois civilities were thus manufactured in a direct relation to the anxieties over the siting of native servants in the education of (white) desire.

In the bodily intimacies of native servants in the colonies was thus deposited metropolitan anxieties of race as a moral threshold. Servants, in particular, embodied the site at which racial and sexual intimacies intersected. 'Servants could steal more than the sexual innocence of European children,' argues Stoler, including the very 'sentiments that underwrote their identifications as European' (1995: 163–64). This was the motor of the anxieties over child masturbation as a fulcrum for the education of desire—that is, the interdependent relations of racial mastery, sexual control, and together, their coincident organization of 'the bourgeois vision of a colonial utopia' (1995: 164). '[N]ative servants [thus] occupied and constituted . . . a pivotal moral role,' argues Stoler (1995: 150). 'Underwriting colonial anxieties,' she concludes, was thus the figure of the servant (2010: 114).

Anne McClintock's (1995) brilliant disentangling of these interpenetrating orders of imperialism and classed/raced sexuality converges, not coincidentally, on Stoler's fulcrum figure of the servant. 'The black woman stands at the threshold of domesticity as a figure of intense ambivalence,' writes McClintock (1995: 268). Olive Schreiner's ambivalent figuring of her 'Old Ayah' is brought into the same frame as both Steyn's Afrikaner man from the Northern Transvaal and Stoler's Dutch charges of native nannies, as McClintock details the strikingly archetypal affective architecture of, what she calls, 'domestic colonialism':

> Part of the white child's earliest identity is structured around the strength and authority, however restricted, of the black mother figure. Coming to adolescence, however, white children are obliged, by colonial decree, to detach themselves from identification with the African women with whom they have been so intimate and thus also from significant aspects of their own identity. Black women come to form the abjected, inner limit of the white child's identity: rejected but constitutive. *In the process, a number of morbid symptoms appear.*
>
> (1995: 270, my emphasis)

Summarized more crisply: 'White children—nursed, tended, caressed and punished by black maids and nurses—receive the memory of black women's power as an ambiguous heritage' (1995: 270). McClintock prefers the vocabulary of ambivalence.[10] Yet, 'morbid symptoms' gesture to the psychosomatic diagnosis of colonial anxiety that burdens the figure of the servant. 'Anxiety, then, is in the first place something that is felt,' wrote Freud.

At the same time, moving away from anxiety as mere morbid symptom, Freud reworked anxiety as *itself* 'an affective state' (Freud 1959: 132). The domestication of racialized-sexualized intimacy is, as Stoler demonstrates, amongst the most potent of colonialism's 'affective states.' Indeed, suggests McClintock, the colonial condition is a nervous one:

> The power of black women is a colonial secret. White domestic life enfolds itself about this secret, as its dreaded, inner shape. Displaced and denied, its pressure is nonetheless felt everywhere, managed by multiple rituals of negation and abasement, suffused with unease. *The invisible strength of black women presses everywhere on white life so that the energy required to deny it takes the shape of neurosis.*
>
> (1995: 271, my emphasis)

The figure of the servant systematizes these colonial ambivalences of race, condensing the anxieties of intimacy. What inheres in colonial domesticity and domestic service, therefore, is not only a particularly powerful equation of race, sex, and intimacy, but the sinews of anxiety that bind them indelibly in the neurotic colonial imagination. Both Stoler and McClintock eloquently decode how imperial power was founded on the crafting of a simultaneity between race as difference, and the anxiety of intimacy, and both demonstrate how few other institutions disrupt and concretize the tensions of racialized intimacy as much as domestic service.

The most brutal and incongruous expression of this was, in many ways, apartheid South Africa, where domestic work represented the site, arguably, of one of the most sustained and affectively loaded interracial encounters between blacks and whites (Cock 1980). Throughout the interpenetrating histories of South African colonialism, the raced-sexed intimacies of domestic service provoked anxiety. The most sustained of these episodes, beginning in the 1880s in Natal and extending into the 1910s in Johannesburg, otherwise known as the 'Black Peril' scares, summarized the colonial neuroses induced by the intimacies of domestic service (van Onselen 1982; Martens 2002). Indeed, colonial men pursued their fear over the siting of black 'houseboys' in sexual proximity to white mistresses with an at times violent obsession. Indeed, the 'Black Peril' scares and the figure of the raced-sexed servant would become the basis for the crafting of the bureaucratic architecture of colonial rule. 'Native registration,' as Jeremy Martens shows, was the direct result of colonial anxieties over the intimacies that inhered in service (2002; see also Lowrie, this volume). And so nothing less than the infamous apartheid 'pass laws'—that paradigmatic mode of institutionalized modern racism in South Africa—had its genesis in the intimate anxieties attending the figure of the African houseboy.

In Johannesburg, the so-called 'Black Peril' scares were in fact so productive that, together with the necessity for cheap African male labor in the rapacious local gold mining industry, it eventually succeeded in evacuating the African houseboy from the scene of white colonial domesticity (Van Onselen 1982). This 'success' of the 'Black Peril' in Johannesburg, compared to other Southern African contexts where the same moral panic obtained but did not succeed in displacing the houseboy from service, would set the scene for what would become the iconically distinctive relation of apartheid domestic service: 'maids and madams,' as the title of Jacklyn Cock's (1980) classic study so efficiently summarized the primary protagonists in the intimate dramas of apartheid's domestication.

Apartheid domestic service, however, betrayed a racial paradox. While the racial requisite of whiteness under apartheid was a fanatical separation of races, white mastery required a servicing of whiteness by black bodies within the sites of intimate domesticity. This gave the cultivation of (racialized) intimacy by black maids added political potency. Recovering intimacy with white employers under apartheid's manic forms of racist separation was more than mere management of work, cynical calculations of beneficiation, or even recuperation of personhood (cf. Ginsburg 2011). It represented nothing less than a refiguration of the raced relations of colonial rule by black workers inside white homes.

In this context, the tensions of intimacy that frame South African domestic workers' recalcitrant entry into democratic political personhood are more dense than an initial reading may suggest. Practices of intimacy by workers in the recesses of private life interact with and shape public statecraft. They render legible the making of an alternate public racial order out of the private spaces of familial domesticity, and thus suggest why the continuing confrontations with the intractable colonial residues of race take shape as, and in, the figure of the servant.

The figure of the servant is potent and recurring not because it confirms colonial rule as the submission to absolute racial dominion. Rather, it is because the servant exposes how submission to mastery has never been a predictable posture. The intimacies shared between masters and servants imbued in the latter the powers of espionage and subterfuge. This brings us back to Queen Sophie versus the 'vulnerable worker,' of the servant's powers or lack thereof.

These alternate renderings of the figure of the maid in the contemporary public culture of South African cities are prescient in converging on the servant as the figure through which to render the intractability of the past in the present. 'Colonial pasts, though effaced, continue to carve out the environmental and psychic debris in which people live, long after colonial polities have been dismantled,' Ann Stoler argues (2010: *xviii*). Whether assertive or subjected, the figure of the servant may be seen to instantiate what Derek Gregory calls 'the colonial present' (2004).

FANTASY AND THE FRONTIER: A CONCLUSION

> The furtive intimacies between black women and their white charges; the forbidden liaisons between black women and their white male employers; the fraught relations of acrimony, strained intimacy, mistrust, condescension, occasional friendships and coerced subservience that shape the relations between African women and their white mistresses ensure that the colonial home is a contest zone of acute ambivalence.
> (McClintock 1995: 271)

Intimacy and estrangement (especially sexual) across the combustible boundary of race is potent. For McClintock, this structures the colonial home as a 'contest zone of acute ambivalence' (1995: 271). For Victoria Haskins, domestic service is a 'contact zone' of racialized intimacy (2001). In a textured reading of domestic service as a site that distils settler colonialism's racial dilemmas of assimilating the native versus consigning them to oblivion, Haskins compellingly reads the Aboriginal servant on the doorstep of the settler home as the colonial frontier.[11] The supple boundaries of that frontier are lubricated by colonial anxieties. Stoler argues that 'servants were such a charged site of European anxieties' because:

> servants policed the borders of the private, mediated between the 'street' and the home, and occupied the inner recesses of bourgeois life; they were, in short, the subaltern gatekeepers of gender, class, and racial distinctions that by their very presence they transgressed.
> (2010: 133)

Inasmuch as the figure of the servant bears the psychic load of colonial neuroses of race, it is through the figure of the servant that politics and aesthetics intervene in the racialized reiterations of the colonial in contemporary South African cities. Like Queen Sophie versus the 'vulnerable worker.' Strength and creativity versus vulnerability and victimhood. But, why is this the recurring trope for figuring the servant?

In McClintock's interrogation of Olive Schreiner's childhood relation to her nanny lies an answer: 'As a white child, [Schreiner] held potential power over the African workers in the home; but these women possessed a secret and appalling power to judge and punish her' (1995: 267). In the colonial relation of native nanny to white child, apprenticeship into white mastery confronted the powers of the black servant in racialized intimacy. 'Old Ayah locked the door and put the key into her pocket,' illustrating 'the unbidden recognition that African women hold the keys to the domestic power of white people' (1995: 268). The servant stands, literally, as the threshold figure at the doorway of the metonymic colonial frontier itself; standing there in the ambiguous posture of subjection *and* power. 'The power of black women is a colonial secret,' wrote McClintock, and the degraded humiliations of service she is forced to endure is orchestrated by a white imagination terrified of the servant's secret power (1995: 268).

Strength and creativity set against vulnerability and victimhood is thus the persistently indexical idiom through which servants condense our colonial pasts; in Queen Sophie and the 'vulnerable worker,' they also augur a postcolonial future. The state's passive, victimized, 'vulnerable,' maid is not only iconic of poor black women statically stalled in subjection, but also precisely the agent of the state's aspiration to a race-corrected future. Mary Sibande's active, capacitated, heroic figure of Sophie recognizes the forging of black womanhood in the furnace of racial subjection, yet her imagination becomes the flight of fantasy to a future beyond. One invokes a politics of empathy, the other a politics of hope. Yet, for all that is radically dissimilar between Sophie and the 'vulnerable worker,' they share a similar psychic field, one dominated by the anxiety of race as an intractable 'colonial present' (Gregory 2004). Both work out their anxiety through fantasy—the fantasy of a racially utopian future iconically embodied in the alternative rendering of the maid-servant, in her relation to injury. Thus, however different Sophie is from the vulnerable worker, in both images, the figure of the maid literally services the fears and anxieties about South Africans' racially dystopic present, and become the means through which its urban public culture fantasizes a future beyond.

Bystrom and Nuttall (2013) see this kind of 'intimate exposure'—the public exposure of private intimacies—in contemporary Johannesburg as very different than the dramatization of 'private lives' in 'public cultures' in the West, citing Lauren Berlant's coinage and critique of the 'intimate public sphere' (Berlant 1997; 2008). Instead, they argue for the productive post-apartheid possibilities of bringing sites of invisibility (racially charged under apartheid)—the bedroom, the bathroom, the kitchen—into visibility, and thus making them subject to, and the subject of, public democratic deliberation.

Yet, this still leaves the question of why it is that the 'public private sphere,' as they call it, so consistently and persistently stages the servant *par excellence* as the site of 'entanglement' (Bystrom and Nuttall 2013: 20). Public politics and aesthetics in South African cities are saturated by the maid. This necessary ubiquity is not easily resolved by positing its productive possibilities for resolving the past in 'the now' of democratic politics, as Bystrom and Nuttall suggest (2013: 20). The figure of the servant stages precisely the irresoluteness of the past, and the indeterminacy of any possible 'after.' In this, the maid is always overdetermined and overburdened. She is the instantaneous icon of the tenacity of an uncomfortable past that South Africans are so unwillingly incarcerated by and yet so desperate to imagine a way out of. Uncomfortably, she manifests the tense, intense, and unresolvable racialized intimacies that mark the millions of middle-class kitchens across the city as a quotidian, but unrelenting, colonial frontier. In that, the so-called maid labors in service not only of homes and families, but nothing less than the social orders of our times.

NOTES

1. A first version of this chapter was presented at the 92nd Harold Wolpe Dialogue, 7 September 2010, Cape Town and, a week later, at the University of Johannesburg's Sociology, Anthropology, and Development Studies Wednesday seminar. I am grateful to Irma Du Plessis for her commentary on the paper at that seminar, and to Victoria Haskins, Claire Lowrie, and the anonymous reviewers for their comments on this significantly revised and expanded version. I am also grateful to the University of the Witwatersrand Friedel Sellschop Award for support towards the writing of this chapter.
2. The project was undertaken by AAW! (Art at Work) Project Management as part of an initiative 'Joburg Art City 2010,' and included 19 building-sized images from the exhibition installed across the city. The project followed the success of the exhibition 'Long Live the Dead Queen' at Gallery Momo in Johannesburg.
3. For a contrary reading of the 'public art' intents of the project, i.e. of the gentrifying logics betrayed by the art's 'covering up' of urban decay, see Singer (2012).
4. See also Alexandra Dodd (2010) for another reading of the specific disruption of colonial categories implied by Sibande's fantastical figuring of 'Queen Sophie.'
5. Interview by author, Johannesburg, July 28, 2010. Transcript held by author.
6. The ethnographic vignettes and interviews throughout this chapter are drawn from PhD fieldwork, discussed in detail with full source information in Ally (2009).
7. The national domestic workers union, the South African Domestic Service and Allied Workers Union (SADSAWU) was formed in 2001, after its predecessor union, the South African Domestic Workers Union (SADWU) was dissolved in 1996. For more on the union as well as on contemporary domestic service in South Africa, see Fish (2006).
8. Note the recent International Labour Organization's Convention 189 on Decent Work for Domestic Workers (cf. Fish, this volume).
9. While white women, black (African) men, 'Coloured' women, and Indian men and women worked as servants across South Africa's varied histories of domestic service, African women came to predominate in the sector from the 1930s. For more on the varied race relations between white employers and their non-white domestic employees, see Preston-Whyte (1969).
10. The most important theorization of ambivalence as a colonial code is, of course, Homi Bhabha's (1984) 'Of Mimicry and Man: The Ambivalence of Colonial Discourse'. It is beyond the scope of this chapter however to put Bhabha's 'ambivalence' into conversation with McClintock's, but it is the subject of my ongoing work. Bhabha, for instance, in 'The World and the Home' (1992) addresses directly the relation between domesticity and intimacy in colonialism. 'In a feverish stillness,' writes Bhabha of the psychic tempo of colonial codes, 'the intimate recesses of the domestic space become sites for history's most intricate invasions' (41). There is thus a productive dialogue to be had between Bhabha, Stoler, and McClintock on this specific theme.

11. Myrna Tonkinson (1988) also makes an important argument for domestic service in settler colonialism as a 'frontier.' Even though the very idea of the 'frontier' is located in—and hence somewhat contaminated by—colonial ideology, it can be analytically productive. As Cooper and Mitropoulos (2009) suggest, it is precisely the semantic potency of the 'frontier' as imperial ideology that makes it useful for an examination of the domestication of empire.

REFERENCES

Ally, Shireen A. 2009. *From Servants to Workers: South African Domestic Workers and the Democratic State.* Ithaca: ILR/Cornell University Press.
Ally, Shireen A. 2011. 'Domestics, "Dirty Work" and the Affects of Domination.' *South African Review of Sociology* 42(2): 1–7.
Badassy, Prinisha. 2006. '". . . And My Blood Became Hot!" Crimes of Passion, Crimes of Reason: An Analysis of the Crimes of Murder and Physical Assault against Masters and Mistresses by their Indian Domestic Servants, Natal, 1880–1920.' *Journal of Natal and Zulu History* 23: 73–106.
Berlant, Lauren. 1997. *The Queen of America Goes to Washington City: Essays on Sex and Citizenship.* Durham: Duke University Press.
Berlant, Lauren. 2008. *The Female Complaint: The Unfinished Business of Sentimentality in American Culture.* Durham: Duke University Press.
Bhabha, Homi K. 1984. 'Of Mimicry and Man: The Ambivalence of Colonial Discourse.' *October* 28: 125–33.
Bhabha, Homi K. 1992. 'The World and the Home.' *Social Text* 31(32): 141–53.
Bystrom, Kerry, and Sarah Nuttall. 2013. 'Introduction: Private Lives and Public Cultures in South Africa.' *Cultural Studies*: 1–20.
Campkin, Ben, and Rosie Cox, eds. 2008. *Dirt: New Geographies of Cleanliness and Contamination.* London: I. B. Taurus.
Cock, Jacklyn. 1980. *Maids and Madams: A Study in the Politics of Exploitation.* Johannesburg: Ravan Press.
Cooper, Melinda, and Angela Mitropoulos. 2009. 'The Household Frontier.' *Ephemera: Theory and Politics in Organization* 9(4): 363–68.
Corrigall, Mary. 2009. 'Mary Sibande: Domestic Fantasy.' 5 August. http://corrigall.blogspot.com/2009/08/mary-sibande-domestic-fantasy.html. Accessed 6 August 2009.
Davis, Angela Y. 1981. *Women, Race and Class.* New York: Random House.
Derek, Gregory. 2004. *The Colonial Present: Afghanistan, Palestine, Iraq.* Malden, Oxford and Carlton: Blackwell.
Dodd, Alexandra. 2010. '"Dressed to Thrill": The Victorian Postmodern and Counter-Archival Imaginings in the Work of Mary Sibande.' *Critical Arts: South-North Cultural and Media Studies* 24(3): 467–74.
Fish, Jennifer N. 2006. *Domestic Democracy: At Home in South Africa.* New York and Oxon: Routledge.
Foucault, Michel. 1988. *The History of Sexuality: Volume 1.* London: Penguin.
Freud, Sigmund. 1959. *Inhibitions, Symptoms and Anxiety: The Standard Edition of the Complete Psychological Works of Sigmund Freud*, edited by James Strachey. New York: W. W. Norton.
Friedan, Betty. 1963. *The Feminine Mystique.* New York: W. W. Norton.
Ginsburg, Rebecca. 2011. *At Home with Apartheid: The Hidden Landscapes of Domestic Service in Johannesburg.* Charlottesville and London: University of Virginia Press.

Haskins, Victoria. 2001. 'On the Doorstep: Aboriginal Domestic Service as a "Contact Zone."' *Australian Feminist Studies* 16(34): 13–25.
Hondagneu-Sotelo, Pierrette. 2001. *Doméstica: Immigrant Workers Cleaning and Caring in the Shadows of Affluence*. Berkeley: University of California Press.
Light, Alison. 2008. *Mrs Woolf and the Servants: The Hidden Heart of Domestic Service*. London: Penguin.
Mabandu, Percy. 2009. 'Ambition Made Flesh.' *Mail and Guardian*, 31 July. http://mg.co.za/article/2009-07-31-ambition-made-flesh. Accessed 6 August 2009.
Martens, Jeremy C. 2002. 'Settler Homes, Manhood and 'Houseboys': An Analysis of Natal's Rape Scare of 1886.' *Journal of Southern African Studies* 28(2): 379–400.
McClintock, Anne. 1995. *Imperial Leather: Race, Gender, and Sexuality in the Colonial Contest*. New York and London: Routledge.
Meagher, Gabrielle. 2002. 'Is it Wrong to Pay for Housework?' *Hypatia* 17: 52–66.
Parreñas, Rhacel Salazar. 2001. *Servants of Globalization: Women, Migration, and Domestic Work*. Stanford: Stanford University Press.
Preston-Whyte, E. 1969. 'Between Two Worlds: A Study of the Working Life, Social Ties, and Inter-Personal Relationships of African Women Migrants in Domestic Service in Durban.' PhD thesis, University of Natal-Durban, South Africa.
Rollins, Judith. 1985. *Between Women: Domestics and their Employers*. Philadelphia: Temple University Press.
Sanjek, Roger, and Shellee Colen. 1990. 'Introduction.' In At Work in Homes: Household Workers in World Perspective, edited by Roger Sanjek and Shellee Colen, 1–13. Washington DC: American Ethnological Society.
Salmon, Lucy Maynard. 1906. *Progress in the Household*. New York: Houghton and Mifflin.
Salmon, Lucy Maynard. 1912. 'Democracy in the Household.' *American Journal of Sociology* 17(4): 437–57.
Singer, Alison E. 2012. '"Sophie Reigns" over Dominant Display Practices: Negotiating Power in Mary Sibande's Installations. MA thesis, University of Texas at Austin, United States.
Steyn, Melissa. 2001. *Whiteness Just Isn't What It Used to Be: White Identity in a Changing South Africa*. Albany: SUNY Press.
Stoler, Ann Laura. 1995. *Race and the Education of Desire: Foucault's History of Sexuality and the Colonial Order of Things*. Durham: Duke University Press.
Stoler, Ann Laura. 2002. *Carnal Knowledge and Imperial Power: Race and the Intimate in Colonial Rule*. Berkeley: University of California Press.
Stoler, Ann Laura. 2010. Carnal Knowledge and Imperial Power: Race and the Intimate in Colonial Rule. With a new preface edition. Berkeley: University of California Press.
Tonkinson, Myrna. 1988. 'Sisterhood or Aboriginal Servitude? Black and White Women on the Australian Frontier.' *Aboriginal History* 12(1): 27–39.
Tronto, Joan C. 2002. 'The Nanny Question in Feminism.' *Hypatia* 17(2): 34–51.
van Onselen, Charles. 1982. *New Nineveh: Studies in the Social and Economic History of the Witwatersrand 1886–1914*. Johannesburg: Ravan Press.

3 Settling In, From Within
Anglo-Indian 'Lady-Helps' in 1920s New Zealand

Jane McCabe

On August 24, 1909, a young woman by the name of Aileen Sinclair arrived at Port Chalmers, Dunedin, the southernmost town of the British Empire. She was under the charge of the Reverend Dr. John Anderson Graham, and together with his daughter they had travelled from Kalimpong in the Darjeeling region of Northeast India. Graham was on a health trip, but more pertinent was his plan to visit the four young men whom he had sent to work on farms in the colony, and to accompany Aileen to her placement with a Dunedin family as a domestic servant.

Aileen Sinclair was the first of sixty-five adolescent 'Anglo-Indian' women (and an equivalent number of young men) who were systematically emigrated to New Zealand between 1909 and 1938.[1] They were all products of St. Andrew's Colonial Homes in Kalimpong, established by Graham in 1900 to make educational and social provision for the mixed-race children of British tea-planters and native women. Although it operated along similar lines to various institutions of the time that sought to remedy the problems of marginal populations by removal and (re)training, Graham's vision differed in that he looked to resettlement in *other* British colonies as a long-term solution. Thus this scheme affords an excellent opportunity to consider the differing colonial contexts of New Zealand and India. In particular, this essay seeks to comment on the distinctions between settler and non-settler colonies in providing long-term solutions to 'problems' that sprung from colonial intrusions.

In this case the 'problem' was that of the growing Anglo-Indian population in India, subject to increasing regulation and derision by British authorities in the wake of the 1857 rebellion. Although Durba Ghosh argues that anxieties about racial mixing in India were present much earlier, scholars generally agree that by the late nineteenth century interracial relationships were an important ground upon which to enforce physical and social distance between ruler and ruled (Ghosh 2006; Buettner 2004: 6). As the product of such relationships, existing Anglo-Indian populations were profoundly impacted by this attitudinal shift. Scholars have produced in-depth studies of their consequent segregation into specific industries, middle management positions and, most markedly, employment in railway 'colonies'

(Bear 2007; Caplan 2001: 60–63). Such studies have however focused on the labor of Anglo-Indian men. This essay aims to bring the labor of Anglo-Indian women into direct dialogue with the rhetoric of imperialism and colonial migration that so dominated the Kalimpong scheme.

The nature of domestic service in British India, and the involvement of Anglo-Indian women in that role, is of key interest here. Many Anglo-Indian women were employed as ayahs or nurses, and Alison Blunt has argued that their high representation in paid employment was an important means of embracing European habits (Blunt 2005: 57–61). Like their Indian counterparts, Anglo-Indian women were seen to have an aptitude in some aspects of mothering, but were more often the focus of considerable anxiety due to fears that their native habits would contaminate the children for whom they cared (Buettner 2004: 39–41; Mizutani 2011: 152–53; see also Stoler 1995: 156–57). While those who had been educated or trained in European institutions were regarded as potentially 'very satisfactory nurse[s],' the 'infectious' Anglo-Indian accent was an ongoing concern (Buettner 2004: 43). These specific anxieties were not present in New Zealand households. While Anglo-Indians would face racial discrimination in the colonies—most notably in the form of immigration restrictions—these concerns were seen to represent generalized racial anxieties which Graham believed could be appeased through their training at the institution.

Although only a small minority of graduates of the Homes would ever be placed abroad, the education and training provided was tailored to 'fit' the children for 'the colonies.' For the girls, this entailed a generalized training in domestic tasks, which became more structured as the institution developed. In 1910 the 'Babies Cottage' opened for infant admissions at the Homes. It was soon deemed to have a secondary function as 'the training house for nursery nurses.' 'The children are as far as possible cared for as they would be in a well-to-do home,' the *Homes Magazine* reported, 'so that the probationers may be able to take up situations as nursery nurses when they leave.'[2] The article concluded by stating that 'the greater number' of the girls working in the cottage 'look forward to making their homes in New Zealand.' While Graham often spoke of the girls' future employment as 'domestic service' when publicizing his scheme, the term was never used to refer to individual graduates. Those placed in India were usually reported to have gained positions as 'nannies' or 'nursery nurses,' while the New Zealand emigrants were more often referred to as 'lady helps' or 'mother helps.' Terminology is argued here to be a useful means of considering the subtle differences that the institution sought to make between the Kalimpong women and other types of domestic servants in India and abroad.

From his initially vague statements about the potential for emigration to 'the colonies,' Graham soon came to regard New Zealand as the ideal destination for his graduates. It was the only settler colony that ever accepted groups of emigrants from Kalimpong, and hence its requirements to some extent informed the development of the institution. Like other settler colonies, this self-governing dominion in the South Pacific was represented by visions of unused land, under-population, and the opportunity to create a society in which 'class was no longer central to social organization' (Olssen and Griffen 2011: 16). Graham was not alone in the potential he found for a mutually beneficial imperial exchange, providing disciplined workers in return for the promise of social mobility on new frontiers (Collie-Holmes 1991: 22–23; Gordon 1999: 9).

Though emigration numbers in this scheme were never high, bringing India and New Zealand together in this analysis goes some way towards addressing the lack of comparative work on colonial states (Heath 2006: 229). Graham's policy of a servant-free institution aligned his scheme neatly with the developing colonial ideal of the servant-free household. The fact that the female emigrants all began their adult lives as domestic servants in colonial households therefore illuminates the very different regard in which such work was held in New Zealand and British India. Where exactly these mixed-race women would *eventually* fit in settler colonial society was a question about which Graham could only theorize. But his persistent faith in the social structures of the young colony to propel the emigrants upwards, from a starting point of domestic service, facilitates the new connections argued here between the notions of expansion, intercolonial dynamics, and the broader imperial formations of race and gender.

BEGINNINGS IN BRITISH INDIA

> But we had an ayah, we all had ayahs. You spent more time with your ayahs. You did the things, played with their children and all that, you mixed with them.
>
> (Isabella Gammie, 2000)[3]

While the Homes in Kalimpong took in children from a variety of circumstances, it was originally established to cater for first generation Anglo-Indian children from the tea-planting districts of Northeast India. The overwhelming majority of those who were sent to New Zealand originated from this background. As children of tea-planters, the Kalimpong girls spent their early childhood in substantial bungalows with their parents, attended by servants and cared for by ayahs (native nursemaids). Social pressures in British India meant that by the turn of the century there was no possibility of making these interracial families legitimate, though Graham found in his travels around the region that the relationships were often 'real and tender.' It was the children who were the chief concern to Graham. The same social pressures that made their parents' relationship temporary meant that they could no longer be sent back to Britain for schooling. Graham disliked the 'local policy' of simply paying the women out when the planters left India, as this left children of European heritage facing highly uncertain futures in India.[4]

For most of the children the moment at which they were sent from the plantation to the Homes was a permanent separation—from their mothers, their birthplace, and for many, their fathers. Letters from the tea-planters written to the Homes seeking admission for their children clearly show that the mothers were reluctant to allow their children to leave, and were in some cases successful in preventing this from happening. When Isabella Gammie's daughter asked her about this moment of separation from her mother, Gammie's immediate response was that they had ayahs whom they 'spent more time with.'[5] Her comment tells us not only that it was usual for the children to have ayahs, but that this relationship mitigated closeness to their mothers, and that separation from these ayahs was another trauma they experienced when sent to the Homes. The salient point here is that all of the children suffered maternal separation at an early age, and most had also memorable exposure to being cared for by an ayah—an experience that likely impacted the way they would later carry out roles as 'nannies' to New Zealand children.

Graham's use of the term 'Homes' reflected his concern that the children would gain some experience of family life in contrast to the typically austere Victorian institution of the day. He was less concerned about the pain of separation from native mothers and native ayahs, which he saw as an essential first step in the process of fitting them for the colonies. Graham's attitudes towards race and miscegenation were typical of his day. As Ann Laura Stoler has argued in her work on the Dutch East Indies, separating mixed-race children from their native mothers was widely perceived as a positive and responsible course of action (Stoler 2002: 88–89). Graham housed the children in cottages with 30 to 40 others, along with in-lieu parents—a housemother and an 'aunty.' But of course cottage life was a very different experience to the cosseted existence of life on the plantation. As one later graduate recalled, 'I didn't know what hit me to be honest. I looked for my mother and she wasn't there. . . . I'm falling out of the bed and she's not there to get me. . . . You were pushed into the swimming pool, dragged off here, dragged off there, and you just didn't know where you were.'[6]

While Graham was concerned with providing a home-like atmosphere for the children, he made no apology for the lack of servants at the institution. In fact the 'servant-free' policy was one of his most oft used catch phrases when selling the scheme to colonial audiences. Graham saw multiple benefits to this policy. It made it easier to keep the institution entirely free of 'injurious native influence,' while ensuring the 'true dignity of manual labour' would be learned by the children in carrying out all domestic duties.[7] This self-sufficiency would also stand the children in good stead for the tough physical existence that Graham believed awaited in the colonies. In an interview printed in a New Zealand newspaper in 1909, Graham complained that in India, 'even the poorest family has some sort of a servant and in the humblest orphanages servants are employed,' describing the Homes' policy in contrast to this practice as 'a startling innovation for India.'[8] Graham was not alone in this disparaging British view of servants in Indian families, as outlined by Swapna Banerjee in her valuable study of colonial Bengal (2004: 42).

Another benefit of not having servants at the Homes was that it would instill a belief that 'work and refinement are not antagonistic.'[9] What Graham saw on the tea plantations upset him because he felt the children should be made worthy of their European blood by receiving an education. But it also upset him because he did not like to see mixed-race children expecting to be attended by servants, and this is crucial in understanding his colonial scheme. In order to insert them into what he saw as their appropriate level in colonial hierarchies, Graham had first to strip them of the inappropriate expectations garnered by their early childhood experiences. He endorsed the principles of Julius Smith, a Burmese missionary, whose article from the *Indian Witness* was reprinted in the *Homes Magazine* in 1902. Smith's writing was peppered with references to the problem of servants in 'pretentious' schools in India, which reinforced the Anglo-Indian tendency to 'despise the simplest duties.'[10] The Anglo-Indian 'problem' had its origins in racial issues but as Satoshi Mizutani has argued, Graham's solution was as much about instilling in the children a 'class-based understanding' of themselves as a racial one (Mizutani 2011: 164).

COLONIAL VISIONS

> We shall probably begin gradually. Sticklers for the colour line need not be frightened. Only the girls of English blood will be sent. If the first batch are found suitable and the conditions of New Zealand suit them, then probably more will follow.
>
> (John Graham, 1909)[11]

Given the strength of Graham's opinions about the place of servants in Indian and Anglo-Indian families, the fact that he incorporated colonial servanthood into his emigration scheme is revealing of the differences between settler and non-settler colonies. The colonial reference in the title of the Homes reflected Graham's early view that emigration held 'the only real hope of amelioration' for these Anglo-Indian children. Graham believed issues of class and caste in India and Britain could not be resolved in the short-term, and therefore looked to Britain's settler colonies for the children in his institution. Only those 'manifestly unfitted for Colonial life' would be 'trained for openings in India.'[12] The colonial destination was also an appealing option for the tea-planting fathers of the children, many of whom grew up in highly mobile 'empire families' and were hence cognizant of the opportunities different colonies could offer. They selected training for 'the colonies' (rather than India) on their children's application forms, and exerted strong pressure on Graham to realize his original vision. Egerton Peters, for example, complained on more than one occasion about a lack of arrangements for his children's promised colonial future. In 1920 Peters wrote that he had sent them fourteen years earlier 'on the plain understanding that they would be sent to the colonies' and pleaded with Graham to send them to New Zealand.[13] He showed particular concern for the fate of his daughter, should Graham 'turn her out to earn a living in India.'[14]

Two factors quickly made it apparent that this vision would never be realized on a large scale. Ironically, the first was the immediate demand from many quarters (tea-planters, Anglo-Indian families, and various orphanages and mission houses in India) for places at the Homes. Rapid growth in pupil numbers saw development of an institution beyond anything Graham had imagined. From an initial plan to house 40 children, the roll had risen to 305 by 1910 and would exceed 600 children by 1925. Graham soon acknowledged that it was not only the 'unfit' who would have to be placed in India (Mainwaring 2000: 17, 37). At the same time the growing 'color question' regarding immigration to the British settler colonies posed a hindrance to Graham's vision. Both Canada and Australia passed legislation in the early 1900s that made it difficult for Indian migrants to cross their borders. Similar legislation was enacted in New Zealand in 1899, although historians of the Indian community in New Zealand agree that the act was ineffectual in terms of reducing numbers (Zodgekar 1980: 185; Leckie 2010: 49). But broadly speaking, the trend towards such restrictions made Graham more cautious in his hopes for emigration.

As Graham's above quote in the *Otago Witness* suggests,[15] the experiences of the early emigrants were to be more than an opportunity to demonstrate their potential as workers and citizens: the reception provided by colonial households and local communities was also a crucial test of the suitability of the colonies for these young women. A written exchange between Charles Holdsworth, a customs official resident in Dunedin, and D. M. Hamilton, an associate of Graham's in Calcutta, provides insight into the attitudes Graham might encounter in attempting to find places for his young graduates in colonial families.

Hamilton sought to convince Holdsworth that a 'problem' population in India could well be perceived as remedial in the New Zealand context, where labor was needed to fuel the development of the colony. Holdsworth expressed considerable uncertainty about the likelihood of finding suitable positions for the emigrants, but added that 'there really is plenty of openings for trained domestic servants . . . but the responsibility of bringing such girls to New Zealand, even if they were trained, would be too much for a private individual.'[16] He suggested involving the churches, referring to local support of missions in India as possibly indicative of a willingness to support the scheme. Holdsworth's suggestion of church involvement did eventuate, with a Reverend Ponder receiving the first two boys in 1908 and placing them with farmers in his parish. It was also through the Presbyterian Church that young women volunteered as workers at the Homes. Ponder wrote an article for the *Otago Witness* in the same year appealing to locals to act beyond a 'mere cosmopolitanism' in supporting the Kalimpong initiative.[17] Appeals for colonial assistance simultaneously promoted the scheme as an opportunity for New Zealanders to display an enlightened attitude, and to take advantage of migrant labor in a colony with a chronic shortage of domestic servants.

Graham was greatly encouraged by the situations in which he found his male graduates on his 1909 visit to New Zealand, and hopeful of similar prospects for the women. In an article printed upon his return to Kalimpong entitled 'Our Girls as Colonists,' Graham lauded the many opportunities in New Zealand for the women to begin in 'household work' and believed that 'after a few years experience, they could easily earn from £40 to £50 a year, with board.'[18] This statement is revealing on several levels. Referring to his graduates as 'colonists' is significant, given that they were classified as 'alien' (or 'Asiatic') and as such have been excluded from the dominant colonizer/colonized binary in New Zealand historiography (Ballantyne 2012: 56–57). Secondly, Graham's sentiment promulgates the egalitarian ideology of settler colonies that insisted upon a link between a strong work ethic and social mobility, an ideology which arguably had limited applicability to white women in the early 1900s (Olssen 2003: 60). In a third (and related) point, Graham was expressing the belief that domestic labor in its own right could facilitate such mobility. In doing so, he was addressing an aspect of the servant 'problem' in the settler colonies—British women migrants assisted into domestic positions who viewed the role as a transitional one, and moved into better occupations or marriage at the first opportunity (Higman 2002: 88).

Graham's visit to New Zealand in 1909 also saw the consolidation of a small but strong network built around church and Indian connections, which would prove vital to the longevity of the scheme. The link to Dunedin is not surprising given the high proportion of Presbyterian Scots resident there. Graham enjoyed the familiarity of the people and the landscape. 'Dunedin seems very homelike to me,' he told the *Otago Witness* reporter, 'as a Scot I delight to hear to the old accent.' He was impressed by its 'solidarity,' finding it 'wonderful that such a place could have been brought into being in only 60 years.'[19] The youth of the colony stood in marked contrast to the weight of history and social convention that Graham found so frustrating in Britain and India. While he saw the Indian practice of keeping servants as wholly negative, in New Zealand it was imagined as an entry point to households that promised a new configuration of social relations. The *Otago Witness* reporter prompted comment from Graham regarding these young women who were understood to 'have no objection to coming to the colonies for domestic service.' 'They would not have the least objection,'

Graham replied. This willingness—to perform a role that white women in the colonies were beginning to refuse—thus presented a crucial counterpoint to the persistent racial stigmas that threatened Graham's vision of colonial settlement.

THE NEW ZEALAND CONTEXT

> I am doing well. . . . Most of the people would hardly believe I come from India; they say I look more of a home girl. My mistress is very pleased with the way I work; she said I am very tidy in the way I dress.
>
> (Dorothy Higgins, 1914)[20]

The scheme gradually began to take hold in New Zealand, with a trickle of migrants sent between 1909 and 1911 followed by the first large 'batch' of thirteen in 1912. The *Homes' Magazine* announced the safe arrival of the 1912 batch, noting 'Mrs. Scott and her committee had no difficulty in arranging places for the six girls who, she reports, have made an excellent impression.'[21] The magazine contains numerous references to the demand for girls. 'Dr. Graham,' wrote Mary Roberts from Marlborough, 'you will soon have no big girls left, such a lot of ladies want girls from our school.'[22] She referred to an article in the local newspaper after which the Homes committee received numerous applications. Over the next four years another twelve young women were sent out, all dispersed around the South Island. In 1916 at the annual meeting of the Ladies Committee in Dunedin, it was recorded that the girls 'ably supplied a felt want' and that there was a 'keen demand for them.'[23]

It was with the arrival of the 1912 group that the term 'lady-help' was first employed. A newspaper article announced the imminent arrival of the 'orphan emigrants,' stating that 'the girls will become "lady helps," for domestic servants are almost unknown in New Zealand, and the "lady help" is treated as one of the family.'[24] The deployment of this term was important. B. W. Higman notes that in Australia, it first appeared in the 1870s to encourage a higher class of women to take on domestic roles; and in the 1920s there was a proposal to accept British lady-helps as an addition to domestic servants. They would bear a lighter workload and higher status, although wages were the same (Higman 2002: 148). Pamela Horn contends that attempts to use such lady-helps to alleviate the servant shortage in Britain were not successful, partly due to the friction it caused between lady-helps and domestic servants (Horn 1975: 29, 153). The term also appeared in a story by the New Zealand writer Katherine Mansfield published in 1920, in which two sisters role-play a domestic scene. 'I don't think you ought to introduce me to the servant,' said one, to which her sister replied, 'well, she's more of a lady-help than a servant, and you do introduce lady-helps' (Mansfield 2001: 41).

Issues of terminology and status were the subject of highly charged debate in the colonies, where the renegotiation of the relationship between mistress and servant was something of a metaphor for the practical expression of social mobility. There was growing unease about the presence of servants, whom Charlotte Macdonald argues were essential to the nineteenth-century New Zealand household, 'yet not members of it' (2000: 42). Macdonald attributes the sharp decline in the proportion of females employed as domestic servants between the 1880s and the early 1900s to several factors, including the impact of the colonial ideal of the servantless household. Families were increasingly able to get by without help and had a desire to escape 'the discomforting presence of strangers at the hearth' (Macdonald 2000: 44). Scholarship on domestic service in New Zealand has clearly shown that alternative employment opportunities for young women at the turn of the century reduced the appeal of domestic work, which was seen as low status, outside union representation, and restricting freedom (Holland 1976: 9, 16; Olssen 2003: 70–73).

The Kalimpong women hence stepped into a somewhat ambiguous role at both a broader societal and familial level. The particular circumstances of their employment do seem to have addressed aspects of the servant problem. Being tied to contracts of one to two years was of great benefit to their employers, and many stayed beyond their required term. This stability indicates their dependence on their employers for finding their place in colonial society. The isolation of plantation life and their years of institutionalization meant that they arrived in New Zealand relatively naïve about how to negotiate broader social structures. Deprivation of family life during their time at the Homes inculcated an appreciation of any sense of inclusion in their host families, reports of which filled the pages dedicated to 'Our Colonials' in the *Homes' Magazine*. Rosie Cooper expressed this sense of indebtedness when she wrote that her mistress wanted her 'to stay another year at least, so I'm staying on. I do not like to leave her, seeing she does not keep well and needs all the help she gets and indeed she is very, very good to me. I'm just like one of the family. Anyway I'll not leave till I get someone to take my place.'[25]

The presence of these Anglo-Indian women in New Zealand families represents a small but significant exception to Macdonald's finding that unlike other colonies, domestic service in New Zealand was almost exclusively European (Macdonald 2000: 50; Holland 1976: 66–69). Apart from a short-lived scheme to train Maori girls for work in 'refined' households, numbers of Indigenous women in domestic service were never high, suggesting that Maori women too were an uncomfortable presence. But the fact that the Kalimpong girls were accepted by numerous families suggests that color itself was not an issue. Indeed their color may have made their presence easier to incorporate in that it made their place in the household recognizable. This too had been a problem with domestic servants in New Zealand, who did not wear uniforms and were derided for forgetting their 'proper place' in daring to dress like their employers (Holland 1976: 25).

The Kalimpong women might have been (and from descendant testimony and the photographic record often were) immaculately groomed and refined of manner, but there could be no doubt to visitors of their place in the household. Such visibility, and the sourcing of outsiders for low status work, reflected the trend towards meeting servant shortages by employing foreigners, not only in settler colonies but also in Britain (Horn 1975: 30; Higman 2002: 96–100).

The relative success of the Kalimpong scheme when compared to similar attempts to place Maori women in white families helps to tease out the racial issues otherwise hidden. It is easy to forget with names like Gertrude Plaistowe and Dorothy Higgins that many of the Kalimpong women were dark-skinned and had pronounced features that were noticeable in colonial society. Graham had worked hard to educate the women to a high degree of literacy and verse them thoroughly in European dress, manners, eating habits, Christian values—all of the indicators of race that could be molded to fit. But their skin color could not be disguised. The fact that Maori women living in white families as domestic servants never took hold, while the Kalimpong scheme did, inflects the particular relationship between colonizers and colonized in New Zealand. As we have seen, Graham's supporters appealed to colonial audiences to take charity a step further by allowing Anglo-Indian women into their homes. Their social distance from the origins of this racial 'problem' surely made that charity easier to contemplate.

SETTLING IN

> Mrs and Mrs Jenkins and I were just talking about sea trips. Mrs Jenkins doesn't think that she would like the sea, Mr Jenkins and I think a sea trip is not bad at all. . . . I love Mr and Mrs Jenkins, they are just like father and mother to me. I am treated just like one of them in the house. I have been here over two years now.
>
> (Dora Moller to James Purdie, 1927)[26]

The 1920s saw consolidation of the Kalimpong community in New Zealand. Many of the early Kalimpong emigrants married New Zealanders and produced families of their own. New arrivals were welcomed into the homes of the 'old girls,' as well as former Homes' staff and families associated with the scheme. While the Immigration Restriction Amendment Act of 1920 threatened to disrupt the flow of Kalimpong graduates to New Zealand, as it transpired, the new permit system was no barrier to the scheme. Between 1922 and 1929 a further thirty young women arrived in New Zealand—the same number as the previous fourteen years. The system of emigrating small numbers and immediately scattering them around the colony continued, and was an effective means of reducing visibility as well as ensuring assimilation. While the Kalimpong women in the cities did get together on their afternoons off, they were otherwise fully immersed in the world of their employers.

Placement of the new arrivals with professional families continued throughout the 1920s. Of the large 1926 batch, several wrote about their situations in Wellington. Connie Walker had 'a good mistress and a darling child to look after'; Margie Smith was in 'a beautiful home at Mr and Mrs Bobbingers' with two children to care for; and Violet Allcard was living with the family of one the barristers who arranged the permits.[27] Eva Masson went to the home of the Mayoress of Blenheim, whom she wrote was 'just like a mother to me. Every day she lets me go to the swimming baths and that always reminds me of Kalimpong.'[28] Margaret Fox wrote the following year that she was 'getting on very much better now since I came over into the big town and I absolutely adore the two wee children I look after. Yesterday we gave a dance. I polished the floor of the dining room, which was used as the ballroom, in the Kalimpong style with bare feet.'[29] It was in these affluent surroundings that many of the women were socialized into New Zealand families and learnt their place in colonial hierarchies.

Not all of the Kalimpong women were placed with professional urban families. Growing confidence in their resilience and the protection of colonial families saw numerous women sent to rural areas, where the demand for help was probably more about need and less about charity. Mavis Haslett worked in a boarding house in a farming district south of Dunedin, where she was very well treated and 'loved the farm work.'[30] Dora Moller, an emigrant of 1921, stayed with her first employer for two years before discovering that she preferred country to town life, even though it meant that she seldom saw others from Kalimpong.[31] From her letters to the secretary of the Homes, we learn that she then settled for several years with Mr. and Mrs. Jenkins as a 'companion help'—another example of the many euphemisms for domestic service employed by those involved in the Kalimpong scheme.[32] Dora's letter relaying her conversation with the Jenkinses conjures an intimate domestic scene, sitting with the elderly couple talking about India. While racial anxieties were an issue in the wider community, the women's correspondence suggests a high level of acceptance within their host families.

Like the great majority of the Kalimpong women, Dora's graduation from domestic service came with her marriage in 1931. 'Nearly all the girls are married,' she wrote in 1929, 'I suppose you have heard I'm thinking about getting married too. I'm marrying a Christchurch boy.'[33] Dora's sister Elizabeth was engaged for several years, but in the interim she continued to work as a live-in domestic for various families.[34] Hence while they may have acted as free agents in the labor market at completion of their initial contracts, these women were very much tied to the work for which they had been groomed. Kate Edbrooke and Esther Graham, whom 'proposed working in Auckland for a time,' apparently found the northern city 'too hot . . . and have returned contentedly to their old situations and to the other Homes girls in Wellington.'³⁵ Permanent relocations were only made when moving with their employer or upon marriage. Of the women who did not marry, all either stayed in domestic service or lived independently upon receiving inheritances from their tea-planting fathers.

KALIMPONG LEGACIES

> The girls from Kalimpong were very much a part of our lives as children.... I remember Molly Roberts first when I was very young but we used to see her later after she married. There is no doubt it was a successful plan and policy bringing so many now fine people to New Zealand.... We owe them much for their part in the family life of ours and so many others' families in our community.
>
> (Hon. Sir John White to Isabella Gammie, 2000)³⁶

Sir John White's assertion that the scheme had brought many 'now fine people' to New Zealand can be seen as an answer to the question Charles Holdsworth posed nearly one hundred years earlier, as to the likelihood of Eurasian children turning out well. His father, C. G. White, was a barrister and former chairman of the Kalimpong committee in New Zealand, and John White remembered well the 'girls from Kalimpong' from his childhood and beyond. His comment speaks to the impact of the Kalimpong women in their child-caring roles and is reminiscent of their own relationships with ayahs in India. John White's sister, who presumably grew up with the same Anglo-Indian nanny, herself employed a Kalimpong graduate in the 1930s. These intergenerational dynamics saw the growth of a vibrant community in Wellington, one that functioned as a substitute extended family for the first-generation New Zealanders from Kalimpong. Their children grew up with stories of India at large gatherings attended by the many and various people they knew as 'aunty' and 'uncle.'

Graham was greatly impressed by this Kalimpong community when he visited New Zealand in 1937. At seventy-five years of age, Graham sought to pay a final visit to as many graduates as possible during a hectic three-week tour of the North and South Islands. In a diary written for his family, he left a relatively candid record of the emigrants' successes and failures.³⁷ Graham wrote in positive terms about those who remained in domestic service, but saved his highest praise for the women who (by his standards) had married well, produced offspring, and lived in contented homes. In this Graham found evidence of their successful socialization as a result of careful placement in Presbyterian families. He visited many in their own homes as well as attending reunions, such as that held in an employer's (the Didsbury's) residence in Wellington. The photograph below shows some sixty Kalimpong old boys and girls not looking at all out of place, with the Didsburys amongst them.

Graham also hoped to persuade New Zealand authorities to allow his emigration scheme to resume. No permits had been granted to his graduates

Figure 3.1 A group of Kalimpong emigrants with the Didsbury Family at the Didsbury residence, Wellington, in July 1937. Gammie Family Archives.

since 1929 due to the onset of economic depression. To this end, in his public speaking engagements Graham couched the scheme in the language of colonial development, imperial cooperation, and concern over the future of British India.[38] He also referred specifically to the labor of the women, from which 'some of the most comfortable households' had benefitted. In a broadcast on national radio, Graham described the women as 'Diplomaed Nursery Nurses' who 'begin as Mothers' Helps.'[39] A descendant of one of the Kalimpong women echoed Graham's words some seventy-five years later, expressing to the author her feeling that the 'Indian girls' would have been 'aghast' to be referred to as 'domestics.' In her view they were 'trained as nurses at the Homes . . . and came out as nannies to professional people.'[40] Terminology was, and continues to be, an important vehicle through which a perceived 'Old World' system of subordination was replaced with a colonial understanding of the same labor performed in a different social context.

CONCLUSION

This scheme was about far more than work. Yet domestic labor was a crucial means of getting these young women off the ships and onto the shores of New Zealand. Their placement in families, too, was about more than adequate performance in their domestic service roles. It was a final point of training in a highly disrupted trajectory from which John Graham believed they would be fully integrated into colonial structures. As has been argued here, Graham justified their entry point as domestic servants in several ways. In the first instance, their racial inferiority meant a subservient position in colonial hierarchies was appropriate. White women in the supposedly classless colonies were increasingly reluctant to take on these roles that in various sites came to be filled by women who were considered marginal by their foreignness, rather than lower-class status. Secondly, the shortage of domestic labor in the colonies gave Graham an extra bargaining tool when making his appeals to colonial audiences. Thirdly, the use of various terms, such as lady-help, companion help, and nanny—none of which used the word 'servant'—were often deployed by those associated with the scheme to mitigate negative connotations.

This paper has examined the workings of a scheme that was distinctive for its transcolonial vision of producing potential settlers for New Zealand from a problem population in British India. Thinking through domestic service as a vehicle of immigration and socialization has posed questions about the relationship between colonizer and colonized in New Zealand. It has also highlighted critical distinctions between settler and non-settler colonies. Specific concerns about the employment of Anglo-Indian women by British families in India were not present in settler colonial households. While domestic service in New Zealand families did not in its own right lead to social mobility, it was the precursor to integration through marriage and community involvement. The eventual place of the Kalimpong women in the respectable working classes of New Zealand represented, in Graham's view, a permanent elevation from the Anglo-Indian enclaves of British India that justified the familial intrusions his scheme involved.

NOTES

1. Anglo-Indian here refers to the mixed-race community of India, as it was officially known from 1911 (see Roychowdhury 2000). For the use of the term in the nineteenth century to denote British people resident in India, see Dussart, this volume.
2. *St Andrews Colonial Homes Magazine* (hereafter *SACHM*), 12(3) (1912): 38–39, Dr. Graham's Homes Archive, Kalimpong, India (hereafter DGHA).
3. Family interview with Isabella Gammie, Wellington, New Zealand, 2000, Gammie Family Archive.
4. John Graham, 'The St Andrews's Colonial Homes,' Typed notes, 6039:15:1, National Library of Scotland, Edinburgh (hereafter NLS).
5. Family interview with Isabella Gammie.
6. Interviewee in *We Homes Chaps*, documentary film by Kesang Tseten, 2001.
7. Graham, Typed Notes, NLS.
8. 'The Land of the Sahib: Kim and His Sisters,' *Otago Witness*, September 1, 1909, 52.

9. 'Kim and His Sisters,' *Otago Witness*, September 1, 1909, 52.
10. 'Correct Education for Anglo-Indians and Eurasians in India,' *SACHM* 2(1) (1902): 45–46, DGHA.
11. Graham, Typed Notes, NLS.
12. Graham, Typed Notes, NLS.
13. Egerton Peters to John Graham, July 20, 1920, Peters File, DGHA (with permission from the Peters family).
14. Egerton Peters to John Graham, October 21, 1914, Peters File.
15. 'Kim and His Sisters,' *Otago Witness*, September 1, 1909, 52.
16. Charles Holdsworth to D. M. Hamilton, October 30, 1905, Charles Holdsworth Collection, Letterbooks, AG-292–004–002/003, Hocken Collections, Dunedin.
17. 'Kim and His Brothers,' *Otago Witness*, August 12, 1908, 88.
18. 'Australia and New Zealand: Notes and Impressions,' *SACHM* 9(3) (1909): 6, DGHA.
19. 'Kim and His Sisters,' *Otago Witness*, September 1, 1909, 52.
20. 'Our Colonials,' *SACHM* 14(2) (1914): 28, DGHA.
21. 'News from Our Emigrants,' *SACHM* 13(1) (1913): 12, DGHA.
22. 'Our Colonials,' *SACHM* 14(2) (1914): 29, NLS.
23. 'Our Girls in New Zealand,' *SACHM* 16(3/4) (1916): 34, NLS.
24. 'Orphan Immigrants,' *Ashburton Guardian*, December 17, 1912, 7.
25. 'For the Old Boys and Girls,' *SACHM* 15(3/4) (1915): 43, DGHA.
26. Dora Moller to James Purdie, June 27, 1927: Moller File, DGHA (with permission from the Moller family).
27. 'For the Old Boys and Girls,' *SACHM* 27 (1/2) (1927): 21, NLS.
28. 'Our Emigrants First Impressions of New Zealand,' *SACHM* 27 (1/2) (1927): 11, NLS.
29. 'New Zealand,' *SACHM* 28 (3/4) (1928): 45, DGHA.
30. 'For the Old Boys and Girls,' *SACHM* 27 (1/2) (1927): 21, NLS.
31. 'For the Old Boys and Girls,' *SACHM* 26 (3/4) (1926): 34, NLSDGHA.
32. Dora Moller to James Purdie, March 8, 1925, Moller File.
33. Dora Moller to James Purdie, July 7, 1929, Moller File.
34. Elizabeth Moller to James Purdie, March 12, 1938, Moller File.
35. 'For the Old Boys and Girls,' *SACHM* 25 (3/4) (1927): 47, NLSDGHA.
36. Hon. Sir John White to Isabella Gammie, April 17, 2000, Gammie Family Archive.
37. 'Pour Les Intimes': Diary of Dr. John Graham, NLS 6039: 7.
38. 'The Call of India': Wellington Broadcast July 4, 1937, NLS 6039: 7.
39. 'The Call of India': Wellington Broadcast July 4, 1937, NLS 6039: 7.
40. Descendent interview, March 11, 2012.

REFERENCES

Ballantyne, Tony. 2012. *Webs of Empire: Locating New Zealand's Colonial Past*. Wellington: Bridget Williams Books.

Banerjee, Swapna. 2004. *Men, Women and Domestics: Articulating Middle-Class Identity in Colonial Bengal*. New Delhi: Oxford University Press.

Bear, Laura. 2007. *Lines of the Nation: Indian Railway Workers, Bureaucracy, and the Intimate Historical Self*. New York: Columbia University Press.

Blunt, Alison. 2005. *Domicile and Diaspora: Anglo-Indian Women and the Spatial Politics of Home*. Malden: Blackwell Publishing.

Buettner, Elizabeth. 2004. *Empire Families: Britons and Late Imperial India.* Oxford: Oxford University Press.

Caplan, Lionel. 2001. *Children of Colonialism: Anglo-Indians in a Postcolonial World.* Oxford: Berg.

Collie-Holmes, Mary. 1991. *Where the Heart Is: A History of Barnardo's in New Zealand 1866–1991.* Wellington: Barnardo's New Zealand.

Ghosh, Durba. 2006. *Sex and the Family in Colonial India.* Cambridge: Cambridge University Press.

Gordon, Linda. 1999. *The Great Arizona Orphan Abduction.* Cambridge: Harvard University Press.

Heath, Deana. 2006. 'Comparative Colonialism, Moral Censorship and Governmentality.' In *Decentring Empire: Britain, India and the Transcolonial World*, edited by Durba Ghosh and Dane Kennedy, 213–42. New Delhi: Orient Longman.

Higman, B. W. 2002. *Domestic Service in Australia.* Victoria: Melbourne University Press.

Holland, Jean. 1976. 'Domestic Service in Colonial New Zealand.' PhD dissertation, University of Auckland, New Zealand.

Horn, Pamela. 1975. *The Rise and Fall of the Victorian Servant.* New York: St Martin's Press.

Leckie, Jacqueline. 2010. 'A Long Diaspora.' In *India in New Zealand: Local Identities, Global Relations*, edited by Sekhar Bandyopadyay, 45–64. Dunedin: Otago University Press 2010.

Macdonald, Charlotte. 2000. 'Strangers at the Hearth: The Eclipse of Domestic Service in New Zealand Homes.' In *At Home in New Zealand: Houses History People*, edited by Barbara Brookes, 41–56. Wellington: Bridget Williams Books.

Mainwaring, Simon. 2000. *A Century of Children.* Kalimpong: Dr Graham's Homes.

Mansfield, Katherine. 2001. 'Prelude.' In *Bliss and Other Stories*, edited by Katherine Mansfield, 11–62. London: Penguin Books.

Mizutani, Satoshi. 2011. *The Meaning of White: Race, Class and the 'Domiciled Community' in British India 1858–1930.* Oxford: Oxford University Press.

Olssen, Erik. 2003. 'Working Gender, Gendering Work: Occupational Change and Continuity in Southern Dunedin.' In *Sites of Gender: Women, Men and Modernity in Southern Dunedin, 1890–1939*, edited by Barbara Brookes, Annabel Cooper and Robin Law, 50–90. Auckland: Auckland University Press.

Olssen, Erik, and Clyde Griffen. 2011. *An Accidental Utopia.* Dunedin: Otago University Press.

Roychowdhury, Laura. 2000. '"Anglo-Indian": Historical Definitions.' In *The Jadu House: Intimate Histories of Anglo-India*, edited by Laura Roychowdhury, 287–97. London: Transworld Publishers.

Stoler, Ann Laura. 1995. *Race and the Education of Desire: Foucault's History of Sexuality and the Colonial Order of Things.* Durham: Duke University Press.

Stoler, Ann Laura. 2002. *Carnal Knowledge and Imperial Power: Race and the Intimate in Colonial Rule.* Berkeley: University of California Press.

Tseten, Kesang, director. 2001. *We Homes Chaps.* DVD. Nepal: Shunyata Film Production.

Zodgekar, Arvind. 1980. 'Demographic Aspects of Indians in New Zealand.' In *Indians in New Zealand*, edited by Kapil Tiwari, 183–97. Wellington: Price Milburn & Co.

4 'Ah Look Afta De Child Like Is Mine'[1]
Discourses of Mothering in Jamaican Domestic Service, 1920–1970

Michele A. Johnson

In twentieth-century Jamaica childcare constituted an important component of the labor performed by female domestic workers. Often competing for positions in circumstances of limited educational and employment opportunities, the women recruited to perform childcare offered a service that was linked to the island's legacies of colonialism and slavery. Domestic workers and many of their female employers shared what Kamau Brathwaite might refer to as an Afro-Creole culture where woman-centered networks often shared the responsibilities of childcare (1974: 31, 38–43; see also Mintz and Price 1976; Green 1986; Bolland 1992). At the same time, however, the workers were required to perform 'motherwork' from which their female employers of all classes sought to be alleviated (see O'Reilly 2006: 133–38). This chapter explores how the discourses of 'mothering' were deployed by female employers in order to extract emotional and physical labor from domestic workers who, in turn, used the rhetoric to elicit dignity in a devalued occupation and to reduce their vulnerability in a competitive, largely unregulated sector. It addresses the experiences of domestic workers and their employers from the 1920s to 1970, covering the periods of labor activism and political unrest in the 1930s, the decolonization of the island in the 1940s–1950s and its political independence in 1962. The study ends in 1970, before *An Act to Repeal the Masters and Servants Law* of 1974 finally revoked the 1842 *Masters and Servants Act* that had framed the working lives of large segments of the population in the post-slavery period. As such, the chapter examines domestic service in Jamaica outside of 'modern' labor regulations, which treated their employers' households as 'workplaces,' and their work as 'real' labor.

In exploring the experiences of servants and employers from the 1920s to the 1970s, this study draws on classified newspaper advertisements[2] and oral histories. Despite some of the limitations associated with oral histories including faulty or selective memories, along with silences, distortions and outright falsehoods (see Vansina 1985; Thompson 2000; Sangster 1994), such testimonies are very useful in identifying servants' experiences. As poor, marginalized women whose concerns were usually deemed unimportant by the record making and keeping classes, their experiences were rarely recorded in traditional archival material. As such, oral testimonies provide one of the only avenues for accessing their histories (see Higman 1985–6; Higman 1999a; Higman 1999b). In order to highlight the voices of domestic workers and their employers, I conducted sixty-five interviews[3] and was given access to fourteen narratives in the African Caribbean Institute of Jamaica/Jamaica Memory Bank (Institute of Jamaica) archives. All the names of respondents have been changed in order to maintain their privacy. Conscious of the need to maintain the voices of the respondents, they appear in English and/or a phonetically presented Jamaican nation-language with translations.

COLONIALISM, SLAVERY AND DOMESTIC SERVICE IN JAMAICA

Twentieth-century Jamaican society was built on foundations of centuries of European colonialism and enslavement of Africans (see Brathwaite 1984). While colonizers were focused on profiting from the exploitation of the enslaved African labor force used in commercial agriculture, they also utilized the enslaved and, initially, some indentured European female workers for domestic work. Whereas the indentured Europeans had graduated into what Lucille Mathurin Mair called 'the ranks of the free and the respectable' by the end of the eighteenth century, almost all levels of free (white) society depended on enslaved and some free(d) Africans, mostly women, to perform domestic labor (2006: 9, 13, 26–28). As Barbara Bush argued, female domestic slaves were believed to have been elevated above the fieldwork performed by their compatriots, but they often experienced close surveillance and personal vulnerability from predatory white men, sometimes resulting in colored (biracial) offspring who were, themselves, frequently utilized as enslaved or free(d) domestic workers (Bush 1981: 253–54; see also Bush 1990). Performing heavily gendered work for enslavers/employers to whom they might be related, the correlation between enslaved coloreds and domestic service was so established that, according to B. W. Higman, while colored slaves constituted about ten percent of the total slave population, by 1834 'at least 60 percent of the slave domestics in Jamaica were coloured' (1983: 126). As Hilary Beckles notes, many enslaved servants were owned/rented by urban-based white women who supported and benefitted from colonialism and slavery (1999: 60–72).

Given what Michael Craton (1993) described as the region's tendency to 'continuity' rather than change, emancipation in 1834 and 'full freedom' in 1838 did not dismantle the colonial socioeconomic and political structures or hierarchies of race/color, class/status and gender which enabled the sustained exploitation of the majority. Instead, imperial 'mother' Britain and the cultural elite, comprised of expatriate Britons, some white Jamaicans and some aspiring acculturated black Jamaicans, attempted (albeit unsuccessfully) to contain and 'improve' the 'free(d)' people through a 'civilizing mission' spearheaded by churches and their connected schools (see Hall 2002: 1–22; Moore and Johnson 2011: 1–10). Among those targeted were black lower-class women who were expected to labor as their foremothers had done, but who were also harangued about exhibiting 'proper' gendered behavior. Limited by intersecting marginalizations of race, class and gender, many black and colored lower-class women worked in agriculture while tens of thousands of others performed domestic service, which became the most common form of female employment in twentieth-century Jamaica (Higman 1983: 117).

For the fifty years on which this study focuses, between one-fifth and one-third of the island's officially 'gainfully-employed' women, and untold numbers not captured by the national censuses, performed domestic service.[4] While in other contexts the combined forces of industrialization and urbanization along with the mechanization and commercialization of household tasks resulted in the decline of domestic service, in Jamaica urbanization occurred independent of industrial development before 1950. This resulted in an abundant supply of domestic workers competing for positions in the homes of 'the emerging bourgeoisie and the better-off working classes' in the urban centers (Higman 1983: 121, 122). While there were some changes in domestic service after 1950 due to increased educational and employment opportunities among women, increased emigration to Britain and North America (for migration of Caribbean domestic workers to Latin America in the earlier period, see Foote, this volume) and a steady shift from residential to 'live-out' and day work, the socioeconomic legacies of colonialism and slavery/servitude continued to color the sector for tens of thousands of women.

Those legacies were apparent in the *Masters and Servants Law* of 1842, which was amended in 1940 to decriminalize contractual breaches and only revoked in 1974.[5] Largely excluded from modern labor legislation until that revocation, domestic servants were not guaranteed the minimum wage, and were subject to unregulated working conditions (see Gaunt 1922; Chapman 1952; Hughes 1962). It was in this context that some women in Jamaica recruited others to perform childcare.

OTHERMOTHERS: CHILDCARE, DOMESTIC SERVICE AND MOTHERHOOD

Among the sites where childcare was highlighted as a part of domestic service was in classified newspaper advertisements where potential employers and servants offered and sought positions. In a sample of classified advertisements in the *Daily Gleaner* and *Sunday Gleaner*, 249 of the sample's 1,652 employers and 1,745 of the 8,510 workers included specific references to childcare,[6] while others assumed its inclusion in 'general maid' positions which were in the majority. Employers sought workers 'to assist with management of one young child,' 'to take entire charge of a little boy and an infant,' or 'to take charge of three children.'[7] Potential servants indicated a willingness 'to care baby,' 'to care children,' 'to care child from 9 days upward,' to 'take care of children on voyage to England or Canada' or to perform childcare with other household duties.[8]

Similarly, childcare was a concern among the employers and domestic workers whose oral histories contributed to this research project. According to businesswoman Mae Virgo, starting in 1954, she hired nursemaids to assist her after the births of her children.[9] When school administrator Maureen Cooper got married in 1957, she said that as a working wife and mother, she 'had to have' one person 'to help with the children along with a general helper.'[10] Social worker Margaret Clarke said that the domestic worker she hired after her marriage in 1961 also performed childcare after the birth of her daughter in 1964.[11] In 1927, Icilda Cole was hired to care for an infant and a small child in Rae Town, Kingston when she replied positively to the question of whether she 'loved' children.[12] And when Lena Ferguson advertised her services in the newspaper in the 1940s, she said she wanted to 'du baby-sitting . . . [to] look afta young baby.' She was hired as nursemaid by a family who employed a domestic staff of four in Stony Hill, St. Andrew.[13]

As Higman argued, the domestic service sector always employed 'large proportions of young people' (1983: 126); however, given the work and weighty responsibilities associated with childcare, the recruitment of very youthful nursemaids was noteworthy. When Doris Watson worked as a nursemaid in Norwich, St. Thomas in the 1920s she was 'twelve-t'irteen' years old; Icilda Cole was hired in Kingston in 1927 when she was fourteen; and Jean Evans worked for a family in Vere, Clarendon from about 1942 'when mi a 12 year of age . . . when mi fe going to school.'[14] Winnifred Black worked in a relative's home in Chudleigh, Manchester after, she said, 'mi mada jus kyaa [carry] mi go dere an leave mi de.'[15] She and other girls were placed by their mothers in arrangements that Judith Blake called 'child dispersal' and Olive Senior referred to as 'child shifting' (Blake 1961: 83–86; Senior 1991: 12), and were often expected to work as nursemaids, although they were sometimes barely older than their wards.

According to H. G. DeLisser, writing in early twentieth-century Jamaica, 'It is when they are about twelve years of age that their mothers begin to think of having them learn something by which they will be able to earn their bread'; they worked as servants in exchange for food, clothing and shelter and began to earn wages when they reached seventeen or eighteen (1913: 99). The system of employing young children as domestic servants was common in other contexts, such as the United States where African-American children were reported to have worked in white homes from the late nineteenth century well into the twentieth century (Sutherland 1981: 53; van Wormer et. al. 2012: 77, 89, 157; Tucker 1988: 44, 156, 168). In this 'schoolgirl system' which emerged in Jamaica at the end of the nineteenth century (Higman 1983: 130–31), girls worked under the tutelage and close surveillance of female employers who were expected by their mothers to care for them. Primarily through this mechanism, according to Higman, as late as 1942, 'almost one-third of Jamaican female domestics were described in the census as "unpaid family workers"' (1983: 130). It was only after 1960 that there was a decline to less than two percent in this category of worker in the census, perhaps as a result of increased expectations for children's educational opportunities and/or a growing reluctance to self-identify as unremunerated domestic workers.

As I have argued elsewhere (see Johnson 2002: 398–401), young servants, many of whom were nursemaids, were attractive to employers because they were believed to be capable of hard work, and were more easily controlled (DeLisser 1913: 100). For young workers and their families, including those mentioned above, their placement as nursemaids/mother's helps provided possibilities out of poverty, agricultural work and offered the chance to be cared for as 'schoolgirls' by surrogate mothers. However, for many, the realities were quite harsh.

Doris Watson was given shelter but was not paid while Jean Evans was paid with 'likl clothes an shoes an ting.'[16] When Icilda Cole was hired to care for an infant and a child at fourteen, she had to fix their breakfast, escort the older child to school, to and from lunch and after school, all while caring for the baby for whom she was responsible, day and night. In addition, she 'wash dem clothes, an look afta an wash fi-ar [employer's] clothes . . . A mi cook, fa she an' de two children.' Sometimes, she said, her female employer (a dressmaker) and her husband left her with the children, 'fi a whole week . . . I an dem [the children] alone is dere.' And 'becau . . . mi use to look afta de children dem, A neva get no day's off.' Despite these conditions, she worked in the household until the infant was ten years old and left only when the employer said she could not pay more than five shillings per week.[17] Recruited as nursemaids while they were themselves children and presumably in need of parental care, these girls knew that they could not afford to take the rhetoric of care and mothering at its face value. As Selena Todd argued in the case of a domestic worker in Britain in the 1930s who said her employer was 'a bit of a Momma' to her, these arrangements 'did not mean a servant forgot that the basis of this relationship was economic' (2009: 192), and was potentially exploitative.

Where younger domestic workers could be caught in severely asymmetrical relationships with their 'maternal' employers (who could also be their relatives), sometimes the expectations of mothering went in the other direction. According to Mary Romero, some of the older women who she interviewed for her research on Chicanas working as domestics in the greater Denver metropolitan area during the 1980s reported that younger (female) employers sometimes saw them as ' "protomothers" . . . expected to perform the emotional labor of "mothering" both the women employers and their families . . . to serve as surrogate mothers' (1992: 6, 8, 106). In these circumstances, domestic workers 'found themselves in the role of a grandmother and delegated responsibility for employers' children in order to relieve the employer/"daughter" of child care' (Romero 1988: 329). As Romero argued, the 'calculated strategy . . . to place domestics into nurturing and caring roles' was further complicated in contexts like the United States where women of color were hired to perform this emotional labor and to fulfill white middle-class female employers' 'psychological needs' by simultaneously confirming their superior status while allowing them to present as 'nonracist' (Romero 1992: 107, 111–12). The levels and layers of exploitation were multiple and complex.

Merlene Frater worked for a family in Kingston during the 1950s and 1960s: she cooked, washed, cleaned and looked after three children; she was, she declared, 'good pon everyting!' Asked if her employer had guided her, she laughed, 'De lady?' and scoffed *'Dem* can cook?! Dem de people de mosly use, ahm, cooking book an all dem ting de. . . . All one whe mi den a work wid, a *me* learn har fe cook.' She laughed again, *'Dem* can cook?' She taught 'Miss Babs' to cook, cared for her children 'for a *long*-long time' and declared that 'dem people de come een like mi own,' but she eventually left the position because, she said, she was not young: 'mi body want res, mi jus leave.'[18] While Miss Babs benefitted from the labor of this 'protomother,' as an older worker, perhaps Frater occupied that niche as a strategy against employment challenges she may have faced in a sector dominated by younger workers. Still, in the end, she left Miss Babs and the children to cope, or recruit another 'protomother,' perhaps confirming Todd's argument that 'we need to take *detachment* from work . . . seriously'; when servants left jobs, they demonstrated that in the final analysis, despite their mothering activities and/or rhetoric, 'it was just a job' (2009: 198).

While the discourse of mothering operated differently whether the workers were children or older women, it acquired additional layers when women who worked as nursemaids were also mothers themselves. In Western gender ideology, ideal motherhood is perceived as a private, fulltime occupation; therefore, according to Eileen Boris, 'the working mother was a contradiction in terms.' However, this was not the case for black women in former slave societies like the United States where they 'were regarded not as mothers, but as workers'; it was their motherhood, not their labor, that was at issue (1993: 106–107). And if these black working mothers were domestic servants, theirs were complicated positions, since they performed the labor associated with ideal motherhood, but not in their homes or for their children. Indeed their paid mothering work was often in contexts of 'long hours, low wages, and . . . sheer drudgery' (Newman 1986: 10) which threatened their *own* personal motherhoods and motherwork. In order to make their domestic labor possible, as Romero and Elizabeth Clark-Lewis point out, some women depended on others to care for their children (see Romero 1992: 32–45; Clarke-Lewis 1994: 30) in a mothering culture that Andrea O'Reilly described as female-defined, -centered and potentially empowering (2006: 11).

Within African-American communities, for example, according to Rosalie Riegle Troester, 'othermothers . . . adult women . . . grandmothers, aunts, or cousins, united by kinship with the blood mother,' assisted mothers with providing care (1984: 13). From this emerged what Patricia Hill Collins described as 'a distinctly Afrocentric ideology of motherhood,' which is neither restricted to biological mothers nor excessively private, but rather constituted by '[o]rganized, resilient, women-centered networks of bloodmothers and othermothers' (1987: 3–5). Among African diasporic women who were working mothers, including domestic servants, a reliance on 'othermothers' was a regular occurrence (see Tucker 1988: 20, 28; Collins 1987: 4–5; van Wormer et al. 2012: 103, 109–10; Silvera 1989: 20).

In the Caribbean context, women's networks are not merely present, but in fact, kinship patterns among Afro-descended communities have long been dominated by matrifocal forms which, according to Marietta Morrissey, emphasize ties between mothers and their families (1998: 81–83). As Christine Barrow argued, whether these familial structures were assessed as sources of 'social pathology,' as a 'functional response to the disorganizing effects of contemporary socioeconomic conditions,' or as 'culturally appropriate solutions to the problems of poverty, unemployment and economic uncertainty,' they have been 'extensive, [and] enduring' (1999: 152, 156; 1996: 71). And mothers who worked as domestic servants were deeply inserted into these family forms and networks.

When Lena Ferguson worked as a nursemaid in Stony Hill, St. Andrew in the 1940s, she said her two children were 'at home . . . wit mi family . . . [in] Westmoreland.'[19] According to Edith Clarke, when domestic workers in her 1950s study became pregnant, 'the girl had to leave her job' and 'would return to her mother's home for the birth of her child, and, if she re-entered domestic service, leave the child with her mother' (1999: 111). This was necessary as, according to Patricia Mohammed, '[s]upport services for domestic workers are non-existent. While looking after other people's children, they use makeshift facilities such as elderly relatives to care for their own' (1986: 46; see also Senior 1991: 9). When Adelle Robinson worked as a domestic servant between 1945 and the 1960s, she said she looked after her children herself but sometimes she had to 'leave dem somewhere . . . [with] neighbours' and that she didn't 'feel any way about dat.'[20] Perhaps she had embraced the survival techniques that had served Jamaican women for generations where, according to Joycelin Massiah, many women cultivated other women especially around 'child care, child watching . . . sharing household chores' (1982: 78) in female-headed households and matrifocal families (see Blake 1961; Clarke 1999; Smith 1956; Smith 1962).

Whereas in some societies domestic service was an early, temporary, bridging occupation and possibly 'a step along the way to marriage, motherhood and private domesticity' (Higman 2002: 260; see also McBride 1974, 1976, 1977; Brown and Smith 1963), in others like Jamaica and for some groups, domestic service could last for long periods or women's entire working lives (see Bunster and Chaney 1985). For those who were also mothers, it was often othermothers who made it possible for them to become what Susan Tucker called 'mother surrogates' (1988: 16) themselves: 'second' or othermothers to their employers' children.

After the birth of her second daughter in the early 1960s, Maureen Cooper employed Linnette who worked for her for twenty years. Linnette did general housework, 'brought up the children'[21] and relieved Cooper of some of the onerous, monotonous, emotional and physical labor assumed to be her lot as a housewife/mother. According to Romero:

> All of the gender-specific aspects of unpaid housework—identified in the housewife experience—are also present in domestic service. Even though domestics are paid workers, they do not escape the sexism attached to housework but rather carry the burden for the middle-class women employers. The never-ending job described by housewives is transferred to workers employed by women who treat domestic service as an opportunity to 'hire a wife.'
>
> (1992: 129–30)

This may have been the hope of Mae Virgo who employed Iris Morris in 1954: in the fifty years that she worked for the family, according to Virgo, Miss Iris was 'a second mother to the children,' in fact, '[s]he come een like a part a de family.'[22]

'... PART A DE FAMILY': EXPLOITATION, RESISTANCE AND THE MOTHERING DISCOURSE

The intricate connections among housewifery, motherwork and domestic service helped to explain the concurrent celebration and devaluation of the emotional and physical labor of unpaid and paid childcare. As Romero argued, employed to do 'women's work' in the home, domestic servants' labor 'is assumed to incorporate both skill as a worker and affection for the employer's family. Because they are women, they are expected to be caring and nurturing, acting in many instances as surrogate mothers to the employer and her children.' Further, said Romero, the

> emotional dimensions of the work, such as child care, are frequently manipulated to expand the worker's obligation beyond instrumental and economic considerations. Employers' references to domestics as 'one of the family' concretizes these gender specific characteristics, equating the work with homemaking.
>
> (1992: 130)

Although Romero's analyses were focused on the experiences of Chicana domestic workers in white American homes, her insights are applicable in the Jamaican context, where racial difference was apparently less of an issue. The complications that could result from these 'familial' discourses were evident when, in a separate interview, Miss Iris was asked about her work: she pointed to her employer's son and replied, 'See mi son de,'[23] while in quieter tones, the 'retired' 80-year-old, who was 'helping' a younger domestic worker in her (former) employer's kitchen, mentioned long work days and her employer's unkept promises for her own home. This was no easy life.

When Edna Philips worked as a domestic servant in Trelawny in the 1950s, she said she was required to wash, clean and 'nurse baby,' a skill of which she was proud. 'A look afta de chile like is *mine*. . . . Dem usually se dat fi how I tek care a chile, A na go av any, an mi really doh av any. Yu si if yu leave yu baby wid mi . . . an yu gone to work, yu no av to fret. . . . Wen yu come een an se, "Come baby, come," im se, "No" . . . a *mi* im come hug-up.'[24] In one job in Anchovy, St. James, she was responsible for eight children 'an de mada, an granmada, an fada.' She said she felt especially attached to the children: 'A mi an de children dem, because dem did *love* mi, love mi more dan de mada yu kno!'[25] According to Philips, the children's mother said 'a no she av dem, a me.'[26] The children's mother probably meant to create affective connections by claiming that it was Philips who had had her children and to extract even more emotional labor and motherwork. While Philips claimed that she and her employers 'jus come like one family' and that she only stopped working for them because they emigrated, when she worked for them she worked alone, did not get days off and was not allowed to have company because, she said, 'when yuh looking afta baby . . . dat was di strickes work.'[27]

According to Abigail Bakan and Daiva Stasiulis, 'In addition to the low status, long hours, isolation and poor pay,' domestic workers often have to contend with 'the affective quasi-familial and asymmetrical relations that develop between employers and (especially live-in) domestic employees' who are said to be 'just like one of the family.'

> The characterization of relations with their employers as familial or quasi-familial is one adopted by some live-in domestic workers. Those engaged in childcare are particularly apt to develop an attachment to the employers' children, who may in turn come to view them as a 'second mother.' Whether performed for love or money, childcare involves emotional labour associated with nurturing, care, guidance and training.
>
> (1997: 10–11)

This was reflected in Paula Aymer's (1997) research among women from the eastern Caribbean who migrated to the Dutch Antilles as domestic workers, some of whom 'were particularly fond of the children they helped raise from infancy.' That attachment, said Aymer, could lead them to remain in substandard working environments; one such worker focused on a child's behavioral improvement which she attributed to her care, and asked, 'How I go leave now? Is my child that' (1997: 105; see also Colen 1987: 184–85; Hondagneu-Sotelo 2001: 152). The possibility for personal conflict was especially heightened for live-in domestic workers who were mothers since, as Pierrette Hondagneu-Sotelo argued, developing 'motherlike ties' with their employers' children allowed them to enjoy 'the affectionate, face-to-face interactions that they cannot experience on a daily basis with their own children' (2001: 27).

For domestic workers who performed childcare, then, there was potential for emotional and labor exploitation in second mothering since claims of, and sometimes the existence of, kinship relations could mask relations of super/subordination. This was highlighted in Patricia Anderson's study of the Jamaican domestic sector in 1985, where workers were 'not only required to perform specific duties, but also to act out the rituals which go along with the ideological definition of housework as "loving service." '[28] Similarly, during Abigail Lawrence's interviews of eight Jamaican domestic workers and seven employers in the 1990s, all respondents re/iterated the discourse of maternal connection by repeated declarations that the worker was 'like a madda' to her employer's children, although these second mothers might be reprimanded if they indulged (and therefore 'spoiled') or disciplined their wards too harshly (1995: 67–72).

Claims of maternal connection should certainly be treated with caution, after all, as Katherine van Wormer asked when faced with white employers in the southern United States who said that they 'loved' their African-American domestic workers who were 'like family,' 'Who else in the family was scrubbing the bathtub or toilet? Who else in the family was getting paid at the end of the week? Who else was dressed in a uniform?' (2012: 274). Given the duplicitous utilization of the tropes of family and second motherhood which never absolved domestic servants from completing their assigned tasks, we can certainly echo Judith Rollins' statement that domestic work is more 'profoundly exploitative than other comparative occupations' (1985: 156).

In addition to possible exploitation, in contexts where the vestiges of colonialism, slavery and racism continue to define many social interactions, the discourses of mothering in domestic service could be especially fraught. For many persons in the United States, references to mothering in domestic service evoke the image of 'the Mammy, the faithful, devoted domestic servant . . . [who] conscientiously "mothers" her white children' (Collins 1987: 4; see Wallace-Sanders 2008; McElya 2007). Where white women were employers of women of color to perform domestic service, as Romero points out, 'the domestic and mistress relationship . . . brings several important factors to play simultaneously: same gender, inter-racial and inter-class oppression' (1988: 319). The assumption that domestic service inevitably meant interclass conflict might be questioned by Micki McElya, who argued that while '[m]ost black women did not and could not similarly employ others to do this work,' increasing numbers of working-class white women became employers of domestic labor in the United States after World War I (2007: 228). However, African-American Martha Calvert's report that when she worked as a domestic worker 'watching someone else kids' in the South in the 1980s, she had a teenager looking after her son (Tucker 1988: 38), leaves uncertain the suggestion that only white (working-class) women made use of domestic service. Indeed, according to Hondagneu-Sotelo, in Los Angeles the increase in high-paying jobs and a concentration of immigrant women (which drove down wages among domestic workers) led to a situation where 'demand is no longer confined to elite enclaves' but had expanded to include employers with modest incomes. Among the new employers were Latina nanny/housekeepers who pay other Latina immigrants 'to do in-home child-care, cooking, and cleaning, while they themselves go off to care for the children and homes of the more wealthy' (2001: 8–9).

Similarly, in Jamaica, according to Higman, 'a significant number of domestics were employed in working-class households by the 1950s, both in town and country' (1983: 122).[29] And while the fissures of race/color also existed in the Jamaican context, the question of a racial divide was complicated by the fact that by the twentieth century the vast majority of the population, including domestic workers and their employers, shared a racial heritage connected to the enslavement of Africans.[30] Although 'racial' differences were sometimes constructed out of color/'shade,' employment in domestic service was often intra-racial. Jamaican domestic servants and their employers often shared an Afro-Creole heritage and sometimes even class/status; they may also have shared a culture of mothering that may have been a challenge to other employers.

Englishwoman Margaret Clarke married a Jamaican in 1961, and soon after, hired Beatrice. She said that for four years their relationship was 'very good, it was always good. Until after I had my daughter.'

> I don't know what it was; there was something about the way—it might have been me, post-natal emotional state or what, I don't know, but somehow or other, I remember we had quite a few run-ins after, ahm, after [the baby] was born. And eventually I got somebody else. Ahm, I got another woman. I can't remember exactly when, but sometime when [the baby] was quite a young baby.[31]

Perhaps there was tension about the increased workload that childcare introduced to Beatrice's duties, or difficulties over notions of 'suitable' childcare or perhaps Clarke's self-diagnosis was correct. However, she quickly grew uncomfortable with her portrayal and tried to correct her narrative: 'The other thing was that Beatrice went to England, so I can't remember if I, it might have been that reason why she left.'[32] While the reasons for Beatrice's departure remain unclear, Clarke's memories of maternal discomfort hinted at what Todd described as 'middle-class women's fear that their maids would *replace* them'; after all, while they might see domestic work and childcare as 'unskilled drudgery,' they feared that 'neglecting these tasks is to fail as a wife, as a mother, and as a woman' (2009: 203). Perhaps Afro-Jamaican employers shared these concerns, but given their mothering culture, were without the means to articulate them. However, they were able to use that culture along with their racial, gender and sometimes class connections with their employees to cement bonds with them and to extract motherwork. According to Bridget Anderson, 'With particular reference to the caring function of domestic labour, . . . it is the worker's "personhood," rather than her labour power, which the employer is attempting to buy, and . . . the worker is thereby cast as unequal in the exchange' (2000: 2). By purchasing domestic workers' personhoods and, in this case, their (surrogate) motherhoods, employers of all classes sought to ensure their children's care and their abrogation of some of the less appealing aspects of childcare.

If employers sometimes used mothering and family tropes to manipulate workers into emotional and physical labor and to emphasize difference and deference (since workers were *just like* but were *not* family), domestic workers who used the terms often had other agendas. According to Romero, the use of 'the family analogy' by domestic workers 'points to aspects of the emotional labor that some workers are willing to accept and those they reject.' While the analogy 'suggests that domestics are engaged in emotional labor involved in nurturing and caring,' it also 'suggests that domestics are treated with respect and are not forced into doing the emotional labor required to create deference.' Further, said Romero, 'some domestics willingly exchange certain types of emotional labor for respect, status, and influence, for instance by manipulating traditional "feminine" qualities attached to housework. By being "motherly," they support and enhance the well-being of others while eliminating many negative and harsh attacks on their self-esteem' (1992: 124, 125).

In a similar vein, Hondagneu-Sotelo argued that while parents try to use the emotional bond between the 'nanny/housekeeper' and the children for whom they cared to get the best possible quality of care for their children, some domestic workers who provided childcare 'used concerns about the children's safety as leverage to strengthen their position' (2001: 150). For Linnette who worked with Maureen Cooper for twenty years and Miss Iris who worked with Mae Virgo for fifty years, and who were celebrated by their employers for mothering their children, the affective bonds both ensured great amounts of labor and that both women were cared for by their employers in their elder years. In a country where the social safety net was/is almost negligible, second mothering could act as insurance against the destitution that overtook many domestic workers.[33] Perhaps by wrapping themselves in mantles of mothering, and creating working/personal relationships, some domestic workers tried to insulate themselves from the volatility of the sector. In doing so, they drew on the 'high status and value' associated with motherwork in Jamaica (Durant-Gonzalez 1982: 15). Indeed, as A. Lynn Bolles said, '[t]raditional values pertaining to the importance of motherhood as a dimension of Afro-Caribbean women's roles are as strong today as they were in the days of slavery' (1988: 9).

For Hondagneu-Sotelo, even though employer/employee relationships remain 'asymmetrical,' personal connections could move them beyond '*maternalism*' which she defined as 'a unilateral positioning of the employer as a benefactor who receives personal thanks, recognition, and validation of self from the domestic worker' to '*personalism*, a bilateral relationship that involves two individuals recognizing each other not solely in terms of their role or office . . . but rather as persons embedded in a unique set of social relations, and with particular aspirations' (2001: 207–208). Still, Romero would join Hondagneu-Sotelo in reminding us that 'the intimate relationship [did] not shift power relations within the households' (1988: 329; see Romero 1992: 105).

CONCLUSION

In twentieth-century Jamaica, childcare was an important element in the range of duties performed by domestic workers. While some worked exclusively as nursemaids, others cared for children along with other duties. Domestic workers experienced and enacted concurrent, complementary and competing varieties of mothering during their careers. Young women (some of them 'schoolgirls') who worked as domestic servants were often expected to mother the children in their care as well as their employers who were sometimes also their relatives. Other domestic workers embraced or were expected to embrace the role of 'protomothers' guiding their (female) employers on aspects of 'domesticity.' Those domestic workers who were themselves mothers, frequently turned to 'othermothers' to care for their own children while they provided childcare for their employers' children.

Since domestic workers in Jamaica often shared the race/color, gender and even class designation of their employers, the barriers between the groups appeared to be perforated so that domestic workers and their employers may have seemed to be redefining and redeploying the Afro-Creole concept of maternal networks for the benefit of the nation's children. However, none of the shared histories and experiences prevented attempts to exploit the workers. These domestic workers competed for positions in an underdeveloped economy with few job opportunities and were unprotected by labor laws. The work they performed was tied to the legacies of a slave society that characterized domestic work as an emblem of servitude and devalued 'women's work' carried out in private homes rather than 'real' workplaces. At the same time, however, the mothering discourse was also strategically utilized by domestic workers to protect themselves in a volatile labor market. In twentieth-century Jamaica, domestic servants and their employers both referred to mothering as a means of gaining their best circumstances: if employers sought to extract domestic and emotional labor in the care of their children, then domestic servants sought to negotiate, within greatly asymmetrical work/personal relationships and a heavily competitive and largely unregulated sector, for some stability and, perhaps, fair treatment.

NOTES

1. Edna Philips, personal interview, Trelawny, 15 August 2004: 'I looked after the child as if it was *mine*.' The names of all interviewees have been changed to protect their privacy.
2. After an examination of local newspapers, *The Daily Gleaner* was chosen because it was the most popular and longest running newspaper in the island. An initial study determined that the second Saturday of every month (up to 1946) drew the greatest number of advertisements; after the introduction of the *Sunday Gleaner* in 1946, the most popular day to advertise was the second Sunday of the month. Since as many as 300 advertisements appeared in some newspaper issues, and an examination of 2,600 issues of the newspaper was prohibitive, a further sample was developed where all the classified advertisements from every second Saturday/Sunday for every month, for every five years were assessed. By this means 10,215 classified advertisements which appeared in the *Daily Gleaner* or *Sunday Gleaner* between 1920 and 1970 were examined. Some of the data extracted from that sample are used in this chapter.
3. Respondents were identified through personal contacts, several churches (including Anglican, Roman Catholic, United, Baptist and Church of Christ), the administrators in twenty homes for the elderly, the thirteen local parish councils, eleven parish Poor Relief Departments and eleven parish infirmaries.
4. *Census of Jamaica and Its Dependencies*, 1921; *Census of Jamaica*, 1943; *West Indies Population Census: Census of Jamaica*, 1960; *Commonwealth Caribbean Population Census: Jamaica*, 1970.
5. *Masters and Servants Law* 1842 (5 Victoria, Cap. 43); *The Masters and Servants Law* 1940 (Law 27 of 1940, Cap. 240); *An Act to Repeal the Masters and Servants Law* also cited as *The Employment (Termination and Redundancy Payments) Act* (Law 31 of 1974); also see *The Minimum Wage Act* also cited as *The National Minimum Wage Order* (Law 339 of 1975). Main Library, University of the West Indies, Mona, Jamaica.
6. Sample, *Daily Gleaner*, 1920–1970. For examples of advertisements by employers and servants see *Gleaner* 13 July 1935, 10 January 1960, 13 April 1935, 11 May 1940.
7. *Gleaner* 10 January 1920, 9 August 1930, 11 April 1925.
8. *Gleaner* 10 June 1950, 10 January 1960, 8 September 1945, 13 April 1935, 11 May 1940. See also *Gleaner* 13 March 1920, 8 August 1925, 8 February 1930, 12 April 1930; see also *Gleaner* 10 April 1920, 8 March 1930, 14 September 1935, 10 February 1940.
9. Mae Virgo, personal interview, Kingston, 31 July 2004.
10. Maureen Cooper, personal interview, Kingston, 30 July 2004.
11. Margaret Clarke, personal interview, Kingston, 29 July 2004.
12. Icilda Cole, personal interview, Kingston, 4 August 2004.
13. Lena Ferguson, personal interview, Kingston, 4 August 2004.
14. Doris Watson, personal interview, St. Thomas, 2 August 2004; Cole, personal interview; Jean Evans, personal interview, St. Ann, 20 August 2004: 'When I was 12 years of age . . . when I should have been going to school.'
15. Winnifred Black, personal interview, Trelawny, 14 August 2004: 'My mother just took me there and left me there.'
16. Watson, personal interview; Evans, personal interview: 'little clothes and shoes and thing.'
17. Cole, personal interview: '. . . washed their clothes and looked after and washed her [employer's] clothes . . . it is I who cooked for her and the two children . . . for the whole week . . . they [the children] and I would be alone there . . . because I used to look after the children, I didn't get any day's off.'

'Ah Look Afta De Child Like Is Mine' 93

18. Merlene Frater, personal interview, St. Thomas, 2 August 2004: '. . . good on everything! . . . The lady? Can *they* cook? Those people mostly use cookbooks and those sorts of things. . . . There was one who I was working with, *I* taught her how to cook. Can they cook? . . . Those people were like my own. . . . My body wanted rest, I just left.'
19. Lena Ferguson, personal interview, Kingston, 4 August 2004: '. . . at home with my family in Westmoreland.'
20. Adelle Robinson, personal interview, Kingston, 4 August 2004.
21. Maureen Cooper, personal interview, Kingston, 30 July 2004.
22. Mae Virgo, personal interview, Kingston, 31 July 2004: 'She was like a part of the family.'
23. Iris Morris, personal interview, Kingston, 31 July 2004: 'See my son there.'
24. Edna Philips, personal interview, Trelawny, 15 August 2004: 'I looked after the child as if it was *mine*. . . . They [people] usually have said that according to how I take care of a child, I would not have any, and I really don't have any. You see if you leave your baby with me . . . and you are gone to work, you don't have to fret. . . . When you come in and say, "Come baby, come," he says, "No" . . . he will hug *me*.'
25. Philips, personal interview: '. . . and the mother, and grandmother and father. . . . It was me and the children, because they *loved* me, loved me more than the mother you know!'
26. Philips, personal interview: 'it was not she who had them, it was me.'
27. Philips, personal interview: '. . . just were like one family . . . when you look after babies . . . that is the strictest [most controlled] work.'
28. The report was based on a 1985 research project led by Patricia Anderson, as part of the Population Mobility and Development Project of the Institute of Social and Economic Research (ISER) at the University of the West Indies, Mona, Jamaica. The findings of the report were then published by the Jamaican cultural women's association *Sistren*. 'Domestic Service: Complex Work Relations between Women.' *Sistren*, 1988, 10 (2&3): 8–9.
29. Higman's calculations are based on Jamaica Department of Statistics, *Household Expenditure Survey, 1953–1954* and *Rural Household Expenditure Survey, 1956*.
30. According to the 1921 census, 1.69% of the population was 'white,' 18.32% was 'coloured,' 76.96% was 'black,' 2.17% was 'East Indian,' 0.43% was Chinese and 0.43% were 'Not Specified'; by 1960, although categories had changed, the picture was similar: 78.3% were 'African,' 0.94% were 'European,' 2.9% were 'East Indian & Afro-East Indian,' 1.3% were 'Chinese and Afro-Chinese,' 13.6 were 'Afro-European' and 2.6 were 'Other.' See *Census of Jamaica*, 1921, 1960.
31. Margaret Clarke, personal interview, Kingston, 29 July 2004.
32. Margaret Clarke, personal interview, Kingston, 29 July 2004.
33. In 2004 when this fieldwork was completed, many former domestic workers were residents in the thirteen parish infirmaries (formerly Poor Houses).

REFERENCES

Anderson, Bridget. 2000. *Doing the Dirty Work? The Global Politics of Domestic Labour*. London and New York: Zed Books.

Aymer, Paula L. 1997. *Uprooted Women: Migrant Domestics in the Caribbean*. Westport and London: Praeger.

Bakan, Abigail B., and Daiva Stasiulis. 1997. 'Introduction.' In *Not One of the Family: Foreign Domestic Workers in Canada*, edited by Abigail B. Bakan and Daiva Stasiulis, 3–28. Toronto: University of Toronto Press.

Barrow, Christine. 1996. *Family in the Caribbean: Themes and Perspectives*. Kingston: Ian Randle Publishers; Oxford: James Currey Publishers.

Barrow, Christine. 1999. 'Men, Women and Family in the Caribbean: A Review.' In *Gender in Caribbean Development*, edited by Patricia Mohammed and Catherine Shepherd, 149–63. Kingston: Canoe Press, University of the West Indies.

Beckles, Hilary McDonald. 1999. *Centering Woman: Gender Discourses in Caribbean Slave Society*. Kingston: Ian Randle Publishers; Princeton: Markus Wiener Publishers; Oxford: James Currey Publishers.

Blake, Judith. 1961. *Family Structure in Jamaica: The Social Context of Reproduction*. New York: The Free Press of Glencoe.

Bolland, O. Nigel. 1992. 'Creolisation and Creole Societies: A Cultural Nationalist View of Caribbean Social History.' In *Intellectuals in the Twentieth Century Caribbean. Vol. 1. Spectre of the New Class: The Commonwealth Caribbean*, edited by Alastair Hennessy, 50–79. London: Macmillan Caribbean.

Bolles, A. Lynn. 1988. *My Mother Who Fathered Me and Others: Gender and Kinship in the Caribbean*. Working Paper #175, Women in International Development, Michigan State University, United States.

Boris, Eileen. 1993. 'What about the Working of the Working Mother?' *Journal of Women's History* 5(2): 104–109.

Brathwaite, Edward Kamau. 1974. *Contradictory Omens: Cultural Diversity and Integration in the Caribbean*. Mona: Savacou.

Brathwaite, Edward Kamau. 1984. 'Caribbean Woman during the Period of Slavery.' Elsa Goveia Memorial Lecture, Cave Hill, Barbados.

Brown, L., and J. H. Smith. 1963. 'Bridging Occupations.' *British Journal of Sociology* 14(1): 321–34.

Bunster, Ximena, and Elsa M. Chaney. 1985. *Sellers and Servants: Working Women in Lima, Peru*. New York: Praeger Special Studies.

Bush, Barbara. 1981. 'White "Ladies", Coloured "Favourites" and Black "Wenches": Some Considerations on Sex, Race and Class Factors in Social Relations in White Creole Society in the British Caribbean.' *Slavery and Abolition* 2(3): 245–62.

Bush, Barbara. 1990. *Slave Women in Caribbean Society, 1650–1838*. Kingston: Ian Randle; Bloomington and Indianapolis: Indiana University Press; Oxford: James Currey.

Chapman, Esther. 1952. *Pleasure Island: The Book of Jamaica*. Kingston: Arawak Press.

Clarke, Edith. 1999. *My Mother Who Fathered Me: A Study of the Families in Three Selected Communities of Jamaica*. Kingston: The Press, University of the West Indies.

Clarke-Lewis, Elizabeth. 1994. *Living In, Living Out: African American Domestics in Washington D.C., 1910–1940*. Washington and London: Smithsonian Institution Press.

Colen, Shellee. 1987. ' "Just a Little Respect": West Indian Domestic Workers in New York City.' In *Muchachas No More: Household Workers in Latin America and the Caribbean*, edited by Elsa M. Chaney and Mary Garcia Castro, 171–94. Philadelphia: Temple University Press.

Collins, Patricia Hill. 1987. 'The Meaning of Motherhood in Black Culture and Black Mother/Daughter Relationships.' *Sage* 4(2): 3–10.

Craton, Michael. 1993. 'Continuity Not Change: The Incidence of Unrest among Ex-slaves in the British West Indies, 1838–1876.' In *Caribbean Freedom: Economy and Society from Emancipation to the Present: A Student Reader*, edited by Hilary McD. Beckles and Verene Shepherd, 192–206. Princeton: Markus Wiener Publishers.

DeLisser, H. G. 1913. *Twentieth Century Jamaica*. Kingston: Jamaica Times.

Durant-Gonzalez, Victoria. 1982. 'The Realm of Female Familial Responsibility.' In *Women and the Family: Women in the Caribbean Project*, edited by Joycelin Massiah, 1–27. Cave Hill: Institute of Social and Economic Research, University of the West Indies.
Gaunt, Mary Eliza Bakewell. 1922. *Where the Twain Meet*. New York: E. P. Dutton and Company; London: J. Murray.
Green, William A. 1986. 'The Creolisation of Caribbean History: The Emancipation Era and a Critique of Dialectical Analysis.' *Journal of Imperial and Commonwealth History* 14(3): 149–69.
Hall, Catherine. 2002. *Civilising Subjects: Metropole and Colony in the English Imagination, 1830–1867*. Chicago and London: University of Chicago Press.
Higman, B. W. 1983. 'Domestic Service in Jamaica since 1750.' In *Trade, Government and Society in Caribbean History, 1700–1920: Essays Presented to Douglas Hall*, edited by B. W. Higman, 117–38. Kingston: Heinemann Education Books Caribbean.
Higman, B. W. 1985–6. 'Theory, Method and Technique in Caribbean Social History.' *Journal of Caribbean History* 20: 1–29.
Higman, B. W. 1999a. *Writing West Indian Histories*. London: Macmillan Education Ltd.
Higman, B. W. 1999b. 'The Development of Historical Disciplines in the Caribbean.' In *UNESCO General History of the Caribbean: Methodology and Historiography of the Caribbean*, VI, edited by B. W. Higman, 3–18. London and Oxford: UNESCO Publishing/Macmillan Educational Ltd.
Higman, B. W. 2002. *Domestic Service in Australia*. Carlton: Melbourne University Press.
Hondagneu-Sotelo, Pierrette. 2001. *Doméstica: Immigrant Workers Cleaning and Caring in the Shadows of Affluence*. Berkeley, Los Angeles, and London: University of California Press.
Hughes, Marjorie. 1962. *The Fairest Island*. London: Victor Gollanez.
Johnson, Michele A. 2002. 'Young Woman from the Country: A Profile of Domestic Service in Jamaica, 1920–1970.' In *Working Slavery, Pricing Freedom: The Caribbean and the Atlantic World since the 17th Century*, edited by Verene Shepherd, 396–415. Kingston: Ian Randle Press.
Lawrence, Abigail R. 1995. "Like a Madda": A Study of the Relationship between Domestic Helpers and their Employers in Jamaica. Unpublished research paper. Brattleboro: Women and Development Program, School for International Training.
Mair, Lucille Mathurin. 2006. *A Historical Study of Women in Jamaica, 1655–1844*. Kingston: University of the West Indies Press.
Massiah, Joycelin. 1982. 'Women Who Head Households.' In *Women and the Family: Women in the Caribbean Project*, edited by Joycelin Massiah, 62–126. Cave Hill: Institute of Social and Economic Research, University of the West Indies.
McBride, Theresa. 1974. 'Social Mobility for the Lower Classes: Domestic Service in France.' *Journal of Social History* 8(1): 63–78.
McBride, Theresa. 1976. *The Domestic Revolution: The Modernization of Household Service in England and France, 1820–1920*. London: Croom Helm.
McBride, Theresa, 1977. 'The Modernization of Women's Work.' *Journal of Modern History* 49(2): 231–45.
McElya, Micki. 2007. *Clinging to Mammy: The Faithful Slave in Twentieth-Century America*. Cambridge: Harvard University Press.
Mintz, Sidney, and Richard Price. 1976. *An Anthropological Approach to the Afro-American Past: A Caribbean Perspective*. Philadelphia: Institute for the Study of Human Issues.

Mohammed, Patricia. 1986. 'Domestic Workers.' In *Women in the Caribbean*, edited by Pat Ellis, 41–46. Kingston: Kingston Publishers.

Moore, Brian L., and Michele A. Johnson. 2011. *'They Do as They Please': The Jamaican Struggle for Cultural Freedom after Morant Bay*. Kingston: University of the West Indies Press.

Morrissey, Marietta. 1998. 'Explaining the Caribbean Family: Gender Ideologies and Gender Relations.' In *Caribbean Portraits: Essays on Gender Ideologies and Identities*, edited by Christine Barrow, 78–90. Kingston: Ian Randle Publishers and the Centre for Gender and Development Studies, University of the West Indies.

Newman, Debra Lynn. 1986. 'Black Women Workers in the Twentieth Century.' *Sage* 3(1): 10–15.

O'Reilly, Andrea. 2006. *Rocking the Cradle: Thoughts on Motherhood, Feminism and the Possibility of Empowered Mothering*. Toronto: Demeter Press.

Rollins, Judith. 1985. *Between Women: Domestics and Their Employers*. Philadelphia: Temple University Press.

Romero, Mary. 1988. 'Sisterhood and Domestic Service: Race, Class and Gender in the Mistress–Maid Relationship.' *Humanity and Society* 12(4): 318–46.

Romero, Mary. 1992. *Maid in the U.S.A.* New York and London: Routledge.

Sangster, Joan. 1994. 'Telling Our Stories: Feminist Debates and the Use of Oral History.' *Women's History Review* 3(1): 5–28.

Senior, Olive. 1991. *Working Miracles: Women's Lives in the English-Speaking Caribbean*. Cave Hill: Institute of Social and Economic Research, University of the West Indies; London: James Currey; Bloomington and Indianapolis: Indiana University Press.

Silvera, Makeda. 1989. *Silenced: Talks with Working Class Caribbean Women about Their Lives and Struggles as Domestic Workers in Canada*. Toronto: Sister Vision.

Smith, M. G. 1962. *West Indian Family Structure*. Seattle: University of Washington Press.

Smith, R. T. 1956. *The Negro Family in British Guiana*. London: Routledge & Kegan Paul.

Sutherland, Daniel. 1981. *Americans and Their Servants: Domestic Service in the United States from 1800 to 1920*. Baton Rouge and London: Louisiana State University Press.

Thompson, Paul Richard. 2000. *The Voice of the Past: Oral History*, 3rd ed. New York: Oxford University Press.

Todd, Selina. 2009. 'Domestic Service and Class Relationships in Britain 1900–1950.' *Past and Present* 203(1): 181–204.

Troester, Rosalie Riegle. 1984. 'Turbulence and Tenderness: Mothers, Daughters, and "Othermothers" in Paule Marshall's *Brown Girl, Brownstones*.' *Sage* 1(2): 13–16.

Tucker, Susan. 1988. *Telling Memories among Southern Women: Domestic Workers and Their Employers in the Segregated South*. Baton Rouge and London: Louisiana State University Press.

van Wormer, Katherine, David W. Jackson III and Charlette Sudduth. 2012. *The Maid Narratives: Black Domestics and White Families in the Jim Crow South*. Baton Rouge: Louisiana State University Press.

Vansina, Jan. 1985. *Oral Tradition as History*. Madison: University of Wisconsin Press.

Wallace-Sanders, Kimberly. 2008. *Mammy: A Century of Race, Gender, and Southern Memory*. Ann Arbor: University of Michigan Press.

5 'Always a Good Demand'
Aboriginal Child Domestic Servants in Nineteenth- and Early Twentieth-Century Australia

Shirleene Robinson

In Australia in recent years, public debates over the historic experiences of Aboriginal people have intensified. The 1997 *Bringing Them Home* report drew attention to the forced removal of generations of Aboriginal children by Europeans (HREOC). In 2006, the *Unfinished Business: Indigenous Stolen Wages* report by the Federal Australian Senate (SSCLCA) extensively documented the exploitation of Indigenous workers, including children. Both reports have shown the impact of colonization is still keenly felt in contemporary Australia. They have also highlighted the centrality of labor, particularly domestic service, to the colonizing project and have revealed that Aboriginal children were particularly vulnerable to state surveillance and control in the colonial system.

Domestic service in European homes constituted one of the main forms of labor undertaken by Aboriginal children in nineteenth- and twentieth-century Australia.[1] As a result, domestic service acted as a key contact zone and significant numbers of Aboriginal children interacted with European colonizers in this way (Haskins 2001: 13–25). In 1924, W. Porteous Semple, the superintendent of the Queensland Aboriginal reserve Barambah, alluded to the scale of this employment, asserting that he had no trouble finding employment situations for Aboriginal girls because for Aboriginal 'domestic labour there is always a good demand.'[2] While Aboriginal domestic servants of all ages were sought after, there was a particularly strong and consistent demand for young Aboriginal girls. At the time that Semple wrote his letter, at least one-third of the domestic servants employed in Queensland were aged under eighteen years (Robinson 2008: 136).

This chapter considers the 'good demand' for young Aboriginal domestic servants across Australia in detail, outlining the significance of Indigenous child domestic employment in this settler society. It argues that the use of young Aboriginal domestic service not only served an economic purpose but was also presented as a means of reforming a population that was designated a 'problem' under the structures of colonialism. The philosophy, which stressed the reformatory potential of labor, drew from 'child saving' ideas prevalent in nineteenth-century Britain. The process of colonization meant that Aboriginal children were designated as subjects who needed reform and domestic service was presented as the most appropriate form of labor for Indigenous girls. Thus, domestic service functioned as a means of colonizing these children by preparing them to assume positions as menial workers, who were ranked lowly on the hierarchy of settler society. While colonists maintained that domestic labor would benefit Indigenous children, in actuality, performing this labor was ultimately a dangerous and damaging experience for Aboriginal children. The chapter concludes its analysis by considering this impact.

A growing body of recent scholarship has expanded understandings of Aboriginal domestic servants in Australia's past (Huggins 1987–1988, 1991, 1995; Evans and Scott 1996; Haskins 2001, 2003, 2009). Regional studies have been particularly important in illuminating the scale, impact and significance of Aboriginal domestic labor (McGrath 1978; Sabbioni 1993; Walden 1995; Haskins 2004, 2007, 2009).

The experience of the Aboriginal children who were employed as domestic servants, however, is a topic that has received much less consideration. The limited work that has been published has tended to adopt a regional state-based approach and to concentrate on the particular vulnerability of child workers (Hetherington 2002; Robinson 2001, 2003, 2008). A nation-wide focus has not yet been adopted and there have not been any sustained examinations of domestic service as a means of colonizing and reforming young Aboriginal workers. By addressing this omission, this chapter expands understandings of Aboriginal domestic service in Australia and also provides further elucidation on the way that relationships between colonizers and the colonized were framed in an intimate zone.

Although the role of domestic service as a means of 'reforming' Indigenous children remains to be investigated, there is a considerable amount of related scholarship on child-saving and child rescue movements, child labor histories, and histories of Indigenous child removal that can inform this topic (Kociumbas 1997; Swain 2006; Kidd 1997: 18–37; Parry 2007; Read 1981; Haebich 2000; Bowden 2006). Such material contextualizes the use of Aboriginal child domestic servants as a means of colonizing 'problem' populations.

THE IDEOLOGY OF 'CIVILIZATION' THROUGH LABOR

Australian ideas about childhood and the reformatory potential of labor originated from nineteenth-century Britain (Kociumbas 1997: 79; Swain 2006: 157–66). The rapid process of industrialization in the eighteenth century had led to social dislocation and a fear of rising crime. British theorists attempted to control or prevent their fears of social collapse from being realized by blaming the perceived increase in crime on 'problem populations.' They argued that the children of 'problem populations' should be retrained in manual labor and provided with a religious education (Platt

1977: 314). This process was represented as the best method of rehabilitating the criminal classes in England (Kidd 1997: 18–32). As a consequence, significant numbers of children from working-class backgrounds in Britain were exploited in homes and workshops in the nineteenth century.

The concept of 'reforming' problem populations was one that reached beyond Britain's national boundaries and became enmeshed with broader colonial anxieties about race and class in sites of colonization. The historical anthropologist Ann Laura Stoler points out that such experiments in social reform and child welfare were conducted across the imperial world and that a range of institutions and processes were utilized to 'rescue young citizens and subjects in the making' (2001: 850, 852). While white children from working-class backgrounds in settler societies were subjected to policies of reform, the imperial and radicalized assumptions of such views meant that the children of Indigenous populations were even more vulnerable to these practices (Swain 2006: 163). Work on the mixed-descent children of the Dutch East Indies and on Native Americans in the United States confirms the link between processes of colonization and efforts to 'train' and 'reform' non-white children (Stoler 2001: 852; Stoler 2002: 112–39). Stoler argues such colonial genealogies of social welfare were grounded in imperial concerns over perceived distinctions between races (2001: 856).

COLONIZATION, ABORIGINAL CHILD REMOVAL AND DOMESTIC LABOR

Imperial concerns over race, coupled with views that children were susceptible to environmental influences, including perceptions of the corrupting influences of Aboriginal mothers and the broader Aboriginal community, meant that Aboriginal children in Australia were defined as a 'problem population' almost as soon as colonization began. By 1810, the start of a decade when debate on future policies towards Indigenous people in New South Wales increased considerably, many members of the public were freely advocating the removal of Aboriginal children from their parents so that they could be 'reformed.' The *Sydney Gazette* newspaper received extensive correspondence on this topic in that year.[3] In 1814, these sentiments influenced the opening of the Parramatta Native Institution (Robinson 2008: 47; Brook and Kohen 1991: 61). By 1840, a Sydney newspaper, the *Australian*, was framing the removal of Indigenous children from their families and their subsequent retraining in manual labor in positive terms:

> If these children are from their earliest age so carefully brought up by the State under scrupulous and judicious management, if they are trained in industry, and above all, in habits of regularity, a permanent good may, under the Divine blessing, be reasonably expected.[4]

This sentiment of 'reforming' Aboriginal children by separating them from their parents and retraining them in manual labor was highly influential in Australian history, and was articulated across the continent by a variety of individuals from diverse backgrounds in different eras. This social context shaped the introduction of legislation across Australia from the late nineteenth century that permitted the removal of Aboriginal children from their family groups resulting in what is referred to in contemporary Australia as 'stolen generations' policies (Robinson and Paten 2008: 508; Haebich 2000).

Embedded racial attitudes meant that Aboriginal children were not protected from exploitation as workers in the same way as European children. Educational reform in the Australian colonies between 1872 and 1894 treated Indigenous children differently to European children. In this era, all of the Australian colonies introduced free, compulsory and secular education for European children. Victoria was the first colony to do this with the *Education Act 1872*, while Western Australia was the last colony to take this action with the *Elementary Education Act 1871 Amendment Act 1894* (Shorten 1996: 8). While these pieces of legislation could have been used to protect Indigenous children from being compelled to perform exploitative labor, this did not occur in any region.

Instead, from the 1890s onwards, the Australian colonies introduced 'protective' legislation pertaining to Indigenous people. This legislation substantially increased the power of the state over Indigenous lives and reinforced the Indigenous child removal policies that had been evident in previous Acts (Haebich 2000: 149–50). Protective legislation also formalized the operation of Aboriginal missions and reserves, which were chronically underfunded and relied on the wages of Indigenous workers to survive.

This was particularly significant in Queensland and Western Australia. As Raymond Evans and Joanne Scott have noted, for much of the twentieth century in Queensland, that state's Indigenous population 'were increasingly supplying the official expenditure set aside for their own dismally imposed segregation and repression' (Evans and Scott 1995: 115). Similarly, in Western Australia, the *Industrial Schools Act* of 1874 enabled missionaries to retain Aboriginal children until they were twenty-one years of age and also encouraged them to send these children out to service and use the money these children earned (Hetherington 2002: 131). Dr. Walter Roth, who took up a position as a Commissioner in Western Australia in 1905 after leaving Queensland, and was later made government medical officer in that state, supported this approach. In an article published in the *West Australian* newspaper on 10 February 1905, he maintained that Aboriginal children as young as six could be indentured as European servants.[5]

By the early twentieth century, the growing number of Aboriginal people who were of mixed-descent was the subject of increased public debate. As the very existence of these people challenged the idea that Aborigines were a 'doomed race,' discussions focused on ways this 'problem' could be dealt with. Removal to missions and reserves served as a way of eliminating the Aboriginal presence from major towns and cities. Furthermore, policies of cultural assimilation, alongside eugenic assimilation by the 1920s, were also presented as 'solutions' to the visibility of Indigenous people (McGregor 2002: 286–302; Ellinghaus 2003: 183–207). In some parts of Australia, such as the Northern Territory, Western Australia and Queensland, the training of Aboriginal girls as domestic servants was presented as a means of making them suitable wives for working-class white men, thus serving as a means of 'breeding out the colour' (Haebich 2000: 195–96; Carey 2007: 162–70).

Material from the Northern Territory in the 1930s reveals the anxieties about the Aboriginal race that were becoming increasingly prevalent in that region by that decade. Dr. Cecil Cook, the Chief Protector of Aborigines in North Australia from 1927 (the Northern Territory after 1931), wrote extensively about the 'problem' of 'mixed race' Aborigines and argued that children with fifty percent or more European heritage should be removed from Aboriginal camps, taken to institutions where they would be trained in manual labor, followed by marriage to 'half-caste' Aboriginal men or white men. This, he argued, would provide the best means of dealing with the Aboriginal 'problem.' Cook's concerns were not solely motivated by racial assumptions. He also alluded to the economic benefits to be accrued if Aboriginal people were 'absorbed' into the lower rungs of white society.[6]

Material published in newspapers across Australia in the early twentieth century reveals the widespread influence of reformatory imperatives and concerns over the perceived 'Aboriginal problem' on Indigenous policy. This published discourse also reveals that domestic service was consistently positioned as the most appropriate means of 'civilizing' Aboriginal children, particularly those of mixed Aboriginal and European (or in some cases Asian) parentage, referred to as 'half-castes.' On 6 August 1909, the Adelaide *Advertiser* newspaper published an article, where J. M. McKay, the Sub-Protector of Aborigines in Alice Springs, expressed these sentiments, stating that:

> A scheme for the amelioration of the condition of the half-caste would be for them to be taken when not older than seven years of age to the city and placed in a good institution where they could be trained for domestic service. They are very docile and teachable. If some philanthropic society could be induced to take up this question and form a separate home for them, they would be protecting these poor children, and at the same time be helping to supply the great demand for domestic servants.[7]

This statement, which casts Aboriginal children as placid, in need of amelioration and receptive to low-level training, reflects the racial sentiment of the era and the way that domestic service was presented as a solution to the 'problem' of Aboriginal children. It also reveals the way, as Victoria Haskins and Margaret D. Jacobs have pointed out, colonizers 'often imagined that the adoption of European-style homes (and the domestic work within them by Indigenous women) would miraculously transform native peoples into 'civilized' colonial subjects' (Haskins and Jacobs 2007: *ix*).

As a result of both a demand for workers and embedded racial attitudes, domestic service was designated as the most suitable form of employment for generations of Aboriginal children. It reflected ideas about the appropriate type of labor Indigenous women should undertake and was presented as a means of 'reforming' this population. Domestic service was a common occupation amongst Australia's female population from the start of settlement until the middle of the twentieth century, when improved technology and wider career options for women made the profession increasingly obsolete (Kingston 1975: 55; Higman 2002: 31). During the nineteenth century, European domestic servants were required to undertake a wide range of tasks, including washing, ironing, cooking, setting the table, washing the dishes, caring for children, making repairs, gardening and chopping wood (Lawson 1973: 135).

Indigenous women were employed as domestic servants almost from the start of settlement in Australia (McGrath 1987: 68–83; Reynolds 1990: 207–13; Huggins 1995: 188). In part, this was due to a scarcity of domestic labor, a common feature across Australia well into the twentieth century (Higman 2002: 27, 31, 95). However, Aboriginal workers did not merely replace white servants. As Jacobs has pointed out, domestic service was a site where colonial relationships were reproduced (Jacobs 2007: 166). Lowrie draws this point out further, arguing that wielding power over domestic servants in the home served as an expression of colonial power (Lowrie 2011; see also Lowrie in this volume). The position of Aboriginal domestic servants as colonized workers was evident from the type of work they were expected to undertake. The tasks they were allocated vastly exceeded the work European domestic servants were allocated. As far as Aboriginal workers were considered, domestic service encompassed 'any type of labour which was not related to stockwork or tasks outside the boundary of the main camp' (Huggins 1995: 12).

By the first decades of the twentieth century, it was evident that state governments were attempting to resolve what they perceived of as the 'half-caste problem' by removing Aboriginal children and training them to take up roles as domestic servants. A Sydney newspaper outlined the way this was occurring when it asserted that:

> What happens is that the girls are taken from the camps and reserves and sent to the Government Institution at Cootamundra, where they are trained for domestic service. They come to the metropolitan area as nurse girls and servants.[8]

The New South Wales state policy established a labor reserve, where Indigenous children were removed from their parents and trained to assume positions as manual workers (Haskins 2003: 106–21).

The use of Aboriginal missions and reserves for the purposes of training Aboriginal people in manual labor, specifically domestic service for Aboriginal girls, was also common in the Northern Territory (Austin 1993: 6; MacDonald 1995: 59–66; Martinez 2006: 122–39; Martinez and Lowrie 2009: 305). A growing body of scholarship has outlined the way that the Kahlin Compound, established outside of Darwin in 1913, functioned as a labor reserve where settlers recruited girls after a period of training (Cummings 1990: 1).

Many reports published in newspapers alluded to the gendered structures of training that were operating in Aboriginal institutions. On 29 June 1937, the *Adelaide Advertiser* newspaper asserted that:

> more than 250 half-castes of all ages are being taught in the special homes established for them at Darwin and Alice Springs. From the Alice Springs institution 16 half-caste youths were found employment with approved private persons, and 12 half-caste girls were found employment as domestic servants during the year. All girls from nine to 12 received instruction in domestic duties, and girls over that age advanced training, which included cooking, bread making, laundry work and dressmaking. Half-caste boys are trained as gardeners.[9]

The emphasis on training in manual labor was also the focus in Aboriginal missions and reserves in Queensland. Here it was not until 1953 that the top grade of education provided on Aboriginal missions and reserves was lifted from Grade 4 to Grade 7 (Long 1970: 100).

Out of all the Australian states, Queensland appears to have kept the most detailed records regarding numbers of Aboriginal domestic servants in the late nineteenth and early twentieth centuries. Employers in that state were required to register Aboriginal workers after the passage of 1897 legislation, but many would have opted to avoid filling out official paperwork in order to avoid the payment of wages (Robinson 2008: 38–40). Nonetheless, statistics that are available in various newspaper articles indicate that the employment of Aboriginal domestic servants in Queensland was remarkably constant. On 28 May 1908, the *Brisbane Courier* noted that there were 'considerably over 100 girls' who were under the supervision of the Aboriginal Department employed as domestic servants in the Brisbane district alone.[10] By 1920, when the Queensland Chief Protector of Aboriginals, John Bleakley, conducted a survey of Aboriginal domestic service in that state, 524 female Aboriginal domestic servants were listed as being employed in Queensland in that year. More than one-third of these domestic servants were aged under eighteen years.[11] Four years later, 677 Aboriginal females were reportedly employed under agreement in Queensland.[12]

During the early twentieth century, newspapers across disparate regions of Australia often referred to the popularity of Indigenous labor, particularly in the field of domestic service. Noting the 'keen demand' for Aboriginal domestic servants across the state of Queensland in 1907, a journalist in that state asserted that 'if 500 girls were available, places could be found for them quickly.'[13] The demand for Aboriginal domestic labor in other states was also strong. On 5 March 1910, the Perth newspaper the *Western Mail* asserted that Aboriginal girls were 'much sought after in the towns and stations.'[14] Thirteen years later, in an article published in the Western Australian on 19 September 1923, F. Aldrich, the Deputy Chief Protector of Aboriginals in Western Australia, noted that the 'demand for half-caste girls as domestic servants in the metropolitan area continued to be far in excess of the number available.' The demand for Aboriginal domestic servants was not limited to the frontier states. On 17 October 1925, the *Sydney Morning Herald* estimated that around 200 Aboriginal girls were employed as domestic servants in New South Wales' metropolitan areas.[15]

Aboriginal domestic servants were also employed in a wide variety of domestic settings. On 2 April 1938, the *West Australian* newspaper noted that the only servants employed at Government House in Darwin were Aboriginal and 'they do all the cooking and wait at table for all the countless guests.' The newspaper did note that a 'Chinese drinks waiter' had to be engaged for one function due to the 'Aborigines' ordinance which makes it an offence for an Aboriginal even to serve intoxicating liquor.'[16] While not the focus of this chapter, the use of Chinese men and boys as servants was common in northern Australia and reveals the way colonization and its associated racial demarcations impacted on other groups in Australia in this period (Lowrie 2013: 35–57; Martinez and Lowrie 2012: 518).

IMPACT OF COLONIZATION THROUGH DOMESTIC SERVICE

Domestic service was consistently presented as the most suitable type of employment for young Aboriginal girls in Australia until after the Second World War. Statistical evidence from Queensland indicates that one in every three Aboriginal domestic servants in the early twentieth century was under the age of eighteen (Robinson 2008: 135). This material is consistent with studies of other states, which show that young Indigenous workers were employed in large numbers in this field (Hetherington 2002: 152; Walden 1995: 196). While colonizers argued that Aboriginal children were being 'uplifted' and 'civilized' through the performance of domestic labor, it is evident that the performance of domestic service was in actuality replicating the worst abuses and excesses of the frontier in a more intimate setting. Instead of 'civilizing' Aboriginal children, the performance of domestic service trapped Indigenous children in a position where they were forced to be dependent on European employers. They were given no real opportunity to take a place as an equal in the newly emerging society.

Existing historical literature that has focused on Aboriginal child labor has emphasized the slave-like elements of this employment, due to the power imbalance between Aboriginal child workers and their European employers (Robinson 2008). There is certainly considerable evidence that these workers had little control over their working lives. In 1904, James Old, the Normanton Protector of Aboriginals in Queensland, told Dr. Walter Roth, the Northern Protector of Aboriginals, that he believed that a large proportion of female Aboriginal workers in that region had been 'given to their owners' when they were about seven or eight years of age.[17]

Aboriginal children who worked for Europeans were expected to perform quite difficult tasks. Tasks were not moderated to take into account the youth of these Aboriginal workers and included cooking, cleaning, washing and minding their employers' children, in spite of their own youth. These tasks were physically demanding and potentially damaging to the children's physical development. There are cases of Aboriginal children employed as domestic servants being required to separate milk, dig postholes, chop the firewood and fetch the water from the river.

There are accounts of young Aboriginal domestic servants performing quite extraordinary duties. On 28 August 1924, for example, the *Sydney Morning Herald* newspaper reported that some months earlier, Mrs. Chapman Glenfield had left Sydney with her twelve-year-old daughter and an Aboriginal domestic servant and had spent fourteen weeks walking to Brisbane. The young Aboriginal domestic servant had clearly been expected to perform her duties on the course of this arduous trek. On several occasions difficulty was experienced locating water but, according to the *Sydney Morning Herald*, 'the problem was solved by the Aboriginal girl, who appeared to be able to locate water whenever she was called upon to do so.'[18] Another Aboriginal child, ostensibly employed as a domestic servant, was charged with keeping goats warm at night by sleeping with them (Robinson 2003: 165). The assignment of such tasks and the mistreatment of young workers indicate that the colonizing project—with its embedded racial hierarchies—continued to play out in the private sphere.

Research conducted on the experiences of Aboriginal child workers in Western Australia and Queensland has shown that these children were frequently subjected to emotional, physical and sexual abuse and that inadequate mechanisms to protect them from this existed (Hetherington 2002: 147; Robinson 2008: 141). In Queensland, for example, until the Royal Assent of an Amendment Act controlling Aboriginal child labor in 1902, there was no legislation that could compel employers of Aboriginal children to pay these workers. Furthermore, no minimum age was set for Aboriginal child workers until 1919 (Robinson 2002: 1–16). This contrasted with the situation of European children in state care in Queensland, who were not sent out to service younger than twelve years of age after

1884 and also had their employment situations regularly monitored by Inspectors. The Queensland government also set minimum rates of pay for European state children in 1880. Furthermore, before state children in Queensland started employment, their employers had to apply to the government for permission and for a check on their suitability (Robinson 2002: 1–16). While the permit system technically required employers of Aboriginal children to also apply for government permission, no suitability checks were required. Furthermore, a great number of employers did not apply for permits and this was frequently condoned by regional Protectors of Aboriginals (Robinson 2008: 62–63). Such differences in the treatment of Indigenous and non-Indigenous child workers are attributable to prevailing racial attitudes.

Many accounts provided by Aboriginal women outline the way they were constantly treated as inferior by white employers. In this way, the racial structures of colonization were being replicated and produced within the intimate zone of the home. Status and position was emphasized in numerous different ways, including through accommodation, food and language. Glenyse Ward, whose memoir (1988) describes her experiences as a domestic servant in Western Australia, ate off a tin plate, was forced to sleep in a cot above the garage and showered where her employer showered her dogs. Margaret Tucker's autobiographical account references similarly poor treatment. She remembers that she was not fed as well as her employer and that she was constantly hungry (Tucker 1977: 112–15). Alice Nannup remembers being referred to as her employer's 'little black girl' (Nannup, Marsh and Kinnane 1992: 101). The writer Wayne King's mother recalled that:

> You were always the Aboriginal servant. I wasn't allowed to walk through the house to get to my room at the back of the house; I always had to use the back entrance. My meals had to be taken separately on the back verandah.
>
> (King 1996: 201)

It is evident that sexual abuse was a continual issue for young Aboriginal domestic servants. Such mistreatment challenged the rhetoric that Aboriginal girls were being 'uplifted' and 'helped' through employment. In 1902, Dr. Walter Roth, Queensland's Northern Protector of Aboriginals, asserted that large numbers of Aboriginal girls were being employed as domestic servants in that state and were:

> being brought up mostly as nurse-girls, kept in a false position by being temporarily treated as 'one of the family'—a fact which will probably account for them receiving no wages—and then, when they get into trouble, are packed off to camp.[19]

It is difficult to imagine how distraught young Indigenous girls being abandoned by the only 'family' they had ever known in such a vulnerable position must have felt. This was not just a situation that occurred in Queensland at the start of the twentieth century either. On 6 July 1933, the *West Australian* newspaper stated 'of the 80 girls who went into domestic service last year, 30 were returned to the mission stations in a pregnant condition.'[20] Victoria Haskins has also charted sexual abuse as an ongoing problem in New South Wales in the late nineteenth and early twentieth century (2004: 33–58).

The constant threat of sexual abuse is also included in many autobiographical accounts by Indigenous women. Agnes Williams told Jackie Huggins that every male employer she had ever worked for had tried to sexually proposition her and that European females would not believe her complaints about this behavior (Huggins 1991: 2). Wayne King's mother recalls that sexual abuse was a very real threat in her daily working life as a young domestic servant in Queensland (King 1996: 199).

There are also a multitude of accounts of Aboriginal domestic servants experiencing physical abuse. A number of Indigenous women have mentioned this in their accounts of performing domestic service (Huggins 1991: 2; King 1996: 199). In 1900, the physical abuse of one child domestic servant was exposed when her employer travelled to Toowoomba on holiday. A fellow resident in the Toowoomba guesthouse where the family was staying became aware of the child's abuse and reported it to authorities. The ten-year-old servant, named Gerribah, confirmed the abuse, telling police that she had been with a Mrs. Boyce:

> For a long time. Comes from Normanton. Used to do housework and mind the children. Mrs. Boyce never gave me any money. Mrs. Boyce used to thrash me with riding whip and hit me in the face. Sometimes I was thrashed because I forgot to do something Mrs. Boyce told me to do, and sometimes I did not know what the thrashing was for. Mr. Boyce used to kick me around the body. Sometimes I was sent without meals.[21]

Although the power balance was firmly controlled by European employers in a colonial system, it is important to note that Aboriginal children who worked as domestic servants did attempt to resist abusive and exploitative employment situations. A fuller account of strategies of resistance has been provided elsewhere, but it is evident that Aboriginal children tried to run away from their situations and showed resistance through mechanisms that included stealing, 'playing up' and destroying the property of their employers (Robinson 2008: 159–63). This resistance reiterates that colonization is an unstable process, subject to tension, negotiation and challenge.

CONCLUSION

Investigations of Aboriginal domestic service shed light on many important aspects of Australia's past, including the non-payment of Indigenous wages and the forced removal of Aboriginal children from their family groups. Such issues are still contentious in contemporary Australia, demonstrating the potent legacies of colonization. This chapter has focused closely on the employment of Aboriginal child domestic servants, arguing that this employment was intrinsically linked to colonizing imperatives. Domestic service was presented as the most suitable occupation for generations of Indigenous children and as a result, domestic service acted as a key contact zone between colonizers and the colonized.

Aboriginal children were employed as domestic servants as a means of reforming a population that was a represented as a 'problem' under the colonial order. The concept of reform through labor drew from 'child saving' ideas prevalent in nineteenth-century Britain. The colonizing impulse meant that Aboriginal children were designated as subjects in need of reform upon British settlement and domestic service was presented as the most appropriate form of labor for Indigenous girls. While settlers maintained that domestic labor would 'uplift' Indigenous children, in actuality, performing this labor was a heavily detrimental experience. Rather than enabling Aboriginal children to move past the devastation of colonization, domestic service acted as a form of colonization in itself, reiterating the imperial racial order in a more intimate context.

NOTES

1. For the purposes of this chapter, individuals under eighteen years are considered to be children. This definition recognizes that concepts of childhood evolved considerably during the nineteenth and twentieth century and allows for a full discussion of the outcomes of child labor on the largest number of individuals who were impacted. This definition is also consistent with international bodies such as the United Nations International Children's Emergency Fund (UNICEF) and the International Labour Organization, who argue that physical labor is damaging to people under the age of eighteen.
2. W. Porteous Semple, Barambah Settlement, to the Chief Protector of Aboriginals, Brisbane, 1 September 1924, in-letter no. 2677 of 19244, HOM/J539, Queensland State Archives [hereafter QSA].
3. 'Answer to the Query—Concluded,' *Sydney Gazette*, 11 August 1810, 2.
4. [Untitled editorial], *Australian* [Sydney], 29 December 1840, 2.
5. 'The Aborigines Question,' *West Australian*, 10 February 1905, 2.
6. Cecil Cook, 'Report of the Chief Protector of Aboriginals' in Report on the Administration of the Northern Territory for the Year ended 30th June 1934, *Commonwealth Parliamentary Papers*, 138, 1934–1937, 12.
7. 'Natives of the Interior,' *Advertiser* [Adelaide], 6 August 1909, 5.
8. 'Aborigines: Australia's Race Tragedy,' *Sydney Morning Herald*, 17 October 1925, 11.

9. 'Problem of the Half-Caste,' *Chronicle* [Adelaide], 1 July 1937, 17.
10. 'Entertaining Aboriginal Girls,' *Brisbane Courier*, 28 May 1908, 4.
11. 'Returns of Aboriginal and Half-Caste Females in Employment in 1920' [date and in-letter no. not provided], A/58912, QSA.
12. 'Aboriginal Department,' *Western Champion* [Barcaldine], 20 September 1924, 11.
13. 'Aboriginals as Domestic Servants,' *Brisbane Courier*, 15 November 1907, 4.
14. 'The Australian Aborigines,' *Western Mail* [Perth], 5 March 1910, 45.
15. 'Australian Aborigines: Australia's Race Tragedy,' *Sydney Morning Herald*, 17 October 1925, 11.
16. 'Half-Castes as Servants,' *West Australian* [Perth], 2 April 1938, 20.
17. James Old, Normanton Protector of Aboriginals, to Walter Roth, Brisbane, 30 January 1904, in-letter no. 226 of 1904, A/44680, QSA.
18. 'Remarkable Walk—Sydney to Brisbane—Women's Achievement,' *Sydney Morning Herald*, 27 August 1924, 14.
19. Walter E. Roth, Annual Report of the Northern Protector of Aboriginals for 1902 [Queensland, 1903]: 10.
20. 'Care of Natives,' *West Australian*, 6 July 1933, 8.
21. Harold Meston, to the Under Secretary and the Colonial Secretary, 13 March 1900, in-letter no. 03622 of 1900, 'Statement Made by "Gerribah," Aboriginal Girl, Aged about Ten Years,' COL/140, QSA.

REFERENCES

Austin, Tony. 1993. *I Can Picture the Old Home so Clearly: The Commonwealth and 'Half-Caste' Youth in the Northern Territory 1911–1939*. Canberra: Aboriginal Studies Press.

Bowden, Bradley. 2006. 'An Economy Ill-Suited to Younger Workers: Child and Youth Participation in Colonial Queensland, 1886–1901.' *Australian Economic History Review* 45: 100–12.

Brook, J., and J. L. Kohen. 1991. *The Parramatta Native Institution and the Black Town: A History*. Sydney: University of New South Wales Press.

Carey, Jane. 2007. '"Not Only a White Race, but a Race of the Best Whites": The Women's Movement, White Australia and Eugenics between the Wars.' In *Historicising Whiteness: Transnational Perspectives on the Emergence of an Identity*, edited by Leigh Boucher, Jane Carey and Katherine Ellinghaus, 162–70. Melbourne: RMIT Publishing.

Cummings, Barbara. 1990. *Take This Child: From Kahlin Compound to the Retta Dixon Children's Home*. Canberra: Aboriginal Studies Press.

Ellinghaus, Katherine. 2003. 'Absorbing the Aboriginal Problem: Controlling Marriage in Australia in the Late Nineteenth and Early Twentieth Century.' *Aboriginal History* 27: 185–209.

Evans, Raymond, and Joanne Scott. 1995. '"Fallen Among Thieves": Aboriginal Labour and State Control in Inter-war Queensland.' In *Aboriginal Workers*, edited by Ann McGrath and Kay Saunders, 115–30. Sydney: Australian Society for the Study of Labour History.

Evans, Raymond, and Joanne Scott. 1996. '"The Moulding of Menials": The Making of Aboriginal Domestic Servants in Early Twentieth Century Queensland.' *Hecate* 22(1): 140–57.

Haebich, Anna. 2000. *Broken Circles: Fragmenting Indigenous Families 1800–2000*. Fremantle: Fremantle Arts Centre Press.

Haskins, Victoria. 2001. 'On the Doorstep: Aboriginal Domestic Service as a "Contact Zone."' *Australian Feminist Studies* 16: 13–25.

Haskins, Victoria. 2003. '"Could You See to the Return of My Daughter?" Fathers and Daughters under the New South Wales Aborigines Board Child Removal Policy.' *Australian Historical Studies* 34(121): 106–21.

Haskins, Victoria. 2004. '"A Better Chance"? Sexual Abuse and the Apprenticeship of Aboriginal Girls under the NSW Aborigines Protection Board.' *Aboriginal History* 28(1): 33–58.

Haskins, Victoria. 2007. 'Domestic Service and Frontier Feminism: The Call for a Woman Visitor to "Half-Caste" Girls and Women in Domestic Service, Adelaide, 1925–1928.' *Frontiers* 28(1&2): 124–64.

Haskins, Victoria. 2009. 'From the Centre to the City: Modernity, Mobility and Mixed-Descent Aboriginal Domestic Workers from Central Australia.' *Women's History Review* 18: 155–75.

Haskins, Victoria, and Margaret D. Jacobs. 2007. 'Introduction.' *Frontiers* 28(1&2): ix–xvi.

Hetherington, Penelope. 2002. *Settlers, Servants and Slaves: Aboriginal and European Children in Nineteenth-Century Western Australia*. Crawley: University of Western Australia Press.

Higman, B. W. 2002. *Domestic Service in Australia*. Melbourne: Melbourne University Press.

Human Rights and Equal Opportunity Commission (HREOC). 1997. *Bringing Them Home: Report of the National Inquiry into the Separation of Aboriginal and Torres Strait Islander Children from their Families*. Sydney: Sterling Press.

Huggins, Jackie. 1987–1988. '"Firing On in the Mind": Aboriginal Domestic Servants in the Inter-war Years.' *Hecate* 13(2): 5–23.

Huggins, Jackie. 1991. 'Experiences of a Queensland Aboriginal Domestic Servant: Agnes Williams Talks to Jackie Huggins.' *Labour History* 61(November): 1–2.

Huggins, Jackie. 1995. 'White Aprons, Black Hands: Aboriginal Domestic Servants in Queensland.' In *Aboriginal Workers*, edited by Ann McGrath and Kay Saunders, 188–95. Sydney: Australian Society for the Study of Labour History.

Jacobs, Margaret D. 2007. 'Working on the Domestic Frontier: American Indian Domestic Servants in White Women's Households in the San Francisco Bay Area, 1920–40.' *Frontiers* 27(1&2): 165–99.

Kidd, Rosalind. 1997. *The Way We Civilise: Aboriginal Affairs—The Untold Story*. St Lucia: University of Queensland Press.

King, Wayne. 1996. *Black Hours*. Sydney: Angus & Robertson.

Kingston, Beverley. 1975. *My Wife, My Daughter, and Poor Mary Ann*. Sydney: Thomas Nelson.

Kociumbas, Jan. 1997. *Australian Childhood: A History*. St Leonards: Allen & Unwin.

Lawson, Ronald. 1973. *Brisbane in the 1890s: A Study of an Australian Urban Society*. St Lucia: University of Queensland Press.

Long, J.P.M. 1970. *Aboriginal Settlements: A Survey of Institutional Communities in Eastern Australia*. Canberra: ANU Press.

Lowrie, Claire. 2011. 'The Transcolonial Politics of Chinese Domestic Mastery in Singapore and Darwin 1910s–1930s.' *Journal of Colonialism and Colonial History* 12(3). http://muse.jhu.edu/journals/journal_of_colonialism_and_colonial_history/v012/12.3.lowrie.html. Accessed September 14, 2014.

Lowrie, Claire. 2013. 'White "Men" and Their Chinese "Boys": Sexuality, Masculinity and Colonial Power in Darwin and Singapore, 1880s–1930s.' *History Australia* 10(1): 35–57.

MacDonald, Rowena. 1995. *Between Two Worlds: The Commonwealth Government and the Removal of Aboriginal Children of Part Descent in the Northern Territory*. Alice Springs: IAD Press.
Martínez, Julia. 2006. 'Ethnic Policy and Practice in Darwin.' In *Mixed Relations: Asian-Aboriginal Contact in North Australia*, edited by Regina Ganter with contributions by Julia Martínez and Gary Lee, 122–39. Perth: University of Western Australia Press.
Martínez, Julia, and Claire Lowrie. 2009. 'Colonial Constructions of Masculinity: Transforming Aboriginal Australian Men into "Houseboys."' *Gender and History* 21(2): 305–23.
Martinez, Julia, and Claire Lowrie. 2012. 'Transcolonial Influences on Everyday American Imperialism: The Politics of Chinese Domestic Servants in the Philippines.' *Pacific Historical Review* 81(4): 511–36.
McGrath, Ann. 1978. 'Aboriginal Women Workers in the NT, 1911–1939.' *Hecate* 4(2): 5–25.
McGrath, Ann. 1987. *'Born in the Cattle': Aborigines in Cattle Country*. Sydney: Allen & Unwin.
McGregor, Russell. 2002. ' "Breed Out the Colour", or the Importance of Being White.' *Australian Historical Studies* 33(120): 286–302.
Nannup, Alice, Lauren Marsh and Stephen Kinnane. 1992. *When the Pelican Laughed*. South Fremantle: Fremantle Arts Centre Press.
Parry, Naomi. 2007. ' "Such a Longing": Black and White Children in Welfare in New South Wales and Tasmania, 1880–1940.' PhD thesis, University of New South Wales, Australia.
Platt, Anthony. 1977. *The Child Savers: The Invention of Delinquency*. Chicago: University of Chicago.
Read, Peter. 1981. *The Stolen Generations: The Removal of Aboriginal Children in New South Wales 1883 to 1969*. Sydney: Department of Aboriginal Affairs.
Reynolds, Henry. 1990. *With the White People*. Ringwood, Victoria: Penguin.
Robinson, Shirleene. 2001. 'The Unregulated Employment of Aboriginal Child Labour in Queensland, 1842–1902.' *Labour History* 82(May): 1–16.
Robinson, Shirleene. 2002. 'Queensland Settlers and the Creation of the First "Stolen Generations": The Unofficial Removal of Aboriginal Children in Queensland, 1842–1897.' *Journal of Australian Colonial History* 4(1): 1–16.
Robinson, Shirleene. 2003. ' "We Do Not Want One Who Is Too Old": Aboriginal Child Domestic Service in Late 19th and Early 20th Century Queensland.' *Aboriginal History* 27: 162–82.
Robinson, Shirleene. 2008. *Something like Slavery? Queensland's Aboriginal Child Workers, 1842–1945*. Melbourne: Australian Scholarly Publishing.
Robinson, Shirleene, and Jessica Paten. 2008. 'The Question of Genocide and Indigenous Child Removal: The Colonial Australian Context.' *Journal of Genocide Research* 10(4): 501–18.
Sabbioni, Jennifer. 1993. ' "I Hate Working for White People."' *Hecate* 19(2): 7–29.
Senate Standing Committee on Legal and Constitutional Affairs (SSCLCA). 2006. *Unfinished Business: Indigenous Stolen Wages*. Canberra: Department of Senate.
Shorten, Ann R. 1996. 'The Legal Context of Australian Education: An Historical Exploration.' *Australia and New Zealand Journal of Law and Education* 2: 2–32.
Stoler, Ann Laura. 2001. 'Tense and Tender Ties: The Politics of Comparison in North American History and (Post) Colonial Studies.' *Journal of American History* 88(3): 829–65.
Stoler, Ann Laura. 2002. *Carnal Knowledge and Imperial Power: Race and the Intimate in Colonial Rule*. Berkeley: University of California Press.

Swain, Shurlee. 2006. 'Centre and Periphery in British Child Rescue Discourse.' In *Rethinking Colonial Histories*, edited by Penny Edmonds and Samuel Furphy, 157–66. Melbourne: The History Department, University of Melbourne.
Tucker, Margaret. 1977. *If Everyone Cared*. Sydney: Ure Smith.
Walden, Inara. 1995. '"That Was Slavery Days": Aboriginal Domestic Servants in New South Wales in the Twentieth Century.' In *Aboriginal Workers*, edited by Ann McGrath and Kay Saunders, 196–209. Sydney: Australian Society for the Study of Labour History.
Ward, Glenyse. 1988. *Wandering Girl*. Broome: Magabala Books.

6 Maids' Talk
Linguistic Containment and Mobility of Sri Lankan Housemaids in Lebanon

Fida Bizri

A specific language, which I call 'Pidgin Madam,' has developed since the late seventies between Sri Lankan live-in housemaids in Lebanon, and their Arab employers. A sociolinguistic examination of this distinctive contact language allows us to consider the maids' intimate vocal space as it appears in the linguistic negotiations at work between them and their employers. The language is revealed, paradoxically, as being both a strategy of containment of the Sri Lankan domestic worker, and a means of her enhanced mobility. The study of Pidgin Madam can potentially enrich our understanding of the creation and nature of languages of dominance and subordination in domestic service.

The housemaid phenomenon in the Middle East (with domestic workers travelling from Africa, South Asia, and Southeast Asia) has been, for the last two decades, the object of growing academic interest. The situation of live-in housemaids in Lebanon (mainly from Sri Lanka, the Philippines, and Ethiopia) has so far been explained in terms either of race and racism (Moukarbel 2009), or of slavery (Jureidini and Moukarbel 2004; Beydoun 2006). The reference to colonization as a framework for understanding the position of housemaids in the Middle East has been sketched by Michele Ruth Gamburd (2000: 30) who saw, in the hidden transcript between Sri Lankan maids and their Middle Eastern female employers, patterns mirroring the colonial relationship between natives and colonizers. Here, I explore the strategies of transformation and adjustment at work in this linguistic encounter between employers and domestic workers in terms of interaction and negotiation. The dynamics of this contact situation can be seen as being shaped within a colonial context, inasmuch as colonial references are mobilized by the actors themselves to interpret the situation they are involved in, and to create difference and hierarchy according to the relative position of their respective countries in regard to Western imperialist powers. In fact, the countries concerned in this phenomenon, falling within what has been termed the 'Third World,' have had different experiences of subordination during the colonial period. While Sri Lanka (Meyer 2003) and the Philippines (Schirmer and Rosskamm Shalom 1999) were part of Western colonial empires for several centuries, Lebanon was the locus of another type of imperial control introduced in the aftermath of World War I by the League of Nations, the mandate (Thompson 2000). Ethiopia, on the other hand, presents a troubling conundrum, in the sense that it was already, by the time of the colonial partition, one of the oldest and largest sub-Saharan states that defeated a European army (Clapham 2001). It had, therefore, a more intricate position on the political chessboard of the colonial period, and was different from other neighboring countries for being 'a Christian island in a Moslem sea' (Clapham 2001: 3). In this encounter, linguistic attitudes towards foreign workers seems to depend on the evaluation that is made of each foreign community. The value of 'self' and 'the other' appears to be determined, among other factors, by a folkloric discourse on historical facts as will be shown below through the interviews conducted with Madams, maids, and placement agents.

CONTEXTUALIZING THE EMERGENCE OF PIDGIN MADAM

The Middle East is unquestionably one of today's most remarkable hubs of labor migration. Whether skilled or unskilled, migration to oil-rich countries has been massive and in continuous flux since the 1970s. The demand for live-in housemaids in the Arabic-speaking world has attracted, in the last four decades, a substantial number of women from Asia and Africa. The women usually come on a two-year or three-year contract. However, considering the unsuccessful balance of a first contract (barely enough to pay the debts covering the expenses of their departure from their home country), they often choose to take up a second contract with the same family or with a new one. Alternatively, they seek work in another Middle Eastern country altogether.

Lebanon is a curious case on the map of domestic migration to the Middle East. Firstly, unlike its Gulf neighbors that also employ migrant domestic workers in large numbers, it is not an oil-rich country. Secondly, when Asian female migration to Lebanon started in the late seventies and early eighties, Beirut was a divided city plunged in a chaotic war, and ruled by militias, with two militarily powerful neighbors, Israel and Syria, who saw it as a vital strategic place (see Traboulsi 2007 for a modern history of Lebanon). The first Asian domestic workers to appear on the scene were from Sri Lanka, and were employed as housemaids while the city was trying to survive its own violence. Several of the Lebanese employers interviewed for this study (especially in Beirut) recall the eighties and nineties in Lebanon, and mention the dissonance between the Sri Lankan presence and the context of war.[1]

With the end of the Lebanese War in 1992, the maid-business expanded to other nationalities (mainly Filipinas and Ethiopians), but Sri Lankans remained for over a decade the main female migrant domestic community (see Jureidini 2009). The Arabic term *serlankiyye*, 'Sri Lankan,' quickly became synonymous for 'maid' in local Arabic slang. Today, when asked about the identity of their maid, many families speak of having 'a Sri Lankan from Ethiopia,' or 'a Sri Lankan from the Philippines,' or even 'a Sri Lankan Sri Lankan.'

The typical Sri Lankan maid who has been coming to Lebanon since the early eighties is Sinhala,[2] and generally Buddhist, but in some cases Christian. She is usually married, having at least one underage child left at home, with her husband unemployed, or cheaply employed in daily labors. The (officially declared) age of Sri Lankan maids ranges between 19 and 45. On their first appointment, Sri Lankan maids usually have no knowledge whatsoever neither of Arabic nor of English, although they are literate in their own language (Bizri 2010).

Foreign maids in Arab households of the Middle East are generally addressed either in Arabic or in English. Arabic is characterized by a multiplicity of dialects spoken in different parts of the Arab world. Colloquial dialects, used for everyday purposes, can substantially differ from each other, as well as from the more standard variety of formal Arabic known as Modern Standard Arabic (MSA) which is restricted to formal communication or cultural exchanges. This situation has been referred to, in linguistics, by the term 'Arabic diglossia' (Ferguson 1959; Ferguson 1991).

In Lebanon, Ethiopians and Sri Lankans are addressed in Arabic, while Filipinas tend to be usually addressed in English. The study of the Arabic spoken by (and to) maids in Lebanon (which I undertook in 1998) showed that the form of Arabic they use presents major differences in respect to what is conventionally accepted as the Lebanese Arabic norm (henceforth referred to as LAR). Furthermore, I found that the Sri Lankan variety of Arabic differs significantly from the Ethiopian, with the Arabic spoken by Ethiopian workers being much closer to LAR. In fact, in spite of its entirely Arabic vocabulary, and although it is considered to be 'some kind of Arabic' by most of its speakers, Sri Lankan Arabic is drastically different from Arabic. Arab employers label it 'maids' Arabic' or 'Sri Lankan Arabic.' Full competence in this linguistic form requires some training, or a minimum exposure. The Madams[3] and their children are the most fluent speakers of this hybrid language amongst Arabs. Diaspora Lebanese residing in countries where this female domestic phenomenon is absent have trouble communicating with Sri Lankans without training.

To capture the specificity of the Sri Lankan case in Lebanon, I focused my study on fourteen Sinhala women, following them over a decade (1999–2010) and recording their Arabic in Lebanon (either alone or in interaction with their Madams), as well as in Sri Lanka. A total of twenty-five hours of spontaneous speech was gathered and transcribed.[4] A purely linguistic approach[5] failed to account for all the Sri Lankan Arabic speech specificities. It seemed that the environment in which Sri Lankan maids acquired their Arabic had a major impact on the Arabic they speak. Therefore, to better grasp the extralinguistic factors at work, a series of metalinguistic interviews were launched with the fourteen selected maids (in Sinhala), and with twenty-seven Madams (in Arabic, French, or English). The interviews discussed the environment in which Sri Lankan maids acquired the language they spoke in domestic service. In addition, interactions between Madams and their newly arrived maids who were learning the language were recorded.

The power-inscribed interactions between maids and Madams appear to be crucial in the formation of this hybrid language. In fact, upon arrival, the maid is quickly made to understand that her main interlocutor will be Madam, with the husband of the house ('Mister') limiting himself to either very formal communications with her (representing, thus, a higher authority in the case of contention) or, in the worst case scenario, to backstage abuse. It is Madam who introduces the maid to the language, as well as to her daily chores.

To bring this language out of its invisible condition, and to distinguish it from Arabic, I have named it Pidgin Madam, henceforth referred to as PM (Bizri 2005, 2009, 2010, 2013). 'Madam,' because the main actors/creators of this language are the Arab Madam and the Sri Lankan maid and because it is the most frequent appellation by which maids refer to their main interlocutor. 'Pidgin,' because this language is a form of an Arabic pidgin, closely related to other pidginized forms of Arabic which are spoken today in the Gulf area including Gulf Pidgin Arabic (Smart 1990; Næss 2008; Bakir 2010), Urdu Pidgin Arabic (Al-Moaily 2008), and Saudi Asian Pidgin (Al-Azraqi 2010). All these varieties developed as a result of foreign migration to the Middle East from the seventies onward, mainly from the Indian subcontinent and Southeast Asia.

In the context of domestic service, PM and the above mentioned Arabic-pidgins can also be compared to similar contact languages born from the colonial context, such as Butler English (Hosali 2000), a pidginized sub-variety of Indian English spoken between Indian servants and their English-speaking masters. In fact, historically, most of the known pidgins arose as a direct consequence of the European colonial expansion between 1500 and 1900. The plantation system in particular, whereby a European minority came to rule a large mass of mostly non-European subordinated workers (imported slaves and indentured laborers), fostered the development of pidgins. The workers, drawn from different linguistic groups, and locked in an asymmetrical power relation with the dominating Europeans, had to informally and urgently learn the European language for communication needs. Although the stock of vocabulary used in these pidgins is usually drawn from the language of the dominant group, the resulting language is characterized by extensive phonological and semantic shifts, and massive structural changes (Baker and Mühlhäusler 1990; Bakker 1995). The comparative simplicity of pidgins in regard to both the target language which the laborers try to learn, and their substrate language, has been interpreted in terms either of 'impoverishment' and 'simplification' (Mühlhäusler 1974), or of 'formal simplicity' (Siegel 1987). Such interpretations underline the quantitative rather than the qualitative aspect of simplicity, that is to say that pidgins have fewer components, and more generalized rules, but are not necessarily easier to process psychologically.

Like its related pidginized varieties of Arabic spoken in the Gulf, PM is also the result of a dominant group subduing a dominated group that had to learn Arabic while having only a very limited and biased access to its norm. In this context, the linguistic contact takes place on the territory of the dominant group. To that extent, PM can also be compared to other industrial labor pidgins such as *Gastarbeiterdeutsch* or guest-worker German (Klein and Dittmar 1979), foreign-workers' varieties of French (Noyau 1976), or 'Foreign-Workers' Dutch' (Altena and Appel 1982).

Whinnom (1971) distinguishes language contact situations that produce pidgins from others that do not. Focusing on types of contact situations rather than on purely internal (linguistic) factors, he compares the contact of linguistic communities to the biological interbreeding of species, distinguishing between three types (1971: 40): 'primary,' 'secondary,' and 'tertiary hybridization.' 'Primary hybridization' refers to dialectal fragmentation, where both parties in contact are social equals. 'Secondary hybridization' and 'tertiary hybridization' are distinguished by power imbalance between parties. 'Secondary hybridization' applies to bilingual situations where a native speaker of a certain language lives as a minority within a dominant community and acquires a mixed form of the dominant language, where the vocabulary of one language is integrated within the grammar of another one. 'Tertiary hybridization,' the only contact situation that produces true pidgins according to Whinnom, involves necessarily, as in the biological analogy, at least three source elements (languages): one superstrate language and at least two or more substrate languages (1971: 106). This scenario typically occurs in trade contacts and in colonial situations, where one language (usually that of the dominant majority) serves as the lingua franca for the communication of several groups in contacts. Whinnom's argument to support this statement is that, if only one substrate is involved, members of the minor group would always be exposed to the norm of the dominant group's language and have, therefore, the possibility of improving their linguistic skills and getting closer to the norm of the target language. In contrast, in situations of 'tertiary hybridization' the incipient and simplified variety of the target language produced by different minor linguistic groups develops its own phonological, morphological, syntactic, and semantic structures which, over the course of time, may become impenetrable to native speakers of the superstrate.

While other varieties of Arabic pidgins spoken in the Gulf area emerge in multilingual contexts, PM itself appears, as one of a series of counterexamples (like Trio-Ndyuka Pidgin) to Whinnom's claim. Here, we can witness the withdrawal of the norm with only one substrate, that is one minor group, the Sri Lankans. In the discussion below I explore how the unequal relation between the employers and domestic workers impacts upon the course of language formation. Such environmental factors are interlinked with the purely internal linguistic ones, determining language change. In that sense, PM can rightly be compared to the other traditionally studied pidgins born within the colonial setting characterized by domination and subordination.

THE CONTEXT-SENSITIVE GRAMMAR OF PIDGINS: THE CASE OF PIDGIN MADAM

Pidgin languages owe their relatively recent scientific prestige to the fact that they are extremely valuable for understanding both the internal organization of linguistic systems, and the impact of social events on the genesis of languages. While showing important traces of substratal influence,[6] PM is not simply the vocabulary of one language (Arabic), with the grammar of another (Sinhala). As is the case with other pidgins, several factors interact to produce the resulting language: to the substratal influence is added the attitude of superstrate speakers (or what is usually known as 'foreigner talk,' that can differ from one language to another, and from one situation to another), the language acquisition environment, the access to the norm and obstacles to it, and linguistic simplification processes. Examining the environment in which maids acquire their Arabic skills allows us to account for several characteristics of PM that, otherwise, would remain incomprehensible.

In fact, PM offers an excellent illustration of the way the social context of feminine servitude and power negotiations are inscribed in the morphology of the language itself. Here, it appears that, in the initial stages of language acquisition, the maids are exposed to Arabic in two contexts: when they are being addressed by Arab interlocutors (mainly the Madams), and when overhearing intra-Arab discussions, excluding them. The domestic workers acquire their Arabic language skills mainly in the first context, when Madams talk to them. The Arabic that the workers feel compelled to react to is, therefore, dominated by those forms most often present in a verbal exchange between a Madam and her maid, namely orders, prohibitions, and questions. Since Arabic has an obligatory gender and number agreement on all verbal, adjectival, and pronominal forms, and since mainly women are involved in this communication (Madams giving orders, maids receiving orders), these directives appear logically all with a feminine singular agreement.

Consequently, verbs that denote actions occurring in present, past, or future times in PM are extensively drawn from the stock of LAR feminine singular imperative verbal forms. This means that the Arabic imperative form gets emancipated from its imperative meaning and gender connotation, to serve as an all-purpose verb. Other Arabic terms accompany this verbal form to contextualize the action (such as *abel* 'before' for past tense, *badēn* 'after' for future tense, and *yemkin* 'maybe' for probability). Similarly, most adjectives in PM derive etymologically from LAR feminine singular forms (fs.).

The examples given below to illustrate the grammar of PM are presented each at three levels: the first line is the transcription of the statement (here, Arabic is pronounced with the Sinhala phonological filter; words sound therefore different from what they should be in LAR[7]); the second line is a literal translation of what each word means (here, since some words/grammatical forms have different meanings in LAR and in PM, the literal translation gives the value of each word in PM, not its original value in Arabic); then a double translation is given, the first (marked PM) relates to what the statement really means in PM, while the second (marked LAR) refers to how Arabic-speakers with no knowledge of PM whatsoever would perceive it.[8]

(1) *ana sawsik tayi mama bēt, aytilayki, lē ma-pi masāre lebənan, ḍrobiya sīre ebnik*
me hu`sband come mother house shout why no-there is money Lebanon hit small son

PM   'My husband went to my mother's house [in Sri Lanka] and shouted, [asking] why there is no money from Lebanon, and he hit [my] little son.'

LAR   'I am your husband, you do go (fs.), my mother is a house, that I shout on you (fs.), why there is no money Lebanon. Do hit her little your son.'

In the example above, the word order differs from that expected in LAR. Furthermore, the verbal form *tayi* 'come,' deriving from the feminine singular imperative LAR form *taʕe* is used to denote a past action done by *sawsik* 'husband,' a masculine subject from a LAR point of view. Similarly, feminine adjectives such as *sīre* (< *zɣīre* 'small'), surprisingly qualify LAR masculine nouns such as *ebnik* 'son,' or even plural ones. From the perspective of PM, however, there is no gender agreement. What appears to LAR speakers as a feminine agreement is simply part of the morphology of the word that was selected amongst the most frequent forms advanced by LAR speakers themselves.

In fact, exposed to a very limited and biased spectrum of LAR, maids resort to some kind of ancillary 'mimetic bricolage' (Bizri 2010): They adopt the linguistic material available 'as a whole,' treating it as one element, irrespectively of the composite nature it may present in Arabic. This also accounts for the form of nouns in PM, which often derive from a complex LAR form: 'noun + 2nd fs. personal pronoun denoting possession.' For instance, under (1), *sawsik*, treated as one unit in PM meaning 'husband,' comes from LAR *ğawz-ik* or *zawğ-ik*, formed of two units: *ğawz-* or *zawğ-* 'husband,' and *-ik* 2nd fs. suffixed pronoun, the whole meaning 'your husband' (talking to a woman). The Arabic feminine possessive suffix *-ik* has lost its possessive meaning and become part of the nominal form.

Such features are also common to many pidgins that developed in colonial contexts. Here, not only does the majority group fail to correct the pidginized form, but they also adopt it themselves, and generate several similar forms while introducing new words. Indeed, it seems that, in her linguistic interaction with her employer, the maid forces the latter to leave behind her structurally dominant role, and to switch to the logic of the exchange, where both participants in the exchange are equal. The mimetism is, therefore, not one-directional, for the linguistic negotiation goes both ways. The maid mimics her Madam's speech when communicating with her, but then in return the Madam, concerned to ensure communication, feels compelled to adapt and imitate the maid's speech, in order to be understood by her. Etymologically imperative verbal forms are definitely not the only verbal forms attested in the speech of Sri Lankan maids, but they are frequent enough to have become emblematic. Some verbal forms in PM bear witness to the active way Arab speakers embrace these pidginized forms and generate them. For instance: PM verbs *mūti* 'to die' or *kāpi* 'to be afraid' (respectively from LAR feminine imperative *mute* 'do die' and *xāfe* 'do be afraid') are a priori not part of the expected input for domestic chores. Instead, such verbs may be considered as converging accommodation strategies (in the sense described by Giles, Coupland and Coupland 1991) advanced by Arab employers, and through which maids perceive a validation of their grammatical system.

Madams also accommodate with substratal influence (the pattern of which they guess and reproduce, without really attributing it to Sinhala). This shows for instance in the use of Arabic prepositions as postpositions in PM, violating thus the canonic word order of Arabic. Under (2), *pō* comes from LAR *fōʔ* meaning 'above,' which normally occurs as a preposition in LAR. Here, however, it comes after *ana* 'me,' to convey the sense of 'above me.' The verb *nēmi* is, again, originally an Arabic feminine imperative verbal form, used here to denote past tense, and a non-feminine subject.

(2) *mister ana pōnēmi*
    Mister me above sleep

PM   'Mister slept on top of me.'
LAR 'Mister, I am above, do sleep [feminine].'

Of course maids are always exposed to a much richer linguistic atmosphere than simply the orders they receive, whether by observing conversations between their employers and other members of the household or outside visitors, or by their exposure to television, whenever permitted. As their relationship with their Madam grows, so does the complexity of conversational subjects tackled. The corpus of recordings collected for this study presents discussions between Madam and maid around different matters such as religion, the maid's personal history, talk about life and death, and so on. However, even after many years in Lebanon, the language used by live-in Sri Lankan housemaids (at least in the fourteen cases under study) does not develop into a more traditional form of Arabic, but remains similar to what has been sketched so far. It seems that the physical and social confinement of the maid within her employer's house nourishes her linguistic containment, and vice versa. It is important to note, in that sense, that 'freelance'[9] Sri Lankan housemaids in Lebanon, being exposed to a wider spectrum of the norm, speak a different variety of pidginized Arabic slightly less far from the norm of LAR (Bizri 2004; Bizri 2010).

When asked to assess (in Sinhala) the different varieties of Arabic that surround them, the fourteen selected maids argued that, in their understanding, all linguistic traits of the Arabic language that are not related to PM were to be labeled 'formal Arabic,' that is, 'another language.' They often give Sinhala diglossia as an example, pointing out that Sinhala has virtually two totally different languages. Learning colloquial Sinhala does not enable one to understand formal Sinhala without preparation. By perceiving the Arabic diglossia, and by recognizing Lebanese Arabic as a different norm, Sinhala maids accept their own exclusion from it. However, by doing so, they subsume under 'formal Arabic' a whole raft of linguistic features which do not belong to that label, being associated rather with standard LAR.

LINGUISTIC RAMPART OR LINGUISTIC PASSPORT?

In accounting for the development of Pidgin Madam, it seems to have been first and foremost a linguistic rampart erected by employer families (particularly the Madams) that would contain the Sri Lankan maid and ensure a security zone within the realm of intimacy.

Michele Gamburd has used the expression 'intimate outsider' to characterize the marginalized position of Sri Lankan domestic workers in Middle Eastern homes (see Gamburd 2000; also Jureidini 2006: 137–40). The Sri Lankan maid in the Lebanese household can also be seen as an intimate 'intruder,' whose role in the private life of the family requires that family to draw upon and build structures that enable them to manage and contain her.

Migrant female domesticity, such as it has been performed by its main actors in the last four decades, creates a situation where total strangers (employers and employees) have to share the same intimate space, and to organize it creating defensive barriers. It is important to keep in mind that having a housemaid, especially from South Asia, is not restricted to bourgeois families. Even low-income families may, in some cases, find it cost-effective to have a maid taking care of the children while the housewife works outside. Very few families (none in the cases interviewed within this study) have a specified space (separate room) in their house for their maid. The maid is everywhere and nowhere, often relegated to a peripheral space—a mattress in the salon where she can rest when everyone has gone to sleep, a corner in the kitchen where she can store her letters and personal belongings, the balcony where she can communicate with other maids.

Upon arrival, the migrant worker is a total stranger, but she is required to get involved, almost immediately, with the most intimate aspects of her employers' life: their children, their food, their laundry, and their hygiene. She is also a silent but potentially embarrassing witness of their moods, secrets, and habits. Although her very presence stems from the wish of the employers, she is felt by them like an intruder, and the need to take measures to remedy the discomfort caused by her presence is strong. As one Madam says: 'Having a Sri Lankan at home, is like being naked in front of her. You have to protect yourself from her, sometimes you have to hide.'[10]

Increasing distance in order to protect intimacy is a two-way process, but it is by and large controlled by the dominant group (in number and in power): the employers. And it is apparently achieved through a set of frequent attitudes aiming at containing the maid. One of them is reducing her to a generic category, such as by the use of the term 'Sri Lankan,' emancipated from its original meaning and ritualized into an index of profession.

Another very common way of introducing the maid to her new identity is baptizing her with another name. This could be either a shortening of her real name, or a rough translation of it. The maid mimics with gestures the meaning of her name, and the employers figure out an Arabic or English equivalent, or they select a totally new name irrespectively of any objective criterion related to the maid's personal history. The maid, for her part, usually accepts her new name willingly. Many interviews with senior maids proved that they sometimes even find salutary this change of names, as it allows them to distance themselves from the troubling aspects of the inescapable promiscuity with the employer's life, as well as from the whole raft of symbolic or actual abuses that may go with it. As one Sri Lankan senior migrant worker put it: 'All this [having been abused] happened to Lina, not to me,' Lina being her Arabic name in one of her stays in the Middle East.[11]

Most importantly, the intruder is contained through language itself. During fieldwork research, many families expressed the need to protect their most intimate affairs by a linguistic artifact the maid cannot get round. Some families speak another language (such as French, or English) whenever they need to communicate cryptically:

> I don't understand when she phones her family and speaks to them in her language. I don't understand when she sends them letters with their own writing and, honestly, sometimes I wonder what she may be telling them about me, about us. Similarly when I talk in French, it's none of

her concern.... In some neighborhoods there are Madams who address their maid in French, but in that case they NEVER talk to her in Arabic. Arabic for these families is like French for me, a language to say secret things.[12]

However, this possibility is not open to all families, nor is it easy to control one's own expression. Here, PM proves practical. Moreover, it is, as a Lebanese child puts it, unknowingly alluding to the mimetism manifest in it, 'easy, because it's like talking back in a mirror.'[13]

Indeed, the guardians of Arabic (Madams) find PM to be efficient and, above all, secure, to a large extent closing the doors of acquisition leading to the norm of Arabic. The maid will never be addressed with 'normal' Arabic; she will always be spoken to in this secure, specialized Arabic. The asymmetry between speakers ends up being inscribed in the language fabric, and the self-facilitating strategies enacted by Arabs themselves become constitutive of the interaction. This linguistic containment is further publicized and encouraged through TV shows and cartoons where the Sri Lankan maid (often serving as supporting cast or scenic backdrop) is always represented as communicating in this language.

From the perspective of the Sri Lankan maids themselves, however, the situation is quite different. Rather than a rampart, this language is a lifebuoy and a passport to further stays in other Arabic countries. Comparisons between the linguistic data collected in Lebanon and data collected in the Gulf area mentioned above reveal that the similarities between all these pidginized forms of Arabic transcend the structural differences between the varieties of Arabic dialects. PM is therefore understood not only in Lebanon, but all over the Arab world where migrant live-in housemaiding has become a tradition. And it may well be this mobility factor that explains why a common PM developed rather than each employer family developing an individual 'secret' language.

Consequently, maids have a vested interest in acquiring a language that proves vital to ensure their employability, both in the short and the long term. Furthermore, it is a status-raising tool and an emblem of success back home. For instance, for Sri Lankan Muslim female domestic migrants in Saudi Arabia and the Gulf area, Arabic language and the Islamic culture it conveys seem to be a valuable asset they use to successfully renegotiate their status in their Muslim villages back home (Thangarajah 2003). For Sri Lankan Sinhala housemaids in the Middle East, it is less the knowledge of Arabic itself that is put forward as an achievement in the process of selfvalorization, than the knowledge of a language which happens to be spoken in many different countries. The international nature of the language gives the maid an international identity. In this particular context, and as a form of Arabic, PM is potential gold.

Indeed, during their often decades-long constant but always temporary wanderings throughout the Middle East, these women who have come to lose everything they held to before they first left their family, consider this language to be their only trophy. They see in it hope for improving their family condition. Although most of their meager earnings are spent back home on daily expenses with no real margin for savings, an appointment abroad ensures a continuous flow of money, as little as it may be. When Sri Lankan women who have been working for over twenty years as housemaids in different countries of the Middle East are asked to assess what they have lost and gained during these years, their answer is unanimous. They lost three things: their family, their youth, and their sense of belonging. On the other hand, they all agree on having unquestionably gained one thing: a language, Arabic, however pidginized it may be. Priyanka explains: 'My husband drank [the money of] nine years of my life in Kuwait and Lebanon. But I don't care now that he's left, because I know Arabic. I know this will always push me forward.'[14]

A TAXONOMY OF HOUSEMAIDS CHARGED WITH COLONIAL CLICHÉS

The Sri Lankan maid in Lebanon remains on the threshold of both the Arabic language and her employers' private life alike. In this context, it is interesting to see that PM is not spoken by Ethiopian housemaids, although they too are mostly addressed in Arabic. This nourishes beliefs such as: 'Ethiopians are more intelligent than Sri Lankans,' and 'Ethiopians speak better Arabic than we [Lebanese] do.'[15] One possible reason for this may be that Amharic, Ethiopian maids' (in most cases, native) language, has some structural similarities with Arabic, allowing them to pick it up more easily. However, from recordings of interactions between Madams and Ethiopian maids, it appeared that Madams do not speak to Ethiopians the same way as they do to Sri Lankans. Ethiopians are granted a wider access to the consensual norm of Arabic. It seems, therefore, that the set of clichés circulating around each group of maids has considerable consequences on the ground, insofar as they shape different attitudes and evaluations in each case.

Recordings and participant observation of interactions between a placement agent in South Lebanon and his clients seeking to employ a maid[16] show how housemaids are part of a societal marketplace in which power comes with ownership of various forms of capital in Bourdieu's (1991) sense. In this value system, Sri Lankans rate lowest for a set of reasons repeatedly mentioned by both the agent and the employer-clients explaining and justifying to me the different criteria of selection. Some arguments are directly linked to colonial history, while others may be corollary of this history (such as the higher ranking of Christianity over other religions).

The low rank of Sri Lankans is often attributed to the fact that 'they have no religion' (understood as monotheistic religion); that 'they are married and have left their kids behind' (rarely mentioned with regard to Ethiopians or Filipinas); that 'their country has had over 400 years of colonization which results in them lying and stealing, instead of asking'; 'With so many years under the British, they barely understand "come and go" in English'; 'they smile obediently when you shout at them.' Notions of cleanness and color are also mobilized: 'They are unclean,' 'their skin has a weird smell difficult to adjust to.'

Ethiopians, on the other hand, are admired for being 'descendants of the Queen of Saba, hence their beauty,' and for being 'Christians.' Ethiopians' Christianity is often mentioned as a 'quality' in Lebanon, even in Muslim households. One veiled Muslim Madam, lamenting the fact that the agent only 'gave' her a Sri Lankan although she had asked for an Ethiopian, says: 'Why hide from the truth? Christians are better than us, they are more civilized.' Maids from all nationalities themselves play on that chord, pretending they are Christians, or tailoring different stories according to their audience's confession.[17] Another reason for admiring Ethiopians is that Ethiopia 'is the only African country that no colonizer could subdue.' Ethiopian maids themselves appear to be proud of this image of their country, often arguing it is because they are not really African, since they are 'not really black.' Filipinas are, also, praised for being 'Christians.' They have been colonized and subdued but 'they nicely picked up good English from Americans,' and 'English [language] is good money'; on the other hand, 'they are so clean that they can be costly to have at home,' warns the placement agent.

During the three-day participant-observation, Madams recounted past experiences with maids of different nationalities where Sri Lankans appear to be 'loyal but not that bright,' 'affectionate but have no self-esteem.' However, it is only when opposed to Sri Lankans that 'Ethiopians are beautiful, civilized,' that they are 'much like us,' 'intelligent people with bad luck,' and that 'one dares not speak to an Ethiopian like to a Sri Lankan, because are fully competent in Arabic.' But then again, in case of discord, the tables can be easily turned, and Sri Lankans may appear under a better light precisely because of these same clichés: 'Ethiopians understand only what they want to understand,' 'they are arrogant, better have a Sri Lankan,' 'Sri Lankans are docile and good-hearted, if you have kids, avoid Ethiopians who tend to be more individualistic.'

In fact, in this taxonomy of migrant housemaids, presented as a racialized hierarchy with a specified market-value attached to it, several shades of inferiorities are observable: Sri Lankans rank as the cheapest category, Filipinas as the highest or most expensive, and Ethiopians somewhere in between.[18] The employer chooses the nationality of the maid according to the 'price' but also according to the set of clichés usually circulating around each nationality. The price itself is set in part according to objective criteria (such as the length of the route leading from the home country to the host destination, as explained by the placement agent), but also according to the local demand, which is directly shaped by these clichés.

CONCLUSION

The live-in housemaid phenomenon in the Middle East, at the intersection of the very intimate and the public, has fostered discourses on many levels: the state, the agents, the host family, the home family, the activist, and the academic. The maid appears to each under a different light. She may be variously a subject of scientific investigation, a walking economic deal, a sacrificial mother, a lazy liar, a loose woman, a victim, or even a modern slave. A maid-template is always there, ready to be embodied every time a woman from Sri Lanka, Ethiopia, or the Philippines goes to the Middle East for housemaiding. The person herself, during her often long odyssey (sometimes up to 25 years or more), constantly negotiates facets of her identity across this profile.

Pidgin Madam provides us with an insight into the complexity of domestic service relationships. As a dividing line in the vocal space between Madam and maid, it may be filed as a straightforward case of 'security fence construction,' a means of dealing with the intricate issue of the 'Us' and 'Them.' The linguistic limen behind which Sri Lankan housemaids in Lebanon are relegated, reveals micro-processes of symbolic domination and resistance alike. In fact, in her liminality, the maid negotiates the dominating linguistic structure surrounding her through a creative bricolage that forges a new pattern in its own right. It is through the negotiation we see here that the official narrative and agenda are constantly challenged and reworked.

Close analysis of Lebanese linguistic attitudes towards migrant housemaids reveals that the choice of the linguistic code to adopt with maids is permeated with beliefs about the value and intellectual/emotional capacities of each community. Linguistic elements interact with popular understandings of history (related to the Western imperial domination background against which this migration phenomenon is taking place), setting the pattern of a social trend. The ways in which colonial references, with all the images they convey, are instrumentalized would certainly differ across the Middle East. Equally, the way historical elements, religion, gender, and language interact to create a taxonomy of maids and produce various linguistic attitudes towards migrant workers is not uniform across countries where related Arabic-based pidgins are spoken.

Such linguistic behaviors are rarely themselves an object of contemplation and speculation. Produced spontaneously, they must be taken to be unaware of themselves, unconscious of their own condition, ephemeral. The reality of the interactions reveals microscopic movements laboring their way within the ready-made template in which maids appear as passive victims, and challenges the trend of creating false binaries between employers and maids, masters and slaves. Here, the maid appears as both powerless and empowered. Although dependent on a financial and moral grading system regarding the rules of which she has no saying, she appears to be a dynamic actor and negotiator. She is, as much as Madam, a co-producer of a newly born language that ultimately proves to be a valuable asset she possesses. She is also a co-producer of the identity of the international maid and of the Madam alike, for, as a Lebanese child points out: 'A Madam without a maid is no Madam at all.'[19] Seen from this perspective, the maid appears to navigate in a positive and socially productive space, challenging common views of her being caught in a deadlock within an unjust system. The strength of character that enables maids to face, at worse, abuse and death, and, at best, the retrospect that 'all these losses were for not much after all' stems from their awareness of their value. When asked why she does not go back to Sri Lanka to mother her own children that she abandoned as infants eight years earlier, Karuna answers worriedly and genuinely: 'But Madam can't do a thing without me.'[20]

NOTES

1. A 32 year-old female employer (Sahar, recorded by the author in Arabic, Beirut, December 2, 2002) recounts: 'I remember I was twelve that day when, after a whole night of intensive bombing, we were allowed to get out of the underground shelter around 7 in the morning. . . . I ran to the balcony to have a look at the street and saw, in the opposite building, a Sri Lankan maid crying in shock while her Madam was cleaning the night's mess caused by the impact of bullets and shell fragments. For the first time, I asked myself what on hell is this black woman doing in my country. . . . Is it that bad in Sri Lanka [for them to come here]?'
2. While in other Middle Eastern countries Sri Lankan housemaids of different ethnical belongings may be present (Tamil, Sinhala, Moors), in Lebanon, the vast majority of Sri Lankan maids are Sinhala. There is no distinction in local Arabic between the term 'Sri Lankan' and that of 'Sinhala,' the former referring to both designations. Sri Lankan Tamils, however, are referred to simply as 'Tamil from Sri Lanka.'
3. Depending on the age of the female employer and the type of intimacy she has with the maid, she may be called either Madam or *māma* 'mother,' even when the maid is older than her. Likewise, the male employer is either Mister or *bāba* 'father.'
4. Recordings were conducted in Beirut, South Lebanon, and North Lebanon; in Sri Lanka, mainly in Bibile, Ampara, Warakapola, Polonnaruwa, Anuradhapura, Horana, and Wadduwa. The bulk of the transcripts has been published in Bizri 2004, 2010, 2013.
5. From an internal perspective, this language shows both simplification processes common to developing linguistic systems, and substratal influence from Sinhala.
6. Sinhala substratal influences in PM can be seen, for instance, in: the phonological treatment; the transformation of LAR prepositions into postpositions; adjectives and relative clauses preceding the head noun; discursive and narrative strategies.
7. PM is characterized, for instance, by: the absence of many LAR sounds like /f/, /š/, /ğ/, etc.; the reinterpretation of other sounds or sound-sequences according to Sinhala phonological rules; and the loss of initial consonants in some clusters such as *mēne*, *lēte*, *pēha*, and *bīre*, respectively for LAR *tmēne* 'eight,' *tlēte* 'three,' *teffēḥa* 'apple,' and *kbīre* 'big.'

8. This translation has no scientific value, but it is meant to give an appreciation of how the utterances may be perceived by Arabs, and to give a glimpse on how far from Arabic PM is.
9. Freelance maids are maids who have decided to live in rented rooms, and to work, paid by the hour, for (often several) Lebanese households during the day time. For more, see Jureidini and Moukarbel 2004.
10. Suad Madam, recorded by the author in French, Beirut, April 1999, published in Bizri 2010: 40.
11. Nanda, interviewed by the author in Sinhala, in Wadduwa, Sri Lanka, April 5, 2000.
12. Suad Madam, interviewed by the author in French, in Beirut, April 1999, published in Bizri 2010: 40. In fact, French is spoken only to maids from Senegal and Madagascar, a minority amongst housemaids in Lebanon.
13. Reem, recorded by the author in Arabic, Saida, South Lebanon, July 8, 2001.
14. Priyanka, interviewed by the author in Sinhala, Polonnaruwa, Sri Lanka, April 28, 2000.
15. These opinions were expressed, in more or less different wordings, in most of the interviews conducted with Madams within the scope of this study.
16. Unless otherwise stated, all quotes in this section were collected by the author in Arabic during a three-day participant-observation in a placement agency in Saida, South Lebanon, July 2–5, 2000 (including an interview with the head agent, and recordings of interactions between the agent and several clients).
17. For instance, Mala (interviewed by the author in Chekka, North Lebanon, July 28, 2000) tells her Christian Madam in PM how she was abused by a former Muslim employer in Lebanon, then adds in Sinhala that the former employer was actually Christian, but that she prefers not to hurt Madam's feelings by saying the truth.
18. Here, my data concord with Jureidini and Moukarbel (2004), and is in opposition to Beydoun (2006) according to whose appreciation Ethiopians in Lebanon rank lower than Sri Lankans. The situation may be different in other Arab countries where Islamic religion is considered more of an asset than it is in Lebanon. Therefore, maids of Muslim faith may be more valued in the Gulf area. Fernandez (2010) mentions Ethiopian women migrants pretending to be Muslim in order to enhance their chances for a job in Saudi Arabia. Gunawathie (interview conducted in Lebanon in PM by the author, transcribed in Bizri 2010: 199–205) says she chose to pray for Allah when she was in Saudi Arabia just to please her Madam for whom she had affection.
19. Reem playing with her Sri Lankan nanny the game of 'Madam and maid,' recorded by the author in Arabic, Saida, South Lebanon, July 8, 2001.
20. Karuna, interviewed by the author, Saida, South Lebanon, July 8, 2001.

REFERENCES

Al-Azraqi, Munira. 2010. 'Pidginization in the Eastern Region of Saudi Arabia: Media Presentation.' In *Arabic and the Media. Linguistic Analyses and Applications*, edited by Reem Bassiouney, 159–74. Leiden: Brill.
Al-Moaily, Mohammad. 2008. 'A Data-Based Description of Urdu Pidgin Arabic.' Master's thesis, Newcastle University, United Kingdom.
Altena, Nelleke, and René Appel. 1982. 'Mother Tongue Teaching and the Acquisition of Dutch by Turkish and Moroccan Immigrant Workers' Children.' *Journal of Multilingual and Multicultural Development* 3(4): 315–22.

Baker, Philip, and Peter Mühlhäusler. 1990. 'From Business to Pidgin.' *Journal of Asian Pacific Communication* 1: 87–115.
Bakir, Murtadha J. 2010. 'Notes on the Verbal System of Gulf Pidgin Arabic.' *Journal of Pidgin and Creole Languages* 25(2): 201–28.
Bakker, Peter. 1995. 'Pidgins.' In *Pidgins and Creoles: An Introduction*, edited by Jacques Arends, Pieter Muysken and Norval Smith, 25–39. Amsterdam: John Benjamins.
Beydoun, Khaled Ali. 2006. 'The Trafficking of Ethiopian Domestic Workers into Lebanon: Navigating through a Novel Passage of the International Maid Trade.' *Berkeley Journal of International Law* 24: 1009–45.
Bizri, Fida. 2004. 'Le parler arabe des domestiques singhalaises au Liban.' PhD dissertation, l'École Pratique des Hautes Études, Paris, France.
Bizri, Fida. 2005. 'Le Pidgin Madame: Un nouveau pidgin arabe.' *La Linguistique* 41(2): 54–66.
Bizri, Fida. 2009. 'Sinhala in Contact with Arabic: The Birth of a New Pidgin in the Middle East.' In *Annual Review of South Asian Languages and Linguistics 2009*, edited by Rajendra Singh, 135–49. Berlin and New York: Mouton de Gruyter.
Bizri, Fida. 2010. *Pidgin Madame: Une grammaire de la servitude*. Paris: Geuthner.
Bizri, Fida. 2013. *Pidgin Madam*. Online Encyclopedia of Arabic Language and Linguistics. Leiden: Brill. http://referenceworks.brillonline.com/browse/encyclopedia-of-arabic-language-and-linguistics.
Bourdieu, Pierre. 1991. *Language and Symbolic Power*. Cambridge: Harvard University Press.
Clapham, Christopher. 2001. 'War and State Formation in Ethiopia and Eritrea.' Paper presented at the *Failed States* conference, Florence, Italy, April 10.
Ferguson, Charles A. 1959. 'Diglossia.' *Word* 15: 325–40.
Ferguson, Charles A. 1991. 'Diglossia Revisited.' *Southwest Journal of Linguistics* 10(1): 214–34.
Fernandez, Bina. 2010. 'Cheap and Disposable? The Impact of the Global Economic Crisis on the Migration of Ethiopian Women Domestic Workers to the Gulf.' *Gender and Development* 18(2): 249–62.
Gamburd, Michèle Ruth. 2000. *The Kitchen Spoon's Handle: Transnationalism and Sri Lanka's Migrant Housemaids*. Ithaca: Cornell University Press.
Giles, Howard, Justine Coupland and Nikolas Coupland. 1991. 'Accommodation Theory: Communication, Context, and Consequence.' In *Contexts of Accommodation: Developments in Applied Sociolinguistics. Studies in Emotion and Social Interaction*, edited by Howard Giles, Justine Coupland and Nikolas Coupland, 1–68. New York: Cambridge University Press.
Hosali, Priya. 2000. *Butler English: Form and Function*. Delhi: B. R. Publishing Corporation.
Jureidini, Ray. 2006. 'Sexuality and the Servant: An Exploration of Arab Images of the Sexuality of Domestic Maids Living in the Household.' In *Sexuality in the Arab World*, edited by S. Khalaf and J. Gagnon, 130–51. London: Saqi Books.
Jureidini, Ray. 2009. 'In the Shadows of Family Life: Towards a History of Domestic Service in Lebanon.' *Journal of Middle East Women's Studies* 5(3): 74–101.
Jureidini, Ray, and Nayal Moukarbel. 2004. 'Female Sri Lankan Domestic Labour in Lebanon: Contractual, Slavery-Like Practices and Conditions.' *Journal of Ethnic and Migration Studies* 30(4): 581–607.
Klein, Wolfgang, and Norbert Dittmar. 1979. *Developing Grammars: The Acquisition of German Syntax by Foreign Workers*. Berlin: Springer.
Meyer, Eric. 2003. *Sri Lanka, Biography of an Island: Between Local & Global*. Sri Lanka: Viator Publications.

Moukarbel, Nayla. 2009. *Sri Lankan Housemaids in Lebanon.* Amsterdam: University of Amsterdam Press.
Mühlhäusler, Peter. 1974. *Pidginization and Simplification of Language.* Canberra: Pacific Linguistics B-26.
Næss, Unn Gyda. 2008. ' "Gulf Pidgin Arabic": Individual Strategies or a Structured Variety? A Study of Some Features of the Linguistic Behaviour of Asian Migrants in the Gulf Countries.' Master's thesis, University of Oslo, Norway.
Noyau, Colette. 1976. 'Les français "approaches" des travailleurs migrants: Un nouveau champ de recherche.' *Langue française* 29: 45–60.
Schirmer, Daniel B., and Stephen Rosskamm Shalom. 1999. *The Philippines Reader: A History of Colonialism, Neocolonialism, Dictatorship and Resistance.* Boston: South End Press.
Siegel, Jeff. 1987. *Language Contact in a Plantation Environment: A Sociolinguistic History of Fiji.* Cambridge: Cambridge University Press.
Smart, Jack R. 1990. 'Pidginization in Gulf Arabic: A First Report.' *Anthropological Linguistics* 32: 83–118.
Thangarajah, C. Y. 2003. 'Veiled Constructions: Conflict, Migration and Modernity in Eastern Sri Lanka.' *Contributions to Indian Sociology* 37(1&2): 141–62.
Thompson, Elizabeth. 2000. *Colonial Citizens: Republican Rights, Paternal Privilege, and Gender in French Syria and Lebanon.* New York: Columbia University Press.
Traboulsi, Fawwaz. 2007. *A History of Modern Lebanon.* London: Pluto Press.
Whinnom, Keith. 1971. 'Linguistic Hybridization and the Special Case of Pidgins and Creoles.' In *Pidginization and Creolization of Languages*, edited by Dell Hymes, 91–115. Cambridge: Cambridge University Press.

7 Foreign Domestic Workers in Singapore
Historical and Contemporary Reflections on the Colonial Politics of Intimacy

Maria Platt

> I'm absolutely appalled by MOM's [Ministry of Manpower's] ridiculous proposal to give maids mandatory off days. Owners employ maids to serve, i.e. they are servants. As such, they ought to be available 24/7 to meet the demands of their owners. One shudders to think of the mischief and ghastly behaviour in which these servants will indulge on their off days. Employer control of the servant will be severely hampered. The servant problem in Singapore has just worsened frightfully with the extremely ill-advised stroke of MOM's pen.

This lament concerning 'the servant problem' and lack of 'employer control' could have easily occurred during Singapore's colonial era. However, this quote from a disgruntled employer of a foreign domestic worker[1] appeared on the site singaporemaid.blogspot.com[2] on March 9, 2012. The anonymous blogger bemoaned the Singapore government's proposal to make a day off mandatory for all domestic workers beginning 2013.[3] For this employer, and many others who express their views on social media sites, a day off creates 'shudders' due to a deeply ingrained policy which requires the control of one's domestic worker, including in the realms of their sexuality. Using Ann Stoler's (1995, 2010) framework regarding the management of intimacy under colonial rule, I show how Singapore as a postcolonial society has come to recreate many of the intimate anxieties of the colonial era Stoler describes. Stoler asserts that 'colonial projects . . . were riveted on the intimate and so concerned about sex' (Stoler 2010: 14). In contemporary Singapore, policing the sexual liaisons (both real and imagined) of domestic workers is a distinctly political project, one that is specified by the government and enforced by employers.

In this chapter I show how anxieties about sexuality in the state-employer-employee nexus are played out. In doing so, I draw largely upon blogs as a means to capture the perspectives of those who employ domestic workers. While comments on such blogs may not be representative of social attitudes towards domestic workers as a whole, they provide a valuable insight into the conundrums employing a domestic worker can present for a sector of Singaporean (mostly) women who use these blogs as an outlet. The blogs

I have drawn upon, Singaporemaid and Kiasuparent,[4] are mainly visited by Singaporeans sharing parenting advice, including 'managing' maids who play a major role in childcare and housework. Although at times, domestic workers themselves have participated in some of the online discussions. These sites often contain unguarded comments regarding the 'maid situation,' including how to manage domestic workers' social and sexual freedoms in Singapore. Thus these blogs work to highlight the intimate anxieties that exist between employers and employees.

In the colonial era, the politics of intimacy were primarily concerned with reifying or reinforcing 'racialized categories' (Stoler 2010: 10). The efforts of the colonial state and individual colonizers to control the sexuality of 'others' was not just about 'domination' but 'was a fundamental class and racial marker implicated in a wider set of relations of power' (Stoler 2010: 45). In contemporary Singapore, the regulation and construction of domestic workers' sexuality and intimacy similarly serves to differentiate them as 'other' and keep them in their 'proper' place as social inferiors. In order to deconstruct this 'othering' the regulation of domestic workers' bodies and sexual selves needs to be read within the broader context of Singaporean society. Postcolonial Singapore has demanded discipline and restraint of all of its citizens, including in the realm of sexuality, with some arguing that it has maintained, and even perfected, the regime of sexual regulation inherited from its colonial predecessors (Oswin 2010: 139; K. P. Tan 2003: 409).

This chapter argues that in this context of discipline and restraint, domestic workers' bodies act as a potential site of sexual transgression. Consequently full-time, live-in domestic workers are perceived to require a high degree of surveillance, especially in the realm of sexuality. In making this argument I show how the politics of intimacy for domestic workers are implicated in the broader politics of gender in contemporary Singapore. Lack of flexible work arrangements and demands placed upon Singaporean women as key actors in social and biological reproduction complicates the ways in which the sexual agency of domestic workers is perceived. I highlight how this situation is further complicated as employers are charged with the practice of state power vis-à-vis circumscribing domestic workers' sexuality. Yet at the same time employers are expected to adhere to the 'day off' policy, which some see as antithetical to policing the bodies of their employees.

REGULATING SEXUALITY AND 'PROTECTING' DOMESTIC SERVANTS IN COLONIAL SINGAPORE

Singapore, a city-state known for its productivity, efficiency and dramatic rise from 'third world to first' (Lee 2000), relies heavily on a significant foreign labor force. This includes around 200,000 female foreign domestic workers who hail predominantly from the Philippines and Indonesia.[5] The mandatory rest day that the blogger laments is a major policy step when one considers that under contracts entered into prior to the beginning of 2013, domestic workers, particularly those from Indonesia, could theoretically undertake a two-year assignment without any legal entitlement to a rest day or other form of holiday.

While the controversy of a rest day is contemporary, the means by which the government seeks to both 'protect' and regulate the domestic worker population has a great deal of overlap with Singapore's colonial order. During the colonial era domestic service was among one of the most common forms of employment for women who emigrated to the Straits Settlements of Singapore, Penang and Malacca (Gaw 1988: 81). Immigrants from China constituted a large part of this domestic workforce and typically fell into one of two categories of domestic service—*mui tsai* and *amah*. The first category *mui tsai*, literally 'girl slave,' were primarily young women from impoverished families in China who were sold to agents and sent to work for Chinese households in Singapore and Malaysia (Lai 1986: 46). The position of mui tsai within the Chinese household was one that could range from being akin to an adopted daughter or 'subject to severe abuse within the domestic context of traditional authority and filial piety' (Wong 1996: 119; Lai 1986). Chen has described the 'strict hierarchical structure' of traditional Chinese society, whereby women who assumed roles akin to domestic workers in Chinese families (daughters-in-law, mui tsai and the like) were typically 'positioned at the bottom of the family structure and treated as slaves deprived of the ownership of their existence' (1996: 142).

The second category of domestic workers, *amah*, were unmarried females from southern China, many of whom came from an anti-marriage movement and took up domestic work in Singapore as a means of maintaining their independence (Lai 1986: 79; Gaw 1988: 89; Chin 1998: 73). In comparison with contemporary domestic workers, the experiences of amahs were markedly different in many ways. Unlike contemporary domestic workers who live-in with their employers, amahs often shared living quarters with their peers (Gaw 1988: 95). These external living arrangements, along with their strong anti-marriage stance, may have reduced fears surrounding amahs' unbridled sexuality (Chin 1998: 76). The majority of mui tsai employed in colonial Malaya were under fifteen years of age (Lai 1986), and hence potentially constituted less of a sexual threat in households than contemporary domestic workers who are typically in their twenties and above. Yet akin to contemporary domestic workers, in the colonial era mui tsai and other female migrant workers such as prostitutes were subject to a range of social controls ostensibly to 'protect' these so-called vulnerable populations.

The overlap between colonial and contemporary politics of intimacy is not surprising if we consider Singapore's long history of immigration and its past as a British colony. Intimacy and its regulation was a key technology of colonial governance (Stoler 1995) including in the Straits Settlements which were among the many British colonial possessions to have a *Contagious*

Disease Ordinance. The ordinance required monitoring of brothels and prostitutes in order to protect British troops stationed in the Straits Settlements from venereal diseases (B. H. Tan 2003: 3). The desire to reduce sexually transmitted diseases within Singapore was reflective of not only 'a strong Victorian interest in sanitary reform' (Warren 2003: 104) but a pragmatic tolerance of the profitable prostitution industry within the growing port city. The *Contagious Disease Ordinance*, whilst ostensibly designed to protect prostitutes from disease and exploitation, worked to shape the social and economic identities of these women. Instead of being seen as legitimate migrant labor 'inextricably bound up with the emergence of Singapore' (Warren 2003: 10), these women were cast as a potential public health concern under the law (B. H. Tan 2003; Warren 2003).

These colonial notions surrounding body politics have resonance in contemporary Singapore where domestic workers are subject to physical (and by extension moral) scrutiny. Domestic workers' employment conditions include mandatory biannual examinations which involve testing for pregnancy and sexually transmitted infections. These tests which impinge upon women's bodies are testimony to what Stoler called 'the policing of sex' to ensure that certain categories of people are 'kept in line' (2010: 45). Current medical guidelines provide that upon examination the domestic worker must give her consent for her employer to access the results of her health check, should the employer wish to do so (Kashyap 2010: 18). Detection of disease or pregnancy leaves the domestic worker open to the prospect of dismissal and/or repatriation (Kaur 2007, 2010). Furthermore, following a positive pregnancy test, the domestic worker may be denied entry to Singapore indefinitely, if her employer chooses to 'blacklist' her by notifying the authorities.

In the 1930s the colonial government broadened the scope of its 'protection' of females to include mui tsai. This led to the promulgation of the *Mui Tsai Ordinance* (1933), which sought to make registration of girls working in this form of domestic service compulsory, as well as providing them with basic wages and working conditions (Lai 1986). However, as Lai notes, these measures were in many regards tokenistic, as the ordinance did not mandate 'a real living wage on which the *mui tsai* could survive' (1986: 51). Furthermore the private nature of domestic work meant that basic measures of the ordinance were hard to enforce, thus many mui tsai would remain vulnerable to exploitation and abuse. As with mui tsai, the relative isolation of the domestic sphere ultimately makes the 'protection' of current day domestic workers difficult. Furthermore domestic workers remain categorized as 'informal' workers not covered by the nation's Employment Act (Kaur 2007: 1). Therefore the government has made steps to 'protect' domestic workers by introducing a standardized work contract, which recommends domestic workers are provided 'with at least eight hours of continuous rest' (Kaur 2007: 44) and in some cases, a day off. However, there are limited mechanisms to ensure that the provisions of the contract are actually met. Much like its colonial predecessors, the current Singapore government maintains a 'distant attitude' towards such workers Devasahayam (2010: 46).

'MANAGING' MAIDS AND CONTROLLING SEXUALITY IN POSTCOLONIAL SINGAPORE

Natalie Oswin argues that the contemporary governmental agenda of control and maintenance of a regulated society, particularly in the realm of sexuality, was perfected by key local elites who rose to power following independence. These local elites were central in 'narrowing the imagination of intimacy in contemporary Singapore' (Oswin 2010: 131). For instance Laurence Leong (2012) points out how oral and anal sex between consenting heterosexual couples was only legalized in 2007 (homosexuality is still outlawed) and Kenneth Tan (2003) reminds us how under the *Miscellaneous Offences Act* it remains illegal to walk around naked in your own home. These repressive policies coincided with rapid industrialization which has been so effective in transforming Singapore economically. Tan argues the nation's economic success has required the population to be 'disciplined, docile and deferential' with little room for desires and excesses (K.P. Tan 2003: 407). Consequently he contends Singapore is underpinned by a 'technocratic rationality seeking to eliminate "irrational" desires and the chaos of erotic instincts' (2003: 403). At the same time, Singapore's economic success has encouraged a rhetoric of gender equality, whereby both men and women are valued equally as individual units of production necessary for national development. Consequently, Singapore has come to rely heavily upon foreign domestic workers to fill the gap in domestic labor previously provided by Singaporean women who have increasingly entered the paid workforce since the 1970s. Wong (1996: 120) estimates that in 1977 female labor workforce participation was at 37.0 percent, while one year later it had risen to 40.1 percent and by 1990 had reached over 50 percent. The initial rise presumably coincided with the introduction of the Foreign Maid Scheme in 1978. This scheme provided avenues for Singaporean households to recruit domestic workers from nontraditional source countries, such as the Philippines and Indonesia.[6]

Regulation and discipline of foreign maids especially in the realm of intimacy and sexuality came to be seen as necessary to ensure the foreign workforce was well managed while simultaneously supporting a highly productive local female workforce. Thus, in 1986 employing a domestic worker became highly bureaucratized, with the release of guidelines which required employers to pay a security bond of SGD $5000. These guidelines also made it mandatory for domestic workers to undergo pregnancy tests every six months and prohibited them from marrying a Singaporean or permanent resident. The security bond could be forfeited by the employer in the instance that the domestic worker absconded, broke the law or got pregnant, after which she would have to be immediately repatriated. The security bond is reflective of Kenneth Tan's (2003) notion of Singaporean 'technocratic rationality' allowing the government, and by proxy the employers, to manage domestic workers within a cultural milieu of discipline and control. The Ministry of Manpower explicates this by noting that: 'The security bond conditions continue to be an important means by which we ensure a well-managed foreign workforce, with good employment standards.'[7]

In 2010 the arrangements surrounding the security bond changed. Should a domestic worker become pregnant or marry a Singaporean or permanent resident, employers no longer forfeit their security bond. If they abscond, employers are only liable for half (SGD $2500) of the bond.[8] However, it appears from online forums and websites which discuss the risk of domestic workers becoming involved in romantic relationships that the public as a whole is not yet aware of these changes to policy. Similarly, some domestic workers I spoke to are still under the impression that falling pregnant would leave their employer liable to a SGD $5000 fine.

The most recent major development shaping the dynamics between employers and domestic workers is the Singapore government's announcement that, effective from January 1, 2013, all employers will be required to give their domestic workers a mandatory weekly rest day when renewing or issuing new contracts. When considering the intimate anxieties that already exist regarding domestic workers, this policy was bound to create a quandary. In colonial times workers' 'sexual and domestic arrangements . . . were public, political and economic issues' (Stoler 2010: 25). Such is the case for contemporary domestic workers, especially given government policy which makes control of the reproductive and sexual potential of domestic workers in employers' economic interest via the security bond. Yet by creating a provision for a mandatory rest day, the government is effectively reducing the ability of employers to scrutinize the bodies of their domestic help. Employer reaction to this loss of power is illustrated by the controversy surrounding the day off policy.

The same week the Singaporean government announced its policy for a mandatory rest day for domestic workers, the media went into a frenzy over the death of a Filipina domestic worker known as Rezy and her Bangladeshi construction worker boyfriend Mohammad. A suspected murder-suicide, their bodies were found bloody and naked in a hotel room in Geylang—an area notorious for prostitution and cheap, pay-by-the-hour 'love hotels.' These hotels are frequented by couples such as Rezy and Mohammad, especially on Sundays, the typical day off for foreign construction and domestic workers. The initial report was followed by a spate of articles; including one in the daily tabloid *The New Paper* (*TNP*) on March 9, 2012 titled 'Foreign love turns fatal in Singapore.' This piece outlined a string of relationships between domestic workers and their lovers (both Singaporean and otherwise) that had ended in tragedy. Such media accounts only served to heighten the anxiety over what domestic workers would 'get up to' on their day off as expressed by the blogger in the opening quote of this chapter.

Further evidence of such intimate anxiety was encapsulated a few days later on March 12, 2012, also in *TNP*. The front page ran with a banner 'Weekly day off for domestic workers' under which it posed the question 'Where will your maid go?' The accompanying photographs presented the reader with two distinct options—the first was a blurry image of a woman (apparently a domestic worker) pressed into an amorous embrace with a man whom we can assume is also a foreign worker. Another smaller picture showed domestic workers attending what appears to be an infant first aid class. These two images serve to reinforce the idea that given a day off domestic workers will follow one of two distinct paths—pursuit of wanton lust, or activities that strengthen their role as a domestic ally. This corresponds with Kenneth Tan's (2003: 420) claims that 'a false but tenacious dichotomy between reason (discipline) and desire (sexuality)' persists in Singapore, and not only affects its local citizenry but those who also seek work there.

The isolated nature of the home as a workplace for domestic workers means that it is difficult to ensure employers provide a day off. In addition domestic workers are sometimes offered financial incentives to not take a day off.[9] Thus because of these intimate anxieties, the success of the day off policy is far from guaranteed.

DISCOURSES SURROUNDING POLITICS OF INTIMACY AND THE EMPLOYER–MAID RELATIONSHIP IN CONTEMPORARY SINGAPORE

The discourses that inform perceptions surrounding the sexual lives of domestic workers need to be read within the broader construction of femininity and womanhood that exists in Singapore. Stoler (2010: 42) notes the role of gender inequalities in underpinning the structure of 'colonial racism and imperial authority.' Similarly the 'othering' of domestic workers, including in the realms of sexuality, is reinforced by gender inequalities in Singapore. While employing a domestic worker ostensibly liberates Singaporean women to participate in the workforce, there are a number of structural dilemmas that influence the way women's participation in work and family life are both constructed and played out. With a plummeting fertility rate, an ageing population and no natural resources or agricultural land to rely upon, maintaining labor productivity is seen as fundamental to the nation's economic survival (Tan 2009). The economic imperative for a dual income household is made all the more apparent by the rising cost of living in Singapore which was touted by the *Wall Street Journal* on February 14, 2012, to be one of the most expensive cities in the world.[10]

Beyond economics, cultural factors such as the notion of filial piety remain strong in Singapore. Consequently, women are still seen as largely responsible for ensuring the care of both children and the elderly. Therefore, while notions of gender equality and access to paid employment are supposedly celebrated in Singapore, in many cases 'women are still being viewed as primarily responsible for reproducing the nation, their bodies seen as machines for producing the future workforce that is so vital to an island-state' (Tan 2009: 45). Singaporean women are required to perform both productive and reproductive labor, and applauded for doing so. They have by and large been quite successful at playing a starring role in a national story which emphasizes prosperity and rapid economic success. Yet the critical supporting role that domestic workers play in making Singaporean women's workforce participation possible goes largely unnoticed. Moreover, their contributions toward reproductive labor, in the form of lightening the load of families with children, are rarely recognized. Therefore, not unlike colonial times where the economic contribution of colonized workers was barely acknowledged, domestic workers largely remain invisible and unrecognized for their role in Singapore's economic success.

Despite the rhetoric which deems domestic help as a necessary ingredient for women returning to the workforce, it is surprising to note that women's access to paid employment remains at just over 50 percent,[11] akin to rates of two decades ago (Wong 1996: 120). Lack of flexible work arrangements in part explains women's lower level of workforce participation. For example, the Singapore civil service and multinational companies, both of which are major employers of women, generally have rigid hours beginning at eight-thirty or nine in the morning and ending at six at night. The strong work ethic that forms part of the cultural fabric in Singapore often demands workers to stay at the office well beyond standard hours. Many women are also charged with the duty of coaching and tuition for their children. This is a demanding task in Singapore given the strong emphasis on educational achievement, which starts in early childhood, often even before children enter primary school. When combined with a discourse around parenting which sees fathering as a minor role rather than as a distinct form of co-parenting (Tan 2009), many women find themselves hard pressed to fulfill both their parenting and employment roles. As a commenter *mapleleaf* reveals on the Singaporemaid blog on March 23, 2012, having a domestic worker does not necessarily free her from the dual burden of caring for children and juggling a full-time job:

> A FTWM [full time working mother] is expected to pull more than her fair share of work and responsibilities at the workplace on top of juggling babies, toddlers, household and maid. I often struggled whether to take urgent leave to attend to my sick child if there's an important meeting to attend at work, because boss will show black face [express disapproval]!
>
> Sad to say, employers here still hold the traditional mindset that the more number of hours you spend at the workplace = better and more

committed employee. Because of that, FTWMs are being discriminated when it comes to job hunting, promotion and pay rise. My company has not hired a mother with babies and small kids for a long time! So there is also added worry of losing our job because it's hard to find another job when employers view you as having too much baggage, but can't blame them as the govt is always talking about competitiveness and productivity! All that bullshit about work-life balance is just that, bullshit . . . sorry for ranting again, I've not slept a wink for the past 4 nights fighting a bad viral fever of my toddler while still struggling at work while my maid gets 8–10 hrs solid rest every night!

Mapleleaf's quote above alludes to the class politics at play in the employee–employer relationship. *Mapleleaf*'s complaint that she is 'struggling at work' while trying to balance her work and family life underscores her role as an 'economic subject' (Leong 2012: 23) in Singapore's quest for productivity. In comparison she sees her maid getting adequate rest every night. This seemingly narrows the class markers and privileges that 'being served' are purported to bring to women who employ domestic help.

Further rest for domestic workers, in terms of a regular day off, only threatens to further destabilize the employer–employee hierarchy, as another comment on Singaporemaid, by *anonymous* (March 22, 2012), emphasizes:

The next step by dear government will be employers cooking and serving for maids on off days. Does this govt do anything to take care of problem maids? Do they have any knowledge how working mothers handle stressful job, babies at home, problem maids? And still have to pay huge levy, salary, maid loans, her expenses? Is there a proper childcare were [sic] moms are able to leave their kids after 7 pm in case their job demands them to sit late in office. Singapore is becoming the worst country to live in. Seriously, let the dear activists come and take care of our kids . . . and take the responsibility of maids getting into trouble after going on off days every week.

This blog comment highlights the complex array of issues that the rest day poses to working Singaporean women. Conflating the issues of 'problem maids . . . getting into trouble' with the threat a rest day can present to the strict domestic hierarchy, *anonymous*'s concern is about her lack of control over her helper. Her complaint also shows how sexual control of one's domestic worker is not always about keeping a sexual rival in check, but rather about reinforcing one's sense of authority in a broader power dynamic. Singapore's quest for productivity and the demands it places upon women is underpinned by state regulation of intimacy and sex. As previous blog comments highlight, this perceived need for regulation is passed onto employers who feel the onus for their maids 'getting into trouble.' Regulating domestic workers' sexuality not only keeps them in line and ensures they are at the ready on the domestic front, it also acts as a means by which employers can 'demarcate . . . positions of power' (Stoler 2010: 42). This key strategy of colonial sexual control relates to contemporary dilemmas regarding domestic workers in Singapore. This dynamic is further complicated in Singapore where women are both subject to the demands of the state in terms of economic productivity and also charged with enforcing state guidelines by policing their domestic worker's sexuality. Thus, the regulation of a rest day by the state is seen as potentially undermining the employers' control and authority over their domestic help. This lack of control over one's maid is seen as having broader implications for women who have to 'sit late in [the] office' and juggle the dual responsibilities of family and work. Consequently, the state's perceived liberal agenda toward domestic workers is also seen as undermining Singaporean women's ability to fully participate as economic subjects.

Concerns regarding domestic workers' physical and social mobility are not surprising if we bear in mind the fact that the security bond and liability of employer was specifically intended to limit the freedom of domestic workers and inculcate them with the 'disciplined, docile and deferential' (K. P. Tan 2003: 407) spirit of Singapore, whilst providing employers with a degree of control over their domestic workers. In this vein control of domestic workers fits with Foucault's idea that states construct sex as something to be 'administered . . . for the greater good of all' (Foucault 1978: 24). Government policies such as the security bond which linked direct financial loss and, in some cases, legal liability to the bodily examination and social surveillance of domestic workers is a striking example of the Foucauldian project in motion in Singapore.

The immediate effect of the Foucauldian approach to domestic workers' sexuality has a direct bearing on women such as Ninik. Ninik has two children back home in Indonesia and has been employed as a domestic worker in Singapore for just over a year. My conversations with her have been brief, as Ninik says she's not allowed out unaccompanied by her female employer. The one exception to this is if Ninik walks her employer's dog in her local neighborhood. During one of these walks Ninik told me that she is rarely left at home by herself and has to accompany her employer on shopping trips and family outings. According to Ninik her employer previously hired a domestic worker who brought her boyfriend to the house when no one else was home—a misdemeanor serious enough to involve the police. Since then Ninik's employer has been extra cautious to ensure that Ninik does not become romantically involved while working in Singapore.

Although Ninik can negotiate a day off, it is not regular, and when she does request time off her employer wants to know her whereabouts and will even text her to find out where she is. On one occasion when Ninik and a friend made an appointment to go to a hair salon her employer quizzed her wanting to know if a boyfriend had offered to pay. Even though Ninik insisted she would be using her own money, her boss felt it incumbent to accompany Ninik and waited outside the salon until she had finished. When talking to Ninik, her frustration at her lack of social freedom was palpable. She said every time she talks on the phone, or to other domestic workers in the neighborhood, her employer wants to know who she was talking to and the content of the conversation. At thirty years old, Ninik is all too aware of the irony that her boss spends more time and energy policing Ninik's movements than she does that of her own eighteen-year-old daughter, who is permitted to have a boyfriend. Ninik has tried to reassure her employer that she is responsible enough to look after herself, including assuring her that she will not jeopardize her employment by getting pregnant. Not only does Ninik's employer police her whereabouts and sexuality, she insists upon viewing the receipts for Ninik's personal purchases, despite the fact that Ninik is using her own money.

This level of fiscal surveillance by employers is also iterated on some blogs. For instance an employer named *Are* in her list of house rules for her domestic worker (which she has published on the Singaporemaid blog on June 5, 2008) notes, 'We will keep all your money for you, and you can keep track with our documentation. When you need the money to buy things, tell us how much and we will pass it to you.' Such rules not only infantilize domestic workers by presuming that they cannot be trusted with their own money, but also render the domestic worker financially dependent. In enforcing rules like these (although based on my research typically extreme), employers reinforce class markers and underscore the power differential between themselves and their domestic workers. Financial exploitation such as this also demonstrates how the state's protection of domestic workers, which includes recommendations that they should have access to their own money and bank books 'at all times' (Devasahayam 2010: 51) often fails to materialize.

Overall the notion of a mandatory day off has raised an overt anxiety amongst employers in the blogosphere who argue that increasing personal and social freedoms for domestic workers will equate to employer's lack of control. For example, one thread under the header 'suspect my maid has hp [hand phone], need help' on Kiasuparents on March 3, 2012, begins with a blogger named *clioclio* and her suspicion that her domestic worker may have a mobile phone. While some people responded in horror that *clioclio* forbade her domestic worker to have a mobile phone in the first place, other contributors, such as *verykiasu2010* on March 4, 2012, warned that having a phone is a 'slippery slope' that could potentially lead workers to start cutting corners at work, spend uncontrollable amounts of money on phone bills, and eventually end up stealing from their employers. Ultimately the thread descended into the social risks such communication technology pose, not only for domestic workers, who, according to *stressedoutmummy*, 'most of the time . . . cannot control the phone usage,' but also to employers' ability to handle their workers. As *clioclio* posted later in the discussion, on March 5, 2012:

> I have seen maids surfing internet and so on, lying on the road side, along main road, and of course, with some male workers . . . just like tourists having picnic under Eifle [sic] Tower. . . .

Implicit in *clioclio*'s post above is the notion that communications technology, which provides domestic workers with a form of social freedom that cannot be tangibly monitored by employers, can create an atmosphere where moral laxity can occur 'on the road side . . . with some male workers.' The use of communications technology also goes towards challenging perceived markers of class hierarchy assumed to exist between employers and their domestic workers in terms of both leisure and consumption. *Miniami* commented on March 8, 2012, on how her domestic worker has three phones, one for surfing the Internet, one to use for calls to the Philippines and the other a local number. *Miniami* ended by lamenting that her domestic worker is 'really richer then [sic] us.'

Attitudes that construct domestic workers as coming to Singapore to reap financial rewards and live the good life 'just like tourists having picnic under Eiffel Tower' serves to cast a mirror upon the austere work ethic and demands of everyday life placed upon many Singaporeans, whose government has embraced the repressive British sex laws with fervor and appropriated them to coincide with notions of 'Asian conservatism' (Leong 2012). As Kenneth Tan (2003: 409) has argued, sexual repression is evidence of a 'new "internal" colonial mentality' that aims to curb unbridled sexuality in Singaporean society, especially among the Malay minority which Tan claims are deemed to be particularly 'sensual and lazy.'

Similar fears regarding domestic workers and the intimate abound. Consequently a sexually repressive gaze is cast upon them. Without the discipline and control of these bodies, some believe that domestic workers will transgress the moral contract of Singapore which expects all citizens to show restraint in the realm of sexuality. Another post from the Singaporemaid blog on September 25, 2010, attests to this. An employer, also using the moniker *anonymous* (this is used by numerous posters on the blogs) complained how her domestic worker, before she was given any rest days, was 'a good girl and doing . . . good work. When she started go out every Sun. She met bad friends who introduced indian men to pay her meals. That's exactly how things got worst [sic].' *Anonymous* then went on to say how she felt obliged to send her domestic worker back home as:

> she refused to cut off her relationship with her lover. I didn't want her to go to other employers because her heart is not here to work but stay with her indian lover. After one month she came back [to] Singapore easily and now she's returned to Singapore. I should have reported to

the police when she brought a stranger to my condo. I didn't report to the police only because I wanted to give her a chance as I felt sorry she has kids waiting for food in Philippines. I gave her more than one chance. Sadly, she only pretended she had stopped cheating [on] her husband and lied to my family.

In response to the above post, and also on September 25, 2012, another *anonymous* contributor empathized, noting that domestic workers are prone to this behavior, and open to the dual pleasures of sex and money:

Good girls . . . can go bad. My experience told me very few of them [domestic workers] are able to resist temptation . . . they don't want to work but wait for the salary day and days off to get some extra money from their lovers by having sex with them.

The above comment is in direct contrast with discourses which cast Singaporean citizens and its workforce as 'economic subjects rather than sexual citizens' (Leong 2012: 23). By not only taking lovers, but also transgressing the sanctity of the domestic sphere, domestic workers subvert this dominant narrative.

CONCLUSION

In their pursuit of romantic relationships, domestic workers embody what Kenneth Tan (2003: 403) contends are the ' "irrational" desires and the chaos of erotic instincts' that the Singaporean government has tried so hard to eliminate. Therefore, the domestic worker with increased social and spatial mobility in the form of a rest day is seen by many as opening up a Pandora's Box in relation to romantic relationships they might forge with male foreign workers. Once opened, some employers feel that domestic workers, who are often already difficult to train and manage, will become even less compliant within the strict social order that governs both the state and many households in Singapore.

The new day off ruling serves to undermine the form of 'internal colonialism' that operates at the corporal level, regulating women's bodies and sexuality. This holds true not only for domestic workers, who are so feared to fall into bad company, but also Singaporean women, who feel the new ruling reduces their capacity to fulfill their reproductive roles. For example, a blogger named *bellathajah* on Kiasuparent (March 6, 2012) reacted to the news of the rest day by saying, 'Is my rest time not important? My desire to have a 4th child is now thrown out of the window. I should be heading to my gynae soon to get tied up.'

The reality is that romantic liaisons between domestic workers and men (local and foreign) are already happening. Unfortunately, due to ways in

144 *Maria Platt*

which the government, and by extension, employers, construct and attempt to regulate the sexuality of domestic workers, their romantic relationships are not solely the business of the couple. This chapter has highlighted how at the heart of these romantic liaisons and the anxiety they invoke, is a complex and entangled 'employer–maid' relationship. This complexity is underpinned by conflicting expectations each group of women face—domestic workers who are expected to silently support the Singaporean family and by extension, the nation, and employers who also struggle to juggle their reproductive and productive responsibilities for what is deemed 'the greater good of all' (Foucault 1978: 24).

NOTES

1. As almost all domestic workers in Singapore are foreigners, throughout this paper I will use the abbreviated term domestic worker when referring to women who migrate to Singapore to work in this sector.
2. The blog http://singaporemaid.blogspot.sg has since been removed. Calls for its removal appeared in late 2011 from foreign worker rights organizations. It was claimed that the site was illegal as the author of the blog had breached the privacy of domestic workers by including personal details, such as their names and work pass numbers under a section called 'Maid Reviews,' whereby employers evaluated their domestic workers' performance. It is unclear when the blog was removed; however, it was still operational until at least mid-2013. Throughout this chapter, the blog singaporemaid.blogspot.com is referred to as Singaporemaid.
3. The mandatory day off is for those who start or renew contracts on or after January 2013. Those whose contracts are yet to expire are currently not entitled to the day off. However, it has been noted by the Ministry of Manpower that it is possible to pay a domestic worker in lieu of a rest day at a rate of approximately SGD15–20 per day.
4. The blog forum on Kiasuparent can be found at http://www.kiasuparents.com/kiasu/forum/index.php
5. Transient Workers Count Too (TWC2), 2011, 'Fact Sheet: Foreign Domestic Workers in Singapore (Basic Statistics).' http://twc2.org.sg/2011/11/16/fact-sheet-foreign-domestic-workers-in-singapore-basic-statistics/. Accessed May 15, 2012.
6. Previously those who worked in the domestic service were local women, or those who came from Malaysia (Wong 1996).
7. Ministry of Manpower (MOM), 2009, 'Press Release: Obligations of Employers of Foreign Workers Tweaked Change in Security Bond Conditions; Higher Cover for Medical Costs.' http://www.straitstimes.com/STI/STIMEDIA/pdf/20090925/foreign.pdf. Accessed May 15, 2012.
8. Ibid.
9. The going rate to compensate a domestic worker in lieu of a rest day in 2013 is currently around $15–20 per day. In many cases the domestic worker has little choice if her employer wishes her to work instead of receive a rest day.
10. 'Singapore among World's Most Expensive Cities,' *Wall Street Journal*, 2012. http://blogs.wsj.com.searealtime/2012/02/14/singapore-among-worlds-most-expensive-cities/. Accessed August 13, 2012.
11. Ministry of Manpower (MOM), 2012, 'Fact Sheet: Women.' http://www.mom.gov.sg/foreign-manpower/Pages/women.aspx. Accessed May 14, 2012.

See also Singapore Department of Statistics, 2011, 'Occasional Paper: Singaporeans in the Workforce, October 2011.' http://www.mom.gov.sg/Publications/mrsd_singaporeans_in_the_workforce.pdf. Accessed October 3, 2012.

REFERENCES

Chen, S.-J. A. 1996. 'Migrant Women Domestic Workers in Hong Kong, Singapore and Taiwan: A Comparative Analysis.' *Asian and Pacific Migration Journal* 5(1): 141–54.
Chin, Christine B. N. 1998. *In Service and Servitude*. New York: Columbia University Press.
Devasahayam, Theresa W. 2010. 'Placement and/or Protection? Singapore's Labour Policies and Practices for Temporary Women Migrant Workers.' *Journal of the Asia Pacific Economy* 15(1): 45–58.
Foucault, Michel. 1978. *The History of Sexuality Volume 1: An Introduction*. New York: Vintage Books.
Gaw, Kenneth. 1988. *Superior Servants: The Legendary Cantonese Amahs of the Far East*. Oxford and New York: Oxford University Press.
Kashyap, Kiran. 2010. 'Revisiting Medical Examinations for Foreign Domestic Workers.' *The College Mirror* 36(3): 418–19.
Kaur, Amarjit. 2007. 'International Labour Migration in Southeast Asia: Governance of Migration and Women Domestic Workers.' *Intersections: Gender, History and Culture in the Asian Context* 15(May). http://intersections.anu.edu.au/issue15/kaur.htm. Accessed September 15, 2014.
Kaur, Amarjit. 2010. 'Labour Migration in Southeast Asia: Migration Policies, Labour Exploitation and Regulation.' *Journal of the Asia Pacific Economy* 15(1): 6–19.
Lai, Ah Eng. 1986. *Peasants, Proletarians and Prostitutes: A Preliminary Investigation into the Work of Chinese Women in Colonial Malaya*. Singapore: Institute of Southeast Asian Studies.
Lee, Kuan Yew. 2000. *From Third World to First: The Singapore Story, 1965–2000*. New York: Harper Collins.
Leong, Laurence Wai-Teng. 2012. 'Asian Sexuality or Singapore Exceptionalism?' *Liverpool Law Review* 33: 11–26.
Oswin, Natalie. 2010. 'Sexual Tensions in Modernizing Singapore: The Postcolonial and the Intimate.' *Environment and Planning D: Society and Space* 28: 128–41.
Stoler, Ann Laura. 1995. 'Sexual Affronts and Racial Frontiers: European Identities and the Cultural Politics of Exclusion in Colonial Southeast Asia.' In *Tensions of Empire: Colonial Cultures in a Bourgeois World*, edited by Frederick Cooper and Ann Laura Stoler, 196–237. Berkeley: University of California Press.
Stoler, Ann Laura. 2010. *Carnal Knowledge and Imperial Power: Race and the Intimate in Colonial Rule*. Berkeley: University of California Press.
Tan, Beng Hui. 2003. ' "Protecting" Women: Legislation and Regulation of Women's Sexuality in Colonial Malaya.' *Gender, Technology and Development* 7(1): 1–30.
Tan, Kenneth Paul. 2003. 'Sexing Up Singapore.' *International Journal of Cultural Studies* 6(4): 403–23.
Tan, Kenneth Paul. 2009. 'Who's Afraid of Catherine Lim? The State in Patriarchal Singapore.' *Asian Studies Review* 33(1): 43–62.
Warren, James Francis. 2003. *Ah Ku and Karayuki-san: Prostitution in Singapore 1870–1940*, 2nd ed. Singapore: Singapore University Press.
Wong, Diana. 1996. 'Foreign Domestic Workers in Singapore.' *Asian and Pacific Migration Journal* 5(1): 117–38.

Part II
Domination and Resistance

Domination and Resistance

Victoria K. Haskins and Claire Lowrie

It has been said that domestic service 'is a social institution which reflects changing patterns of domination' (Andall 2000: 292). Certainly relations of domination and subordination are deeply embedded in the relationship between domestic servant and employer. Colonial patterns of dominance can be traced to, most obviously, racism and racial theory, with gender and class complicating the picture somewhat, for instance, when poor colonial settlers, soldiers and petty officials could (and did) employ colonized domestic workers, and white domestic servants could be put in charge of overseeing them, or when colonizer women demanded deference from colonized male workers, or white children were able to order about, and even physically punish, their colonized carers. In the contemporary world of global migrant domestic labor, colonial racial hierarchies justifying inequalities and exploitation of domestic workers retain significant power even though the inflections have changed. In the words of Raffaella Sarti, 'the very worst pattern of relationship [that Europeans] created in extra-European countries through colonization and imperialism' has been 'imported' back to Europe (Sarti 2005: 33). Meanwhile in the Middle East, Africa, Asia and the Americas, new forms of domination, based on new racial/ethnic/geographic permutations but embedded in colonialist constructions of racial hierarchy, have sprouted prolifically in the wake of colonialism.

The essays in this section all deal directly with questions of domination and the exercise of power. They demonstrate that colonialist domination does not emanate from one source or direction: the generation and imposition of repressive power is multilayered, and can include the legal and other official institutions ostensibly there to protect those who work in service, and the attitudes of the broader public that marginalize and discount domestic work, as well as the behaviors and attitudes of individual employers. Read together these chapters (and many of the others in this collection also) illustrate the Foucauldian concept of power as dispersed and pervasive, produced by 'regimes of truth' and enmeshing domestic workers past and present within a system that would construct them as almost entirely powerless.

Nevertheless, just as intimacies breed anxieties, domination produces forms of resistance. The focus of the authors is on the struggle for domestic workers' rights and power, on both individual and collective levels. Fae Dussart takes a transnational approach in her analysis of the efforts of individual servants to seek legal redress against abusive employers. In both India and England during Britain's high imperial era of the late nineteenth century, servants used the colonial and national court systems available to them to test public sanction of their rights and the limits of employers' punitive powers over them. She draws on English-language newspapers as her sources, comparing the representations of servants' rights and what constituted legal treatment of colonized versus white working-class servants in these powerful vehicles and constructors of 'truth.' Shifting to present-day New York and the formation of the Caribbean, Latina and African workers' group Domestic Workers United, Alana Glaser provides an ethnographic perspective on the emergence of transnational women's activism from the periphery to the center, and the way that resistance and solidarity are generated through performances of protest: Her findings also recall what we know of Jamaican women's strategies to refuse oppression (see Johnson, this volume). All three of these chapters point, particularly, to the importance of performativity in public space for colonized domestic workers' assertion of their rights.

Michael Aird's evocative photo-essay gives a different perspective on the question of domination and resistance in domestic service. Sharing photographs of his own family members and of other Aboriginal domestic servants in Queensland working under the weight of draconian, so-called protective legislation in the early twentieth century, Aird contends that these cherished and mostly private images are evidence of how women actually used domestic service to resist colonial domination that aimed at the disintegration of their family life. A contest over the meaning and significance of female domestic service for Indigenous peoples in settler colonial nations is also the subject of Mary Jane Logan McCallum's chapter. McCallum addresses the retention of Canadian First Nations girls in residential schools, where their labor was being exploited by the schools or offered out to local settler families, creating a labor deficit for their own families and communities. Like Aird, McCallum focuses on the everyday acts of resistance by Indigenous people to the destruction of their communities, in this case, through the letters of protest the girls' parents wrote to the schools. The final essay in this section, Claire Lowrie's analysis of the historical resistance of Chinese male domestic workers to white women's control as employers, challenges assumptions (past and present) that this conflict was solely, or even primarily, a gender struggle over power in the home. Instead, she argues that conflicts need to be considered in the context of both white women's contested role in colonial regimes and the nationalist and communist political struggle by Chinese people across Southeast Asia at the time, highlighting that the resistance of domestic workers in colonial contexts cannot be separated from wider colonial and anti-colonial politics.

Read together, the essays here raise tantalizing questions for further research. Is the collectivist activism we see of the transnational domestic workers' rights organizations fundamentally different from the resistance of the colonial period, even if the systems of domination have tended to persist? It seems that resistance to domination in domestic work no longer centers on the abolition of the occupation itself (if it ever did). Could the shifting of both historical and contemporary representations of domestic workers, and of domestic service itself, be critical in the struggle for domestic workers' rights?

REFERENCES

Andall, Jacqueline. 2000. *Gender, Migration and Domestic Service: The Politics of Black Women in Italy*. Aldershot: Ashgate.

Sarti, Raffaella. 2005. 'Domestic Service and European Identity.' In *Proceedings of the Servant Project*, vol. V, edited by Suzy Pasleau and Isabelle Schopp, with Raffaella Sarti. Liège: Éditions de l'Université de Liège.

8 'Strictly Legal Means'
Assault, Abuse and the Limits of Acceptable Behavior in the Servant–Employer Relationship in Metropole and Colony 1850–1890

Fae Dussart

Domestic servants' connections to other worlds—whether to working-class friends and family in Britain or to Indigenous society in India—could appear inscrutable and threatening to their employers. This was despite (or perhaps because of) the fact that, especially in India, these connections were essential to the functioning not only of the household, but also the Empire. Servants mediated between above and below stairs, public and private, domestic sphere and marketplace, Indigenous and colonial, working and middle- or upper-class, administering much of the essential traffic between these interdependent sectors and cultures. Although the balance of power in the servant–employer relationship was weighted in the employers' favor, in both India and in Britain the dependence of the employer on the servant created a space in which small acts of servant resistance were possible. Offended servants could spoil food, deliberately fail to hear or understand instructions, spread gossip and generally sabotage the smooth running of the household. However, such methods constituted revenge, rather than justice. At times a servant or an institution representing servants' interests would seek public sanction as to what a servant's rights were and where the limits of acceptable behavior on the employers' part should be drawn. Domestic servants often stood in the dock in nineteenth-century courts in both India and Britain, on charges of petty larceny or breach of contract and not infrequently on charges of prostitution, infanticide, concealment of birth and even murder. However, they also occasionally brought prosecutions against their employers, sometimes for assault.

In recent decades, a range of scholars have analyzed the place of domestic service in the operation of our historical and contemporary social world. Within this body of work, analysis of domestic service and colonialism, broadly defined, is a growing field (with increasing numbers of analyses of colonialism and domestic service focusing on British imperial households in India (see Chaudhuri 1994; Blunt 1999; Collingham 2001; Procida 2002; Banerjee 2004, and in this volume; Buettner 2004; Leong-Salobir 2011; Dussart 2013). In this chapter I seek to add to this scholarship by comparing the different ways in which domestic servants in India and England used the courts, and the way their cases were differently represented in the Indian colonial and the British press respectively.

Court cases are of interest as the courtroom was a 'functional site of power for the contested formation of . . . social identities' (D'Cruze 1998: 4–5) and a place in which representations of private experience were publicly judged. This chapter considers some occasions when employers in India and in Britain stood in the dock, prosecuted by their servants, or by other authorities on their servant's behalf. Although the balance of power in the servant employer relationship was overwhelmingly in favor of the employers in both metropole and colony, I suggest that servants in both sites used the courtroom as a space in which to publicly contest the limits of their employer's authority. Servants did not always win their cases, but the fact the cases were brought for judgment at all bears examination. Comparing metropole and colony reveals the specificity of constructions of 'violence' within the master/mistress/servant relationship. Such constructions intersected with dominant discourses of gender, race and class in the second half of the nineteenth century to produce differentiated ideas about what the relative rights and responsibilities of servants and employers were across imperial space. The relative status of servants and their employers, in relation to discourses of gender, race, class and domesticity, shaped the process and outcomes of the court cases in each site, and their representation in the contemporary press.

The chapter makes use of newspaper articles in an attempt to access the elusive servant voice and to examine the content and representation of court cases involving servants and employers in both metropole and colony. Newspaper articles are a problematic source due to the likelihood of editorial bias and their appeal to a selective segment of the literate population. However, as John Tosh has written, 'no text has ever been composed in isolation' (Tosh 2000: 124). As products of particular sociocultural contexts, textual representations can tap into, challenge, and/or reconstitute ideas about behavior and identity within the wider society to which they relate. In doing so they can suggest alternative possibilities and images for discursive and behavioral emulation, rejection or development. Thus, newspapers could both represent and shape reality (Chartier 1982: 30; Vann and Van Arsdel 1989: 5). Looking at the newspapers of the day may limit us to the opinions of the literate reading public, or even to the opinion of an editor, but with careful reading and attention to we can trace conflicts and ambivalences within a paper's pages and in this way gain access to the making of nineteenth-century identities.

The print media in India and Britain varied considerably. Britain's *The Times* newspaper was a national daily directed at middle- and upper-class readers of a conservative bent. It was thus the mouthpiece of employers of servants rather than servants themselves. The colonial newspapers considered here, including *The Pioneer, The Englishman, Indian Daily News* and *The Civil and Military Gazette* were regional papers, though their uniformity in the major news stories their editors chose to cover is often striking.[1] These were geared to the tastes of a specifically Anglo-Indian readership and reflected the concerns of a white population who considered themselves as a pioneering minority superior to and at times threatened by the Indigenous colonial subjects they lived amongst.[2] Alan Lester has suggested that colonial newspapers were important in connecting disparate colonizing communities in different sites of empire with one another and with the metropole (2001: 6). I would suggest that the colonial newspapers I discuss here were also important in connecting communities *within* such sites, responding to and reflecting the anxieties of colonizers and helping to constitute a dominant and homogenous 'Anglo-Indian' identity as distinct from and as superior to 'the Indian.' At the same time, it is important to recognize that Indian and British subjects rarely conformed to homogenous constructions and often openly challenged them in line with wider debates over the moral purpose of imperialism, and the relative rights of individuals within increasingly contested hierarchies of gender, race and class.

CAPITALISM, COLONIALISM AND DOMESTIC SERVICE IN BRITAIN AND INDIA

The master/mistress/servant relationship was essential within the imperial formation of Britain and India, and to the hierarchies of gender, class and race that underpinned the progress of both capitalism and colonialism as they manifested in both metropole and colony in the nineteenth century. In India, following the transfer of control of the subcontinental colony from the East India Company to the Crown, the Queen's proclamation of 1858 had committed the Government of India, in theory, to a policy of racial equality:

> We hold ourselves bound to the natives of our Indian territories by the same obligations of duty which bind us to all our other subjects. . . . We declare it to be Our Royal Will and Pleasure . . . that all shall enjoy the equal and impartial protection of the Law.[3]

However, the preservation of certain privileges for Anglo-Indians in India contradicted such apparently inclusive aims. As Mrinalini Sinha has pointed out, in the second half of the nineteenth century it was increasingly clear to the colonial authorities that 'continued British political and economic exploitation of India depended on the maintenance of certain exclusive racial privileges for European British subjects in India' (Sinha 1995: 39). India was of very real economic importance to Britain. The challenge to Britain's economic dominance from other European nations and the huge increase in Britain's financial investments abroad in the second half of the nineteenth century put the colonial authorities in a difficult predicament, compromised by liberal aspirations and the political and economic exigencies of the moment. Furthermore, educated Indians were beginning to organize politically. By the mid-1870s, politically conscious Bengalis had begun touring India to promote regional solidarity (Dobbin 1965: 93). Nascent Indian nationalism and Anglo-Indian anxiety about the security of British control of India formed the backdrop to the representations of cases of assault by Anglo-Indian employers on their Indian servants.

In Britain meanwhile, the establishment of a free market and the associated logic of individualism and competition were challenging received notions of hierarchy and patriarchy (Davidoff 1995: 74). Feminists and members of the growing labor movement were developing new ideas about the rights of women and workers. This fed into employer anxieties about their authority over their servants. For example, A. Amy Bulley, an advocate of women's education and trade unionism, identified a 'great upheaval' which was 'stirring the labouring class to its very depths,' writing that she referred 'to the rebellion in the ranks of domestic service' (Bulley 1891: 177). Bulley was not unique. In the final decades of the nineteenth century the 'Servant Problem' was a common theme in newspapers and journals and encompassed both what servant employers saw as an increasing scarcity of servants and their perceived uppityness.

Domestic service was a key occupational category for women during the second half of the nineteenth century, forming the second largest occupational group in the economy.[4] They were largely employed in upper- and middle-class households, although many artisan and respectable working-class households employed a single general servant or maid-of-all-work, often cheaply from institutions such as workhouses and houses of mercy (Prochaska 1981). According to Mrs. Nassau Senior's 1874 report on the education of girls in pauper schools for the Local Government Board:

> [t]he low rate of wages given to these girls . . . makes them sought after by many people who, a few years ago, would have done their own housework, whose income does not permit them to keep a superior servant, and who often look on their little servant as a mere drudge.[5]

Indeed, the plight of such girls, when abused by their employers, frequently made it into the pages of the newspapers. It is difficult to say whether this was a true reflection of life in families who were more 'rough' than 'respectable,' or merely an editorial response to the prejudicial expectations of *The Times* readership. Certainly, orphan pauper girls appear to have been particularly vulnerable to poor treatment wherever they worked.

The class categories by which society in nineteenth-century England was stratified were transformed in the Indian colonial context. Social rank depended on official position on the whole, and military families ranked below those in which the husband held a government position (Collingham 2001: 20). Status in the metropole was of relatively little consequence in determining social ranking in India, but the signifiers of high rank, such as the ability to employ servants, were similar.[6] Literary and visual representations of Anglo-Indians attended by retinues of servants proliferated in the early nineteenth century, fueling the stereotype of the indulged European aristocrat and the court of the 'oriental' prince. Englishness was redefined in India, as a uniquely Anglo-Indian way of life which endorsed European power in an 'Indian idiom' (Majeed 1992: 22).

Though Anglo-Indian life in India was increasingly anglicized in the second half of the nineteenth century, British people travelling to India after 1858, who tended to be of lower middle- and middle-class status, took with them ideas about how elite households should function. Once in the colony, they found themselves able to employ far greater numbers of servants than they might have been able to afford in Britain, claiming differences in climate and custom necessitated a large complement of household staff, though, as Edward Braddon remarked, it was 'one of the social follies of Indian life . . . that you must keep three [servants] to do the work of one' (Chaudhuri 1994: 550; Braddon 1872: 49). Domestic service in colonial India employed over two million people at the time of the 1881 Census of British India and the majority of these servants were male (for further discussion of the prevalence of male servants in tropical British colonies, see Lowrie in this volume). The different gender dynamics of domestic service in England compared with India was noted in the census. In a report on Madras it was observed that there were 'only 445 females to 555 males' in domestic service, while in England there were 894 female domestic servants to 106 male domestic servants per one thousand.[7] The prevalence of adult male Indian domestic servants in Anglo-Indian households skewed the politics of dependence which framed metropolitan domestic service, affecting the representation of employer violence towards servants in colonial texts.

VIOLENCE AGAINST SERVANTS: MORAL AND LEGAL PRINCIPLES

As part of the evangelical drive to reform manners in the early nineteenth century, ideal respectable living entailed a retreat from violence. Self-control was represented in a range of texts as a defining characteristic of Britons in both metropole and colony. Whereas the 'relationship between many Anglo-Indian masters and Indian servants in the early nineteenth century appears to have been characterized by casual brutality,' as the century progressed such behavior was, at least publicly, seen by some as damaging to the authority of the British in India (Collingham 2001: 109, 110). Advice manuals published from the 1840s onwards advised Anglo-Indian employers to be firm with their servants without resorting to physical chastisement, which was increasingly seen as 'un-British and unlikely to yield the desired result' (Procida 2002: 91; for an example see Stocqueler 1844: 198). Elizabeth Collingham has suggested that violent behavior 'threatened the principle of racial separation which was the hallmark of the process of anglicization' as it created an inappropriate 'intimacy between the Indian and his assailant' (2001: 110). In contrast, advice manuals published in Britain in the second half of the nineteenth century do not tend to mention the issue of physical chastisement at all, perhaps because it was (erroneously) assumed that masters and mistresses would not be inclined to strike British servants, or perhaps because in Britain racial consanguinity between employer and servant made the use of physical chastisement less problematic than in India.

In spite of the advice against using violence to discipline servants in India, it appears that the practice was fairly common and appears to have occurred in both lower- and upper-class households. An 1876 editorial in *The Pioneer* stated that 'the truth is . . . that there is hardly a large household in India which could be kept in order by strictly legal means' and advised 'every European here' to 'take care that he never strikes a servant in a way that can possibly have more than a superficial effect.'[8] Some Anglo-Indians criticized the practice. For example, Constance Frederica Gordon Cumming wrote in 1884 that 'to see an Englishman fly into a passion with a native and strike a man who dares not hit him back, is humiliating indeed. If not cowardly, it certainly is horribly derogatory to British dignity, and quite the most painful sight you are likely to witness' (Ghose 1998: 190).

In courts in Britain as the nineteenth century progressed, judges were 'increasingly seeking to set more stringent standards of self-control, refusing to tolerate kinds of violence supposedly accepted elsewhere' (Wiener 1999: 190). Nevertheless, an employer's right to 'discipline' and 'chastise' his or her dependents was still legally endorsed in Britain. In 1845 the case of *Turner v. Mason* established that it was 'a master's province to regulate the conduct of his domestic servant' as he saw fit. The provision was somewhat ambiguous, as 'regulation' could take a range of forms from physical and verbal punishment to material deprivation. This ambiguity in the servant–employer relationship became problematic in cases of abuse, because in order that a verdict might be reached it was necessary to define the limits of an employer's jurisdiction over his or her servant and to mark the boundary between legitimate physical punishment and offensive violence within the servant–employer relationship. The *Apprentices and Servants Act of 1851* made no mention of physical abuse in its provisions; it merely endorsed a servant's dependent status by making employers legally obliged to supply 'necessary Food, Clothing, or Lodging' to servants under the age of eighteen. Thus, unless they were prosecuting their employers for failure to provide food, clothing or lodging as minors, if servants sought redress for physical abuse they had to bring cases of assault for prosecution.

In India the employer–servant relationship was covered by breach of contract and breach of trust laws, which covered employer–employee relationships generally and which protected the employer rather than the employee (Anderson 2004: 428–30).[9] Though they do not appear to have had any specific employment rights, the servant, like any British subject, had a right to freedom from assault under the Indian Penal Code.[10] Indian servants did sometimes bring cases of assault against their employers. This appears to have happened with greater frequency in the last three decades of the nineteenth century, perhaps as a result of a greater willingness on the part of Indians to assert rights, which commentators linked to increasing political activism at this time. Indeed, in 1883 opposition to the Ilbert Bill, which sought to empower Indian judges to try Europeans in criminal cases in rural areas in India, coalesced around a fear that Indian servants would 'annoy their employers by dragging them into court.'[11] Opponents of the Bill argued that European women would be left 'at the mercy of unscrupulous servants,' and this could dangerously undermine colonial authority, as 'An Englishwoman' suggested disingenuously in a letter to *The Englishman* newspaper: 'We women may not be politicians, we may be very illogical, but we surely, some of us, have sufficient knowledge of the position of the English in India to understand that anything that weakens the prestige of our name is detrimental to our safe holding of the country.'[12] Such anxieties resulted in major changes to the bill which became law in 1884.

REPORTING SERVANT ASSAULT IN INDIA AND BRITAIN

Cases of assault brought by Indian servants against their employers did not carry the same sensational value for the Indian press as the abuse of servant girls did in British papers, due to the different gender and racial statuses of Indian compared with British servants. In India cases of assault brought by servants tended to feature as small entries in the 'Police' columns in Anglo-Indian newspapers, when they featured at all. In Britain, the details of cases involving the maltreatment of servant girls were often sensationally entitled with statements such as 'Disgusting Cruelty' or 'Gross Case of Cruelty.'[13] Almost every year between 1850 and 1890 two or three cases, invariably involving servant girls, were warranted sufficiently newsworthy to appear in the pages of the *Times*. Though Pamela Horn has argued that 'spectacular cruelty' against servants declined in the nineteenth century, the records of local newspapers suggest that prosecutions of employers for violence against their servants were not an infrequent occurrence at petty and quarter sessions (2004: 134). Carolyn Steedman's work on the eighteenth and early nineteenth centuries suggests that servants readily went before a magistrate to claim redress from their employers when they felt it necessary (2009: 196). Nonetheless, more often than not servants stood in the dock rather than the witness box, having been accused by employers for leaving their 'places' without due notice. There is a grim irony in the fact that it was not infrequent for a servant to state as her reason for her breach of the hiring agreement that she had suffered poor treatment at the hands of her employer. If the court disbelieved such claims the servant could be fined or even sentenced to three months' hard labor (Hill 1996: 102).

The cases of abuse of servants appearing in the pages of the British national dailies in the period 1850 to 1890 were extreme, and cannot be taken as representative of the experience of most domestic servants. Such accounts of abuse fitted into the popular narrative of the poor friendless orphan child immortalized in the fiction of the period by writers such as Charles Dickens, and perhaps attracted press attention for this reason. Nonetheless, the cases discussed here were not fictional, and mapping the extremities can illustrate underlying contests relevant to the spectrum of 'appropriate' relations between employers and servants. Comparison with media treatment of cases of assault brought by Indian servants adds another dimension to this spectrum, showing how the legitimacy of violence within the employer–servant relationship was differently figured across imperial space.

In many of the cases in Britain an employer's brutality was precipitated by some perceived failing on the part of the servant to fulfil his or her work duties. In 1851 Hannah Hinton was beaten 'because she had not got the fire lighted at 7 o'clock in the morning.'[14] In 1852 Elizabeth Malcolm was beaten because she was 'stupid and slow.'[15] Fanny Square Keys' mistress hit her because 'she did not do something she was told.'[16] Emily Fox was beaten because 'I was not strong enough to carry the boiler.'[17] Similarly, in India an employer's perception that a servant was failing to fulfil work duties could provoke violence. In 1883 a cook in Calcutta brought a case of assault against her mistress, claiming that her mistress had 'assaulted her with clenched fists' when she had declined to 'cook seven or eight dishes for a party of visitors . . . saying she was unable to prepare same alone.'[18]

In smaller households in Britain the family and the servants could not avoid sharing space and work, which exacerbated tensions, resulting in violence. In the case of Susan Russell, whose mistress, Ann Radcliffe, was charged and found guilty of grievous bodily harm at the Central Criminal Court in 1868, the violent presence of the mistress while the servant works is striking. In her testimony Susan, the only servant in the household, described:

> cleaning a grate in a bedroom about 2 o'clock [on Sunday], and the prisoner entered the room. She was then kneeling, and the prisoner kicked her behind, being cross that she had not cleaned the stove before that time. Her master was in the room at the time, and sent her home at once.[19]

The mention of the master of the household in Susan's testimony is interesting in this context as he appears to have protected her, or at least to have removed her from violent situations:

> On the previous Friday the prisoner boxed her ears and her master sent her downstairs. Her master went out, and after that she was cleaning

some saucepans in the kitchen, when the prisoner poured some water into a teacup from a kettle on the hob and threw it over her neck, which it blistered, and also her bosom.[20]

Though it is not possible to say with certainty what had provoked Ann Radcliffe's abuse of Susan, the intimacy of the violent acts in such cases reflects the proximity of master/mistress and servant and points towards emotional tensions; the mistress's fear and jealousy of, and the consequent need to subjugate, the servant/Other.

In these cases the authority of an employer to 'regulate' a servant extended into a right to physically chastise a servant for not doing a job well. Indeed, in many of the cases the employers justified their actions by drawing attention to the servant in question's faults and upheld their right to punish those defined as their social inferiors and dependents as they saw fit. For example, Mr. John Pemberton argued that his servant 'was deceitful and given to lying, and had other evil propensities' and defiantly claimed that 'whatever censure . . . the world might pass on him, he . . . would inflict corporal punishment on the girl whenever he thought she deserved it.'[21]

A servant's defiance when being verbally disciplined could also be used by Anglo-Indian employers as defense for their violent action. On 3 August 1883 a case was heard at a Calcutta Police Court in which a servant accused his employer, Mr. Jones, of assaulting him when he pressed a demand for his wages. Mr. Jones admitted striking the servant, but claimed that this had happened, not because the servant demanded payment, but because the servant 'neglected to bring him his tiffin, on which he remonstrated with him. The latter, however, became very insolent, whereupon he slapped him.'[22] Mr. Jones was fined two rupees, a nominal punishment which points towards the ambivalence surrounding what kinds of behavior were understood by Anglo-Indians to be legitimate within the relationship between Anglo-Indian employer and Indian servant.

Although violence towards colonized subjects was frowned upon by some Anglo-Indians, anecdotal evidence suggests that physical chastisement of servants continued to be fairly common throughout the nineteenth century. As Collingham has written, 'British sensitivity to the slightest hint of a challenge to their dignity or authority meant that they frequently met any act which suggested insolence with physical violence' (2001: 143). According to Florence Marryat, the wife of an Indian Army officer, the 'usual behaviour [of Indian servants] is so aggravating that, however much I may condemn, I cannot wonder at any one losing control of their temper when with them.' She described feeling

> the keenest sympathy with the action of an officer in our regiment, who, aggravated at the slow and solemn manner in which a young Mussulman in his employ was carrying a pile of plates from the luncheon-table out at his back door, jumped up, and regardless of the fate of his crockery,

gave the tardy domestic such an energetic kick that he sent him flying, plates and all, down a flight of some dozen steps, into the garden, vastly astonished, I have little doubt, at the unexpected impetus which had been given to his footsteps.

(1868: 31–32, 35)

The casualness with which Marryat described this act of aggression and the way in which 'the fate of the crockery' was implied to be more significant than the injuries the servant might have sustained in falling down the steps suggests such behavior on the part of Anglo-Indians was more tolerated than it might have been in Britain. It was usual for Anglo-Indian employers found guilty of assault against Indian servants to receive lenient sentences (Sanyal 1893: 2).[23] For example, in July 1876 Mr. Hutchinson, a Calcutta broker, was found guilty of assaulting his servant and was fined twenty rupees as punishment for his crime. In the spring of the same year a Mr. Fuller, an English Pleader at Agra, caused the death of his syce by striking him on the head and knocking him to the ground. It was claimed that the syce had suffered from an enlarged spleen, which had ruptured when he fell and caused his death and Fuller was fined only thirty rupees as punishment. By contrast, in February 1868 at the Central Criminal Court in London, Ann Radcliffe was sentenced to five years penal servitude for 'cruelly ill-using and doing grievous bodily harm to one Susan Russell' her maidservant.[24]

Surprisingly the leniency of the punishment received by Mr. Fuller in Agra did not go unchallenged. On July 15, 1876, a Minute was published in the *Supplement to the Gazette of India* in which the Governor General in Council (Lord Lytton, the Viceroy) criticized the decisions made by the Joint Magistrate of Agra, Mr. Leeds, and the High Court, and argued that a fine of thirty rupees was not only an inadequate punishment for Fuller's crime, but one that damaged the reputation of British justice in India. Lytton claimed that Mr. Leeds seemed 'to have viewed an assault resulting in the death of the injured man in just the same light as if it had been attended by no such result,' evincing 'a most inadequate sense of the magnitude of the offence of which Mr. Fuller was found guilty.' Lytton also took the opportunity to express 'his abhorrence of the practice, instances of which occasionally come to light, of European masters treating their native servants in a manner in which they would not treat men of their own race.' He went on to claim that:

This practice is all the more cowardly, because those who are least able to retaliate injury or insult have the strongest claim upon the forbearance and protection of their employers. But bad as it is from every point of view, it is made worse by the fact, known to all residents in India that Asiatics are subject to internal disease which often renders fatal to life even a slight external shock.[25]

This statement, even while it condemned acts of violence towards Indian servants, constructed them as members of a physically weak race. The European, by implication, was strong and powerful and should use his power to protect, not abuse, his racial inferiors who, owing not only to their powerless position as servants but also to their physical inferiority as Indians, were more in need of protection than men of British origin. In this way the employer's role was constructed as a paternalistic one, in line with wider discourses on the ideal structure of employer–servant relations in both metropole and colony.

Lytton's Minute caused 'vehement wrath, on the part of the Anglo-Indian community, and elicited from the Anglo-Indian press . . . a swarm of protests and articles, attributing it to an ill-considered sentimental impulse, profound ignorance of Indian law, and reckless disregard of the majesty of the High Court.'[26] These letters and articles reveal the ambivalence of Anglo-Indian employers as to the legitimacy of violence within the servant–employer relationship in India. Almost all letters and articles claimed to agree that 'nobody has any right to box a servant's ears in this country any more than in Europe' and that the 'brutal and cowardly habit, so common in India, of resorting to violence on the slightest provocation, and often on no provocation at all, is one that cannot be too unsparingly denounced'.[27] However, most of the letters and articles then went on to contradict themselves, making excuses for Mr. Fuller's conduct and outlining justifications for why his sentence had been fair under the circumstances.[28] In this vein, an editorial in *The Indian Daily News* suggested that Fuller's crime was not that serious: 'The offence of which Fuller was guilty, resulted quite accidentally from a slight exercise of personal violence.' According to this editorial, the really significant offence had been perpetrated by Lytton in criticizing Mr. Leed's judgment: 'The Government resolution taken as a whole, constitutes a serious offence against the proper administration of justice in India, and an undesirable reproof of the highest judicial interpreters of the law in the country.'[29] The statement that the resolution constituted an 'undesirable reproof' of the judiciary in British India reveals that the concern here was with maintaining the prestige of the British; for the *Indian Daily News* writer, 'the proper administration of justice' presumably meant finding in favor of the Anglo-Indian. The fear underlying such an attitude as that expressed by this editorial writer was probably justified. Indian voices were increasingly vociferous in complaining about the injustices embedded in the administration of law in India. A furious letter from Kamala Kanto Ghosh, also published in the *Indian Daily News*, articulated the growing anger felt by many Indians:

> Have you, Sir, ever heard that an Englishman was hanged or transported to the Andaman for murdering an Indian? But I doubt not you have heard of many cases, where Englishmen were found guilty of such foul deeds. Is it anarchy that such acts are being done and overlooked?

Are we not men that justice will never be done to us, that our lives will be regarded like those of dogs? Are we not possessed of the same organs, same feelings, with the whiteskinned Englishmen? Why then, Sir, is justice trampled down under feet in such cases? Why then, Sir, you, who pretend to be the defender of justice, remain dumb when such cases occur? The English nation are proud of their civilization, but are these the actions of civilized men?[30]

An article in the *Civil and Military Gazette* argued that the lack of any legislation protecting employers from vindictive servants was the reason employers were driven to violence because 'absence of law as between master and servant provokes occasional manslaughter as no man can manage an Indian household without an occasional blow for acts of which the law refuses to punish.' The author went on to absolve Mr. Fuller of blame for killing the syce by suggesting that the 'trick of throwing themselves down as the consequence of a blow which would hardly kill a fly is no novelty in India, and probably in this case it was the fall voluntarily inflicted by the syce and not the blow which caused death.'[31] Despite a nod to humanitarian concerns at the outset, the general thrust of this and other articles provoked by the Fuller case was that in Anglo-Indian households violence was not only justified, but necessary in controlling a servant, who might otherwise 'absolutely refuse to perform the duties for which he is engaged.'[32]

In Britain, ambivalence over the justice of convictions and sentences appears much less marked than in India. For example, in 1868 Mary Barry charged her employer Miss Ann Turner with assault. Mary had worked for Miss Turner and her sister for just over a year and had left their employ a couple of months before bringing the charge. In her evidence Mary claimed that she 'ought to have got up at 6 in the morning, but sometimes did not, and when that occurred she was kept without her breakfast and dinner . . . [her mistress] had repeatedly struck her with a thin cane on her hands and shoulders, giving her two or three blows each time.'[33] However, in cross-examination Mary revealed that she 'was very sorry when her mistress discharged her,' which may have suggested to the court that her accusation was malicious. In their defense, the barrister representing the Misses Turner claimed that they had hired Mary Barry after 'seeing the girl and her mother outside St Mary's Catholic Church apparently very poor' and had 'benevolently interested themselves in their welfare' by engaging the girl to work for them:

They used their best endeavours to teach the girl the duties of a domestic servant, and were obliged to use some slight correction. She had never been treated with the least cruelty . . . what had been done was for the cleanliness of her own person and a desire to get her out of slovenly and bad habits. It was admitted that on one occasion two or three blows had been given on her shoulders with a light cane. She was slovenly and obstinate and needed correction.[34]

In this evidence Mary Barry's employers asserted their right to physically punish the servant they had so benevolently taken on as their dependent and attempted to train. It is suggested that they have fulfilled their responsibility as domestic employers—feeding, paying and training the girl—but that her failure to fulfil their expectations of her as a willing and obedient servant legitimized their use of physical punishment. However, while the case against them was dismissed, in his closing remarks the presiding magistrate stated clearly that there 'was an idea prevalent . . . that mistresses had a right to use corporal punishment. In former times such things were permitted, but that fashion had now passed away . . . it would have been better when they found they could do nothing with [Mary] to have sent her away.'[35]

So, although the court sympathized with the Misses Turner's position, the magistrate made it clear that times had changed and employers no longer had a right to chastise their servants' bodies as they might their own child. Rather, they must dismiss her from her workplace as a failing employee. Mary Barry may not have won the damages she sought, but the assertion implicit in her accusation—that physical punishment now constituted an illegitimate use of authority—had been vindicated. In contrast to the response to Lytton's words in the Fuller case in India, in Mary Barry's case there were no letters to the newspapers, no editorials, no outcry, though it must be noted that the situation may have been different if Mary Barry had won her case.

Unlike in India, in Britain cases brought by servants or their representatives often pivoted upon the limits of responsibility and dependence within the employer–servant relationship. Where perceived neglect of duty was a flashpoint in the Indian context, food was an issue in almost all the British cases, with most of the servants complaining of receiving scanty or spoiled food and providing details in cross-examination of the food they had been given. Emily Fox claimed her employers Mr. and Mrs. Gumb had provided her with:

> cold potatoes and cabbage for breakfast, and the same for dinner, and two or three times a week a very little meat. . . . They had fried potatoes and bacon for breakfast, and hot potatoes and cabbage and meat for dinner. They had tea and bread and butter. They were kept locked in the safe. My potatoes and cabbage were kept in the same safe. Mistress treated me very unkindly.[36]

We can imagine the poor girl's mouth watering as she watched her employers enjoy their food. However, her employers' defense was that as a pauper, the food she received in their employ 'was equal to that she had been accustomed to have in the union.'[37] Similarly, in her case against her schoolmistress employer, Eleanor Houseman testified that she 'had porridge for breakfast mixed with charcoal, and sometimes it tasted like cod liver oil. . . . She never had enough to eat . . . she used to steal food out of the cupboard or off the table when she was hungry.'[38] Despite a doctor testifying that the girl was seriously underweight, the defense argued that 'though it was not sumptuous food, it was such, perhaps, as a woman in her position might have to give to a servant.'[39] The implication of the defense in both these cases was that the servant's position as a servant defined the terms of her dependence and her employer's responsibility. According to the defense, the servant was not entitled to the same food as the family she lived with and worked for precisely because she was a servant. As a person of inferior status she ate inferior food. The servants, by drawing attention to the distasteful or meager food they received, were implying they had a right, within the context of their dependence, to decent food. The court was being asked to decide if these terms were reasonable or not.

The most sensational cases frequently involved young pauper servants hired out from workhouses and orphanages (such cases were usually brought by the Guardians of the Poor). This may be because the stigmatized status of paupers increased the likelihood of their suffering abuse at the hands of their employers, but it seems more likely that without the family and community support networks available to non-pauper servants, opportunities to escape violent employers were less available to pauper girls. For example, in 1856 a Mrs. Grills of Steptoe, South Devon, 'the wife of a respectable farmer' was charged with, and found guilty of, assaulting her fourteen-year-old pauper servant Fanny Square Keys, who had been hired from the Kingsford Union to 'tend the pigs and calves and to look after a little child.' According to Fanny's testimony she had been repeatedly violently punished by her mistress for trifling faults. However, when visited by the relieving officer she told him 'that she was very well treated and liked her place, but she said she did this because she was so much afraid of her mistress.'[40] Similarly sixteen-year-old Sophia Jarvis, who in 1863 brought a charge of cruelty against her mistress Mrs. Mary Langdon Thomas, claimed that she was always 'in company with one or other of the her mistress's family and therefore had not had the opportunity of running away until the 19th of December.'[41] With no family to run away to when she made her escape, she went to the Industrial School of St. George the Martyr at Mitcham, whence she had been hired. Though this isolation meant that pauper girls were more vulnerable to violence in their places, it may also have meant that abused pauper servants sought redress in the courts as they could not find a resolution to their predicament other than to turn to the authorities charged with their protection.

CONCLUSION

The greater tolerance of acts of violence towards Indigenous servants in India evidenced by the leniency of the punishments meted out to employers found guilty of assault, and the lack of sympathy for the victims in such cases, as compared with the horror expressed in British newspapers at cases of abuse involving young servant girls in Britain, was linked to the gender and racial status of the servants involved. Physical chastisement of Indian servants was seen as more legitimate than that of British servants precisely because they were Indian. The opinion expressed in *The Pioneer* newspaper that 'cuffs and stripes, and all kinds of corporeal maltreatment are recognised in India by Indians as well as Europeans, as more in accordance with the natural fitness of things than such phenomena would be thought in Europe' was not a unique one amongst Anglo-Indians.[42] Furthermore, many more Indian servants were male than in Britain—the assaulted male servant did not possess the same vulnerability as the friendless, abused, young servant girl. It seems likely that the maleness of Indian servants, as compared to British maids, underwrote the racial difference upon which the legitimacy of physical chastisement was predicated.

As Shani D'Cruze has argued, '[t]he fact that such incidents result in court cases illustrates resistance on the part of servants . . . and also a sense of outrage—that that specific assault . . . was contestably an illegitimate use of authority in a society where physical chastisement of dependents (particularly children) was commonplace' (1998: 92). Though D'Cruze is referring specifically to Britain, her statement can also be applied to the nineteenth-century Indian context. The process of the court cases represented a kind of negotiation; though the choice to go to court may not have been as rationally thought out as this, in suing their employers the servants were implicitly asserting that the limits of acceptable behavior on the part of their employers had been reached, and were asking the court to clarify the ambiguities in what were the servant's and what were the employer's rights within the relationship. Though the servants may have appeared powerless to protect themselves from abuse, the very fact that they brought cases for public judgment in courts constituted a significant challenge to the absolutism of their employer's authority.

Dominant ideas about the respective rights and responsibilities of servants and employers, expressed in the newspapers considered here, were developed across imperial space and owed much to the trans-imperial trope of the problematic domestic servant, who frustrated the benevolent, pedagogic efforts of his or her beleaguered master and/or mistress to 'improve' her or him, and the class or race she or he was seen to represent. Drawing on this trope, the rhetoric of moral reformation was employed by colonial and metropolitan masters and mistresses to elide their use of abuse in effecting social control. In the metropole, the idea that domestic service should be a transformative experience, through which the 'improvement' (if not social advancement, quite the contrary, in fact) of the servant might be effected, was significant in employers' defense of abusive behavior. In India, servant employers were more explicitly concerned with the maintenance of colonial prestige within, and beyond, the walls of the home. These employers framed their assaults upon their servants as the inevitable by-product of ruling ungrateful subjects who were unwilling to submit to the colonial yoke. In both sites, employers used abusive behavior to endorse the construction of their class and racial status and power over the Other that their servants represented.

The identification of shifts in the limits of acceptable behavior, manifesting here in the relationship between servants and employers as it played out in the public sphere of the courtroom and in the pages of newspapers, indicates a world in flux: a colonial society threatened by Indigenous nationalism, and a metropolitan patriarchal and class structure responding reluctantly to emergent ideas about work and rights. Even while violence was assumed by servant employers as an explicable, even necessary, feature of domestic mastery, tensions progressively emerged with official bodies on this issue, as the question 'what kind of rule is legitimate?' was debated by both Indians and Europeans in different ways towards the end of the nineteenth century. These issues continue to be debated today, as domestic workers worldwide seek to mitigate their particular vulnerability by demanding legal redress for the protection of their rights in a neocolonial or postcolonial context.[43]

NOTES

1. During the period covered in this article *The Pioneer* was published from Allahabad, *The Englishman* and *Indian Daily News* from Calcutta and *The Civil and Military Gazette* from Lahore and Simla.
2. I use Anglo-Indian throughout this article according to its contemporary usage to refer to white Britons resident in India, who may or may not have also referred to themselves as British, English or European depending apparently on context. For the use of the term in the twentieth century to refer to people of mixed British and Indian descent, see McCabe, this volume.
3. *Proclamation by the Queen in Council to the Princes, Chiefs and the People of India*, 1 November 1858, 1–3.
4. For statistics on the scale of domestic service in Britain across the period see 1851General Reports of the Censuses of Population, *Parliamentary Papers* [hereafter G.R.C.P. P.P] vol. LXXXVII (1853); 1871 G.R.C.P. P.P vol. LXXI (1873); 1881 G.R.C.P. P.P vol. LXXX (1883); 1891 G.R.C.P. P.P vol. CVI (1893–94); 1901 G.R.C.P. P.P vol. CVIII (1904).
5. Local Government Board, *Third Annual Report: Report by Mrs Nassau Senior on the Education of Girls in Pauper Schools, Parliamentary Papers* vol. XXV (1874), 338.
6. In terms of India, the focus in this article is on white British servant employers and their Indian servants. Analysis of the relationships between Indian employers, who formed the majority of servant employers in colonial India, and their Indian servants would likely complicate the analysis as Swapna Banerjee's work in this area suggests (Banerjee 2004: 189–92; see also Banerjee in this volume).
7. *Report on the Census of British India Taken on the 17th February 1881*, Vol. I, 391.
8. Editorial, *The Pioneer*, 19 July 1876.
9. See *Legislative Acts of the Governor General in Council Vol. I, 1834–1851*, IOR/V/8/117 OIOC; *Legislative Acts of the Governor General in Council Vol. III, 1859–1861*, IOR/V/8/119 OIOC.

'Strictly Legal Means' 169

10. See Act XLV of 1860, Chapter XVI in *Legislative Acts of the Governor General in Council Vol. III*, IOR/V/8/119 OIOC.
11. Letter from 'An Englishwoman,' *The Englishman*, 14 March 1883.
12. Letter from 'An Englishwoman,' *The Englishman*, 14 March 1883.
13. 'Disgusting Cruelty,' *The Times*, 12 February 1857; 'Gross Case of Cruelty,' *The Times* 20 September 1856.
14. 'Cruelty to a Servant,' *The Times*, 13 January 1851, 5.
15. *The Times*, 11 November 1852, 8.
16. 'Gross Case of Cruelty,' *The Times*, 20 September 1856, 7.
17. 'Spring Assizes,' *The Times*, 12 March 1866, 11.
18. *The Englishman*, 14 July 1883.
19. 'Central Criminal Court,' *The Times*, 29 February 1868, 11.
20. 'Central Criminal Court,' *The Times*, 29 February 1868, 11.
21. *The Times*, 11 November 1852, 8.
22. 'Police,' *The Englishman*, 4 August 1883.
23. *Return Showing the Number of Assaults Committed by Europeans on Natives and by Natives on Europeans in the Five Years 1901–1905*, File no. 3445, L/P&J/6/781, OIOC.
24. 'Central Criminal Court,' *The Times*, 29 February 1868.
25. Letter from Arthur Howell, Esq., Officiating Secretary to the Government of India, to the Secretary to the Government of the North-Western Provinces in *Supplement to the Gazette of India*, Calcutta, Saturday 15 July 1876, no. 31, p. 763, IOR/V/11/41 OIOC.
26. Lytton to Salisbury, 30 July 1876, *Lord Lytton. Letters Despatched. 1876*, MSS Eur/E218/18 OIOC.
27. Editorial, *The Pioneer*, 19 July 1876; Editorial, *Indian Daily News*, 21 July 1876.
28. See for example the editorial articles in *The Pioneer*, 19 July 1876, and *The Englishman*, 24 July 1876.
29. Editorial, *Indian Daily News*, 21 July 1876.
30. Kamala Kanto Ghosh, Letter, *Indian Daily News*, 25 July 1876. See also the letter from 'Native' in the *Indian Daily News*, 29 July 1876.
31. 'Master and Servant,' *Civil and Military Gazette*, 22 July 1876, 7.
32. 'Master and Servant,' *Civil and Military Gazette*, 22 July 1876, 7.
33. *The Times*, 7 April 1868, 11.
34. *The Times*, 7 April 1868, 11.
35. *The Times*, 7 April 1868, 11.
36. 'Spring Assizes,' *The Times*, 12 March 1866, 11.
37. 'Spring Assizes,' *The Times*, 12 March 1866, 11.
38. 'Central Criminal Court,' *The Times*, 7 August 1880, 11.
39. 'Central Criminal Court,' *The Times*, 7 August 1880, 11.
40. 'Gross Case of Cruelty,' *The Times*, 20 September 1856, 7.
41. *The Times*, 15 January 1863, 11.
42. Editorial, *The Pioneer*, 19 July 1876.
43. In June 2011 the International Labour Organisation adopted the Convention on Domestic Workers, setting labor standards for decent work. It entered into force in September 2013. For further discussion see Fish, this volume.

REFERENCES

Anderson, Michael. 2004. 'India 1858–1930. The Illusion of Free Labour.' In *Masters, Servants and Magistrates in Britain and Empire, 1562–1955*, edited by Douglas Hay and Paul Craven. 422–54. Chapel Hill: University of North Carolina Press.

Banerjee, Swapna M. 2004. *Men, Women and Domestics: Articulating Middle-Class Identity in Colonial Bengal*. Delhi: Oxford University Press.

Blunt, Alison. 1999. 'Imperial Geographies of Home: British Domesticity in India, 1886–1925.' *Transactions of the Institute of British Geographers* 24: 421–40.

Braddon, Edward. 1872. *Life in India: A Series of Sketches Showing Something of the Anglo-Indian, the Land He Lives in, and the People among Whom He Lives*. London: Longmans, Green.

Buettner, Elizabeth. 2004. *Empire Families: Britons and Late Imperial India*. Oxford: Oxford University Press.

Bulley, A. Amy. 1891. 'Domestic Service. A Social Study.' *Westminster Review* 135(2): 177–86.

Chartier, Roger. 1982. 'Intellectual History or Sociocultural History? The French Trajectories.' In *Modern European Intellectual History: Re-appraisals and New Perspectives*, edited by Dominick LaCapra and Steven L. Kaplan, 13–46. Ithaca and London: Cornell University Press.

Chaudhuri, Nupur. 1994. 'Memsahibs and Their Servants in Nineteenth-Century India.' *Women's History Review* 3(4): 549–62.

Collingham, Elizabeth M. 2001. *Imperial Bodies: The Physical Experience of the Raj, c.1800–1947*. Cambridge: Polity Press.

Davidoff, Lenore. 1995. *Worlds Between: Historical Perspectives on Gender and Class*. Cambridge: Polity.

D'Cruze, Shani. 1998. *Crimes of Outrage: Sex, Violence and Victorian Working Women*. London: UCL Press.

Dobbin, Christine E. 1965. 'The Ilbert Bill: A Study of Anglo-Indian Opinion in India, 1883.' *Australian Historical Studies* 12(45): 87–102.

Dussart, Fae Ceridwen. 2013. '"To Glut a Menial's Grudge": Domestic Servants and the Ilbert Bill Controversy of 1883.' *Journal of Colonialism and Colonial History* 14(1). http://muse.jhu.edu/journals/journal_of_colonialism_and_colonial_history/v014/14.1.dussart.html. Accessed September 15, 2014.

Ghose, Indira. 1998. *Memsahibs Abroad: Writings by Women Travellers in Nineteenth Century India*. Delhi: Oxford: Oxford University Press.

Hill, Bridget. 1996. *Servants: English Domestics in the Eighteenth Century*. Oxford: Clarendon.

Horn, Pamela. 2004. *The Rise and Fall of the Victorian Servant*. Stroud: Sutton.

Leong-Salobir, Cecilia. 2011. *Food Culture in Colonial Asia: A Taste of Empire*. London: Routledge.

Lester, Alan. 2001. *Imperial Networks: Creating Identities in Nineteenth Century South Africa and Britain*. London: Routledge.

Majeed, Javed. 1992. *Ungoverned Imaginings: James Mill's the History of British India and Orientalism*. Oxford: Clarendon Press.

Marryat, Florence. 1868. *'GUP': Sketches of Anglo-Indian Life and Character*. London: R. Bentley.

Prochaska, F. K. 1981. 'Female Philanthropy and Domestic Service in Victorian England.' *Historical Research* 54(129): 79–85.

Procida, Mary A. 2002. *Married to the Empire: Gender, Politics and Imperialism in India, 1883–1947*. Manchester: Manchester University Press.

Sanyal, Ram Gopel. 1893. *Record of Criminal Cases as between Europeans and Natives for the Last Sixty Years*. Calcutta: Bengal Press.

Sinha, Mrinalini. 1995. *Colonial Masculinity: The 'Manly Englishman' and the 'Effeminate Bengali' in the Late Nineteenth Century*. Manchester University Press: Manchester.

Steedman, Carolyn. 2009. *Labours Lost: Domestic Service and the Making of Modern England*. Cambridge: Cambridge University Press.

Stocqueler, Joachim H. 1844. *The Handbook of India, a Guide to the Stranger and the Traveller, and a Companion to the Resident*. London: W. H. Allen & Co.
Tosh, John. 2000. *The Pursuit of History: Aims, Methods and New Directions in the Study of Modern History*. Harlow: Longman.
Vann, J. Don, and Rosemary T. Van Arsdel. 1989. *Victorian Periodicals: A Guide to Research*. New York: Modern Language Association of America.
Wiener, Martin J. 1999. 'The Sad Story of George Hall: Adultery, Murder and the Politics of Mercy in Mid-Victorian England.' *Social History* 24(2): 174–95.

9 Imperial Legacies and Neoliberal Realities
Domestic Worker Organizing in Postcolonial New York City

Alana Lee Glaser

On a warm July Saturday, I enter the recreational room of a Brooklyn church shortly after three o'clock in the afternoon for a monthly Domestic Workers United (DWU) meeting. The afternoon sun streaming in through the floor length windows barely illuminates the remainder of the dim, cavernous room. This afternoon, Katherine, a published poet and musician, reinterprets a full-time nanny/housekeeper job description as a poem, performing it for the group of thirty mostly middle-aged, Caribbean and Latina members gathered. Katherine, one of the stewards of DWU's cultural committee, is well known for her impromptu performances, many of which reinterpret job postings and employer instructions to dramatic and humorous effect. She delivers each line of the employment advertisement in melodic, Trinidadian-accented speech, transforming the makeshift meeting hall into an improvised open-mic stage. She reads from the employer's instructions: 'Before you go out for the night please be sure the kitchen eating area [is] clean, dishes cleaned, and kitchen counters.' Looking up at her secular congregation, she incredulously remarks 'and the four children haven't been mentioned yet!'

Responding to Katherine's performance, her audience recognizes the substandard, labor extraction-oriented conditions of employment, conditions which the neoliberal immiseration of underdeveloped nations has facilitated by pushing impoverished, job-desperate women into the migrant stream to support families and children remaining in Caribbean, South American, Asian, and increasingly African countries (Dickey and Adams 2000; Anderson 2000; Bakan and Stasiulis 1997). By introducing the refrain 'and the four children haven't been mentioned yet,' Katherine casts judgment on the job posting's author by mocking the detailed descriptions of cleaning duties while drawing attention to the fact that the potential employer—presumably a parent of the four children mentioned in the job announcement's headline—fails to include any criteria or description of the childcare responsibilities associated with the job. In repeating this refrain back to her, as Katherine instructs us to do, we, the audience, enact the ironic melding of postcolonial obstacle and opportunity that brings immigrant domestic workers together in this church auditorium, while also signifying resistance to the hierarchies of class, gender, citizenship, mobility, and race that structure New York City domestic work (Brown 2011).

The formation of Domestic Workers United (DWU) is the result, I argue, of a postcolonial pan-ethnic coalitional politics and a critical response to both US imperial history and contemporary neoliberal economic ideology, as are individual workers' strategies for addressing uneven workplace conditions in the homes where they work. My analysis draws on interviews conducted with West African and Caribbean women working as health aides, nannies, elder care providers, and service workers in New York City between 2010 and 2012 as part of my dissertation project—an institutional ethnography within the organization Domestic Workers United and among its members and collaborators.

DOMESTIC SERVICE, US IMPERIALISM, AND THE FORMATION OF DWU

Formed in 1999 under the auspices of two organizations, the Committee Against Asian-American Violence, and Andolan, DWU is an organization of 'Caribbean, Latina, and African nannies, housekeepers, and elderly caregivers,' providing legal assistance, leadership, and nanny training for its members with the broader aim of bringing 'dignity and recognition' to domestic work (Boris and Nadasen 2008). In concert with their long-term partners, DWU successfully campaigned for the passage of the nation's first bill protecting home-based workers. Dubbed 'the nanny bill,' the Domestic Workers Bill of Rights took effect in New York in November 2010 after a decade of lobbying. DWU's organizing has evolved into a 'Know Your Rights' campaign co-sponsored by the Department of Labor and carried out by DWU's 'member-organizers' through novel neighborhood-based approaches and a public awareness campaign. The Bill of Rights extends minimum wage and workplace safety and harassment laws to domestic workers, mandates overtime pay, and provides one day of rest per week. It also provides a legal avenue through which abused domestic workers can seek retribution in the form of back payment of unpaid wages and monetary compensation. The emergence of the organization and its legislative, coalition politics, thus, illustrates creative resistance to the overdetermined experiences of low wage work in a city at the center of a neoliberal, imperial state. At the start of this century, DWU was positioned at the fulcrum of a rejuvenated but highly vulnerable, legally unprotected industry 'staffed' by a migrant, female, impoverished workforce of color.

The emergence of DWU in the late nineties needs to be understood as part of the global inequalities and patterns of migration produced by US neocolonial interventions in the global South. As Ann Laura Stoler has noted, the label 'empire' is not one that is easily applied to the US. Various scholars have questioned 'whether the broader band of territorial annexations, occupations, and hemispheric divisions make the United States an empire or not' (Stoler 2006: 9). Much can be gained, however, from analyzing contemporary domestic service in the US in the context of neocolonial interventions of the US government overseas.

Over the past thirty years, after decades of decline, US domestic service has undergone a resurgence, alongside neoliberal international economic policy and the attendant internationalization of the US service economy. Amid ongoing military and economic influence abroad, the impact of economic neoliberalism at home—characterized by deregulation, trade liberalization, and declining welfare protections—has hollowed out US middle classes, intensifying domestic polarizations of wealth and poverty (Harvey 2005). Exacerbated by the 2008 financial crisis and ongoing recession, US job growth is restricted to low wage sectors, accelerating a decades long decline in the real wages of US male 'breadwinners' (Ehrenreich and Hochschild 2003: 3). As fewer families can afford to subsist on a single income, working mothers and adult female children continue to find themselves the primary caretakers of children, elderly parents, pets, and households. Thus, striking a 'patriarchal bargain,' families—and particularly mothers—who can afford to (and often even those who cannot) turn to the market to outsource previously unremunerated household labor by hiring nannies, housekeepers, and home health aides, many of whom are migrant women, thereby enacting international inequalities fashioned by neoliberal policies (Kandiyoti 1991).

By the late nineties, when DWU formed in response to individual worker advocacy campaigns, the United States had been 'the globe's major imperial power' for half a century, with regional imperial influence extending back to the nineteenth century (di Leonardo 2000: 68). The migration of West African and Caribbean domestic workers to NYC in the late twentieth century is related directly to the intensification of US economic and military interventions in the global South in the period following the Second World War. With the decolonization of countries throughout the global South, US free market expansion (entailing the opening of new markets through economic coercion and force) undermined the budding independence of decolonizing nations, and destabilized and indebted states across the Caribbean, Africa, Latin America, and Asia (Mamdani 2005). The political and social instability caused by military interventions, the establishment of patron regimes, backing of coups and warlords, and disbursal of foreign aid, during decades of Cold War and then later the War on Terror, resulted in the migration of Caribbean and West African people to the US in ways that are akin to former colonial subjects relocating to the metropole following decolonization (Stoler 2006: 8).

Migration to the US was fuelled further by what sociologist Saskia Sassen identifies as 'ideological linkages' between the US and the countries in which it established export industries and military bases, and allocated foreign aid. Disrupting national economies and reorganizing available local industries as well as traditional family life, Sassen contends that out-migration to the US—much like migration from former colonies—results from the imposition of foreign economic and cultural interests that carry new opportunities for domestic as well as international labor migrations (Sassen 1991: 34). The economic impact of Washington Consensus austerity measures over the past three decades weakened local economies while opening countries to foreign capital (Harvey 2003).[1] A combination of Structural Adjustment Program-induced defunding, privatization of state resources, and the reorganization of 'traditional work structures' that followed the introduction of export production, has driven emigration from the global South as an economic necessity (Sassen 1991: 41).

The suite of economic reforms included in the Washington Consensus policy and the patterns of migration which it has produced are often understood as key aspects of neoliberal globalization or the 'intellectual/political stance that presumes that capitalist trade "liberalization" . . . will lead inevitably to market growth, and *ceteris paribus*, to optimal social ends' (di Leonardo 2008: 5). But, given the uniformly asymmetrical direction of capital flows *from* the global south, we might also consider it in Kwame Nkrumah's terms as neocolonialism, defined as ' "giving" independence to . . . former subjects, to be followed by "aid" for their development':

> It devises innumerable ways to accomplish objectives formerly achieved by naked colonialism. It is this sum total of these modern attempts to perpetuate colonialism while at the same time talking about 'freedom.'
>
> (1965: 239)

Notably, Nkrumah identifies the United States as 'foremost among the neocolonists' (1965: 239). Presciently summarizing the combination of economic and military might that fifty years later David Harvey would term 'the new imperialism,' the former Ghanaian President and Pan-African leader argues that US international influence constituted an 'invisible government, arising from Wall Street's connection with the Pentagon and various intelligence services' (2003: 240).

LEGAL EXCLUSION AND COMMUNITY UNIONISM

In the US and elsewhere, workers, responding to the neocolonial and neoliberal structures in which their labor is embedded, develop resistance strategies that incorporate gendered and identity-based claims. Largely migrant, often female workers take on both employers and the state in addressing the multifaceted constraints on organizing to improve working conditions in casual sectors (Collins 2006). DWU is a prime example of this type of US social movement or community unionism. Community unionism leverages power in a context where 'firm-by-firm organizing is inadequate,' as in the 1990s, a decade characterized by a national anti-union climate, mobile firms decamping to non-union states and overseas, and highly vulnerable immigrant workers (Fine 2000–2001: 61). For New York City domestic workers, both the New York State *Labor Relations Act* and the *Wagner Act* still prohibit collective bargaining or negotiating, a legacy of Jim Crow-era race relations when predominantly African-American agricultural and domestic workers were excluded from the bargaining provisions of US labor legislation (Ngai 2004). As historian Premilla Nadasen (2009) recounts of DWU's origins and coalition strategy, community unionism marshals wider circles of influence (such as religious, cultural, ethnic, and transnational groups) and engages broader tactics than typical shop floor labor organizing. By deploying both class-based and identity-based organizing claims, DWU's community unionism model aims to ameliorate the exploitative conditions of domestic labor through legislative reform and grassroots tactics.

Domestic Workers United meeting rooms, therefore, are raced and gendered spaces. Reflecting the demographics of the NYC domestic worker industry, the group is entirely female, save a couple male volunteers, and Caribbean-led. More recently, the organization recruited Latina members, who serve on the board as well as committees. At the time of my research, most monthly meetings hosted about fifty women while smaller committee groups could range from five to thirty. In New York, domestic worker organizing follows ethnic/national lines with groups of Filipina, Brazilian, and South Asian women organized in cultural associations that function as labor advocacy and activist platforms for domestic worker rights.

DWU members migrate to the US with complex and diverse identifications and experiences of race, often shaped by formal colonization histories, but in the multicultural mix of New York, they experience further racialization in ways that align them with seemingly disparate immigrant and domestic groups. As sociologist Pei-Cha Lan reflects on her own experiences studying in the United States and conducting field research on domestic work in Taiwan, in the 'hierarchical order of globalization,' migrant women with diverse immigration trajectories and histories become '"Third World Women" after landing on the alien continent of a racialized landscape' (2006: *xi*). It is precisely this sense of sharing similar experiences based on ethnic difference, migration, and gender along with their shared geopolitical histories of oppression that unite DWU members across other salient differences, such as language, and provide the basis for moving from individual employment dissatisfaction to communal political action.

ISOLATED WORKERS, GENDERED JUDGMENTS, AND COLLECTIVE COMPLAINT

Katherine's audience, now growing increasingly independent, interrupts her, 'and the four children haven't been mentioned yet.' 'Yet,' Katherine reflects back to us. Experiencing the co-construction of this narrative poem, the room erupts in a giddy rumbling, as these diverse domestic workers communally craft their collective judgment of the employer's advertisement, affirming their shared experiences: *we've all worked for this type of person before.* 'The rooms should be cleaned up and vacuumed one to two times a week, and all the lights on the ceiling and the molding,' Katherine looks up gracefully at her one outstretched arm before breaking into a fit of laughter at the suggestion that one be expected to clean crown moldings on a biweekly basis. Building steam, she raises her voice; 'cleaned,' she repeats before cutting herself off. Exasperated, 'and the four children haven't been mentioned yet,' she booms to a room now filled with knowing laughter and inaudible comments.

Given the isolated nature of the worksites, and the physically and emotionally demanding aspects of this work, domestic workers frequently voice dissatisfaction with their positions, complaining about various aspects of the labor relationship as well as the unprotected status of the industry (Colen 1989). While structural in nature, domestic work relationships often are experienced in highly personal terms due to the intimacy of care work (Boris and Parreñas 2010; Colen 1989). Given the 'highly personalized' and individual nature of these employment relationships, the domestic workers with whom I spoke recounted their employers' shortcomings alongside or in place of workplace complaints. During an interview with May, an aggrieved domestic worker, I asked about workplace satisfaction and terms of employment. Although she faced multiple labor law violations and general lack of consideration—including unpaid hours, unpaid overtime, ever-expanding job requirements, and abrupt termination—she described her employer Pam in terms of personal failings rather than employment grievances. I heard about Pam's negligence, vanity, drinking, and laziness *before* I was told about her violation of employment law. 'She's not a parent,' May disapprovingly asserted. 'She adopted the little boy and she has no knowledge of being a parent. She had four huge cats in the house. And she brought the baby and she does not take care of the baby. A real parent would want to spend time with the kids. Not her. Not her.'

Pam's former employees, visibly distressed by their memories, relayed in great detail the unkempt state of Pam's apartment, the residual filth of her four oversized felines, and the pain they experienced upon arriving each morning to find the baby crying alone in his urine soaked sheets with a soiled diaper and 'sour' odor. According to May, his mother's explanation that 'he did a poop last night so I didn't think he'd have a poop today,' cemented her criminal inattentiveness. 'Every day the baby goes. A baby go three, four times, as soon as the baby eat food,' May explained to me, opening her eyes wide to communicate her incredulity at Pam's lack of parenting skills and maternal instinct.

Despite evidence of Pam's extreme parental neglect, the ways in which May discussed her employment in Battery Park reverberates with other (less dramatic) stories I heard from domestic workers throughout the city.

Nannies consistently characterized parents—and particularly mothers—as fit or unfit, caring or absent, devoted or distracted as a means of leveraging their own professional expertise and instinctive knowledge of caretaking while undermining their employers' authority. The nannies with whom I conducted my research frequently experienced multiple forms of disenfranchisement—many lost apartments over the two years in which I knew them, others shared stories of social isolation, and in many cases, sacrificed years of mothering their own children to work abroad in the US. Workers' judgments, therefore, not only managed gendered power dynamics (as fathers rarely figured into domestic workers' estimations) in the household/family where they worked, but mediated the social distance between affluent employers and their struggling employees.

Rhetorical strategies—such as evaluating the personal or parental shortcomings of private employers—function to alleviate the strain of employment relationships in an isolated workforce and unprotected industry. Further, when leveled at caretaking skills and aptitude, these evaluations both trade on and inscribe notions of the 'natural' role of women as mothers and caregivers. In so doing, these judgments not only displace formal workplace grievances but criticize female employers' failure to appropriately inhabit gendered, nurturing norms and behaviors (Lan 2006). Gendered judgments, such as these, share a long pedigree with women's tactics in a number of colonial contexts (Sen 2008). These 'everyday acts of resistance' reveal the ways in which, despite formal hierarchal divisions between women, colonized subjects resisted subjugated social positions by disparaging European women's sexual behavior, parenting, and comportment (Scott 1985: *xvi*). These judgments both establish colonized women's superiority in explicitly gendered arenas and condemn colonizing influences (Sen 2008).

Laughing so hard that she walks away from her crowd, Katherine shows us only her back as she leans forward to catch her breath, shaking her head back and forth in disbelief. Composing herself and returning to the eager audience, she begins 'on mornings you should do a very thorough dusting.' But she must immediately stop herself, as the frivolity of the description (particularly in the absence of any mention of the four wards) as well as the energy of the room has distracted her mid-prose again. In an aside, she notes, 'if the four children ever come home . . .' trailing off into inaudible but shared grumbling, as if to say *there is no way to care for four children, while doing all of this housework*.

CONCLUSION

In DWU meetings, individual workers' complaints are politicized by performances like Katherine's, conversations among workers, and trainings that contextualize and historicize domestic work. Further, the communal setting provides the occasion to collectively experience, express, and object to asymmetrical working conditions and the broader global processes that facilitate them. Of her research among home healthcare providers in California, anthropologist Maria de la Luz Ibarra argues 'caring for an elderly ward is about creating a more just world, of critiquing through deeds the inequality of globalization that makes human intimacy so difficult' (2010: 118). Similarly, New York nannies' criticisms leveled at employers, often mothers, function to both undermine employers' gendered abilities and to criticize the priorities of middle- and upper-class employers. In this respect, Katherine's refrain comments disapprovingly on the lack of attention to the children while also allowing a communal condemnation of the material excesses represented in the intricate cleaning instructions.

Unlike nannies' individual frustrations with employers and home heath aides' dedication to and care for their elderly and ill wards, the indictment of parental priorities and excesses represented in Katherine's poem takes place in a politicized space alongside broader critiques of structural inequality, unbridled free market ideology, and the resulting insecurity and displacement of 'Third World Women' (Lan 2006). The performance of these shared sensibilities in DWU group meetings is explicitly intended to carve space for migrant women of color, Third World Women, and, as DWU advertises itself, 'Caribbean, Latina and African nannies, housekeepers and elderly caregivers' to mobilize. Through these collective claims, therefore, DWU members *organize* as women of color, domestic workers, and caregivers (Boris and Parreñas 2010). Members like Katherine transform otherwise isolated complaints into communally experienced events, thereby bridging the possibility for collective action outside of this circumscribed space.

DWU is novel in that it strives to unite Caribbean, Latina, and African domestic workers, suggesting the organizational opportunities occasioned by a distinctly postcolonial encounter and exchange. Understanding the postcolonial character of DWU's activism in New York serves not only to highlight that these workers have immigrated to the United States from multiple formerly colonized countries, but also to enable an insight into how a postcolonial frame influences the coalitional strategies employed by DWU's pan-ethnic organizing. In organized gatherings and individual interviews, the DWU members with whom I spoke are simultaneously critical of the neocolonial conditions that have robbed them of their 'right to stay home' and laudatory of DWU's political potential engendered by the same historic and economic forces (Bacon 2013). DWU members understand both sides of the same globalized coin—the ways in which imperial legacies and present neoliberal policies manifest in their life histories, workplace strategies, and political organizations.

Back in the Brooklyn church, Katherine begins to read from that post again. 'The kitchen should be kept clean, but one to two times a week should be thoroughly cleaned. The hallway should be cleaned and [inaudible] as needed. The fridge *up*stairs,' preempting the following line, Katherine pauses, shaking her head with a wide, generous chuckle. Her laughter—implying amusement at the extravagance of two refrigerators in one household—begins in her throat but moves to her gut, becoming breathless, as she again bends forward to collect herself before circling her impromptu stage to compelling theatrical effect. For those of us not in the know, the anticipation builds. Returning to her audience for the third time now, she apologizes, 'excuse me,' acknowledging that she finds the absurdity too great to contain. She may be a poet and a performer, but she is only human after all. Beginning once again, 'the fridge *up*stairs. And *down*stairs should be cleaned out [interrupts herself laughing again] once a week. With the food thrown out and the shelves and bins cleaned out.' She looks up. *Now* we are all in the on the joke.

NOTE

1. While somewhat polysemous in its usage, the Washington Consensus refers to a set of economic polices imposed first regionally in Latin America and later throughout indebted, decolonized countries. The policies include privatization, deregulation, trade liberalization, and opening to foreign investment while reforming national expenditures and subsidies, tax policies, and interest rates (Harvey 2003, 2005).

REFERENCES

Anderson, Bridget. 2000. *Doing the Dirty Work? The Global Politics of Domestic Labour*. New York: Zed Books.
Bacon, David. 2013. *The Right to Stay Home*. Boston: Beacon Press.
Bakan, Abigail B., and Daiva K. Stasiulis. 1997. *Not One of the Family: Foreign Domestic Workers in Canada*. Toronto: University of Toronto Press.
Boris, Eileen, and Premilla Nadasen. 2008. 'Domestic Workers Organize!' *WorkingUSA: The Journal of Labor and Society* 11(4): 413–37.
Boris, Eileen, and Rhacel Salazar Parreñas. 2010. 'Introduction.' In *Intimate Labors: Cultures, Technologies, and the Politics of Care*, edited by Eileen Boris and Rhacel Salazar Parreñas, 1–12. Stanford: Stanford University Press.
Brown, Tamara Mose. 2011. *Raising Brooklyn: Nannies, Childcare, and Caribbeans Creating Community*. New York: New York University Press.
Colen, Shellee. 1989. 'Just a Little Respect: West Indian Domestic Workers in New York City.' In *Muchachas No More: Household Workers in Latin America and the Caribbean*, edited by Elsa M. Chaney and Mary Garcia Castro, 171–94. Philadelphia: Temple University Press.
Collins, Jane. 2006. 'Redefining the Boundaries of Work: Apparel Workers and Community Unionism in the Global Economy.' *Identities: Global Studies in Culture and Power* 13: 9–31.
de la Luz Ibarra, Maria. 2010. 'My Reward is Money: Deep Alliances and End-Of Life Care among Mexicana Workers and Their Wards.' In *Intimate Labors: Cultures, Technologies, and the Politics of Care*, edited by Eileen Boris and Rhacel Salazar Parreñas, 117–31. Stanford: Stanford University Press.
di Leonardo, Micaela. 2000. *Exotics at Home: Anthropologies, Others and American Modernity*. London: University of Chicago Press.

di Leonardo, Micaela. 2008. 'Introduction: New Global and American Landscapes of Inequality.' In *New Landscapes of Inequality: Neoliberalism and the Erosion of Democracy in America*, edited by Jane Lou Collins, Micaela di Leonardo and Brett Williams, 3–20. Santa Fe: School for Advanced Research Press.

Dickey, Sara, and Kathleen M. Adams. 2000. 'Introduction: Negotiating Homes, Hegemonies, Identities and Politics.' In *Home and Hegemony: Domestic Service and Identity Politics in South and Southeast Asia*, edited by Kathleen M. Adams and Sara Dickey, 1–30. Ann Arbor: University of Michigan Press.

Ehrenreich, Barbara, and Arlie Russell Hochschild. 2003. *Global Woman: Nannies, Maids, and Sex Workers in the New Economy*. New York: Metropolitan Books.

Fine, Janice. 2000–2001. 'Community Unionism in Baltimore and Stamford.' *WorkingUSA* 4(3): 59–85.

Harvey, David. 2003. *The New Imperialism*. Oxford: Oxford University Press.

Harvey, David. 2005. *A Brief History of Neoliberalism*. Oxford: Oxford University Press.

Kandiyoti, Deniz. 1991. 'Bargaining with Patriarchy.' In *The Social Construction of Gender*, edited by Judith Lorber and Susan A. Farrell, 104–18. London: Sage Publications.

Lan, Pei-Cha. 2006. *Global Cinderellas: Migrant Domestics and Newly Rich Employers in Taiwan*. Durham: Duke University Press.

Mamdani, Mahmood. 2005. *Good Muslim, Bad Muslim*. New York: Doubleday Press.

Nadasen, Premilla. 2009. '"Tell Dem Slavery Done": Domestic Workers United and Transnational Feminism.' *Scholar and Feminist Online* 8(1). http://sfonline.barnard.edu/work/nadasen_01.htm. Accessed September 15, 2014.

Ngai, Mae M. 2004. *Impossible Subjects: Illegal Aliens and the Making of Modern America*. Princeton: Princeton University Press.

Nkrumah, Kwame K. 1965. *Neo-Colonialism, the Last Stage of Imperialism*. New York: International Publishers.

Sassen, Saskia. 1991. *The Global City: New York, London, Tokyo*. Princeton: Princeton University Press,

Scott, James. 1985. *Weapons of the Weak*. New Haven: Yale.

Sen, Indrani. 2008. *Memsahib's Writings: Colonial Narratives on Indian Women*. Hyderabad: Orient Longman.

Stoler, Ann Laura. 2006. 'Intimidations of Empire: Predicaments of the Tactile and Unseen.' In *Haunted by Empire: Geographies of Intimacy in North American History*, edited by Ann Laura Stoler, 1–22. Durham: Duke.

10 Tactics of Survival
Images of Aboriginal Women and Domestic Service

Michael Aird

Figure 10.1 Sophie Mumming from Woorabinda, Fortitude Valley, c.1906. Photo by Roland Ruddle. neg68943, courtesy John Oxley Library, State Library of Queensland.

Figure 10.2 Katie Williams, Beaudesert, 1924. Photo by Peter Hyllisted. Courtesy Doris Yuke collection.

In the early 1990s I curated an exhibition and publication titled *Portraits of Our Elders* which documented photos dating back to the 1860s, a time when Aborigines had little control over the way in which they were portrayed, through to a time when they had a degree of control over how they were seen—well-dressed, confident Aboriginal women inside photographic studios in the 1920s. These photographs were a part of the political process that Aboriginal people were going through.

A photo of my grandfather's aunties, Katie, Lilly and Clara Williams, gave me the idea for the exhibition. The beauty of these women, and the confidence they demonstrated, inspired me to put together an exhibition of formal studio portraits of Aborigines. I have seen many people look at this photograph and ask questions about the clothes the women are wearing. The answer to this question is that they worked hard and bought these fashionable and expensive clothes themselves. The clothes, the makeup, and the act of walking into a photographic studio as a paying customer are what I call 'tactics of survival' (Aird 2000: 194)—actions that that these women made in order to protect themselves and their families from the very real threat of government intervention. These women lived through an oppressive period of government 'protection' policies, with the very real threat of official intervention, their children being removed, and at times whole families being taken from their traditional country to missions or reserves.

Figure 10.3 Katie, Lilly, & Clara Williams, c.1920. Photo by Peter Hyllisted. Courtesy Doris Yuke collection.

There is no doubt that every Aboriginal family in Queensland has been in some way affected by the far reaching powers of the *Aboriginal Protection and Restriction of Sales of Opium Act of 1897*, and successive Aboriginal protection policies. Many Aboriginal girls and women were placed in domestic service 'under the Act' in the first half of the twentieth century. In the 1920s, Evelyn Monkland was sent to Brisbane to begin work as a domestic servant.

Figure 10.4 Evelyn Monkland at Barambah Aboriginal Settlement, c.1925. Photo from the Betty McKenzie collection. © Image courtesy of Queensland Museum. EH433.

> I came to Brisbane, I think it was 1922, I was only 17. Mrs Semple got me the job in New Farm for her cousin, they were wealthy people, the Mansons, their family owned cattle stations. There were flats, there were six flats, all very wealthy people. Person downstairs was always written up in the papers and that kind of thing. I cooked and did everything, did the washing, had to wash and scrub the floors.
>
> (Evelyn Serico [nee Monkland], January 24, 2001, in Aird 2000: 24)

Figure 10.5 Emma Sommerset with her daughters Eva and Doris and her employers' son, Brisbane, 1915–1920. Courtesy Doris Yuke collection.

Figure 10.6 Emma Sommerset with her daughters Eva and Doris and her employers' son, Brisbane, 1915–1920. Courtesy Doris Yuke collection.

While 'under the Act' in the early 1900s and working as a domestic servant, Emma Somerset had two daughters, Doris and Eva. Emma was fortunate enough to be able to find employment in the Brisbane region that enabled her to keep her daughters with her. Emma accumulated a collection of photographs that documented herself in work situations with her young daughters by her side. By the 1920s Emma managed to be exempted from the provisions of the Aboriginal Protection Act and she married Ted Williams, an Aboriginal man from the Beaudesert district in southeast Queensland.

Figure 10.7 Emma Sommerset with her daughters Eva and Doris, Brisbane, c.1914. Courtesy Doris Yuke collection.

Agnes Williams nee Bell grew up under the Act at Cherbourg Aboriginal Settlement. As a young girl, aged only about thirteen years old, she was sent out to work as a domestic servant on rural properties. In 1947, 'Agnes Williams received a cheque with her exemption from the settlement for nine pounds and five pence. That was all there was after ten years domestic service' (Huggins and Huggins 1994: 39).

Figure 10.8 Agnes Bell and members of the Daylight family, Cherbourg, 1940s. Courtesy Ted Williams.

Figure 10.9 Agnes Williams, Tamrookum, 1991. Photo by Michael Aird.

Agnes Williams was not allowed to go home even for her mother's funeral. She cried and cried and was broken hearted and has always felt cheated about that. I really feel for her. Her family shunned her for not attending because they thought it was her fault for not coming home. She was caught in a hopeless situation. If she dared run away or went on unauthorized leave she'd be sent to goal.

(Huggins and Huggins 1994: 39)

Figure 10.10 Dina Johnson with Nell and Bert Cameron, Moray Downs, 1905. Courtesy Bill Cameron.

Figure 10.11 Nell Cameron, Sydney, 1930s. Courtesy Bill Cameron.

Nell Cameron was born in 1902. Her mother was Aboriginal and her father was a property owner from central Queensland. When her father died in 1912, Nell, her two brothers, and her mother were sent away from the family property by her father's brothers. They were placed under the Aboriginal Protection Act and removed to Barambah Aboriginal settlement, later known as Cherbourg. Nell received an exemption from the Act in 1921 and secured employment as a domestic servant, working for her non-Aboriginal relatives.

> I was raised by my father's sister [Nell Cameron]. I call her Mum. Before I was born she went to Sydney to work in the 1930s as a maid for the Nichols family. We are related to them through my grandfather. . . . She came back to Brisbane and got a job at the Bellevue Hotel. She became friends with the owner, Mrs Admans, and about 1943 or '44 she was made the chief maid upstairs, in charge over all the other staff upstairs. Mum was very proud of that. She was a very hard worker. She puts me to shame I never learnt anything from her as far as hard work is concerned.
>
> (Bill Cameron, May 3, 2000, in Aird 2000: 44).

Figure 10.12 Nell Cameron on verandah of the Bellevue Hotel, Brisbane, 1942. Courtesy Bill Cameron.

During the 1950s Nell gave up her position at the Bellevue Hotel and moved to central Queensland to take on the responsibility of caring for her brother's young son, Bill Cameron. In order to support herself and Bill she took up the position in the laundry at St. Brendan's, a Christian Brothers school at Yeppoon. This was a live-in position for Nell and her adopted son, and it also included free tuition for Bill. So as circumstances changed in her life, Nell had to give up her position as a senior maid in one of the most prestigious hotels in Brisbane, to working in the laundry of a rural boys' boarding school. Then in 1969 when Bill completed school they moved to Brisbane so that Bill could secure a career in the public service. Nell spent the rest of her life devoted to Bill's welfare, never marrying nor having children of her own. Bill would occasionally talk of how his family was denied any entitlement to his grandfather's estate, but instead they were simply sent off to an Aboriginal reserve.

Figure 10.13 Nell Cameron being escorted to the opera by her employers' son, Brisbane, c.1949. Courtesy Bill Cameron.

Figure 10.14 Grace Jones, Teneriffe, 1992. Photo by Sharyn Rosewarne. Courtesy Queensland Newspapers.

Grace Jones nee Dowe was born at Childers in 1902, and came to Brisbane to take employment as a domestic servant for her former schoolteacher, who had recently married a widower with five children. It was in Brisbane that Grace met her husband, Selwyn Jones, who died while their two sons were still young.

For most of Grace's life she had three jobs to support herself and her two sons. As Grace stated in an interview in 1992, 'I had a happy time, going from pillar to post, and we never got a penny from the government' (*The Courier Mail*, May 11, 1992). Grace never drank or smoked, but admitted to having a few bets on the horses. In an interview in 2000 her son John made this statement:

> During the war there was no such things as widow's pensions and workers dole or anything like that. In those days we lived in Commercial Road, not far from the Waterloo Hotel and during the war the American Navy commandeered that area. So Mum worked, starting at half-past-four or five in the morning, washing American clothes. She was a real battler. She worked tirelessly. After she finished work about five o'clock in the afternoon, we came home from school and we would help her prepare a meal. Then she would start working at this Chinese restaurant till one in the morning.
>
> (John Lee Jones, May 26, 2000 in Aird 2000: 22)

These photographs document the important role Aboriginal women played by working hard to earn an income while also struggling to keep their families together. Proving that they were useful to the European economic system, while also generally conforming to European norms, such as becoming Christians, sending their children to school, and dressing well, are just some examples of 'tactics of survival.' It is the decisions that women in my own family have made that have influenced the lives of several generations of my family, and why we have remained in our traditional country.

REFERENCES

Aird, Michael. 2000. *Brisbane Blacks*. Southport: Keeaira Press.
Huggins, Jackie, and Rita Huggins. 1994. *Auntie Rita*. Canberra: Aboriginal Studies Press.

11 'I Would Like the Girls at Home'

Domestic Labor and the Age of Discharge at Canadian Indian Residential Schools

Mary Jane Logan McCallum

Survivors of Canadian Indian residential schools and their descendants will often recall discharge from the schools occurring at the age of either sixteen or eighteen. While the difference between the ages of sixteen and eighteen is small, for young adults these years are part of a critical stage of life, and so it is worthwhile thinking through this common recollection. In fact the discharge of students from residential schools at the ages of sixteen or eighteen was a significant point of contention both for parents and other relatives of students as well as for school officials. This chapter examines the struggle over age of discharge between 1920 and 1940 through the lens of correspondence between parents and other family members, the Department of Indian Affairs (DIA) and school staff about the return of female pupils. Parents and other relatives of the students initiated the exchange, requesting that pupils nearing or past the age of sixteen be returned to them because they were needed at home. In response, school staff wanting to retain students to the age of eighteen and beyond insisted that female students needed the further domestic training, moral uplift and protection offered by the schools so that they could be 'fitted' to undertake employment as domestic servants upon discharge. In fact it was often the need of the schools for the domestic labor of female students that was the real concern. On both sides of the issue, gender mattered and the struggle illuminates the importance of young Indigenous women to both economies of colonization and to Indigenous communities.

The residential school system operated between 1879 and 1986 and was a joint initiative of the federal DIA and Catholic and Protestant churches. The system was established as part of the federal responsibility for First Nations education outlined in the British North America Act at Confederation in 1867. Formal education was also an element negotiated into many of the treaties signed between First Nations people and the Crown in the years 1870–1877. The expectation was that education, maintained by the federal government but implemented and controlled by First Nations, would benefit First Nations communities in the future. However, the federal government interpreted its responsibilities in the area of education as helping to facilitate the 'civilization,' Christianization and assimilation of Indigenous people, rather than acknowledging education as a treaty right (Carr-Stewart 2001: 125–43). Residential schools, with their capacity to board children, were favored because they disrupted the influence of Indigenous parents and communities on children and encompassed students in a 'circle of civilization' (Milloy 1999: 33) or a totalizing environment of learning established by the church and the state. Accordingly, in addition to boarding facilities and classrooms, many of the schools had farms and a number of other facilities to teach industrial and vocational education including large kitchens, laundries and gardens.

In 1931, at the height of the Indian residential school system in Canada, there were approximately eighty schools in operation; forty-four were run by Roman Catholics, twenty-one were run by Anglicans, thirteen were run by the United Church of Canada and two were Presbyterian schools (Royal Commission on Aboriginal Peoples 1996: 331–332). It is difficult to place an exact figure on the number of schools, but the Truth and Reconciliation Commission of Canada has identified 139 for its purposes, recognizing that this does not represent the total number of schools that operated in Canada. There were more than 150,000 First Nations, Inuit and Métis children who attended the schools in every province and territory except Newfoundland, Prince Edward Island and New Brunswick. The earliest schools were opened in the east, but more than half of the schools were located in western Canada (Truth and Reconciliation Commission of Canada 2013; Aboriginal Affairs and Northern Development Canada 2013). Chronically underfunded, these schools provided inadequate education. Worse, histories of the schools by ex-pupils and others have shown that at the schools, children faced widespread cultural, physical and sexual violence, deprivation of food, and exposure to unhealthy conditions that fostered diseases like tuberculosis and the Spanish flu, malnutrition and accidental deaths and injuries.

There is a rich historiography of the residential school system that explores the profound connection between colonialism and Indian educational policies and traces the more personal, familial and community-based impacts of the history of residential schooling (see Regan 2011; Furniss 2011; Racette 2009; Milloy 1999; Fournier 1998; Kelm 1999; Miller 1997; Dyck 1997; Graham 1997; Grant 1996; Knockwood 1992; Haig-Brown 1988). Within this literature, an emphasis on education as a tool of colonization, especially cultural assimilation, has tended to overshadow the central place of gendered labor within the institutions and, ultimately, the vital role that the appropriation and regulation of Indigenous labor plays in colonial dispossession. From the 1880s until well after 1951, manual labor and academic study shared equal space in the curriculum of residential schools, also known as the half-day system. A strict division of labor by gender at the schools reflected broader ideologies in Canadian society in which one's work and workplace were supposedly inherited according to gender. Thus, at the schools, female education included housework, sewing and mending, food preparation, washing and ironing. For female students, manual labor was supposed to prepare them to have a 'civilizing' influence on their homes and communities when they became wives and mothers. The acceptance of females at residential schools was in fact originally defended on this premise. Moreover, domestic training was thought to prepare First Nations women to enter the labor market and the broader socioeconomic order as domestic servants (Barman 1995: 343).[1] The third justification for the half-day system was that residential schools were fully dependent upon the manual labor of students (Milloy 1999: 169)—especially older ones. It was also for these reasons that school officials argued for the extension of schooling until students had been placed in domestic service or were married.

Prolonged training, even against the will of students and their families, had profound impacts on Indigenous families and communities. While the historiography of Indian residential schools in Canada is rich, analysis of Indigenous domestic labor and colonization is thin. This reflects a tendency on the part of Canadian historians to write First Nations labor out of Canadian history; moreover, the little scholarship on labor tends to focus on men's work (McCallum 2013). Furthermore, literature on domestic labor history in Canada also tends to bypass Indigenous women's widespread engagement in domestic labor (see for example Kinnear 1998: 110). Yet as I argue elsewhere, domestic training was a fundamental element of Indian education and there was a significant demand for the domestic labor of Indigenous women throughout Canada (McCallum 2013). Sources on this history are few and far between. One important source is correspondence between Indian Affairs officials and parents and guardians of students about the discharge of students and the appropriate 'place' of female students aged sixteen to eighteen.

CORRESPONDENCE

It was practically impossible for First Nations to have any input into colonial Indian policy, which was controlled by the Canadian government largely through the DIA. However the practice of colonial law was highly local, and, it appears, often negotiated and clarified in correspondence between DIA officials located in Ottawa, local Indian agents and school staff, and, sometimes, First Nations people themselves. Throughout the years under study, requests by parents and other relatives for the return of students from residential schools were common and persistent. Indian Commissioner for the prairie provinces William Morris Graham stated in 1926 that 'we have at least 100 applications a year here from Indians, to have children dismissed from school before they are 18 years of age.'[2] In 1929, an Alberta Indian agent explained that 'the parents ask that [the girls] leave at the age of 16 and in most cases they are persistent during the next two years in this request.'[3] Nonetheless, letters by Indigenous people to the Department of Indian Affairs constitute a small element within the archive of DIA correspondence; DIA records mostly consist of conversations about Indigenous people among non-Indigenous people. Thus these letters are very special, particularly to those who read archival records for Indigenous voices. Letters constitute an important part of our written record—which is often presumed to be non-existent and, when acknowledged, is often wrongly presumed to be thoroughly colonized and thus inherently unhelpful to Indigenous research (Russell 2005).

While biography, autobiography and Indigenous literature bring Indigenous writing into focus, everyday formalized compositions such as letters to the DIA are often overlooked as sources of information about the past perhaps because they are so difficult to locate. Once they are located, however, at least within the DIA records, these letters stand out physically: while the vast majority of the files are type-written on standard government or school letterhead, First Nations letters are handwritten on different types of paper, ranging from floral stationery to blank and lined paper of various sizes. Likewise, they stand out in terms of content. Unlike daily correspondence of federal bureaucrats, which tends to be prescriptive, directive and administrative, First Nations letters are more descriptive of the day-to-day lives of Indigenous people, and are thus much more private and personal than what is written by employees of the DIA. These letters can, therefore, ultimately change our perspective on the past. They challenge a traditional view of government policy and Indigenous history that tends to assume that Indigenous people were illiterate and largely unexpressive, and that the objectives of Indian policy were synonymous with the results of the legislation, and caused Indigenous people to, as I read so often in undergraduate essays, 'lose their identity.' Cultural and historical loss was part of the violence of the residential school system—but so too were everyday forms of Indigenous expression and resistance, including letter writing.

In the context of age of discharge disputes, First Nations people wrote to the Department of Indian Affairs for one reason—they wanted those who were in charge to re-evaluate a decision that was negatively impacting their lives. In letters requesting the return of young women, parents and others outlined particular struggles in the context of their arguments for the need of the students' help at home. This reflects the importance of Indigenous women to Indigenous communities socially, culturally, economically and politically (Anderson 2011). It also reflects a specific historical context in which destitute and dislocated households were commonplace; and within which the absence of young women in the home constituted a substantial burden to Indigenous families. One example was the case of Mrs. D., who had pneumonia in the spring of 1937. She wanted her sister, Eva, who was seventeen years old, discharged from school so that she could 'care for her two children and housework while she rests.'[4] The reference to Eva's age of seventeen was likely meant to substantiate Mrs. D's request by connecting it to the legal complex that regulated First Nations people—the Indian Act.

'I Would Like the Girls at Home' 195

The Indian Act (still active today) is a consolidation of pre-Confederation Indian legislation into a nationwide framework and is part of a legal complex that equips the Canadian federal government to operate as a colonial power. The first official Indian Act, *An Act to Amend and Consolidate the Laws Respecting Indians*, became part of the Statutes of Canada in 1876. The Act defines who is and who is not a 'Status Indian' (or an individual who is recorded as an Indian in the Indian Registrar, and thus is eligible for treaty rights, participation in band government and access to Indian land and resources); what is a 'Reserve' (or a tract of land vested in the Crown and set apart for the use of Indians); and a wide-ranging set of regulations, disabilities and penalties that applied to 'Status Indians' and to 'Reserves.'

In terms of education, the Indian Act included clauses about the establishment, operation, management and maintenance of Indian schools, the transportation of children to and from school, the per capita grant system, compulsory school attendance, and penalties for noncompliance. It also outlined age of discharge rules. The 1886 Indian Act described a two-part school attendance law pertaining to age. The first part was that the Governor-in-Council could make regulations to have Indian agents or others commit 'children of Indian blood under the age of sixteen years' to industrial or boarding schools. The second part was that children were to be 'kept, cared for and educated for a period not extending beyond the time at which such children shall reach the age of eighteen years.'[5] Children could be sent to the school until they were sixteen, but kept there until they were eighteen. For a brief period from 1920 to 1930, compulsory attendance only applied to 'every Indian child between the ages of seven and fifteen years.' Moreover, the statement about keeping students until they were eighteen was removed.[6] This change caused backlash from principals and school staff across the country who were frustrated that the age limit had been shortened. In spite of the clear language in the law, staff continued the practice of compelling students over fifteen to attend, although they were uncertain of the limits of their powers to do so and often sought DIA approval and support.

In 1930 the law changed again. The age of discharge was brought back to sixteen and the clause about detaining students until they were eighteen was also reinstated. Now section 10(1) of the Indian Act read:

> Every Indian child between the full ages of seven and sixteen years who is physically able shall attend such day, industrial or boarding school as may be designated by the Superintendent General for the full periods during which such school is open each year; provided that where it has been made to appear to the satisfaction of the Superintendent General that it would be detrimental to any particular Indian child to have it discharged from school on attaining the full age of sixteen years, the Superintendent General may direct that such child be detained at school for such further period as may seem to be advisable, but not beyond the

full age of eighteen years, and in such case the provisions of this section with respect to truancy shall apply to such child and its parents, guardians or persons with whom such child resides during such further period of school attendance.[7]

Mrs. D's request for her sister's help during her illness was thus subject to the law. But the law on the matter of seventeen-year-olds was unclear and ultimately the decision was in the hands of the government. A clause added to the Indian Act in 1920 had allowed for exceptions to compulsory schooling in the event that a child was sick, had passed the entrance exam for high school, or was needed to assist in 'husbandry or urgent and necessary household duties.'[8] This clause reflected compulsory schooling legislation for non-Aboriginal people in Canada. With regard to First Nations children, the application of the exception was subject to the approval of the Department of Indian Affairs, an added layer of control and coercion that did not apply to non-Aboriginal students. In Eva's case, however, the principal did not want to discharge her, preferring that she continue her studies at the school. He felt that over the summer Eva could take a domestic science course that would prepare her for 'suitable employment in a private home.'[9] In such cases, principals commonly prevailed upon parents and guardians that further training was in the best interests of the students. Department of Indian Affairs Superintendent of Education Russell T. Ferrier explained to Indian agent G.A. Stevenson of Selkirk, Manitoba:

> You will realize that the majority of residential school pupils will considerably benefit by remaining in such schools until they are eighteen years of age or even older—this is especially true of the girls for reasons which will readily suggest themselves to you. For these reasons, the Department expects Indian Agents, Principals and others interested in Indian education to make every possible endeavour to persuade parents to leave their children in residential schools for a longer period than that prescribed by the Act.[10]

In the end, it was decided that Eva could have a one-month leave only, and that her training and future placement as a domestic were more important than the immediate needs of her family.

This case clearly outlines how residential schools readily displaced the labor of young adults from their families to other people's homes and the schools themselves. The taken-for-granted way that officials refused parents and other family members who needed their labor at home suggests a deeper, ingrained pattern of hostility towards any efforts by Indigenous families and communities to be self-supporting and economically viable. In a colonizing context, young Indigenous women are in fact only considered 'useful' when their labor is harnessed to non-Indigenous projects. This pattern had the effect of creating a deficit for Indigenous families and communities that is consistent with the arguments made by Indigenous political thinkers in the 1970s and 1980s (see Cardinal 1969; Manitoba Indian Brotherhood 1971; Kirkness 1978; Goodwill 1989). At this time, critics outlined how racist and colonial governance and land policies created a separate and unequal economic system for Indigenous people. Usually segregated from economic centers and unable to raise capital except through the Department of Indian Affairs, Indigenous people living on reserves fared much worse economically compared to the rest of Canada. In terms of capital and labor opportunities, this served to drain reserves of Indigenous money and human resources. While this argument initially tended to center on men, men's work and men's income, literature on Indian control of Indian education, health and employment has challenged us to think more broadly about who and what was affected by this disparity.

The refusal to allow for Eva's discharge was indicative of practices at residential schools that stood apart from non-Indian schools in Canada. For example, it was not until 1970 when all provinces across the country had a minimum age of discharge from as old as fifteen or sixteen (Oreopoulos 2006). Moreover, public school laws did not contain options to refuse the release of students who were over the age limit of attendance. One explanation for this difference was the Department's and Churches' missionary zeal, which encouraged the extension of education, seen as a key tool in assimilation, for longer periods of time. But the Department also had very specific and gendered justifications for retaining students that were essential to the broader project of colonization.

The rationale for decisions by the department was that the education of young Indigenous women was to fit them for domestic service to non-Indigenous people and thus young Indigenous women required training at residential schools until the point at which they were fully employed. This was a closed, circular and self-serving rationale and First Nations challenged this vision with some difficulty. By the time a letter of objection was written to the Department, a number of steps had already been taken to retrieve children from an institution. The process would have usually begun with a request to the principal—it was when this resulted in refusal (or no response), that parents or guardians contacted the Department directly. The Department would then follow up with the principal or other school or Department staff before responding to the parent or guardian. If school staff wanted to refuse the request, they would then make a case against the parents to the Department and ask for their advice. There was a great effort to follow chain of command at the Department, which had the obvious effect of bypassing First Nations people. This makes their letters to the Department all the more valuable and important, as they are the result of much effort and frustration in having their voices and arguments heard. Moreover, letters written by mothers or other female relatives are represented among the most marginalized voices. While Indigenous women engaged in a range of informal political, social and cultural structures, they had no options to engage in formal political structures as they were excluded from voting or running in band, municipal, provincial and federal elections. Nonetheless, their letters directly confront school staff and challenge the DIA's entitlement to make decisions on behalf of their children.

In 1937, Mrs. W. anxiously wrote directly to the DIA concerning her daughters Gladys and Velma, who were sixteen and fourteen years old. She wrote, 'I am in bad health and I cannot do work at home. My husband is dead and [I] have no one to help me besides. I have to go out and work and I would like the girls at home [so they can] help me.' She continued, 'They are not at present going to school . . . so they may as well be helping me at home. . . . The older girl is dissatisfied in school and it would be best for them to come home.'[11] She then adds, 'They can go to school here as we have a new teacher at our school.' When the Indian Department contacted the principal of the school, he responded that it was:

> simply a matter of the mother thinking that they are old enough to do some work and they could therefore perhaps be of use at home. While they were younger she was quite satisfied to have us look after them and now they are old enough to make a contribution to the life of the school she would like to have them at home . . . I beg to point out that it is imperative that we should have a percentage of pupils old enough to carry on the work of the school without any one of them being at all burdened. These two girls are not yet fitted to go out to work and would only become a liability upon the reservation without anything to really occupy their time.[12]

It seems entirely reasonable for parents to send children to school until the point at which they would be useful at home. Moreover, with the option of day schooling available to Gladys and Velma, the Department's argument about the importance of education is doubtful. Rather, the principal simply refused to return Gladys and Velma for two oft-repeated reasons: first because older students' domestic labor was needed at the school and second, because students should not leave the schools until they had obtained employment.

The maintenance and operation of Indian residential schools hinged on student labor. The principal of the Port Alberni Indian Residential School in British Columbia complained bitterly about the lowering of the age of discharge, and thus the ability of parents to withdraw students from the schools 'from the point of business management.' He wrote:

> The whole school plant has been constructed on the understanding that they remain till 18. I find myself with a farm and stock . . . a large steam heating plant . . . a large laundry plant, a large baking outfit, a cooking outfit for 120 people, a sewing and dressmaking Department to do sewing for the 100 children. To help with this work we have 5 boys and

girls who are over 14 years of age and ... some of these are looking for jobs in the canneries.[13]

The dependence of the schools on female domestic labor was both an effect of a colonial vision that aimed to reform Indian girls and women, and a mechanism of colonization—or a tactic by which further dispossession and subjugation could be implemented. Subjugation required the displacement of women's labor and at the same time, colonizing operations required the labor of women.

There is some evidence to suggest that the burden of maintaining operational schools fell disproportionately on the shoulders of female students. Schools were funded by the Department on a per capita grant system and thus school principals were required to justify the presence of pupils over the age limits and did so in annual reports each year to headquarters. The 1936 report on students sixteen or older from the Brandon Indian Residential School in Manitoba illuminates some gender disparity in discharge practices. Of the total of sixty students at that school who were sixteen years of age or older, over half were female (approximately 57 percent) and almost three quarters (73 percent) were recommended to stay. Twenty-six of the thirty-four female students, or 76 percent, were recommended to continue; eighteen of the twenty-six boys were recommended to continue, just slightly below 70 percent. There were some similarities in justifications for retaining both female and male students, such as an interest in continued schooling, access to medical care, and because they were 'good workers.' But there were also some gendered rationales. For example, the principal was more likely to comment on male students needing to continue because they were 'slow in development' mentally, physically or both. In contrast, it was only female students whose continuance was justified by the rationale that they 'needed protection and guidance.'[14] Significantly, in two cases that year, female siblings who were recommended for continuance because it was impossible to secure employment for them near their school were ultimately discharged once the Department was informed that 'suitable homes' were waiting for them.[15] This indicates that while age was a legal category guiding discharge law, in practice discharge was related to a number of other factors including the point at which students began working for wages.

Students and graduates engaged in a continuum of different kinds of work that included unpaid and paid labor. Many female students worked at the schools and in the private homes of many of the missionaries, principals, teachers and other Department and school staff. This kind of work is described by Jane Willis (1973: 177–81) who worked as a domestic for the wife of the principal of St. Philip's Anglican Residential School in Fort George, Quebec. This work involved childcare, including feeding, washing and dressing children and taking them out for a walk, putting them down for naps and sending them out to play as well as housework, including dusting, sweeping, mopping, laundering, ironing, polishing silver, washing windows and washing dishes. Hospitals, nursing stations and mission stations also depended on the domestic labor of Indigenous women, work that was almost always part-time and poorly paid, and arranged by school principals and teachers. In some cases, employment placement was actually an expectation after attending a residential school. For example, Elders at Sandy Bay, Manitoba, remember that some of the female students were taken after they finished school to work at St. Boniface Hospital in Winnipeg. One Elder worked in the annex as a nurse's aide and also in the kitchen with two of her friends. She recalls that 'when some of the girls finished school, the Father came and got us to work for the farmers in Lavinia. . . . Other girls were also taken to St. Boniface to go and work. I worked in the annex as a Nurse's Aide, I emptied bed pans and made beds every morning. I also worked in the kitchen.' Another Elder remembers being taken to St. Boniface by the priest to work at the tuberculosis sanatorium when she left school at the age of eighteen (Beaulieu 1996).

Indigenous women's domestic labor was in demand at the farms and homes of settlers in the area of the schools, and in southern Canada the schools also fed labor into urban economies as well. This is exactly what the schools aimed to do.[16] From the late nineteenth century, when the residential school system developed, student labor was contracted out to local people, some of whom were patrons of the schools—often this was called 'working out.' This system has been examined in the US context, where it appears to have been far more extensive. Originally founded by Captain Pratt at Carlisle Indian School in the 1890s, the 'outing system' had changed dramatically by the 1930s from placing pupils with philanthropic Christian families who wanted to teach students 'the customs of civilized life,' to supplying areas around the schools with Indian labor, which was considered cheaper and more easily controlled (Trennert 1983). These assumptions, forms of apprenticeship and contracting patterns prevailed in various parts of the US, Australia and Canada at this time (Haskins 2001, 2007, 2012; Robinson, and Aird, in this volume; Jacobs 2007; Huggins 1987–88, 1995; White 1987; Titley 1986). The outing system was discussed in the Canadian context as early as 1898 at a Conference on Indian Missions, at which Mr. Monroe, of Regina, explained that the system operated over the summer and workers sent their earnings to their parents. Monroe believed that 'a great deal of the work and of the money on the reserves was lost if the future of the children was to be on the reserves.' He continued, 'The Indians in white peoples' homes would be at least equal to white children from rescue homes.' In other versions of the system discussed, students were sent 'out' for various lengths of time from all or part of the summer to the entire year and pay ranged from nothing, to a suit of clothes.[17] Historian J.R. Miller argues that to the Department, outing encouraged 'acquiring increased proficiency in the English language . . . [and] the habits and ways of thought pertaining to the whites. Moreover, it kept young women isolated from their own people at an age when marriage was a possibility'

(1997: 255–57). Miller also points out the Department's ambiguous views of apprenticeship—it raised the problem of controlling the after-school time and spending money of students. This 'problem' was to continue to frame the Department's decision-making in terms of both discharge decisions and labor placement. Yet Indian agents, principals and others continued to take 'requests' for Indigenous domestic servants—often remarking that demand exceeded supply—and engaging in the placement of Indigenous women in domestic service. In fact, the Department was not only involved in the training of Indigenous domestic servants in its schools, but also in recruiting, contracting, supervising and regulating Indigenous women's domestic labor (McCallum 2008).

There was some conflict between the schools' need for student labor and the demand from local white employers for that labor. At schools which required the per capita of each student to continue their operations and did not have enough older students to maintain the schools, principals were less willing to give up the student to domestic service. But records indicate that often domestic service placement was in fact the preferred route, as opposed to continuing schooling. In a study of a domestics placement scheme in Ottawa, Canada, in the early 1940s, I found that some students were placed out of Ontario residential schools and into domestic work at Ottawa homes, hospitals and schools even before the end of the school year, suggesting that work not only far outranked in importance their education at the schools but also that the demands of white employers outranked those of schools. In conflicts, the Department consistently sided with employers; and when domestics were deemed 'disobedient' or otherwise problematic, they would be returned by the department to residential schools for further 'training.'[18]

While residential schooling was seen to feed directly into waged domestic service, long stays at the schools were also substantially justified on the premise that Indigenous women's education would prepare them to become 'good' wives and mothers and to take on the work themselves of 'civilizing' communities after they graduated or otherwise left the schools. This would entail prolonged education and protection at the schools and the continued separation of children from homes that were deemed unsuitable. In 1936, '*Widow* Mrs. A.' wrote to the Indian Department, 'I wish to inquire of you to grant me my wish by allowing my sixteen year old daughter to leave school to come to help me as I have two little children with me and I have no other support. I have a chance to go out to work if I had her home and I know she is willing to work also and help me support us.' She explained that the family had no home, and that the daughter and mother had planned to work together to get a home. 'We are tired of roaming from place to place,' she wrote.[19]

Correspondence to the DIA such as that of 'Widow Mrs. A.' provides a rare glimpse into the impact of federal Indian policy at the level of family and community from the perspective of women. It was not uncommon for the children who were at residential schools to have come from struggling families. In many cases, their parents were separated, ill or deceased, and there was no means of a reliable source of steady income. First Nations communities suffered from much higher rates of mortality from tuberculosis and other infectious diseases than the non-Aboriginal population, due to general poverty, lack of access to clean water and overcrowded living conditions. Under these circumstances, many First Nations women—especially widows or separated women—worked for wages. This suited traditional patterns in which families relied on older members for assistance in raising younger children. However First Nations have a much lower than average life expectancy and there were especially low numbers of people over the age of sixty-five in First Nations communities.

In such a situation, the presence and labor of young women would be essential. It is in this phase of life, Kim Anderson (2011: 97–125) explains in her book on life stages of Métis, Cree and Anishinaabek women in the 1930s to the 1960s, that Indigenous women took on the 'responsibility of ensuring sustenance for the community and care for the young and old.' She finds that after puberty, adolescent girls were seen to be part of an adult stage of life and responsible for various tasks associated with adult women. At this stage, they traditionally took on responsibilities for the care of children from childbirth upward. They also took on ceremonial and medicinal responsibilities. Young Indigenous women additionally engaged in different forms of labor including gathering, preparing, preserving and distributing food, making and repairing clothing and equipment and, as we see a move towards cash economies, waged labor. Some worked at selling furs, berries, Seneca root, rugs and baskets, work that was done in large groups or cooperatively. However, it was also common for unmarried women to take on independent full-time jobs. Studies on the legacies of the residential schools have examined the intergenerational impacts of not having access to a continued traditional education. Struggling family and community economies of the early twentieth century would have only compounded this process.

The DIA's fear that young Native adults may 'backslide' outweighed its conviction that they needed continued training or placement in domestic service and appears to be the strongest justification for refusal of discharge. Instead of addressing Mrs. A's request for her daughter to leave the school, Agent Moore described her character and home conditions ('not the best') in a letter to the Department. Not only had Mrs. A lost her Mothers' Allowance (an insufficient Ontario government payment to 'worthy' mothers) due to immorality, he argued, and had an eleven-year-old placed at a residential school, she was also living with a man with whom she had another child. On this account, Moore argued it was best to leave her daughter at the school 'as long as possible.'[20]

Scholars have argued that settler colonialism and nation building are gendered projects and demanded of women the physical, mental and emotional labor not only of bearing, raising and socializing children but also of creating and maintaining households and people, from infancy to old age (Perry 2011; Carter 1997, 2009; Simonsen 2006). The domestic sphere and domestic labor commonly featured in rationalizations to refuse the discharge of female students for the same rationalizations. The phrase 'home conditions' was used commonly and the term seems to encompass a wide range of circumstances that included the death or separation of parents, homes lacking modern facilities, small overcrowded spaces, and unemployed heads of households.

Judgments of 'unsatisfactory' conditions were also applied to First Nations communities more generally, and the peril faced by young women in both was not ungendered. The concern about return was also informed by distinct racialized ideas of the 'natural inclinations' of First Nations people. It was felt that female pupils would leave the schools only to find 'trouble' waiting for them, or that they would be an economic or social 'liability' to reserves. This commonly seems to have been about fears of unmarried couples living together, 'illegitimate children' and the influence of irresponsible parents along with the rowdy on young adults, who had spent the majority of their lives in the highly disciplined, sheltered and regulated environment of residential schools. In these situations, it was thought best that female students receive further training in domestic service until they could be placed in 'suitable' jobs as domestic servants.

When the bill to amend sections of the Indian Act, including increasing the age of discharge to eighteen, was debated in the House of Commons in 1930, the justification seems to have merely repeated the broader justification for assimilation policy and the schools more generally; it was a way for students to 'continue to live in the atmosphere in which [they had] been brought up in the school.'[21] It was also framed as a safety net for sixteen-year-olds who did not have homes, families and communities waiting for them when and if they returned. It is unfortunate that the debates did not include a discussion of the frequent and persistent requests by parents for the return of their children. Superintendent of Education Russell Ferrier explained the change in the law using two cases in which the schools were 'morally obligated' to refuse parents' requests for their daughters. In one case, the department refused to discharge Kathleen from school upon repeated requests by her father because Kathleen's mother was dead and her father 'eked out an existence, begging, etc.' in a nearby city. In the other case the DIA refused to return two seventeen-year-old pupils to their mother, Mrs. C. who, Ferrier was convinced, 'wanted her daughters to join her in a life of prostitution.' While he lacked the legal right to do so, Ferrier felt a 'moral obligation to thwart the efforts of an irresponsible parent,' and felt that the DIA should grant school officials the power to keep 'such children' in school until their eighteenth birthday, at which point 'they would be better able to choose wisely for themselves.'[22] By Ferrier's reckoning, if the girls were returned to their mother, 'the best that would happen to them would be early marriage to Indian men or doubtful whites, who are favored by the mother and the man with whom she is living, and a consequent reversion to reserve habits and life.' In contrast, at present the girls were studying at a nearby Collegiate and living in a Christian home 'where their evening activities are thoughtfully supervised.'[23]

When faced with no other option, some parents went to solicitors in order to have their children returned. A local barrister had sent a letter on behalf of Kathleen's father, for example, to the Deputy Superintendent General, requesting Kathleen's discharge.[24] Mrs. C. also went to a Winnipeg solicitor to enforce the age restrictions of the Indian Act. In such cases, Ferrier urged the DIA respondents to convince the solicitors that school was the best option, and to disclose all personal information collected by the DIA about the parents. The DIA did not intend to back down on such cases, even in the event that it was unsuccessful in convincing the solicitor to drop the case.[25] This illustrates the coercive power of colonial authorities to make decisions on behalf of Indigenous families and communities, even in the face of efforts to resist. The Department was profoundly invested in the domestic training and labor of Indigenous women and was prepared to go to great lengths to ensure that this investment paid off, once it was set in motion.

OTHER VOICES

Struggles over age of discharge provide a sketch of colonization and domestic service in the context of residential schools in the early twentieth century. These two points of view, while dominant, do not represent the entirety of opinions about the proper place of young First Nations women in Canada. Dissenting voices were scarce—yet there were a few. Compulsory manual labor at residential schools was not free of critics who felt that it hindered academic education and overtaxed the students. In addition, some department officials agreed with parents on discharge cases; however, they did so mostly in cases where there was no room at the school for extra students. Other reasons included complaints that female students over sixteen were sullen, baneful, revengeful or rowdy, or an overall nuisance and even a demoralizing influence on younger girls. In a few other instances the case was made that discharge was in the interests of establishing good relations between First Nations people and the DIA. Only one letter suggested that detaining students under the pretenses of education was actually deceptive, and that more children than not would be better off at home.[26] I found no evidence of any parent or guardian requesting that their children stay past the age of sixteen at the schools, despite it being clear that many of the students did not have homes to return to when they became old enough to leave and many of those who stayed past this age had very few other choices. It is significant that for many families, especially during the Depression, residential schools were the only means of ensuring children were fed and clothed. Indeed, historian Brenda Child finds that in the United States,

Indian boarding schools had their highest enrollments during these years (Child 2013: 99).

The almost singular focus of domestic training for female students at Indian schools came under some scrutiny after World War II. In 1942, a special House of Commons Committee on Postwar Reconstruction and Reestablishment was struck to conduct several hearings to identify issues of importance that would likely face Canada following the war and solutions that reflected Canadians' postwar reality. In this period, the marked inequality of First Nations people within Canada became a matter of national concern and the Committee considered the efficacy of a segregated system of Indian education—in particular residential schools. One of the chief questioners, Dorise Nielsen (a Member of Parliament from Saskatchewan), voiced her objection to the conventional opinion that Indian girls were 'best fitted for domestic service,' stating, 'It seems to me that there is something wrong with our whole attitude towards these young girls. Why should Indian girls be more fitted for domestic service than any other type of girl? Why should we not endeavor to fit these girls . . . in the usual life of the country and to go into various forms of service?' She continued, 'Why not give them every opportunity and facility, if they are capable of absorbing it?' Nielsen's larger argument was about the importance of equal opportunity in education and employment in order that Indigenous people could be absorbed by the larger Canadian nation (quoted in Shewell 2004: 149). This view was indicative of a shift in Indian policy in the postwar years towards integration, reflected in an increasing preference for day schools over residential schools, and the integration of Indigenous children into provincial schools—a move that would encourage a grand transition from reserve life to the so-called Canadian way of life. Significantly, even in a period of integration, training for domestic service followed through as a mainstay of curriculum for Indigenous female students and domestic service remained a key area of employment for Indigenous women.

CONCLUSION

Indigenous scholars argue that Indigenous women are doubly disadvantaged in societies that are colonial and patriarchal (Anderson 2000; Smith 2005; Green 2007; Sunseri 2011; Huhndorf and Suzack 2010). Yet the irony is that while Indigenous women were assigned a low status in these societies, their place within them was vitally important. This becomes very clear in the age of discharge disputes of the early twentieth century. The labor of young Indigenous women was crucial to the economies of colonization. The physical operation of residential schools was fully dependent on the labor of female students who sewed uniforms, cooked, cleaned, laundered and gardened. This training was to prepare them for jobs as domestics outside of the schools, where they were greatly in demand by surrounding communities. At the same time, Indigenous communities were struggling in the early twentieth century, and this was compounded by the absence of young women who were refused discharge from residential schools. Letters from parents requesting the return of daughters illustrate their centrality to family economies, and the roles young women would have undertaken there. These included helping out with young children while mothers worked, helping out with caring for the sick and also engaging in paid labor to contribute to family economies. In Canada, education for and employment in domestic service were to play a key role in the colonization of Indigenous people. Efforts to displace and also replace domestic labor reflect the gendered and racialized nature of colonial projects as well as the central place of Indigenous women within our history.

NOTES

1. Discharge forms for students in the schools had columns for 'Trade or Industry Taught and Proficiency in it': 'Domestic' was all that was put in the column for many of the female students who were discharged. In 'Reasons for discharge' columns, there included the following: reached age limit, asked for by mother, sent to sanatorium, run away, incorrigible, parents request for them, and to go to day school.
2. Library and Archives Canada (hereafter LAC), Record Group 10—Indian Affairs (hereafter RG 10), volume 7184, file 1/25–1–5–7 pt. 1, letter to the Secretary J.D. McLean from W.M. Graham, Indian Commissioner, February 19, 1926.
3. LAC, RG 10, volume 7184, file 1/25–1–5–7 pt. 1, letter to the Secretary from Indian Agent at Gleichen, Alberta, February 22, 1929.
4. LAC, RG 10, volume 6209, file 468–10 pt. 1, letter from Medical Superintendent Caradoc to the Secretary, Indian Affairs Branch, March 12, 1937.
5. The Statutes of Canada, 43 V, c28, s138.2, 1886.
6. The Statutes of Canada, 10–11 George V, c50, s10, 1920.
7. The Statutes of Canada, 20–21 George V, c25, s10, 1930.
8. The Statutes of Canada, 10–11 George V, c50, s10.2 and s10.3, 1920. By the 1951 Act, the time allowed for the third exemption was no less than six weeks.
9. LAC, RG 10, volume 6209, file 468–10 pt. 1, letter from Medical Superintendent Caradoc to Secretary, Indian Affairs Branch, March 12, 1937.
10. LAC, RG 10, volume 7184, file 1/25–1–5–7 pt. 1, letter from Russell T. Ferrier, Superintendent of Indian Education, to C.A. Stevenson, Indian Agent Selkirk, Manitoba, June 30, 1927.
11. LAC, RG 10, volume 6209, file 468–10 pt. 1, letter to Indian Department from Mrs. Louisa Williams, August 13, 1937.
12. LAC, RG 10, volume 6209, file 468–10 pt. 1, letter to Philip Phelan from Oliver Strapp, September 25, 1937.
13. LAC, RG 10, volume 7184, file 1/25–1–5–7 pt. 1, letter from Principal Pitts, Indian Residential School, Alberni, October 4, 1929.
14. LAC, RG 10, volume 6258, file 576–10 pt. 9, letter to the Secretary, Department of Indian Affairs, from J.A. Doyle, Principal of Brandon Indian Residential School, May 27, 1936.

15. LAC, RG 10, volume 6258, file 576–10 pt. 9, letter to J.A. Doyle from J.D. Sutherland, June 16, 1936.
16. LAC, RG 10, volume 6205, file 468–1 pt. 2, letter to Department from Principal McVitty, Mount Elgin Institute, May 31, 1929, and volume 6205, file 468–1 pt. 1, letter to Rev. Dr. Sutherland, Muncee, The Institute, from Principal McVitty, Mount Elgin Institute, December 10, 1908.
17. 'Indian Missions: Closing of the Conference in St. Andrews Church,' *Manitoba Morning Free Press*, Saturday, November 7, 1898, 5.
18. See for example two conflicts over vacation time: LAC, RG 10, volume 3199, File 504, 178–5, letter to Mr. Morris from C.A. Primeau, June 11, 1943, and letter to C.A. Primeau from R.A. Hoey, June 14, 1943.
19. LAC, RG 10, volume 6209, file 468–10 pt. 1, letter to Indian Department from Mrs. Ethel Abram, Southwold, Ontario/Oneida, September 16, 1936. Original emphasis.
20. LAC, RG 10, volume 6209, file 468–10 pt. 1, letter to secretary, Indian Affairs Branch, from A.D. Moore, Indian Agent, September 27, 1937.
21. Debates of the House of Commons, Dominion of Canada Session 1930 Volume 1, March 31, 1930, 1108.
22. LAC, RG 10, volume 7184, file 1/25–1–5–7 pt. 1, memorandum from Superintendent of Education Russell Ferrier, February 16, 1929.
23. LAC, RG 10, volume 7184, file 1/25–1–5–7 pt. 1, letter to Mr. Bunn, Inspector of Indian Agencies, Winnipeg, from Russell T. Ferrier, Superintendent of Indian Education, December 26, 1924.
24. LAC, RG 10, volume 7184, file 1/25–1–5–7 pt. 1, letter to Mr. Sweet, Barrister, Brantford from Duncan Campbell Scott, Deputy Superintendent General, February 5, 1927.
25. LAC, RG 10, volume 7184, file 1/25–1–5–7 pt. 1, letter to Mr. Bunn, Inspector of Indian Agencies, Winnipeg, from Russell T. Ferrier, Superintendent of Indian Education December 26, 1924.
26. LAC, RG 10, volume 7184, file 1/25–1–5–7 pt. 1, letter to Secretary Indian Affairs J.D. McLean from W.M. Graham, Indian Commissioner, March 3, 1926.

REFERENCES

Aboriginal Affairs and Northern Development Canada. 2013. 'List of Recognized Institutions.' www.aadnc-aandc.gc.ca/eng/1100100015606/1100100015611. Accessed August 8, 2013

Anderson, Kim. 2000. *A Recognition of Being: Reconstructing Native Womanhood.* Toronto: Sumach Press.

Anderson, Kim. 2011. *Life Stages and Native Women: Memory, Teachings, and Story Medicine.* Winnipeg: University of Manitoba Press.

Barman, Jean. 1995. 'Separate and Unequal: Indian and White Girls at All Hallows School, 1884–1920.' In *Children, Teachers and Schools in the History of British Columbia*, edited by Jean Barman, Neil Sutherland and J. Donald Wilson, 337–57. Calgary: Detselig Enterprises.

Beaulieu, George. 1996. *Sandy Bay Anishinabek: The Elders Tell Their Stories.* Manitoba: Sandy Bay Education Foundation.

Cardinal, Harold. 1969. *The Unjust Society.* Vancouver: MG Hurtig.

Carr-Stewart, Sheila. 2001. 'A Treaty Right to Education.' *Canadian Journal of Education* 26(2): 125–43.

Carter, Sarah. 1997. *Capturing Women: The Manipulation of Cultural Imagery in Canada's Prairie West.* Montreal: McGill-Queen's University Press.

Carter, Sarah. 2009. *The Importance of Being Monogamous: Marriage and Nation Building in Western Canada to 1915*. Edmonton: University of Alberta Press.

Child, Brenda. 2013. *Holding Our World Together: Ojibwe Women and the Survival of Community*. Reprint Edition. New York: Penguin.

Dyck, Noel. 1997. *Differing Visions: Administering Indian Residential Schooling in Prince Albert 1867–1995*. Halifax: Fernwood Press.

Fournier, Suzanne. 1998. *Stolen from Our Embrace*. Vancouver and Toronto: Douglas & Mcintyre.

Furniss, Elizabeth. 2011. *Victims of Benevolence: The Dark Legacy of the Williams Lake Indian Residential School*, 2nd ed. Vancouver: Arsenal Pulp Press.

Goodwill, Jean. 1989. 'Indian and Inuit Nurses of Canada.' *Canadian Woman Studies* 10(2&3): 117–23.

Graham, Elizabeth. 1997. *The Mush Hole: Life at Two Residential Schools*. Waterloo: Hefle Publishing.

Grant, Agnes. 1996. *No End of Grief: Indian Residential Schools in Canada*. Toronto: Pemmican Publications.

Green, Joyce. 2007. 'Taking Account of Aboriginal Feminism.' In *Making Space for Indigenous Feminism*, edited by Joyce Green, 20–31. London: Zed Books.

Haig-Brown, Celia. 1988. *Resistance and Renewal: Surviving the Indian Residential School*. Vancouver: Arsenal Pulp Press.

Haskins, Victoria. 2001. 'On the Doorstep: Aboriginal Domestic Service as a "Contact Zone."' *Australian Feminist Studies* 16(34): 13–25.

Haskins, Victoria. 2007. 'Domestic Service and Frontier Feminism: The Call for a Woman Visitor to "Half-Caste" Girls and Women in Domestic Service, Adelaide, 1925–1928.' *Frontiers: A Journal of Women Studies* 28(1&2): 124–94.

Haskins, Victoria. 2012. *Matrons and Maids: Regulating Indian Domestic Service in Tucson, 1914–1934*. Tucson: University of Arizona Press.

Huggins, Jackie. 1987–88. '"Firing On in the Mind": Aboriginal Women Domestic Servants in the Inter-war Years.' *Hecate* 8(2): 5–23.

Huggins, Jackie. 1995. 'White Aprons Black Hands: Aboriginal Women Domestic Servants in Queensland.' *Labor History* 69(November): 188–95.

Huhndorf, Shari M., and Cherly Suzack. 2010. 'Indigenous Feminism: Theorizing the Issues.' In *Indigenous Women and Feminism: Politics, Activism, Culture*, edited by Cheryl Suzack, Shari M. Huhndorf, Jeanne Perrault and Jean Barman, 1–20. Vancouver: University of British Columbia Press.

Jacobs, Margaret. 2007. 'Working on the Domestic Frontier: American Indian Domestic Servants in White Women's Households in the San Francisco Bay Area, 1920–1940.' *Frontiers: A Journal of Women Studies* 28(1&2): 165–99.

Kelm, Mary Ellen. 1999. *Colonizing Bodies: Aboriginal Health and Healing in British Columbia, 1900–50*. Vancouver: University of British Columbia Press.

Kinnear, Mary. 1998. *A Female Economy: Women's Work in a Prairie Province 1870–1970*. Montreal: McGill-Queen's University Press.

Kirkness, Verna. 1978. *Evaluation Report: Education of Indians in Federal and Provincial Schools in Manitoba*. Ottawa: Department of Indian Affairs and Northern Development.

Knockwood, Isabelle. 1992. *Out of the Depths: The Experiences of Mi'kmaw Children at the Indian Residential School of Schubenacadie, Nova Scotia*. Lockeport: Roseway Publishing.

Manitoba Indian Brotherhood. 1971. *Wahbung: Our Tomorrows*. Winnipeg: Manitoba Indian Brotherhood.

McCallum, Mary Jane Logan. 2008. 'Labour, Modernity and the Canadian State: A History of Aboriginal Women and Work in the Mid-Twentieth Century.' PhD thesis, University of Manitoba, Canada.

McCallum, Mary Jane Logan. 2013. *Indigenous Labour and Indigenous History, 1940–1980*. Winnipeg: University of Manitoba Press.
Miller, J. R. 1997. *Shingwauk's Vision: A History of Native Residential Schools*. Toronto: University of Toronto Press.
Milloy, John. 1999. *A National Crime: The Canadian Government and the Residential School System—1879–1986*. Winnipeg: University of Manitoba Press.
Oreopoulos, Philip. 2006. 'The Compelling Effects of Compulsory Schooling: Evidence from Canada.' *The Canadian Journal of Economics* 39(1): 22–52.
Perry, Adele. 2011. *On the Edge of Empire: Gender, Race, and the Making of British Columbia 1849–1871*. Toronto: University of Toronto Press.
Racette, Sherry Farrell. 2009. 'Haunted: First Nations Children in Residential School Photography.' In *Depicting Canada's Children*, edited by Loren Lerner, 49–84. Waterloo: Wilfred Laurier Press.
Regan, Paulette. 2011. *Unsettling the Settler Within: Indian Residential Schools, Truth Telling, and Reconciliation in Canada*. Vancouver: UBC Press.
Royal Commission on Aboriginal Peoples. 1996. *Report of the Royal Commission on Aboriginal Peoples: Looking Forward, Looking Back*, vol. 1. Ottawa: Canada Communications Group.
Russell, Lynette. 2005. 'Indigenous Knowledge and Archives: Accessing Hidden History and Understandings.' *Australian Indigenous Knowledge and Libraries* 36(2): 169–80.
Shewell, Hugh. 2004. *'Enough to Keep Them Alive': Indian Welfare in Canada, 1873–1965*. Toronto: University of Toronto Press.
Simonsen, Jane E. 2006. *Making Home Work: Domesticity and Native American Assimilation in the American West, 1860–1919*. Chapel Hill: University of North Carolina Press.
Smith, Andrea. 2005. *Conquest: Sexual Violence and American Indian Genocide*. Cambridge: South End Press.
Sunseri, Lina. 2011. *Being Again of One Mind: Oneida Women and the Struggle for Decolonization*. Vancouver: University of British Columbia Press.
Titley, Brian. 1986. 'Indian Industrial Schools in Western Canada.' In *Schools in the West—Essays in Canadian Educational History*, edited by Nancy M. Sheehan, J. Donald Wilson and David C. Jones, 133–53. Calgary: Detselig Enterprises Limited.
Trennert, Robert. 1983. 'From Carlisle to Phoenix: The Rise and Fall of the Indian Outing System 1878–1930.' *The Pacific Historical Review* 52(3): 267–91.
Truth and Reconciliation Commission of Canada. 2013. 'Residential School Locations.' http://www.trc.ca/websites/trcinstitution/index.php?p=12. Accessed August 8, 2013.
White, Pamela Margaret. 1987. 'Restructuring the Domestic Sphere—Prairie Indian Women on Reserves: Image, Ideology and State Policy 1880–1930.' PhD thesis, McGill University, Canada.
Willis, Jane. 1973. *Geneish: An Indian Girlhood*. Toronto: New Press.

12 White Mistresses and Chinese 'Houseboys'

Domestic Politics in Singapore and Darwin from the 1910s to the 1930s

Claire Lowrie

The 1910s to the 1930s marked a time of change and upheaval across the colonial world. While small numbers of white women had long played a role in empire as wives, missionaries, travelers and workers, the period saw significant increases in the numbers of British, European, American and Australian women visiting and settling in colonies throughout Southeast Asia and the Pacific (Bulbeck 1992: 207; Knapman 1986: 142; Stoler 2002: 33). Colonial administrators regarded the increasing numbers of white women visiting and settling in the colonies as a welcome development; however, these women were publicly condemned in the local press and often by their own husbands and fathers as unsuitable colonizers (see for example Knapman 1986: 16).

Negative assessments of white women were certainly prolific in the neighboring British colonial ports of Singapore and Darwin for which there exists a wealth of memoirs, travel accounts, newspaper articles and oral histories produced about and by British and white Australian women. Drawing on these sources, this chapter explores how white women in Singapore and Darwin pursued household management with vigor, perhaps in part as an attempt to prove their worth to the colonial venture in the context of intense public criticism. But try as they might to assert their control over the home, white women in Singapore and Darwin were confronted by Chinese male servants who they claimed continually contested their authority. This chapter argues that white mistresses' persistent claims that their Chinese male servants were increasingly insolent and assertive need to be considered in context of the nationalist, anti-colonial and communist ideologies which overseas Chinese communities were grappling with in this era.

The absence of accounts from Chinese 'houseboys' and cooks themselves makes it impossible to determine whether these servants were actively seeking to usurp the power and authority of the white mistress. Chinese servants in Darwin and Singapore had always advocated for fair wages and good working conditions and reports of Chinese servants stealing from and assaulting employers can be found from the late nineteenth century. Some mistresses dismissed the insolence of their Chinese servants as stemming from a patriarchal dislike of taking orders from a woman. Nonetheless, the

White Mistresses and Chinese 'Houseboys' 211

increasingly resistant response of Chinese men to white mistresses in the twentieth century went beyond gender politics.

Chinese nationalism and more radical political developments, including trade unionism and communism which gained strength in the wake of the Chinese Revolution of 1911, placed a great deal of emphasis on the need to challenge the exploitation of ordinary workers and criticized imperialism in all of its forms (Yong and McKenna 1990; Yong 1997; Ban 2001; Bayly and Harper 2004). The influence of these ideologies on Chinese workers in Singapore and Darwin is illustrated by their active involvement in labor strikes and demonstrations in the 1920s and 1930s. The influence of ideas about working men's rights and the wrongs of colonial oppression ensured that Chinese men were even less willing than in previous periods to play the part of the loyal and servile Chinese 'boy.'

The focus of historians on the highly publicized anxieties regarding the possibility of interracial sex between white mistresses and their non-white male servants has yielded impressive insights into the gendered and sexualized nature of colonial power relations. In colonial situations in India, Malaya, Singapore, Australia, Papua New Guinea, Natal and the United States, the potential for sexual encounters (consensual and otherwise) between white women and non-white men provoked intense public concern which at times spilled over into racial violence (Sinha 1995: 2, 7; Bulbeck 1992: 206; Inglis 1975: 54–55; Keegan 2001: 459; Hodes 1997: 2–3). As Anne McClintock has argued, the sexual 'contagion' of white women by 'native' men represented a symbolic and practical threat to 'white male and imperial potency' (1995: 33). Male servants, who were widely employed in European homes in tropical colonies up until the 1930s, were considered to be particularly threatening in that they had intimate access to white women, 'unguarded and unsupervised by White men' (Martens 2002: 396; Bagnall 2002: 21; for further discussion of the preference for male domestic servants in tropical colonies see Higman; Dussart; and Nilan, Artini and Threadgold in this volume). Thus, European colonists attempted to both signal and downplay the threat to white patriarchal and colonial power which 'native' male servants represented by referring to them in demeaning and infantilizing terms as 'houseboy' and 'boy' regardless of their age (Martinez and Lowrie 2009: 307; Haskins and Maynard 2005: 206; Chin 1998: 71; Proschan 2002: 436, 449; Louie 2002: 3; Morrell 1998: 616).

By focusing on the political significance of everyday encounters between white women and Chinese men in Singapore and Darwin, however, this chapter offers new insights into the mistress–servant relationship in colonial societies. While the public discourse may well have been preoccupied with sex, British and white Australian women's accounts of their Chinese male servants in Singapore and Darwin contain notably little discussion of sexual intimacy, attraction or fear. A much more marked feature of these accounts is a struggle between white women and Chinese servants for power and control in the home.

Drawing on Ann Laura Stoler's (2002) conception of the colonial home as a highly charged political space, this chapter explores how the competing ambitions of British, Australian and Chinese nationalist and imperialist politics affected the relationships between white mistresses and Chinese servants. I argue that at the same time as white women were attempting to master their servants in order to fulfil their colonial and postcolonial destinies, Chinese 'houseboys' and cooks were asserting their status not as subordinate servants but as workers with rights, in line with a world view influenced by anti-colonial and communist values.

TRANSCOLONIAL TRADITIONS OF DOMESTIC SERVICE IN SINGAPORE AND DARWIN

The neighboring British colonial ports of Singapore and Darwin were in many ways very different colonial societies. Darwin was part of a settler colony where the intended outcome of colonization was permanent white settlement based on the dispossession of the Indigenous populations. Singapore was by contrast an exploitation colony where the aim was to export commodities rather than achieving permanent settlement. The different colonial objectives in Singapore and Darwin became more obvious following Australian Federation in 1901, after which Darwin became part of a settler nation rather than a British colony. But while there were significant differences between the two port towns, there were also marked similarities and a history of connection and interaction. A shared tropical climate, similar multiethnic populations and an exchange of trade and migrants along the steamship lines which ran between them resulted in the cultivation of a similar tropical colonial culture. Indeed, the white elites of Darwin who hoped that the port town might one day be 'the Singapore of Australia' actively embraced a lifestyle that mirrored that of the British in Singapore, by donning white plantation suits and *solar topees* (pith helmets) and by employing a multiethnic entourage of domestic servants (Searcy 1984: 70).

For the relatively small numbers of British and white Australian colonists in Singapore and Darwin, as with colonists in other tropical European colonies, the presence of multiple servants in the home not only related to the ready availability of relatively cheap domestic labor in tropical colonies but was considered essential to managing the ravages of the tropical climate (Buckley 1969: 357; Martinez and Lowrie 2009: 308). The ability to employ large numbers of so-called 'colored' servants was also viewed as a symbol of the power and status of white colonizers (Martens 2002: 394; Stoler 2002: 133; Locher-Scholten 1998: 135; Munn 2004: 372–73). From the mid-nineteenth century into the 1920s in British tropical colonies such as Singapore, Malaya, Hong Kong, India and Northern Rhodesia, a minimum of three and often more than six servants were employed in modest white colonial households (Butcher 1979: 79–80; Munn 2004, 372–73;

Blunt 1999: 429; Hansen 1989: 45). By contrast, in Britain one servant was the norm throughout the eighteenth and nineteenth centuries (Steedman 2009: 28). While up to five servants were employed in upper-class homes in Britain at the turn of the twentieth century, following the First World War middle-class families were lucky to afford even one (Blunt 1999: 429; Butcher 1979: 142). In Darwin, elite white families employed at least five servants and working-class families employed two (Rosenzweig 1996: 42, 46, 51, 52). In contrast, in the southeastern Australian colonies at the turn of the century, upper/middle-class white families employed only one servant (Higman 2002: 45).

Domestic work in Darwin and Singapore was organized around a hierarchy of race and gender. Male servants were preferred over female servants at least up until the 1920s, as was typical across European tropical colonies in Southeast Asia, Africa, India and the Pacific. In temperate British colonies and former colonies, including the southeastern regions of Australia and New Zealand, local-born white women, migrant women from the United Kingdom and smaller numbers of Indigenous women formed the bulk of the servant class (Higman 2002: 61; Hamilton 1993: 71–91; Pickles

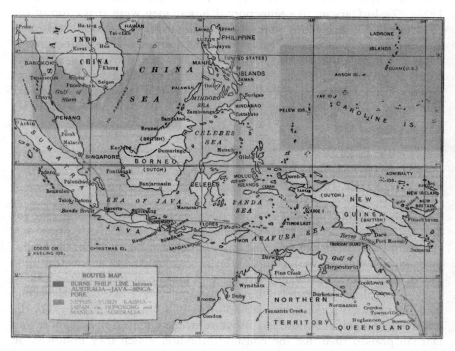

Figure 12.1 Burns Philp Steamship Line between Singapore and Darwin. *Picturesque Travel*, Burns Philp and Company, no. 6, 1925. From the collections of the National Library of Australia.

2001: 22–44). The preference for male servants in tropical colonies was also distinctly different from Britain and Europe where a feminization of domestic service had taken place by the early nineteenth century (Meldrum 2000: 118–20; Steedman 2009: 13; Sarti 2006: 188–89; Fairchilds 1984: 185–86).

Historians have provided a variety of reasons for why male servants were employed in greater numbers than female servants in hot climate colonies, including the strenuous nature of the work, the more ready availability of male laborers and fears about the (perceived) sexual threat female servants presented in male dominated white households (Constable 1997: 42; Martens 2002: 393; Hansen 1989: 30; Banerjee 2004: 30; Munn 2004: 369). Whatever the reason for the initial preference for male domestic servants, the 'houseboy' came to be associated with the luxury which Europeans expected in the tropics.

In Singapore in 1883, male servants accounted for 95 percent of the servant population (Bird 1990: 116). Most 'houseboys' and cooks employed inside British homes were Chinese from the Hainanese dialect group. Malay and Indian men were usually employed in menial and outdoor tasks as *punkah* pullers, water carriers, gardeners and drivers, reflecting prevailing racial conceptions of these workers as 'less civilised' (Chin 1998: 71; Lai 1986: 77). In Darwin, like Singapore, Chinese men were at the top of the hierarchy of servants. They were drawn from the majority 'coolie' class and included individuals from the Sze Yap, Heung-san and Hakka dialect groups (Daly 1887: 233; Jones 2005: 58). Aboriginal men and women were incorporated into the lowest scale of this racialized hierarchy of domestic service, the men being mostly employed as outdoor manual laborers in gardening, laundering and water-carrying (Lockwood 1968: 104, 105; McGrath 1987: 33, 53).

LOYAL CHINESE 'BOYS'? THE MASTER–SERVANT RELATIONSHIP, 1890S–1910S

Racialized notions of Chinese 'houseboys' as the most loyal and efficient domestic servants ensured that they came to be the most highly prized servants not only in Darwin and Singapore but also in Hong Kong, the Philippines and Hawaii, as well as in California and Vancouver at least until the end of the First World War (Martinez and Lowrie 2012: 520–25; Salmon 1892: 95; Palmer 1989: 67; Dubinsky and Givertz 2003: 75). The white men who made up the primary employers of Chinese 'houseboys' in the years before significant numbers of white women arrived in Singapore and Darwin praised them for the constant attention which they bestowed on their masters and their ability to preempt their needs.[1] Yet alongside claims of devotion and servility were accounts of theft and violence perpetrated by Chinese servants against their masters.[2]

In Singapore public angst about the alleged criminal nature of the 'houseboy' prompted calls from 1886 for Chinese servants to be registered so that their employers might be able to identify them (thereby having more control over the process of hiring and firing them). A registration ordinance was passed in 1888 but was never implemented, due in part to the refusal of servants to register and an active campaign of resistance by Hainanese *kongsi* organizations (secret societies) (Song 1984: 238–39, 482). The central role which Hainanese *kongsi* played in recruiting domestic servants made a mass strike of domestic servants a very real possibility and as such their resistance to the scheme was taken seriously (Peleggi 2012: 21). While their key role lay in organizing the migrant labor workforce, Chinese *kongsi* were demonized by the colonial government as criminal organizations and were banned from 1890 (Trocki 1990: 3, 11–12, 38).

Figure 12.2 'Chinese Man Servant with His European Master,' Singapore, 1908. Courtesy of the National Archives of Singapore.

216 Claire Lowrie

Figure 12.3 'Chinese Staff Employed by Dr Gilruth. Ah Chow (Seated), Ah Bong (Table Boy), Ah How (Dobie) and House Boy,' Darwin, c.1912–1919. Gilruth Collection, Northern Territory Library.

As I have argued elsewhere, the emphasis which white men in Singapore and Darwin placed on their Chinese servants as servile and loyal attendants was a strategy white men used to reaffirm their status as uncontested masters in the face of constant challenges by their servants (Lowrie 2013: 48, 51–52). Such strategies are reflected in the photographs of servants commissioned by British and white Australian employers. Unnamed Chinese 'houseboys' studiously serving their white masters or standing at the ready were popular subjects for photographers in both Darwin and Singapore.[3] Yet even in such a choreographed medium the unstable nature of the master–servant hierarchy was visible. In the image from Singapore (Figure 12.2), the white man is the epitome of a colonial master dressed in pristine tropical whites and with a nearby solar topee marking his status as a ruler. Yet his Chinese servant hardly matches the ideal of the submissive 'boy.' He stares down the camera with a stance which is at once servile (fan in hand) yet also assertive (hand on hip).[4]

The example from Darwin (Figure 12.3)—an image from Administrator John Gilruth's family album—attests to the wealth and power of this elite family who could afford to employ an entourage of Asian servants including three Chinese men and another male servant possibly of Timorese or Ceylonese origin. Rather than the deference or servility one might expect of loyal 'boys,' however, these men stare at the camera with disinterest or even apathy. The inclusion of the surnames of the three Chinese servants ensures that the viewer sees them as individuals rather than anonymous and silent servants.

Further indications of tension in the master–servant relationship can be found in Chinese 'houseboys'' reputation for alleged sexual perversion (Proschan 2002: 626, 629; Aldrich 2003: 204–205). White men in Darwin and Singapore sought to come to terms with the sexual anxiety and curiosity sparked by their intimate contact with Chinese servants by depicting them as feminized and eunuch-like 'boys' (Lowrie 2013). There are indications, especially in terms of the photographic record, that concerns about the perceived sexual threat which the Chinese 'houseboy' represented may have been amplified following the increase in the numbers of white women settling in Singapore and Darwin from the 1910s onwards. While white women were regularly pictured with their female servants in Singapore and Darwin, images of white women with Chinese male servants seem to be nonexistent.[5] For British and white Australian colonists, the close contact which white women shared with their Chinese male servants behind closed doors was perhaps best left to the imagination. Certainly there was robust public commentary on Chinese men's sexuality in Darwin and Singapore during this period, particularly concerning Chinese masters of servants (see Lowrie 2011; Lowrie 2008: 344–56) and this may have impacted on white mistresses' perceptions of their Chinese domestic servants. Yet reference to the issue in white women's accounts of their servants is rare indeed.[6] A far more prevalent complaint was their difficulty in asserting power over their Chinese male servants.

As Ann Laura Stoler has so compelling illustrated, exercising power in the home was an important expression of colonizer status. At the same time, however, intimate contact and conflict between non-white servants and their employers had the potential to destabilize the hierarchical distinctions on which colonial society was based (Stoler 2002: 123, 216, 129, 133; Stoler 2001, 831). Newly arrived white women in Darwin and Singapore found themselves struggling against a tirade of publically aired anti-white woman rhetoric which questioned their ability to be effective colonizers. The refusal of Chinese men to submit to their mastery presented a further challenge to white women's colonial and postcolonial legitimacy and, as such, the struggle for control over the home became the focus of their attention.

IDLE *MEMS* AND WEARY WIVES: WHITE WOMEN IN THE TROPICS

From the 1910s, the numbers of British women in Malaya and Singapore was on the rise, and similar demographic changes were also occurring in Darwin.[7] In Singapore, the European female population included small numbers of single working women such as teachers, missionaries, nurses, doctors and prostitutes. The bulk of the female population, however, were the wives of government officials, merchants, bankers, lawyers, doctors and military men (Butcher 1979: 141–42; Marriott 1991: 348). Similarly, British and white Australian female missionaries, domestic servants and governess occasionally traveled to Darwin for work. However, most white women living in the port town were the wives of the officers of the British Australian Telegraph Company, government officials, traders and merchants (Hammond 1998: 15; Lockwood 1968: 62, 93).

Throughout the nineteenth century, tropical colonies had been viewed as unsuitable for the long-term settlement of the 'white race' with white women and children considered to be particularly vulnerable to its perceived degenerating affects (Anderson 2005: 75). By the 1920s, however, developments in tropical medicine which brought diseases like malaria under control ensured that the tropical climate was not viewed as an impediment to the settlement of white women to the same degree as in previous eras. Along with improvements in housing and infrastructure, this encouraged more women to travel to colonies like British Malaya (Butcher 1979: 135). The increasing numbers of white women traveling to the colonies also stemmed from the new social and political freedoms which were emerging in the wake of the first wave feminist movement and the First World War as well as changing ideas about women's place in the colonial project. Empire had long been viewed as the prerogative of white men. From the late nineteenth century, however, the supposedly innate domesticating and nurturing qualities of white women was increasingly seen as essential to the colonial civilizing mission. In colonies and former colonies, the imperialist and nationalist rhetoric of the era emphasized that white women had a duty to 'civilize' white men and 'native' others on the frontier. In particular, their presence was intended to mediate against 'miscegenation' (Haskins 2007: 124; Lake 1996: 12–20; Keegan 2001: 460; Spear 1999: 51; Rafael 1995: 642; Grimshaw 1989: *xii*).

For the administrators of Singapore and Darwin at least, the increasing numbers of white women was a positive development. While in Singapore, the white woman's key role was seen in terms of stabilizing a male-dominated society, in Darwin white wives and mothers were also charged with the responsibility of transforming a frontier society on the edge of Asia into a flourishing site of white settlement (Holden 2000: 73; McGrath 1980: 237). On the ground, however, the ambivalence many British and white Australian men felt about the 'intrusion' of white women meant that they often represented white women as being unable to fulfill their prescribed purpose. In memoirs, fictional accounts, editorials in local newspapers and government reports mostly (though not always) written by white men, white women were represented as inadequate. The discourse of the inadequate white woman took different forms in Darwin and Singapore due to differences in the availability of 'appropriate' servants—preferably male, certainly Asian and ideally Chinese.

In Singapore, by the 1920s Chinese 'houseboys' were hard to come by and expensive, particularly following 1930 when immigration restriction was introduced to limit the numbers of male labor migrants entering the colony (Chiang 1994: 239). However, the increasing numbers of Chinese female migrants in the colony and the lower wages they were prepared to accept ensured that 'houseboys' were readily replaced with Chinese female servants called *amahs*.[8] The easy availability of domestic servants in Singapore culminated in claims that British women were idle *memsahibs* or *mems*, drawing on imagery first used in India. The mem was regularly described as 'a menace to the Empire.' In addition to being seen as lazy, 'pleasure mad' and 'easy-going' women whose lives were filled with 'unfettered enjoyment,' they were also condemned for heightened bigotry that resulted in 'aloofness' between ruler and ruled.[9] As one male commentator to the *Singapore Free Press* exclaimed in 1925: 'What on earth Mems find to do with themselves all day, beats me! . . . Amah takes the kids off her hands and the servants run the house for her, so there is simply nothing left for her to do. And yet she doesn't even so much as trim her own hats!'[10]

In Darwin, by contrast, white women were rarely condemned for being idle. This was because, as Charlotte Urquhart, wife of Frederic Urquhart, the Administrator of the Northern Territory (1921–1926), explained: Darwin was 'like the East without the East's comforts.'[11] Mrs. Fairfax Finniss, an elite white woman, made similar observations. Referring to the 'idea prevalent in the minds of many people that all white women in the tropics enjoy a life of abundant leisure, free from any household responsibilities other than those of issuing orders to a retinue of dusky or yellow-skinned servitors,' she proclaimed 'it isn't true of tropical Australia.'[12] Quite the contrary, for while in the thriving cosmopolitan city of Singapore, servants were readily available and relatively cheap, in Darwin white colonists maintained that 'good help' was hard to come by, especially from the 1910s onwards.

The decline in the availability of Chinese domestic servants in Darwin was due not only to the *Immigration Restriction Act* in 1901, which stopped immigration from Asia, but also the introduction of policies of economic discrimination which were introduced following the Commonwealth government's takeover of the Northern Territory in 1911 and aimed to replace Chinese workers with white unionized workers. Chinese laborers in Darwin were forced to either return to China or to travel to the southern states of Australia to find work (Martinez 1999: 2; Powell 1988: 156; Jones 2005: 53, 102). The few Chinese male servants who remained in the town were able to command high wages ensuring that only the wealthiest white residents could afford to employ them. While Chinese male servants were increasingly replaced by Aboriginal men and, where possible, mixed-race girls, these servants were considered by the white colonists to be 'unsatisfactory,' 'indifferent' and 'unreliable.'[13]

The white women of Darwin might not have been seen in terms of the idle mem of Singapore but their image did not reflect the vital white mother of nationalist imaginings either. White women of the tropical north were depicted by the authorities in quite the opposite terms—as weary housewives. In a letter lobbying the Commonwealth Government to relax the *Immigration Restriction Act* in the tropical regions of Australia in order to allow the entry of indentured Asian domestic servants, one politician maintained that: 'A young married woman who follows her husband to these tropical districts, who has to cook and go into the washhouse, bear and look after her children, is wan, old, weary and unhealthy at thirty.'[14] On the other hand, other white men in Darwin, particularly trade unionists who were vehemently opposed to the use of Asian domestic labor, openly contested claims of the 'unhappy lot of housewifes [sic] in the tropics.' As one male writer to the local newspaper claimed in 1921, 'the great majority' of white women 'we have come into contact with are altogether too "Happy" and too "dignified" to do their own cooking and invariably either go out to dine, or get blackboys to bring their meals from the nearest pub or restaurant.'[15]

White women (and sometimes white men) contested these depictions of inadequate white women that proliferated in the press.[16] However, the belief that white women were not up to the task of 'domesticating the empire'—either through laziness or exhaustion—remained largely unchallenged and ensured they were at pains to prove themselves as effective household managers. Rather than the obedient 'boys' of their imaginings, however, white women encountered Chinese men who they claimed were increasingly assertive and even intimidating.

A STRUGGLE FOR CONTROL: THE MISTRESS–SERVANT RELATIONSHIP, 1910S–1930S

In their accounts from the 1920s and 1930s, British women in Singapore and Malaya maintained that while the Chinese servants of the 'old days' matched the stereotypical 'silent, efficient Oriental menial of the magazine stories,' the servants of their time were insolent, demanding and disrespectful (Butcher 1979: 113).[17] Thus, according to one 'harassed mem' of Malaya writing to *The Straits Times* in 1930, 'the Hylam "boy" (old-style) was an ideal servant' while the new Hainanese servants were lazy and disobedient. She maintained that even her old 'Hylam cook' had encouraged her to employ Malay rather than Chinese household labor as 'the modern youth of his country were all suffering from the same complaint—swollen head, which prevented them from learning anything but how to swank!'[18]

Similar changes in Chinese male servants were observed by white women in Darwin. In an article about Darwin life printed in a local newspaper in 1927, Mrs. Finnis complained of her Chinese cook's insolence: 'You must be careful to give your cook courteous notification if you desire to bring a guest home to dinner,' she wryly exclaimed. Her cook's assertiveness, she suggested, was different from 'the good old days' when Chinese men were apparently more respectful.[19] The past Mrs. Finnis was nostalgic for was documented by 'Murray Eyre,' who lived in Darwin from 1887 to 1888 and reflected on her experiences in the *Pall Mall Gazette* in 1907. According to Eyre, Chinese 'houseboys' performed their tasks 'cheerfully and willingly'; when unexpected guests arrived for dinner 'the house-boys vied with each other in carrying out their parts smartly.' As one local put it in response to Eyre's description of life in Darwin, the 'picture of the Chinese cook and 'houseboys' as they appeared in "Murray Eyre's" time is in rather amusing contrast to the degenerate class as we know them in these days of monopoly, insolence, laziness, and dirt.'[20] Another example of the supposed 'insolence' of Chinese servants is provided in Jessie Tamblyn's recollections of her family's Chinese servant in the Northern Territory the late 1910s who argued with her mother over his technique of ironing her father's white linen suits. The servant maintained that his way of spitting water on the clothes to get the desired sharp corners was a 'good way' and was unwilling to change his approach.[21]

At the same as white mistresses claimed that their Chinese servants were becoming insolent and disrespectful, employers in general lamented the growing expense of employing Chinese 'houseboys' and cooks. One famous outburst published in Singapore's *Straits Times* in 1933 violently rebuked Chinese men for demanding high wages and called for servants to be registered to give employers more control over hiring and firing them: 'Horrors! Dogs must be licensed. Why not servants? And make them pay for their own licenses. If they ask for such high wages as $30 a month, muzzle "em"' (quoted in Chin 1998: 72). In Darwin too, white employers complained about the increase in wages for Chinese servants from approximately six pounds a month in 1911 to fourteen pounds in 1917 (Masson 1915: 42, 44). In this case, however, it was not usually Chinese men but the Commonwealth government's commitment to immigration restriction that was blamed.[22]

In their attempts to account for the growing assertiveness of Chinese servants in Singapore and Darwin, white men and women pointed to the managerial enthusiasm of the white mistress and the difficulties male servants had in adjusting to a female employer. In Singapore and Malaya, British men tried to prevent their wives and daughters from managing the household, encouraging them to 'sit back and let the "boy" carry on.'[23] Following her arrival in Penang in the late 1920s, Lucia Bach's father refused to let her learn Malay, the intermediary language used to communicate with Chinese, Malay and Indian servants throughout Singapore and Malaya.[24] He told her:

> You are not to speak to the servants. All these men servants are good and excellent servants until a wife comes along, or a woman. When a woman starts to boss about the house, the servants leave.[25]

Such attitudes were typical of the anti-white woman rhetoric of the era that condemned white women for destroying the supposedly harmonious relationships white men had developed with 'natives' during the early colonial years (Knapman 1986: 16; Holden 2000: 74; Stoler 2002: 33). Some white women themselves suspected that their enthusiasm for household management made it difficult to hold onto their male servants. In an article in *The Straits Times* in 1939, Ednah Prall attempted to account for the 'vanishing cookies,' pondering: 'Have we Mems peeped, spied and "sanitized" his kind out of existence?'[26] One British woman, on a Malayan outpost, advised her fellow white women that the best way to keep servants was to employ 'tact' and leave them to their own devices. As she put it: 'When "Cookie" for instance, is enjoying his after-tiffin opium pipe, I do not break in rudely on his beatific dreams.' Likewise, when arguments broke out between the servants she did not interfere.[27]

Other women maintained that the difficulties male servants had in adjusting to a white mistresses related not to the approach of the white woman, but to the servant's patriarchal beliefs. Emily Innes, based in Malaya in the late nineteenth century, explained that her Chinese, Malay and Indian servants were not 'accustomed to English mistresses; they all had the true Oriental contempt for women at the bottom of their hearts.' While they would obey her in the presence of her husband, the *Tuan* (boss), when she was alone with them they would disregard her orders (1974: 19).

In Darwin, just as in Singapore, it was suggested that white women's challenges with their servants were in part related to the difficulties Chinese men had in adjusting to the managerial mistress. Jeanie Gunn's memoir of the Northern Territory, *We of the Never-Never*, published in 1908, is full of her struggles with her two Chinese cooks Sam and Cheon. Gunn recalled that Sam, who had been employed many years prior to her arrival, made a habit of sabotaging her in an attempt to expose her as incompetent household manager in front of her new husband. The tension between them escalated and Sam resigned from the job. While Gunn's relationship with her new Chinese cook Cheon was far more amicable, she was bemused by the fact that he did not behave as a servant at all. Cheon constantly patronized her and refused to 'be instructed,' acting as 'a born ruler' and 'master' (Gunn 1908: 51, 93, 94).

The claims of white women in Singapore and Darwin that their Chinese servants were intentionally and actively seeking to usurp their power and authority might be at least partly attributed to white women's insecurity, in the context of intense public criticism about their contribution to the colonial project in Singapore and nation building in Darwin. Resistance, defiance and (in Singapore at least) some degree of collective bargaining aided by *kongsi* organizations was nothing new, but it is possible that Chinese men's defiance of their female employers was a new reaction to their difficulties in adjusting to the managerial approach of the white mistress. Possibly, these men had internalized the negative attitudes towards white women that were in circulation in the public discourse and, in all likelihood, discussed in the homes in which they were employed. The lack of reports from *Chinese* mistresses about troublesome Chinese 'houseboys' suggests that their disdain was targeted at white women specifically.[28] However, white women's expressed concerns about male servants also need to be considered in the nationalist and communist politics of the 1910s to the 1930s.

RADICAL POLITICS AND CHINESE 'HOUSEBOYS'

With the downfall of the Qing dynasty in 1912 and the founding of the Chinese Republic, Chinese men around the world, including in Singapore and Darwin, cut off their *queues*, the long braid of hair they had been forced to wear from the beginning of the Manchu Qing dynasty as a symbol of loyalty and subservience (Turnbull 1977: 109; Alcorta 1984: *xi*). Removing the queue symbolized their rejection of Manchu traditions, especially Confucian notions of superior–inferior, obedience and conformity. British colonists in Singapore had embraced the wearing of the queue by Chinese servants and the submission to colonial authority that it embodied. As such, they viewed its removal with some trepidation, expressing concern that demands for political freedoms would soon follow (Butcher 1979: 114; Turnbull 1977: 329).

This trepidation was reflected in growing anxiety about servant behavior, indicated by a renewed and concerted campaign for servant registration from 1911 to 1913.[29] Despite the claims of employers about a spate of thefts, inadequate service and the use of forged letters of recommendation, however, instances of theft by servants actually dropped in 1912.[30] Further angst about newly politicized and potentially dangerous servants is illustrated by the reaction of the British to the Singapore mutiny of 1915 when a regiment of Indian sepoys mutinied, sparking fears of an 'uprising of all natives' (Butcher 1979: 123–24; Ban 2001: 23). To their surprise, British residents returned home at the conclusion of the mutiny to find their servants going about their duties as usual (Song 1984: 482–83). Yet alongside these seemingly unfounded fears about rebellious servants, there was evidence that Chinese male servants in Singapore were becoming active in nationalist and anti-colonialist politics.

In Singapore, following the Chinese revolution, the *huaqiao* (overseas Chinese) community demonstrated their loyalty to Sun Yat Sen and his new *Guomindang* (National Party) in China by forming an independent Guomindang to provide financial and moral support to the new republic (Yong 1992: *xix*). Mirroring the emerging divisions within China itself however, Singapore's Guomindang came to be associated with the conservative interests of wealthy Chinese. In response, alienated Chinese workers turned to more radical branches of nationalism which culminated in the formation of the Nanyang (South Seas) General Labour Union in 1926 (Yong and McKenna 1990: 83–88). The Union combined an anti-British and anti-imperialist platform with communism and had branches in Singapore, Malaya, Sarawak, Siam and the Dutch East Indies. It was a precursor to the Malayan Communist Party which was formed in 1930. Despite the fact that they were a minority group in Singapore, the Hainanese dominated the union. Many of them were domestic servants (Yong 1997: 68–70; Bayly and Harper 2004: 53).

Domestic servants were also active in the Hainanese night schools that began to be established in Singapore during the 1920s and in which education was directed at raising the political consciousness of workers along communist lines (Yong 1997: 68, 141; Ban 2001: 87). Together with the Nanyang General Labour Union, the colonial authorities maintained that the night schools were behind a number of violent demonstrations, boycotts and strikes that took place in Singapore during the 1920s. The most significant incidents were the trolley bus boycott of 1927 and the shoemakers' strike of 1928, both of which, according to the colonial government and the Special Branch of Police, constituted active attempts to destabilize British rule (Ban 2001: 91, 105, 111). According to the local press and at least some employers of domestic servants, Hainanese male servants played a key role in these disturbances (Dixon 1935: 137).[31] This claim seems to be supported by three separate raids on servants' quarters which were conducted by the Special Branch of Police during 1928: Five domestic servants were arrested for possession of seditious literature inciting riots and the overthrow of British colonialism, as well as the possession of ammunition and explosive materials (Ban 2001: 111–12).[32]

By the 1930s Hainanese 'houseboys' were closely associated with the Malayan Communist Party. In one famous incident on April 29, 1930, the Special Branch of Police raided the servants' quarters at the home of a Mr. and Mrs. Dunn and arrested a large proportion of the Malayan Communist Party, including the Dunns' two Hainanese cooks (Ban 2001: 121; Bayly and Harper 2004: 53; Yong 1997: 146).[33]

In Darwin, the radicalization of Chinese workers was not as marked as it was in Singapore. Policies of immigration restriction and economic discrimination, pursued in the context of the White Australia Policy, had ensured that the Chinese laboring class was smaller as a proportion than in Singapore and more constrained in terms of collective organization. Yet here too, the Chinese community embraced nationalist sentiment, joined labor unions and participated in communist-organized demonstrations. As with Singapore, the Chinese community set up a Guomindang in support of Sun Yat Sen's republic. While the Guomindang membership was dominated by well-educated young Chinese (often the children of prominent local merchants), unlike in Singapore, its members managed to balance a focus on nationalist and communist beliefs and were active in promoting workers' rights (Martinez 2011: 208; Rolls 1996: 258, 447).

Darwin's Chinese community was likely influenced by the development of Australian trade unionism which blended a focus on working men's rights with that of nationalism (Alcorta 1984: *ix*; Powell 1988: 155–57). Indeed, the development of Chinese nationalism in Darwin emerged alongside the development of the white union movement. The common values of Chinese and white Australian nationalism, however, only went so far. Both the Darwin branch of the Australian Workers Union (AWU), which was established in the town in 1911, and the Northern Australian Workers Union (NAWU), which was established in 1927, were deeply committed to building a white 'working man's paradise' through the exclusion of what they perceived as 'cheap coloured labour.' This ensured that Chinese men, and indeed all those deemed to be part of a 'coloured race,' were banned from joining either organization (Martinez 1999: 1, 9).

Despite their official exclusion from the AWU and the NAWU, the degree to which Darwin's Chinese community was influenced by the values of unionism is illustrated by their active participation in demonstrations organized by the unions such as the march of unemployed waterside workers of Darwin in 1930, during the Great Depression (Martinez 2011: 208; Martinez 1999: 9). Furthermore, while they were excluded from joining the two most powerful unions in Darwin, Chinese workers, primarily those who worked on the wharf, could and did join the Industrial Workers of the World (IWW) (Powell 1988: 156–57; Martinez 1999: 4).[34] While it is not possible to ascertain whether domestic servants were members of the IWW, they could not have been ignorant of the very public struggle around working men's rights and nationalism that was being waged in their community.

While Chinese male servants in Darwin and Singapore were never the loyal 'boys' of the colonial imagination, white mistresses' claims that they were increasingly assertive and insolent may well be indicative of a more politicized servant resistance emerging in the context of the nationalist, anti-colonial and communist mobilizations of the period. This is not to suggest that all Chinese male servants working in this period were imbued with the spirit of rebellion. Indeed, while Chinese 'houseboys' were becoming less available in both Singapore and Darwin by the 1920s, they were nonetheless highly sought-after as servants, indicating that their reputation as efficient, if not loyal, was retained. Furthermore, while they largely disappeared from private homes, Chinese men continued to be widely employed in service roles as cooks and waiters in hotels in northern Australia and Singapore. Yet, their preference to work in hotels rather than private homes, in which personal surveillance was less marked, alludes to a desire to be treated as workers rather than personal servants at the beck and call of their employers. Indeed, Maurizio Peleggi has shown that those employed in hotels in Singapore as waiters, cooks and 'houseboys,' like Chinese staff employed in private homes, illustrated an increased willingness to strike for better wages and conditions in the wake of the Chinese revolution (2012: 21–22).

CONCLUSION

With the virtual disappearance of Chinese men from the domestic workforce by the late 1930s, conflicts between white women and Chinese 'houseboys' would become a thing of the past. Yet in this earlier period, white mistresses found themselves engaged in a constant struggle for power and authority in their home. Between the lines of white women's complaints about Chinese servants' insolence we can read the wider political context of anti-colonialism. In the context of the imperialist, nationalist and communist developments of the 1910s to the 1930s, the home became a site of political struggle between white women and Chinese men. As white women sought to assert control over the home in order to fulfil their colonial and postcolonial duty, Chinese servants resisted these attempts, demanding respect and autonomy in line with their emerging nationalist identity as workers with rights. Looking beyond the public discourse surrounding the mistress–male servant relationship, drawing on white women's accounts and considering the circumstances of Chinese men's lives not only provides new historical insights into domestic politics within the colonial home but may also inform understandings of the strategies of resistance employed by domestic workers in the contemporary era.

NOTES

1. For Singapore see Mackellar 1912: 74. For Darwin see Sowden 1882: 136.
2. For Singapore see: 'A Dishonest Boy,' *The Straits Times*, July 4, 1899; 'A Ferocious "Boy,"' *Straits Times*, July 1899; *The Singapore Free Press and Mercantile Advertiser*, August 2, 1907; 'The Missing Purse,' *Singapore Free Press and Mercantile Advertiser*, April 25, 1914; 'A Godown Pilferer: Chinese Houseboy Caught in the Act,' *Straits Times*, June 17, 1915. For Darwin see: 'Legal Information: Police Court,' *North Australia*, March 18, 1888; 'Our Domestic Servants,' *Northern Territory Times and Gazette*, October 14, 1882; 'The Discouragement of White Labor: Cruelty to Native,' *Northern Standard*, April 25, 1922; 'Station Hand Shot: Chinese Cook Imprisoned,' *The Advertiser*, April 21, 1926.
3. For Singapore see photographs: 'Chinese Boy Serving His Master,' accession number 94727, National Museum of Singapore (hereafter NMS), 1910; 'Group of White Men with Their Servants,' accession number 606, NMS, c. 1900. For Darwin see: 'Houseboy,' Jean A. Austin Collection, photograph number 0412/0003, Northern Territory Library and Information Service (hereafter NTLIS), c. 1912–1918.
4. 'Chinese Man Servant with His European Master Taken at the Studio,' Accession number 125997, National Archives of Singapore (hereafter NAS), 1908.
5. For Singapore see Falconer 1987: 156. For Darwin see photograph: 'Woman and Maid,' date unknown, Jean A. Austin Collection, photograph number 0412/0025, NTLIS. In the case of Singapore there are images of white women in rickshaws with the rickshaw driver. The women are, however, often flanked by their white husbands and/or fathers. See for example: 'Miss Dyke in a Rickshaw,' accession number 45567, NAS, c. 1880; 'Rickshaw Pullers with Their

Passengers,' accession number 213837, NAS, 1908; A. Bennett Collection, accession number 608, NAS, c. 1900.
6. I found only one example of a white mistress discussing or alluding to issues of sexuality and Chinese male servants in Singapore and none from Darwin: 'Women's Notebook: Are Malaya "Mems" Well Served?' *Straits Times*, February 11, 1937.
7. In British Malaya (including Singapore) there were three European men to one white woman in 1911. By 1931 there were two European men to one white woman (Butcher 1979: 134, 142). In the Northern Territory as a whole in 1911, the white population stood at 1729, of which 26 percent were women. By 1921 the proportion of women had increased to 37 percent and by 1938 it stood at 48 percent (Powell 1988: 142, 187–88).
8. While male servants demanded thirty dollars a month, amahs were prepared to work for five to fifteen (Gaw 1988: 78).
9. '"Memsahib": A Menace to the Empire,' *Singapore Free Press and Mercantile Advertiser*, December 19, 1906; 'The Menace of the Memsahib,' *Eastern Daily Mail and Straits Morning Advertiser*, December 21, 1906; M. Martin, 'The Life of the Outstation Men,' *Straits Times*, April 13, 1939; 'An Asiatic Mem,' *Straits Times*, September 9, 1946.
10. 'Lilies of the Field,' *Singapore Free Press*, December 11, 1925.
11. 'Life in Darwin: Mrs Urquhart's Experiences,' *Northern Standard*, March 26, 1926.
12. 'Lure of the South: Darwin Past and Present,' *Northern Standard*, February 4, 1927.
13. 'Letter to Mr Gregory from P McM Glynn,' June 14, 1917, A1/15, 1920/6227, National Archives of Australia (hereafter NAA); 'Report from Administrator Gilruth to the Department of External Affairs,' June 12, 1917, A1/15, 1920/6227, NAA.
14. 'Letter to the Hon. Minister for Home and Territories from H. Gregory,' March 23, 1920, A1/15, 1920/6227, NAA.
15. 'Candid Criticism: Ministerial Sidetracking,' *Northern Standard*, March 19, 1921.
16. For Singapore see 'Housework for European Mems: Differing Views,' *Straits Times*, September 6, 1946. For Darwin see Masson 1915: 181; Gunn 1908: 6.
17. 'The Servant Problem: A Pocket Guide for New Mems,' *Malayan Saturday Post*, November 1, 1926.
18. 'The Servant Problem in Malaya,' *Straits Times*, February 15, 1930.
19. 'Lure of the South: Darwin Past and Present,' *Northern Standard*, February 4, 1927.
20. 'An Unknown Corner of the Empire,' *Northern Territory Times and Gazette*, August 16, 1907.
21. 'Transcript of Interview with Jessie Tamblyn,' 1981: 24–25, NTRS 226, TS 126, Northern Territory Archives Service (hereafter NTAS).
22. 'Where Servants are a Luxury,' *The Advertiser*, March 31, 1914.
23. 'The Servant Problem in Malaya,' *Straits Times*, February 15, 1930.
24. 'Malay for "Mems,"' *Straits Times*, February 20, 1936; 'Mems Learn to Speak to Servants,' *Singapore Free Press*, March 27, 1950.
25. 'Transcript of Interview with Lucia Bach,' 1982: 41–42, NAS: 000184/25, NAS.
26. Edna Prall, 'Vanishing Cookies,' *Straits Times*, September 14, 1939.
27. 'Life of a Planter's Wife: It has Its Compensations,' *Straits Times*, October 22, 1936.
28. Very few Chinese women resided in Darwin and there is no evidence that those who did employed Chinese male servants. In Singapore, however, Chinese

mistresses such as May Wong reported dismissing one of her female Chinese servants for being 'a bit of a commune' but recalled no specific issues with her Chinese male servants: 'Interview with May Wong,' 1982, NAS: 00093/18/08/09.
29. 'Registration of Servants: To the Editor,' *Singapore Free Press and Mercantile Advertiser*, July 25, 1911; 'Registration of Servants,' *Straits Times*, July 17, 1912; 'Servant's Register: The Poll of Employers in Singapore,' *Straits Times*, July 30, 1912; 'Registration of Servants: An Enthusiastic Supporter,' *Singapore Free Press and Mercantile Advertiser*, January 8, 1913; 'Registration of Servants,' *Straits Times*, May 24, 1913.
30. 'Police and Crime,' *Singapore Free Press and Mercantile Advertiser*, August 26, 1912.
31. 'Why Employ Hylams,' *Straits Times*, September 29, 1928.
32. 'Red Propaganda: Serious Allegations of Sedition,' *Straits Times*, March 2, 1928; 'Police Raid: Alleged Seditious Literature,' *Straits Times*, March 22, 1928; 'Domestic "Reds": Hylam Servants in Court,' *Straits Times*, May 1, 1928.
33. 'South Seas "Reds" in Malay,' *Straits Times*, June 9, 1930.
34. Alf Pain, 'Letter to the Editor: Darwin Dispute,' *Northern Territory Times and Gazette*, September 30, 1915.

REFERENCES

Alcorta, F. X. 1984. *Darwin Rebellion, 1911–1919*. Darwin: University Planning Authority.
Aldrich, Robert. 2003. *Colonialism and Homosexuality*. London: Routledge.
Anderson, Warwick. 2005. *The Cultivation of Whiteness: Science, Health and Racial Destiny in Australia*. Carlton: Melbourne University Press.
Bagnall, Kate. 2002. 'Across the Threshold: White Women and Chinese Hawkers in the White Colonial Imaginary.' *Hecate* 28(2): 9–32.
Ban, Kah Choon. 2001. *Absent History: The Untold Story of Special Branch Operations in Singapore 1915–1942*. Singapore: Raffles.
Banerjee, Swapna M. 2004. *Men, Women, and Domestics: Articulating Middle-Class Identity in Colonial Bengal*. Oxford: Oxford University Press.
Bayly, Christopher, and Tim Harper. 2004. *Forgotten Armies: The Fall of British Asia*. London: Allen Lane.
Bird, Isabella. 1990. *The Golden Chersonese: The Malayan Travels of a Victorian Lady*. Singapore: Oxford University Press.
Blunt, Alison. 1999. 'Imperial Geographies of Home: British Domesticity in India, 1886–1925.' *Transactions of the Institute of British Geographers* 24(4): 421–40.
Buckley, Charles Burton. 1969. *An Anecdotal History of Old Times in Singapore*. Kuala Lumpur: University of Malaysia Press.
Bulbeck, Chilla. 1992. *Australian Women in Papua New Guinea*. Cambridge: University of Cambridge Press.
Butcher, John. 1979. *The British in Malaya, 1880–1941: The Social History of a European Community in Colonial South-East Asia*. Kuala Lumpur: Oxford University Press.
Chiang, Claire. 1994. 'Female Migrants in Singapore: Towards a Strategy of Pragmatism and Coping.' In *Women and Chinese Patriarchy: Submission, Servitude and Escape*, edited by Maria Jaschok and Suzanne Miers, 238–61. Hong Kong: Hong Kong University Press.
Chin, Christine. 1998. *In Service and Servitude: Foreign Female Domestic Workers and the Malaysian 'Modernity' Project*. New York: Columbia University Press.

Constable, Nicole. 1997. *Maid to Order in Hong Kong: Stories of Filipina Workers*. Ithaca: Cornell University Press.
Daly, Dominic. 1887. *Digging, Squatting and Pioneering Life in the Northern Territory of South Australia*. London: Sampson Low, Marston, Searle and Rivington.
Dixon, Alec. 1935. *Singapore Patrol*. London: George G. Harrap.
Dubinsky, Karen, and Adam Givertz. 2003. '"It Was Only a Matter of Passion": Masculinity and Sexual Danger.' In *Gendered Pasts: Historical Essays in Femininity and Masculinity in Canada*, edited by Kathryn McPherson, Cecilia Morgan and Nancy M. Forestell, 65–79. Toronto: University of Toronto Press.
Fairchilds, Cissie. 1984. *Domestic Enemies: Servants and Their Masters in Old Regime France*. Baltimore: John Hopkins University Press.
Falconer, John. 1987. *A Vision of the Past: A History of Early Photography in Singapore and Malaya*. Singapore: Times Editions.
Gaw, Kenneth. 1988. *Superior Servants: The Legendary Cantonese Amahs of the Far East*. Singapore: Oxford University Press.
Grimshaw, Patricia. 1989. *Paths of Duty: American Missionary Wives in Nineteenth-Century Hawaii*. Honolulu: University of Hawaii Press.
Gunn, Aeneas. 1908. *We of the Never-Never*. London: Hutchison and Co.
Hamilton, Paula. 1993. 'Domestic Dilemmas: Representations of Servants and Employers in the Popular Press.' In *Debutante Nation: Feminism Contests the 1890s*, edited by Susan Magarey, Sue Rowley and Susan Sheridan, 71–91. St Leonards: Allen and Unwin.
Hammond, Melinda. 1998. 'No Place for a Lady: A Lady's Lot in Palmerston in the Nineteenth Century.' *Journal of Northern Territory History* 9: 11–27.
Hansen, Karen. 1989. *Distant Companions: Servants and Employers in Zambia, 1900–1985*. Ithaca: Cornell University Press.
Haskins, Victoria. 2007. 'Domestic Service and Frontier Feminism: The Call for a Woman Visitor to "Half-Caste" Girls and Women in Domestic Service, 1925–1928.' *Frontiers* 28(1&2): 124–64.
Haskins, Victoria, and John Maynard. 2005. 'Sex, Race and Power: Aboriginal Men and White Women in Australian History.' *Australian Historical Studies* 126: 191–216.
Higman, B. W. 2002. *Domestic Service in Australia*. Carlton: Melbourne University Press.
Hodes, Martha. 1997. *White Women, Black Men: Illicit Sex in the Nineteenth-Century South*. New Haven: Yale University Press.
Holden, Philip. 2000. *Modern Subjects / Colonial Texts: Hugh Clifford and the Discipline of English Literature in the Straits Settlements and Malaya, 1895–1907*. Greensboro: ELT Press.
Inglis, Amirah. 1975. *The White Women's Protection Ordinance: Sexual Anxiety and Politics in Papua*. London: Sussex University Press.
Innes, Emily. 1974. *The Chersonese with the Gilding Off*. Kuala Lumpur: Oxford University Press.
Jones, Timothy. 2005. *The Chinese in the Northern Territory*. Darwin: Charles Darwin University Press.
Keegan, Timothy. 2001. 'Gender, Degeneration and Sexual Danger: Imagining Race and Class in South Africa.' *Journal of Southern African Studies* 27(3): 459–77.
Knapman, Claudia. 1986. *White Women in Fiji, 1835–1930: The Ruin of Empire?* Sydney: Allen & Unwin.
Lai, Ah Eng. 1986. *Peasants, Proletarians and Prostitutes: A Preliminary Investigation into the Work of Chinese Women in Colonial Malaya*. Singapore: Institute of Southeast Asian Studies.
Lake, Marilyn. 1996. 'Frontier Feminism and the Marauding White Man.' *Journal of Australian Studies* 49: 12–20.

Locher-Scholten, Elsbeth. 1998. 'So Close and Yet So Far: The Ambivalence of Dutch Colonial Rhetoric on Javanese Servants in Indonesia, 1900–1942.' In *Domesticating the Empire: Race, Gender and Family Life in French and Dutch Colonialism*, edited by Julia Clancy-Smith and Frances Gouda, 131–53. Charlottesville: University Press of Virginia.

Lockwood, Douglas. 1968. *The Front Door: Darwin 1869–1969*. Adelaide: Rigby Limited.

Louie, Kam. 2002. *Theorising Chinese Masculinity: Society and Gender in China*. Cambridge: Cambridge University Press.

Lowrie, Claire. 2008. 'Domestic "Slaves" and the Rhetoric of "Protection" in Darwin and Singapore during the 1920s and 1930s.' *Journal of the Oriental Society of Australia* 39–40(2): 334–56.

Lowrie, Claire. 2011. 'The Transcolonial Politics of Chinese Domestic Mastery in Singapore and Darwin 1910s–1930s.' *Journal of Colonialism and Colonial History* 12(3). http://muse.jhu.edu/journals/journal_of_colonialism_and_colonial_history/v012/12.3.lowrie.html. Accessed July 11, 2014.

Lowrie, Claire 2013. 'White "Men" and Their Chinese "Boys": Sexuality, Masculinity and Colonial Power in Darwin and Singapore, 1880s–1930s.' *History Australia* 10(1): 35–57.

Mackellar, C. D. 1912. *Scented Isles and Coral Gardens*. London: John Murray.

Marriott, Hayes. 1991. 'The Peoples of Singapore: Inhabitants and Population.' In *One Hundred Years of Singapore*, edited by Walter Makepeace, Gilbert Brooke and Roland Braddell, 341–57. Singapore: Oxford University Press.

Martens, Jeremy. 2002. 'Settler Homes, Manhood and "Houseboys": An Analysis of Natal's Rape Scare of 1886.' *Journal of Southern African Studies* 28(2): 379–400.

Martinez, Julia. 1999. 'Questioning "White Australia": Unionism and "Coloured" Labour, 1911–1937.' *Labour History* 76: 1–19.

Martinez, Julia. 2011. 'Patriotic Chinese Women: Followers of Sun-Yat Sen in Darwin, Australia.' In *Sun-Yat Sen, Nanyang and the 1911 Revolution*, edited by Lee Lai To and Lee Hock Guan, 200–218. Singapore: ISEAS.

Martinez, Julia, and Claire Lowrie. 2009. 'Colonial Constructions of Masculinity: Transforming Aboriginal Men into "Houseboys."' *Gender and History* 21(2): 305–23.

Martinez, Julia, and Claire Lowrie. 2012. 'Transcolonial Influences on Everyday American Imperialism: The Politics of Chinese Domestic Servants in the Philippines.' *Pacific Historical Review* 81(4): 511–36.

Masson, Elsie. 1915. *An Untamed Territory: The Northern Territory of Australia*. London: MacMillan and Co.

McClintock, Anne. 1995. *Imperial Leather: Race, Gender and Sexuality in the Colonial Contest*. New York: Routledge.

McGrath, Ann. 1980. '"Spinifex Fairies": Aboriginal Workers in the Northern Territory, 1911–1939.' In *Women, Class and History*, edited by Elizabeth Windschuttle, 237–67. Melbourne: Fontana/Collins.

McGrath, Ann. 1987. *Born in the Cattle: Aborigines in Cattle Country*. Sydney: Allen and Unwin.

Meldrum, Tim. 2000. *Domestic Service and Gender 1660–1750: Life and Work in the London Household*. London: Harlow.

Morrell, Robert. 1998. 'Of Boys and Men: Masculinity and Gender in Southern African Studies.' *Journal of Southern African Studies* 24(4): 605–30.

Munn, Christopher. 2004. 'Hong Kong, 1841–1970: All the Servants in Prison and Nobody to Take Care of the House.' In *Masters, Servants and Magistrates in Britain and the Empire, 1562–1955*, edited by Douglas Hay and Paul Craven, 365–401. Chapel Hill: University of North Carolina Press.

Palmer, Phyllis. 1989. *Domesticity and Dirt: Housewives and Domestic Servants in the United States*. Philadelphia: Temple University Press.

Peleggi, Maurizo. 2012. 'The Social and Material Life of Colonial Hotels: Comfort Zones as Contact Zones in British Colombo and Singapore, ca. 1870–1930.' *Journal of Social History* 46(1): 1–30.
Pickles, Katie. 2001. 'Empire, Settlement and Single British Women as New Zealand Domestic Servants during the 1920s.' *New Zealand Journal of History* 35(1): 22–44.
Powell, Alan. 1988. *Far Country: A Short History of the Northern Territory*. Burwood: Melbourne University Press.
Proschan, Frank. 2002. 'Eunuch Mandarins, Soldats Mamzelles, Effeminate Boys and Graceless Women: French Colonial Constructions of Vietnamese Genders.' *GLQ* 8(4) 435–67.
Rafael, Vincente L. 1995. 'Colonial Domesticity: White Women in United States Rule in the Philippines.' *American Literature* 67(4): 639–66.
Rolls, Eric. 1996. *Citizens: Flowers and the Wide Sea*. St Lucia: University of Queensland Press.
Rosenzweig, Paul. 1996. *The House of Seven Gables: A History of Government House, Darwin*. Darwin: Historical Society of the Northern Territory.
Salmon, Lucy. 1892. 'A Statistical Inquiry Concerning Domestic Service. *Publications of the American Statistical Association* 3(18–19): 89–118.
Sarti, Raffaella. 2006. 'Forum: Domestic Service Since 1750.' *Gender and History* 18(2): 187–98.
Searcy, Alfred. 1984. *In Northern Seas*. Darwin: Northern Territory Department of Education.
Sinha, Mrinalini. 1995. *Colonial Masculinity: The 'Manly Englishman' and the 'Effeminate Bengali' in the Late Nineteenth Century*. Manchester: Manchester University Press.
Song, Ong Siang. 1984. *One Hundred Years' History of the Chinese in Singapore*. Singapore: Oxford University Press.
Sowden, William. 1882. *The Northern Territory As It Is*. Adelaide: W. K. Thomas & Co.
Spear, Jennifer. 1999. '"They Need Wives": Metissage and the Regulation of Sexuality in French Louisiana.' In *Sex, Love and Race: Crossing Boundaries in North American History*, edited by Martha Hodes, 35–59. New York: New York University Press.
Steedman, Caroline. 2009. *Labours Lost: Domestic Service and the Making of Modern England*. Cambridge: Cambridge University Press.
Stoler, Ann Laura, 2001. 'Tense and Tender Ties: The Politics of Comparison in North American History and (Post) Colonial Studies.' *Journal of American History* 88(3): 829–65.
Stoler, Ann Laura. 2002. *Carnal Knowledge and Imperial Power: Race and the Intimate in Colonial Rule*. Berkeley: University of California Press.
Trocki, Carl. 1990. *Opium and Empire: Chinese Society in Colonial Singapore, 1800–1910*. Ithaca: Cornell University Press.
Turnbull, C. M. 1977. *A History of Singapore, 1819–1988*. Kuala Lumpur: Oxford University Press.
Yong, C. F. 1992. *Chinese Leadership and Power in Colonial Singapore*. Singapore: Times Academic Press.
Yong, C. F. 1997. *The Origins of Malayan Communism*. Singapore: South Seas Society.
Yong, C. F., and R. B. McKenna. 1990. *The Kuomintang Movement in British Malaya*. Singapore: Singapore University Press.

Part III
Legacies and Dreams

Legacies and Dreams

Victoria K. Haskins and Claire Lowrie

That colonization left behind more than just traces in the countries that had been colonized (European street names, for instance, or botanical gardens), but also deep wounds that continue to shape social, political, cultural and economic realities within ostensibly sovereign and self-governing nations is well understood. In a direct sense the legacies of colonialism are most often considered in terms of political structures of governance. Withdrawing colonial regimes installed bifurcated political structures that mediated continuing, if less visible, global systems of economic domination, reproducing systems of racial and class inequalities. But colonial legacies are also embedded in cultural and social systems of power, in the sense of practices and symbols (including the street names and parks) that continue to foster a sense of connection and identification, however painful and conflicted, with the former colonizing regime or country. The nature and patterns of domestic work today often bear the imprint of the colonial past, most noticeably perhaps in the way that global patterns of migration build upon and replicate the old connections between colonizer and colonized (Parreñas 2001: 2) and also in the continuities of systems of racial dominance and exploitation. But domestic work, crucially, is in itself often considered to be one of the more problematic legacies of colonialism.

The persistence, indeed revival, of domestic service and particularly the continuation of patterns of exploitation in some ways stands for the failure of decolonization: at least, its unfinished nature. The ongoing exploitation of domestic workers represents how dreams of independence, equality, freedom and respect that flourished in the wake of early decolonization efforts from the mid-twentieth century have yet to be realized. Some, however, consider the situation of migrant domestic workers today not so much as being a colonial inheritance, but rather as a more recent product of 'neo-colonialism' (Tronto 2011). A Marxist concept that appeared first in the context of French policy in Algeria in the late 1950s, neo-colonialism refers to the continued postcolonial control and exploitation of former colonies and dependencies, not only by former colonial powers, but by new global powers (especially the United States in Latin America, the Caribbean and Asia), and multinational corporations and institutions. The disparities of power *between* former colonies today, played out in the seemingly gratuitous abuse of migrant domestic workers employed in the stronger new 'postcolonial' nations, might also be considered in some ways a neo-colonial phenomenon. In any case, as Cynthia Enloe pointed out some years ago, the fact that '[l]iterally hundreds of thousands of women from Third World countries are cleaning the homes and minding the children of *other*, more affluent Third World women' underscores the inadequacies of any simple binary model for understanding colonialism in the present (1990: 193; see also Harzig 2006).

In this final section of our collection, seven contributors consider the kinds of colonial legacies and neo-colonial dreams that are reflected in different domestic service situations. The opening chapter in this section, by Swapna Banerjee, offers a close historical reading of the life-narrative of Baby Halder, the Indian domestic worker whose autobiography published in the early twenty-first century has been a major international publishing success. Banerjee likens her to the Victorian domestic servant Hannah Cullwick, immortalized by Leonore Davidoff (1979) as an icon of gender and class and, later, by Anne McClintock (1995), who claimed this extraordinarily transgressive woman for postcolonial theory. Arguing that Baby Halder not only negotiated but appropriated a 'cult of colonial domesticity' for empowerment, Banerjee reflects upon Halder's life experiences as told by herself, as a way of examining the continuities and changes for domestic workers in India from colonial times to the present, as they struggle to control their own lives and destinies. Banerjee's evocative and nuanced study of how one woman negotiated the realities of being a domestic servant in contemporary India, and found her own voice in the process, provides a resonant metaphor for the ongoing struggles of domestic workers for decolonization in an ostensibly postcolonial world.

The next three chapters direct our attention to the continuing importance of racialization in understanding colonization and domestic service both past and present. Rosie Cox examines the policies around the hiring of au pairs from Eastern Europe in the UK, arguing that these workers and their countries of origin are subject to 'neo-colonial' imaginings by the British government. Locating their experience on an historical trajectory whereby non-English but 'white' domestic workers provided the solution to the need for domestic labor in the mother country, even as non-white workers serviced British homes in the colonies, Cox elaborates the contradictions this entailed and the way that colonial processes of racialization brought to bear upon these workers today in an attempt to resolve them. The following two historical essays consider domestic service where a transition from older to newer forms of colonial power relations was underway. Together they provide tantalizing insights into the uneasy position of domestic workers in the context of national modernities. Charlotte Macdonald looks at a period in New Zealand history during and immediately after the Second World War, when the New Zealand government experimented with the exercise of colonial power by bringing in Indigenous women from the Cook Islands in the Pacific to work as servants. Teasing out the connections between race, citizenship and domestic labor, Macdonald highlights, in something of an echo of McCabe's earlier study, the vexed issues around these young women's status and the ways in which they resisted repatriation. Nicola Foote's essay is about the experiences of black migrant workers from the British Caribbean colonies, who served in the 'enclave' households of North Americans employed by US corporations in Latin America. Foote highlights how various colonialist representations of domestic workers (including those connected with slavery in the American South) intersected to shape a particular preference for certain non-white domestic workers over others. In all three chapters we see a peculiar racialized phenomenon: the ideal domestic worker is categorized as being simultaneously one race/ethnicity and yet not. Thus the Eastern European au pairs in English homes are 'white but not-white,' the Cook Islander Maori 'housegirls' in New Zealand homes were 'Indigenous but not-Indigenous,' and the British Caribbean domestic workers working for North American expatriates in Latin American, 'black but not-black.' In all three cases, we see the kind of colonialist fantasies that employers indulge in when looking to recruit certain groups of women for service, and the insight that these 'quite but not-quite' racialized migrant domestic workers are preferred over any others may be critical for understanding the relationship between colonization and domestic service. The importance of racial categories in delineating the domestic worker's status as excluded from full citizenship remains paramount.

Pam Nilan, Luh Putu Artini and Steven Threadgold consider the employment of Balinese service staff on contemporary tourist cruise liners: not strictly domestic service in the sense we use it (private household employment) but as the authors of this chapter show, the cruise ship industry employing these workers trades upon a fantasy of colonial domestic servitude to entice white working-class passengers to come on board and playact colonial mastery. Again, racial criteria come to the fore in the selection of the ideal worker (dark-skinned but not too dark), and, as interviews with the young men and women who work on these ships highlight, neo-colonialist relations of power are recreated through the process, especially and indeed definitively between the multinational corporate employers and the Balinese communities from which they recruit. Drawing upon the voices of both cruise workers and the passengers they serve, Nilan, Artini and Threadgold offer a sharp insight into the way that imagined histories of colonialism are manipulated to buttress new forms of global inequity and exploitation.

The question of how colonial legacies and neo-colonial dreams play out in the present is one that invites a constant rethinking of our definitions and assumptions about domestic work. Perhaps we are seeing a kind of elaborate and transnational interaction between historical and contemporary forces that are producing new kinds of domestic service relationships, as well as changing the way we view those in the past.

REFERENCES

Davidoff, Leonore. 1979. 'Class and Gender in Victorian England: The Diaries of Arthur J Munby and Hannah Cullwick.' *Feminist Studies* 5(1): 86–141.
Enloe, Cynthia. 1990. *Bananas, Beaches and Bases: Making Feminist Sense of International Politics*. Berkeley: University of California Press.
Harzig, Christine. 2006. 'Domestics of the World (Unite?): Labor Migration Systems and Personal Trajectories of Household Workers in Historical and Global Perspective.' *Journal of American Ethnic History* 25(2&3): 48–73.
McClintock, Anne. 1995. *Imperial Leather: Race, Gender and Sexuality in the Colonial Contest*. London: Routledge.
Parreñas, Rhacel Salazar. 2001. *Servants of Globalization: Women, Migration and Domestic Work*. Stanford: Stanford University Press.
Tronto, Joan. 2011. 'Privatizing Neo-Colonialism: Migrant Domestic Care Workers, Partial Citizenship and Responsibility.' In *Europeanization, Care and Gender: Global Complexities*, edited by Hanne Marlene Dahl, Marja Keränen and Anne Kovalainen, 165–81. Basingstoke: Palgrave Macmillan.

13 Baby Halder's *A Life Less Ordinary*
A Transition from India's Colonial Past?[1]

Swapna M. Banerjee

Baby Halder, a domestic worker from Gurgaon, Delhi, broke new ground by authoring her autobiography. *Alo Aandhari (Light and Darkness)* (2002), originally written in Bengali, unabashedly told the life-story of a neglected daughter, girl, wife, and mother echoing the experiences of millions of working women like her.[2] The translation of her text in English, *A Life Less Ordinary* (2006), and its renditions in twenty-three other languages not only turned Baby Halder into an international celebrity, it also signaled a seminal moment for researchers on domestic workers in India. Records of domestic workers in India's long past are mediated and fragmentary, lurking in the interstices of memoirs, autobiographies and other ego-sources produced by employers, instruction manuals, censuses, and various genres of imaginary literature. Indeed, in the genealogy of domestic service in India from the antiquity to the present, there is hardly any narrative left by a male or female servant.[3] Baby Halder's telling of her own life thus allowed me to navigate the lives of domestic workers in India from the colonial times (1757–1947) up to the present.

This chapter proposes to read *A Life Less Ordinary* as a critical feminist practice that enables us to address the question of self-writing and the persistent historical problem of domestic service from the point of view of the subaltern. Working from the details of Baby Halder's life in contemporary India, I will tease out the historical specificities that informed the author's experiences and track the trajectory of changes and continuity to the present. Baby Halder comes from the state of West Bengal, which in the past housed the British imperial capital in the city of Calcutta (now Kolkata) until 1911, and was the first state in India to have an encounter with Western 'modernity.' In Bengal, Western-educated men and British officials launched a series of reforms during the nineteenth century in an attempt to free women from oppressive social practices and to advance them in a path of progress and education (Borthwick 1984; Chakrabarty 1993; Chatterjee 1993; Forbes 1996; Sarkar 2001). Thus as the major social, economic, and educational center, Bengal fostered a culture of bourgeois domesticity among its burgeoning middle-class that selectively combined Victorian domestic ideals with reinvented notions of chaste and sacrificing Hindu womanhood. This distinctive form of colonial domesticity exalted the role of the 'wise mother' and the 'good wife' and it distinguished its 'new woman' from all other women by positioning the former as superior to common working women: both the uneducated, unrefined traditional Indian women, and Western and Westernized Indian women (Chatterjee 1993: 129). Although envisioned for the upper-caste groups, the model of the 'new woman' percolated down the lower social groups even in the colonial period. The process was evident when women from agricultural caste groups in Bengal withdrew from their field-related services to attain 'respectability' and status (Banerjee 2004: 89). As a consequence, Bengal continued to have lower rates of women's participation in work in the late colonial period. It also privileged certain kinds of professions such as domestic service (and prostitution) as women's work.

I will examine Baby's life in the light of the colonial past and consider how she negotiated and appropriated the cult of this colonial domesticity and deployed it to maximize her labor power as a domestic worker. My reading of Baby Halder in the light of the past challenges the historicist assumption that the past can only be understood in its own terms. It also disrupts the binary between the colonial and the postcolonial by establishing the lingering continuities as well as the marked changes set forth in the wake of India's independence and partition from British colonial rule in 1947 and more urgently, by the liberalizing economic policies of the postcolonial Indian state.

FEMINIZATION OF DOMESTIC SERVICE IN INDIA

Current historical literature recognizes that the so-called process of modernization brought about uneven developments in women's lives (Poovey 1988). This is particularly evident in colonial India where technological changes and innovations, attended by bourgeois ideologies of civility and respect, impacted differently and unevenly on lives of different groups of women. As explained above, in colonial Bengal women from upper castes and classes made significant strides in gaining political and social rights, albeit within ideological parameters. By the first decade of the twentieth century, a select group of these 'new women,' called *bhadramahila* (respectable ladies), built women's organizations, opened schools, wrote in magazines, and participated in nationalist politics (Forbes 1996: 28). But the lives of working-class women deteriorated as they were subsequently pushed into domestic service, which in spite of providing food and shelter in an unwholesome and often unfamiliar urban environment, allowed very little scope for upward mobility. From 1930 onwards, Bengal employed the highest number of domestic workers in colonial India and more than 70 percent of its workforce were women (Banerjee 1990: 278).

In contrast to the West where live-in domestic service was the single woman's primary occupational domain in the nineteenth and early twentieth centuries, men had continued to dominate the profession in colonial Bengal until the first quarter of the twentieth century (women were present before then, but in a much restricted number). The male predominance in domestic service in Bengal was a combined result of the agrarian crisis that uprooted agricultural laborers and the incursion of foreign trade sponsored by colonial rule undermining traditional caste-based occupations of Indigenous artisans, traders, and craftsmen. Male domestics were the displaced workers hailing mainly from the rural and the adjacent areas of Bengal. Female domestics were mostly young widows, or women abandoned by their husbands and, becoming 'destitutes,' who sought refuge in an urban environment. These women often left their children with their natal or in-laws' families in the rural areas from where they came. Some married women with husbands and children also figured, but they mostly worked part time. In such cases, their husbands were urban workers, or were employed in family estates where their wives worked as maids (Banerjee 2004: 80).

The feminization of the domestic workforce in the first four decades of the twentieth century was a strikingly 'modern' phenomenon unleashed by a wide range of political-economic and sociocultural forces in the interwar period. Until 1911 working-class women followed independent caste-based occupations and about 41 percent of them were engaged in 'making and selling' industrial goods. The increasing mechanization of the economy initially signaled a partial shift of lower-class women from the traditional sphere of agricultural labor into the modern industrialized sector. This was followed by a steady marginalization from industrial occupations as well, and hence from the productive process itself. Women's share in total employment fell from 29 percent in 1901 to 17 percent in 1911 and 12 percent in 1921. By 1931, women were pushed out of industrial employment, and domestic service had become the only important nonagricultural occupation for them. With the economic downturn for women, the practice of hiring domestic workers by the growing middle-class in Bengal as a mark of their status remained a significant sociocultural factor to absorb the women labor force into domestic service (Banerjee 2004: 89).

In the later years the massive disruption of the colonial political economy that had ensued from India's independence and partition in 1947 was followed by a major demographic shift in the subcontinent, particularly from the eastern Bengal (now Bangladesh) to West Bengal, unleashing a huge supply of unskilled female labor available for domestic service at a considerably lower cost than before. In the absence of any organized movement or unions safeguarding the domestics, the 'cheapening' of their labor cost enabled the postcolonial employers of the present generation to enjoy the continued luxury of domestic service in India much like the European officials and the Indian middle-class of the colonial era. The trend of feminization of domestic service has continued into the late twentieth century. Between 1983 and 1999, female domestics in the workforce increased to 89 percent (Kaur 2004: 19), and recent studies show that in 2004–2005, there were 30.5 million women domestics in urban India, indicating a rise of two percent from 1999 and 2000 (John 2013: 6). It is within this historical process of feminization of domestic service in the twenty-first century that I situate the story of Baby Halder.

BABY'S LIFE: A BRIEF HISTORY

My reading of Baby Halder's life is based on Urvashi Butalia's translation of her text and is reinforced by my interview with her on May 31, 2012. I will occasionally juxtapose Baby's account with vignettes of another interview I conducted in June 1995 with Mrs. Kumuda Pal, a live-in domestic worker who worked for a family in Kolkata for three generations across the colonial and postcolonial periods.[4]

Born in the early 1970s in a working-class household in West Bengal, Baby was abandoned by her mother at age four and grew up with an irresponsible and apathetic father.[5] A child who loved to go to school and immerse herself in books, Baby only had an intermittent education until sixth or seventh grade and was married off to an abusive and indifferent husband when she was twelve or thirteen. Within a year she became a mother, to be followed by a miscarriage and two other children. Leaving a violent and loveless marriage, Baby came to Delhi with her three children in search of employment in the late 1990s (Halder 2006: 126–27). Baby told me that given her limited education, domestic service was the only viable occupation for her. The proximity to her brother living in Delhi guided her choice.[6]

The employers' household provided Baby and her children with a roof over their heads in an unknown city. The opportunity of boarding and lodging was always a motivation to take up domestic service for single, 'destitute' women even in the colonial period. My other interviewee, Kumuda Pal, also saw her life and choices colored by similar experiences. Born into the potter caste *(kumor)* in a suburb of West Bengal, Kumuda was married off at age seven, to be widowed at thirteen without any children. Kumuda had no memory of her father who passed away when she was very young. Although her husband had some land, most of it had to be sold off to pay for the treatment of his asthma. Upon the death of her husband, Kumuda came back to her brother, but friction with her sister-in-law drove her to seek domestic service as a means of livelihood and shelter. A classic case of a family retainer, she would work for different branches of a single family from the late 1940s to early 2000s.[7] Interestingly, one of Baby's primary reasons for moving away from her brother's house in Delhi was to avoid conflict with her sister-in-law. More than half a century later, Baby's adoption of domestic service attests to the availability of cheap women's labor for reasons of survival and the persistent cultural bias in defining domestic work as a woman's niche.

Baby's initial experience in a series of employer-households in Delhi was far from acceptable. A live-in domestic single-handedly raising three children, Baby fulfilled the demands of her *memsahib*, her mistress,[8] by serving in every conceivable capacity—running errands, cooking and serving, taking care of the pets, and even escorting her daughter to the bus stop to and from work. Meanwhile her own children were subjected to brutal living conditions, including being confined in an attic (Halder 2006: 127–36). Soon thereafter, Baby was fortunate to find a kind, warm, and compassionate employer. Mr. Prabodh Kumar, a retired professor of Anthropology and the grandson of the famous Hindi writer, Munshi Premchand (1880–1936), became a mentor and a father figure in Baby's life. Baby calls him *Tatush*, the Polish term for father; Prabodh Kumar's wife is Polish and his children address him as 'Tatush' as well. Discovering Baby's interest in books, Prabodh Kumar gave Baby the autobiography of rebel Bangladeshi poet Taslima Nasrin, *My Girlhood*, to read. He also gave her a pen and a notebook, urging her to write about her own life. Baby recounted to me that this was the single most important event in her life. Overcoming initial resistance due to her lack of experience of writing of any sort, Baby poured out her heart in the notebook, chronicling her memories at the end of a long day's work. Mr. Kumar translated and edited the rough drafts of Baby's texts, checked them with his literary friends, and put them out for publication without Baby's knowledge (see Majumdar 2006). Before long, to Baby's great surprise, her writings saw the light of the day, eventually earning her international acclaim.

ALO AANDHARI (LIGHT AND DARKNESS) AKA *A LIFE LESS ORDINARY*: A BOOK OF HER OWN?

Baby's book, embodying transcultural practices and involving the mediation of her employer, can be read as an endeavor of 'a brown man saving a brown woman,' without the presence of the colonial/white master (cf. Spivak 1988: 297). Martine van Woerkens (2010) reads Baby's text in the light of the colonial period when Indian men tried to give their women a new life and a voice (Chatterjee 1993). Furthermore, the intervention of Prabodh Kumar in Baby's life urging her to write her life reminds us of Hannah Cullwick (1833–1909), the maid from Victorian England and her middle-class husband, Arthur Munby.[9] Arthur Munby, the civil servant and writer, with a deep fascination for working-class women, secretly maintained the relationship with Hannah Cullwick for almost forty years and pressed Hannah to document her life in writing.[10] Separated by a century and unfolding in very different contexts, Baby's experiences evoke more dissimilarities than sameness with Hannah Cullwick. Nonetheless, the role of the paternalistic employer for Baby Halder and the husband for Hannah Cullwick compels us to rethink the nature of their relationship with the female domestics.

Anne McClintock has meticulously scrutinized Arthur Munby's motivation for his involvement with Cullwick along the lines of class, gender, and racial power, in the 'peculiarly Victorian and peculiarly neurotic connection between work and sexuality.' As a Victorian gentleman, Munby displayed an obsessive interest in watching, sketching, photographing, and collecting data on working-class women, particularly those who did the 'filthiest, most sordid and most menial work,' to capture the lost world of steadily dissipating female labor in nineteenth-century England and the 'passing away of aristocratic mastery over the female serf' (McClintock 1995: 83; 131). Baby Halder, in contrast, inherits a different (if connected) cultural legacy where Western-educated male professionals in nineteenth-century India, broadly termed as middle-class, took up the leadership role of making 'their' women 'modern.'

Baby's employer Prabodh Kumar inherits the colonial legacy of the middle-class intelligentsia and transgresses his social boundary through his paternalistic role for his subaltern employee, managing her life through literary intervention that made 'ordinary' Baby 'extraordinary.' Unlike Munby, his intention does not seem to be 'purely sociological: to find archetypes by which to represent the entirety of female labor' (McClintock 1995: 81) but perhaps to present the world with the individualized voice of one of the many female domestics who dominate the informal sector of India's current service economy. Instead of trying to rescue and rehabilitate the image of the common women or being driven by a nostalgia for a feudal master–servant relationship as displayed by Munby, Prabodh Kumar wanted to construct a different kind of quasi-familial employment relationship with his employee. Prabodh Kumar not only nurtured and encouraged Baby's self-expression and talent as a writer, he also mobilized his resources to get Baby's work out. The instrumentality of Prabodh Kumar in driving and managing the project remains without a doubt.

The question that looms at this point is to what extent is Baby's 'voice' original? To what extent is it lost in translation? To disentangle my web of thoughts, I directly posed the question to Baby. Baby vehemently retorted that every word in the book is hers: 'The incidents are culled from my own experiences. When I first started writing, the language was rough. Now I write whenever I can, even in the middle of my cooking. But Tatush provides all the titles. I may not have education, but Mother Saraswati (the Goddess of Learning), has endowed me with intelligence.'

Baby's writings are characterized by a fluid and unbounded sense of self. While reading Baby Halder's autobiography we need to understand that self-writing in South Asian linguistic traditions cannot simply be equated with the Euro-American self-writing practices, even at the turn of the twentieth century. Although strong and assertive, Baby Halder's restraint and self-erasure point to a long-standing culture of non-selfhood in the subcontinent and her text offers not a unique individual self but that of an endlessly reproducible plastic kind of 'self' that was affirmed by her own interview with me. Baby's voice and subjectivity cannot be located in an individualism created out of the binaries of the Self and the Other and the Subject and the

Object. Her life-action-narrative are both oppositional and non-essentialist: She urges, 'Feminist or not, I oppose injustice.' Her situatedness outside of an organized group does not imply her loss of agency. Throughout her life she inhabited multiple positions in multiple locations—as a daughter, sister, wife, mother, and a domestic worker, she has lived in Jammu and Kashmir, Murshidabad, Durgapur, and Delhi. She forges solidarity through her plurality as a subject, in transition and in movement. She understands and opposes multiple oppressions by interrogating and resisting various sources of power. Her complex positioning can be best described in the words of Norma Alarcon as the 'multiple-voiced subjectivity' (Grewal 2002: 235).

In the history of self-writing in India, Baby's text is not the first to be written by a subaltern. There is a large corpus of writing by *dalit* women (women of lower social groups) coming from different corners of India. Furthermore, Baby's work appears in a thoroughly entrenched literary culture of personal narratives written by Bengali women, both Hindus and Muslims. At one end of the spectrum is Rashsundari Devi's (1999 [1868]) *Amar Jiban (My Life)*, the first published autobiography by a Bengali woman and perhaps the first full-scale autobiography written in the Bengali language; at the other end is Bangladeshi doctor turned poet-cum-feminist Taslima Nasrin's (2002 [1999]) *Amar Meyebela (My Girlhood)*, that won one of the highest literary awards in India (the Ananda Puroshkar) in 2000, while being banned in her native country Bangladesh, for voicing anti-Islamist sentiments.

Baby Halder's work is very different from that of Rashsundari Devi and Taslima Nasrin. Unlike Rashsundari Devi's *My Life*, a completely 'self-absorbed,' 'non-dialogic,' 'devotional quest' (Sarkar 1999: 5), Baby Halder's *Alo Aandhari* is not just 'a book of her own,' but spoke for the millions of 'ordinary' women like her. Baby's recounting of her neglected childhood, the trauma of growing up, her brutal marriage and work life, her friendship with several other working-class men and women resonated with the experiences of millions of other Indian women, rich and poor (for an abusive childhood of an upper-class woman, see Sen 2001). After her book's popularity, other domestics came and told her that it was as if they were talking in her book; Baby's ventriloquism indeed voiced the life-stories of fellow domestics. Her autobiography has inspired many other women like her to write about their own lives (Halder 2008: Preface). In contrast to Nasrin, Baby did not write to specifically inform about gender inequities, biases, and discriminations. Instigated by her intellectual employer and his literary friends, Baby discovered herself through her writing; writing became a passion and a cathartic exercise, targeted at a literate yet unknown audience.

Even as a subaltern narrative in Bengali, Baby's work is unique. However, *Alo Aandhari* brings to mind the personal narratives of the famous Bengali actress Binodini Dasi (1862–1941) of the colonial times. Binodini Dasi's *My Story* (1912) and *My Life as an Actress* (1924–1925) provided us with a rare testimony to the travails of working women, particularly that of the first generation of Bengali actresses, who usually came from impoverished and dubious backgrounds. Rimli Bhattacharya, the translator and editor of Binodini's works, has pointed out that Binodini Dasi's *My Story* was an account of personal pain written immediately after the demise of her protector; and her second work *My Life* emerged from the 'conscious desire to recall and record an age gone by' and was specifically addressed to younger actresses (Dasi 1998: 19–20). As a well-known actress in colonial Bengal, yet excluded from the circle of the 'respectable ladies,' Binodini assumed a self-conscious outsider position in Calcutta, the heart of the colonial metropolis. She lashed out against the dominant Bengali patriarchy and framed her narratives in pain and from a sense of betrayal by her middle-class patrons (Chatterjee 1993: 135–57). Baby, in contrast, is a (post)colonial subject situated at the lower end of the socioeconomic order, and an isolated outsider. While Baby's life-story encapsulates pain and struggle, her writings did not emerge from pain or an interaction with members beyond her class. Rather the encouragement by her employer sustained her writings. Nor did she focus on particular moments, as Binodini did. Binodini, as a public persona, stayed local in the metropolis of Calcutta and registered her dissent against members of the upper-class; but Baby crosses local borders to explore her fate, traverses multiple cultures, and effectively communicates with the larger world through her writing. Her transculturalism is evident in her adoption of middle-class values of restraint, caution, and detachment, never lodging a complaint against her father, mother, or husband, as we shall see.

NEGOTIATING DISPLACEMENT AND CHALLENGING INJUSTICE

Conspicuous by their absence in Baby's account are any references to her own caste, class, religion, hierarchy, and power. She notes the different castes of people around her, but elides the question of her own caste or religion. With the rise of the Hindu fundamentalist politics and the demolition of Babri Masjid in Ayodhya in 1992, religious identity, particularly as Hindus and Muslims, became a key marker of Indian citizens in postcolonial India. Caste politics also became rampant in the 1980s and 1990s with the Mandal Commission Report on 'the socially or educationally backward,' and the furor unleashed in its aftermath.[11] Those factors seemed not to impinge directly on Baby, either in personal life or in the choice of her career.

Moreover, geopolitical space occupies an important place in Baby's narrative. Although Bengali by birth, Baby Halder is not from the city of Kolkata, the city that still harbors the highest number of female domestics (Qayum and Ray 2003). She hails instead from Murshidabad, an important district of West Bengal, which enjoyed preeminence as a seat of Muslim power in pre-British India. Her migration from West Bengal to Delhi was a translocal act indicating passage from the local to the global—Delhi, the metropolitan capital of India, is also becoming the fastest and the largest consumer of domestic service in India. This move (also happening from other peripheral areas to the urban centers besides Delhi), parallels the migration of domestic workers of the colonial period from rural hinterland to the imperial capital in Calcutta and other important cities.

Historically speaking, as a native of Murshidabad, Baby inherits two kinds of displacement and dispossessions. Murshidabad was the capital of the Muslim *nawabs* (governors) until the city lost out to the British in the late eighteenth and early nineteenth century and Calcutta emerged as the imperial stronghold (Chowdhury 2004). As a district sharing its border with Muslim-dominated East Pakistan (eastern Bengal) in the wake of India's partition in 1947, Murshidabad was the seat of another political turmoil in the early 1970s when Bangladesh emerged as an independent nation-state (1971). Not only did Murshidabad witness a tremendous influx of refugees from across its eastern borders, its own Muslim population also faced serious threats of eviction. Inhabiting this volatile area, Baby ventured out further to a completely new cultural and linguistic environment and made herself part of a larger pool of labor thereby becoming more marginal and vulnerable in a complicated social and cultural milieu. Her articulation in Bengali in a predominantly Hindi-speaking environment, and then getting heard internationally through several acts of translations, further transcends regional, ethnic, and national boundaries, and attests to her translocalism. If translocalism involves establishing 'connections between two or more specific localities as created and established by migrants' (Hoerder 2013), Baby Halder's life offers a powerful scenario of crossing boundaries, straddling different worlds, and linking her 'local' self to the 'global.' However, her reticence on matters of unequal power structure and gender hierarchy, of the myriad diversities, discriminations, and differences based on caste, class, ethnicity, language, and religion among others, point to a careful restraint that she practices in her writing. I argue that this restraint, almost contradicting her simultaneous urge for self-expression and justice, conceals the desires that frame her life—instead of critiquing the social system, she outlines her desires to attain and enjoy the quality and privileges of a 'respectable' life (Steedman 1986).[12]

Baby displays an indomitable spirit to interrogate and to resist; she defies all odds, yet does not show overt signs of protest. This was borne out in her conversation with me—instead of blaming her father and her husband, she recognized them as crucial individuals who shaped the trajectory of her life. Instead of holding a grudge, she described them as products of their social upbringing and victims of their own circumstances. Reflecting on the struggles her own mother endured as a dependent wife, Baby wrote:

> Ma asked Baba's friends for help but none of them were in a position to take on the burden of another family. Ma also thought of taking up a job, but that would have meant going out of the house, which she had

never done. And after all, what work could she do? Another of her worries was: what would people say? But worrying about what people will say does not fill an empty stomach, does it?

(Halder 2006: 2)

Baby told me that if her elder sister, who had fallen victim to another violent marriage (Halder 2006: 123), were alive, she would have dragged her out of the failed relationship and shown her that there is another world, there is a better way to live one's life. As Baby's own life reveals, in all her acts of courage and defiance, she never worried about 'what people would say.'

Once Baby had made the transition to Delhi, her chief impediment to getting a job was her single status. Seeing her constantly harassed by the question why she was without her husband, her elder brother suggested that she return to her home and bring her husband back with Delhi with her. Baby's response to his suggestion is revealing:

> And I thought, if this was what I had to do, I may as well have stayed there with him. Surely, I hadn't travelled all this way, and gone to all this trouble, just to go back to where I'd started? . . . All of them thought that it would have been better for me to die than leave the home of my swami, my lord, my master. No one so much has tried to understand why I had left. *More than anything, I wanted that my children should have a good life. It is not enough to give birth, for birth brings with it a responsibility: the responsibility to enable a person to grow into a human being* [my emphasis].
>
> (Halder 2006: 123)

It was the desire to improve the lives of her children (one which her husband did not share) that motivated Baby to continue the search for work despite the obstacles presented by being a single woman. As she put it: 'I thought, well, if people think I'm doing the wrong thing, let them. I'll just keep on looking for work and some day, somehow, I'll find it. . . . I would find work: I was determined to' (Halder 2006: 123).

Instead of yielding to an unfavorable situation, Baby pressed hard, displayed courage, and questioned her state. Her feminism manifests through her sense of self-worth and optimism, in her ability to take charge, and in determining the course of her own life. Nowhere in her text and conversation does she regret her status as an underprivileged woman. Her unabashed proclamation of her 'single' status marked by sexual restraint and 'purity' speaks to her strength as an individual and her allegiance to the hegemonic middle-class culture that demands physical purity and restraint from women. Her own account of her life reverses the two contrasting prototypes of working-class women as hapless victims of inexorable socioeconomic conditions and as aggressive, sexually promiscuous individuals acting as a threat and a counterfoil to middle-class women and respectability.

Baby both sustains and disrupts the myth of the ideal family fostered by India's middle-class. Baby displayed a commitment to the ideology of 'social feminism' that emerged in the context of the newly educated 'respectable women' of the colonial era (Forbes 1996: 7)—she tied her rights and autonomy to her familial obligation. Baby personified the model of an ideal mother that was once reserved only for upper-class women. Her critique came in her everyday forms of resistance: she protested as a wife and a mother trying to rescue herself and her children from an abusive husband and father. After the birth of her third child, to prevent further pregnancies she took control of her own body and underwent a surgery without the consent of her husband (Halder 2006: 97). I contend, therefore, that Baby's autobiography is an act of critical feminist practice. She is neither an ardent social critic nor a rebel trying to transform the system. But her feminism is embedded in her extraordinary acts of courage, in her own ways of offering resistance, and most importantly, in questioning the odds and discriminations that she faced all her life. Baby defied gender stereotypes, challenged prevailing customs, but gave in to the persuasions of motherhood, the specter of which haunted her since she was a child.

MOTHERHOOD, RESPECTABILITY, AND DOMESTIC WORK

A Life Less Ordinary offers possibilities of multiple readings, but I emphasize the trope of the loss of her mother and the responsibility of motherhood that appear as a refrain in her narrative. Baby was moved by a desire to be an ideal mother—the mother who bestowed 'motherly' care that she lacked in her personal life. In her own words, her childhood ended with the sudden disappearance of her mother. She clung to the memories of her mother by holding on to the coin that the latter pressed into her hand before she left. Later in life she imagined how her hardship would have been alleviated if her mother were alive. However, in real life when Baby encountered her mother at a mature age, she immediately felt the unbridgeable distance between them—the love, affection, and protection that she often invoked about her mother was a myth from which she derived her faith and emotional sustenance. Baby's mother followed certain dictates of respectability but she did not abide by any prescribed norms of motherhood and abandoned her children without looking back. Baby constantly exalted the virtue of being a mother and led her life following that mission.[13] The discrepancies between Baby and her mother can be attributed to the intergenerational gap but perhaps, more importantly, they demonstrate how the ideology of domesticity and motherhood acted as a restrictive yet enabling force socially, culturally, economically, and politically (see Banerjee 2010).

Baby's work is interspersed with accounts of children, of her own and those of other relatives and siblings, not to mention her own experience as a child—a victim of ruthless neglect, lack of education, child-marriage, pregnancies, and motherhood. In fact, more than half of Baby's narrative is one of a 'denied childhood,' shorn of pleasures and happiness, and filled with fear, torture, and anxieties, as well as physical and emotional anguish. She tried to overcome the repetition of these horrific experiences in the life of her children, but of little avail. For circumstances beyond her control, her eldest son could not get regular schooling and hired himself as a child-worker in different positions. Sometimes Baby would lose touch with him, not knowing where he was. Baby's book documents, perhaps inadvertently, the condition under which poor and disadvantaged children grow up in India. They are not only subject to child labor and unhealthy living conditions, but are witnesses to various kinds of abuses and exploitative practices (Halder 2006: 63–64). Baby's accounts thus bear testimony to some of the most pressing issues in the subcontinent and worldwide.[14]

Furthermore, as Baby is possessed by the specter of her own mother and her own compelling commitment to motherhood, her father figures more frequently in her lived experiences and writings.[15] Baby represents him ungrudgingly, and without any element of idolization and the father evolves from a reckless, abusive, temperamental 'bogeyman' into a more complex character with sentiment, affection, and obvious humanly limitations and dependencies. He is a 'subaltern' man, located at the bottom of the society, lacking both material and spiritual capital and inhering many layers of hierarchy and subordination in both the present and the colonial past. At the same time Baby's total lack of trust or expectation from male members close to her life, on the one hand, and her own self-reliance defying patriarchy, on the other, further reinforces her claims as a 'free,' independent, and single mother.

Baby's life embodies old values and new confidence. Her narrative explodes the myth of the ideal family providing comfort and succor, a haven and a refuge, that the nationalist ideologues so carefully crafted during the colonial era and the legacy of which continues to the present (Chatterjee 1993; Sarkar 2001). The rhetoric of the *Sangh Parivar* (*parivar* meaning family) of the right-wing Hindu fundamentalist party still attests to the political implication of the metaphor of 'family' in the present. Motherhood and the struggle for survival are both entwined in Baby's life.

Committed to the values of 'respectability' and motherhood that the colonial patriarchy produced, Baby emphasized in her conversation with me that the profession of domestic service allowed her to 'stay clean,' by which she meant, protected from sexual exploitation.[16] Unlike her mother, she succeeded in overcoming the stigma associated with working women and her life as a single working mother bridges the dichotomy and ambiguity that prevailed in the superficial divide between the home and the world in colonial Indian culture. Subscribing to the ideology of 'respectability' that the colonial patriarchy produced, Baby's life upheld that she was no less respectable than her employing mistresses—sexually chaste, morally sound, clean, efficient, and articulate. Furthermore, overcoming the stigma associated with domestic service as 'dirty jobs,' she raised her children along 'middle-class' values. By foregrounding her experience of domestic work, Baby elevates the status of domestic service by using the profession as a stepping-stone for further improvement in life—a process that had unfolded in other geopolitical locales of the western hemisphere much earlier (see Banerjee 2004).

CONCLUSION

Baby helps break the silences of women domestics of the late colonial era and the problems they grappled with—economic urgency, lack of familial support, abusive and exploitative work environment, and a need for their own sustenance, combined with the responsibility of raising children and family. If Baby's life sheds light on the experience of growing up as a girl-child in an underprivileged environment in the present, it also gives us insights into how women and children from similar backgrounds overcame these challenges in the past.

Baby's life affords us an insight into the temporal and spatial transition from colonial past to the postcolonial present. A linear reading across time allows us to witness the coming of age of a postcolonial nation-state—from a ravaged and undermined status to a more assured and complicated political economy acting as a key player in the ongoing process of globalization. As part of a global workforce, Baby participates in social reproduction that underwrites the profession of caregiving and domestic service (Laslett and Brenner 1989). Baby's adoption of domestic service as a means of survival indicates the persistent cultural bias in sexual division of labor upholding domestic work as women's work; at the same time it demonstrates a rising demand for domestic service created by working women of the upwardly mobile middle-class whose claim to status partly lay on hiring paid help for housework. In real life, Baby punctures a patriarchal reality. By assuming the role of the breadwinner as a domestic worker, by seizing the role of decision-making for her family, Baby challenges the gender stereotypes of a predominantly patriarchal society. In fact, a large section of part-time domestics in urban India today are 'married' yet single women, not supported by their spouse, single-handedly shouldering the financial responsibility of raising children and running the household (Ray and Qayum 2009: 61). Straddling the intersection of myriad forces—disruption of family life, political-economy driven by late capitalism transporting her beyond her familial locale, her commitment to motherhood, and the intervention of the print media and powerful intellectuals who made 'ordinary' Baby 'extraordinary'—Baby lays bare a story not that unfamiliar in the social terrain of India, but consistently elided in history.

By foregrounding Baby, I continue my engagement with recuperating the history of domestic workers—from indirect representation to direct self-assertion; from a synecdochic presence to a protagonist. Baby consciously told her own life in the guise of an autobiographer, not as a social critic or an activist. Her life-story enables us to transition from the personal to the political—wielding the pen, she unabashedly presented to the public the injustices and oppression that riddle the life of working-class women. Baby's positionality as a writer, the success of telling her own life-story by leveraging the rudimentary education she received, catapulted her from the hidden corners of the home to the limelight of international attention. Understandably, Baby considers education as the only weapon that would fortify working-class women to resist injustices afflicting their lives. No wonder, after much contemplation, she dedicated her first book to her school teachers who taught her Bengali language and literature. She dreams of a better future for her children as professionals and not as unskilled workers. But as she told me in her interview, she herself will continue to be a provider of service (*seva*) to her mentor Prabodh Kumar.

I have posited Baby Halder's life-work as a critical feminist practice to expand the awareness of alternate counter-hegemonic feminist practices specific to their own location and their emancipatory possibilities by subverting, challenging, upsetting, and destabilizing the status quo. As Inderpal Grewal and Caren Kaplan have alerted us, 'If the world is currently structured by transnational economic links and cultural asymmetries, locating feminist practices within these structures becomes imperative' (2002: 3). Baby fights against specific and multiple hegemonies of an oppressive patriarchal system of her father, husband, and the society at large. Interestingly, she is also fueled and nurtured by a powerful patriarchal minority, the empathetic employer and his friends (an exception rather than the norm) who made 'invisible' Baby 'visible' by making it possible for her 'to live, work, write and publish within a hegemonic culture' (Grewal 2002: 251).

Baby's story can be read as one of unequal developments in India where a vast majority of the female workforce (72 percent), many of them underage and hence children, work as domestic workers. Needless to say, they hardly enjoy any protection or legal rights from the government. Initially, the Bill on the *Protection of Women Against Sexual Harassment at Workplace*, passed on December 17, 2010, did not even include domestic workers. Later, at the urging of the National Domestic Workers Movement, the Women and Child Development ministry decided to include the 47.5 million domestic workers under the Bill in March 2012. The Bill was finally approved by the Union Cabinet in May 2012, and it included domestic workers within its purview.[17] In an age when international newspapers regularly print the hapless stories of abused domestic workers in India, Baby's commentary breaks the conspiracy of silence. Baby now avers with confidence and pride—'I am a domestic worker and not a writer. It is no less to be a domestic help and it is extremely important that I write.'[18]

NOTES

1. I thank the two anonymous reviewers as well as Victoria Haskins, Claire Lowrie, and Sheryl Kroen, for their valuable suggestions in shaping this article.
2. Baby Halder's autobiography *Alo Aandhari* (*Light and Darkness*) was first translated from Bengali and published in Hindi with the aid of her employer Prabodh Kumar Shrivastava in 2002. The Bengali version came out in 2003.
3. Ray and Qayum (2009) have emphatically justified the use of the term 'servant' instead of domestics or domestic workers. See also Haskins and Lowrie's 'Anxieties and Intimacies,' in this volume.
4. Baby Halder, interview with author, May 31, 2012; Kumuda Pal, interview with author, June 1995, Kolkata: transcripts are held by the author.
5. In India it is customary to refer to domestics by their first names.
6. Halder interview.
7. Pal interview.
8. It is instructive to note that Baby addressed her male and female employers as 'sahibs' and 'memsahibs,' terms that were used to denote white men and women in the British period; the prevalence of these terms in Indian language to denote positions of power allude to the colonial baggage citizens of free India still carry with them (Halder 2006: 126–29, 132–37). For a discussion of the negative connotations the term 'memsahib' embodied in the colonial period see Lowrie's chapter in this volume.
9. A better transcultural comparison for Baby Halder could be Margaret Powell (1907–1984), the British maid who wrote her autobiography *Below Stairs* (1968) that became a best seller and the inspiration for the TV show *Upstairs Downstairs*. However, the trajectory of Halder's life is quite different from that of Powell's.
10. For the continuing relevance of domestic service in twentieth-century England see Delap 2011.
11. For details on the Mandal Commission, see Chapter 5 of the official website of the Ministry of Social Justice and Empowerment in India. http://socialjustice.nic.in/pdf/Chapter5.pdf. Accessed October 3, 2013.
12. As Carolyn Steedman reminds us, this is a trope not uncommon in the writings and experiences of working-class women in other cultures as well. I invoke Steedman not to echo Western feminist principles but to identify common aspirations and experiences of working-class women that cut across borders.
13. Baby Halder's continuing 'engagement' with her mother is also evident in her second book, *Eshat Rupantar* (2008).
14. According to a report by UNICEF, 74 percent of child domestic laborers in India are between the ages of 12 and 16 and Baby's son was one of them: see Rao (no date).
15. Baby Halder's second book *Eshat Rupantar* (2008) is mostly about her encounter with her father after the publication of her first book in Hindi.
16. Halder interview. Baby admitted to me the hazards of sexual exploitation particularly for live-in young maids, as evidenced in Ray and Qayum 2009. But for her, she considered domestic service as the 'safest' opportunity for survival and raising a family.
17. This Bill provides protection not only to women who are employed but also to any woman who enters the workplace as a client, customer, apprentice, and daily wage worker or in ad hoc capacity. Students, research scholars in colleges and universities, and patients in hospitals have also been covered. *Hindustan Times*, March 18, 2012; *The Times of India*, May 11, 2012; http://articles.timesofindia.indiatimes.com/2012–05–11/india/

31668111_1_workplace-bill-molestation-and-eve-teasing-vishaka-vs-state. Accessed September 19, 2012.
18. Halder interview.

REFERENCES

Banerjee, Nirmala. 1990. 'Working Women in Colonial Bengal: Modernization and Marginalization.' In *Recasting Women: Essays in Indian Colonial History*, edited by Kumkum Sangari and Sudesh Vaid, 269–301. New Brunswick: Rutgers University Press.
Banerjee, Swapna M. 2004. *Men, Women and Domestics: Articulating Middle-Class Identity in Colonial Bengal*. Delhi: Oxford University Press.
Banerjee, Swapna. 2010. 'Debates on Domesticity and the Position of Women in Late Colonial India.' *History Compass Journal* 8(6): 455–73.
Borthwick, Meredith. 1984. *Changing Role of Women in Bengal, 1849–1905*. Princeton: Princeton University Press.
Chakrabarty, Dipesh. 1993. 'The Difference—Deferral of (A) Colonial Modernity: Public Debates on Domesticity in British Bengal.' *History Workshop* 36(1): 1–34.
Chatterjee, Partha. 1993. *The Nation and Its Fragments*. Princeton: Princeton University Press.
Chowdhury, Sushil. 2004. *Nababi Amal-e Murshidabad*. Kolkata: Ananda Publishers.
Dasi, Binodini. 1998. *My Story and My Life as an Actress*. Edited and translated by Rimli Bhattacharya. New Delhi: Kali for Women.
Delap, Lucy. 2011. *Knowing Their Place: Domestic Service in Twentieth-Century Britain*. London: Oxford University Press.
Devi, Rashsundari. 1999 [1868]. *Amar Jiban*. Kolkata: Writers Workshop.
Forbes, Geraldine. 1996. *Women in Modern India*. Cambridge: Cambridge University Press.
Grewal, Inderpal. 2002. 'Autobiographic Subjects and Diasporic Locations: *Meatless Days* and *Borderlands*.' In *Scattered Hegemonies: Postmodernity and Transnational Feminist Practices*, edited by Inderpal Grewal and Caren Kaplan, 231–54. Minneapolis: University of Minnesota Press.
Grewal, Inderpal, and Caren Kaplan. 2002. 'Transnational Feminist Practices and Questions of Postmodernity.' In *Scattered Hegemonies: Postmodernity and Transnational Feminist Practices*, edited by Inderpal Grewal and Caren Kaplan, 1–36. Minneapolis: University of Minnesota Press.
Halder, Baby. 2002. *Alo Aandhari*. Kolkata: Roshnai Prokashan.
Halder, Baby. 2006. *A Life Less Ordinary*. Translated by Urvashi Butalia. New Delhi: Zubaan Books in collaboration with Penguin.
Halder, Baby. 2008. *Eshat Rupantar*. Kolkata: Roshnai Prokashan.
Hoerder, Dirk. 2013. 'Translocalism' in *The Encyclopedia of Global Human Migration*. DOI: 10.1002/9781444351071.wbeghm540. Accessed October 3, 2013.
John, Koti. 2013. 'Domestic Women Workers in Urban Informal Sector.' *Abhinav: National Monthly Refereed Journal of Research in Arts and Education* 2(2): 1–16. www.abhinavjournal.com/images/Arts_&_Education/Feb13/1.pdf. Accessed September 25, 2013.
Kaur, Ravinder. 2004. 'Empowerment and the City: The Case of Female Migrants in Domestic Work.' *Harvard Asia Quarterly* 8(2): 15–25.
Laslett, Barbara, and Johanna Brenner. 1989. 'Gender and Social Reproduction: Historical Perspectives.' *Annual Review of Sociology* 15: 381–404.

Majumdar, Parama. 2006. 'A Prof. Discovered a Subaltern Writer.' *Merinews*, May 25. http://www.merinews.com/article/a-prof-discovered-a-subaltern-writer/178.shtml. Accessed September 24, 2012.
McClintock, Anne. 1995. *Imperial Leather: Race, Gender, and Sexuality in the Colonial Context*. London: Routledge.
Nasrin, Taslima. 2002 [1999]. *Amar Meyebela*. Kolkata: People's Book Society.
Poovey, Mary. 1988. *Uneven Developments: The Ideological Work of Gender in Mid-Victorian England*. Chicago: University of Chicago Press.
Powell, Margaret. 1968. *Below Stairs*. London: Peter Davies.
Qayum, Semin, and Raka Ray. 2003. 'Grappling with Modernity: India's Respectable Classes and the Culture of Domestic Servitude.' *Ethnography* 4(4): 520–55.
Ray, Raka, and Semin Qayum. 2009. *Cultures of Servitude: Modernity, Domesticity and Class in India*. Stanford: Stanford University Press.
Rao, Jyoti. No Date. 'Assessing Child Domestic Labour in India.' *UNICEF India: Child Protection*. www.unicef.org/india/child_protection_2053.htm. Accessed September 25, 2013.
Sarkar, Tanika. 1999. *Words to Win: The Making of Amar Jiban: A Modern Autobiography*. New Delhi: Kali for Women.
Sarkar, Tanika. 2001. *Hindu Wife, Hindu Nation*. Delhi: Permanent Black.
Sen, Haimabati. 2001. *Haimabati Sen: 'Because I Am a Woman': A Child Widow's Memoirs from India*. Translated and introduced by Tapan Raychaudhuri and Geraldine Forbes. New Delhi: Chronicle Books.
Spivak, Gayatri Chakravorty. 1988. 'Can the Subaltern Speak?' In *Marxism and the Interpretation of Culture*, edited by Cary Nelson and Lawrence Grossberg, 271–313. Urbana: University of Illinois Press.
Steedman, Carolyn. 1986. *Landscape for a Good Woman: A Story of Two Lives*. New Brunswick: Rutgers University Press.
van Woerkens, Martine. 2010. 'Baby Halder.' In *Nous Ne Sommes Pas Des Fleurs: Deux Siecles de Combats Feministes en Inde*, edited by Martine van Woerkens, 279–99. Paris: Albin Michel.

14 From Our Own Backyard?
Understanding UK Au Pair Policy as Colonial Legacy and Neocolonial Dream

Rosie Cox

Au pairs have long been an important part of the British solution to a perceived 'servant problem,' a problem which is as much about the tensions arising from having 'other' people within the private home as it is about labor supply. An au pair (meaning 'as an equal') is meant to live with a host family and provide help with childcare and housework in exchange for 'pocket money' and the opportunity to learn more about the host culture. This chapter examines a recent change in the regulation of au pairing in the UK, the abolition of the au pair visa in 2008, and seeks to understand it as part of a historical continuity in attitudes towards who is and who is not appropriate to carry out domestic work in private homes. The long vexed question of who is an appropriate domestic worker is characterized by a desire to negotiate closeness and distance through imaginings of sameness and difference. Within Britain, in contrast to many colonized areas, this negotiation of difference has been mapped onto domestic workers as a favoring of 'othered' white workers and a series of white, non-English groups have been preferred to work inside middle-class homes. The positioning of Eastern Europeans as the new au pairs continues these imaginings.

In 2004, when the Accession Eight (A8) countries of Eastern Europe joined the EU,[1] only three countries from the existing European Union (EU15) granted A8 nationals immediate free access to their labor markets: Ireland, Sweden and the UK (Anderson, Ruhs, Rogaly and Spencer 2006). While this policy was applauded by antiracists and those concerned about migrants' rights in the UK, the government rhetoric surrounding it revealed more of an imperial swagger than it did a humanitarian impulse (McDowell 2009). The Government made clear that A8 workers were welcome as cheap labor rather than as fellow and equal Europeans and the restrictions put on their access to welfare[2] made clear that only those who would work were welcome at all. The UK Government positioned itself as powerful compared to its weaker, poorer neighbors. This approach made concrete the neocolonial imaginings of the A8 as a source of cheap labor and a market for UK goods and services and the UK as the powerful beneficiary of these flows. Recent UK government policy has focused on allowing EU migrants access to labor markets while restricting access to others, particularly those who are considered 'unskilled.' This approach meets the demand for low-waged labor whilst also keeping down the numbers of 'visible,' that is non-white, migrants who come to the country and also keeps official immigration figures low, as EU nationals are not counted as immigrants.

As Bridget Anderson argues, recent debates around EU migrants have racialized their whiteness (Anderson 2013, 2007; see also McDowell 2009). Different 'white' groups are brought into existence by the demands of the labor market and the operation of immigration regulation. In the current instance, 'EU members,' or 'A8 workers,' have been constructed as groups who are more or less welcome within in the UK to carry out certain forms of work, including domestic work in private homes. At other times other 'white' groups have been included in the home/homeland in similar ways (Walter 2004).

There are commonalities in the way that government policy has reacted to shortages in the supply of domestic workers by steering non-British, 'white' women into the sector and this chapter locates au pairing today in a history of racialized domestic service which has produced acceptable 'white' groups to live and work in middle-class homes. Throughout the chapter I argue that 'other' 'white' women have been deliberately steered into domestic labor by UK immigration policies because non-British 'white' women offer a solution to the problem of negotiating closeness and distance within the home. As 'white' women they are acceptable in an intimate space but their immigrant status and 'otherness' can be used to provide a justification for why they are carrying out denigrated work. Whilst the chapter focuses on a contemporary example, it invites historians to consider how British domestic service in the past was racialized, and closely connected to colonialism, and the significance of 'whiteness' in this history.

AU PAIR POLICY TODAY

In November 2008 the UK introduced a new immigration system, the Points Based Immigration Scheme (PBS), which replaced existing immigration routes including the au pair visa. Given the popularity of the au pair scheme and the large number of middle-class, and therefore relatively politically powerful, people who employed au pairs, abolishing this migration route might seem perverse. In practice, however, au pairing has not been eradicated but rather has been expanded while being moved further from government regulation and support. This change to the organization and positioning of the au pair scheme can be thought of as the latest chapter in the long-standing construction of some (white) people as suitable domestic workers and others as not. The deregulation of au pairing is based on an assumption that au pair roles will be taken by EU workers, particularly those from the A8 countries. These workers, like so many before them, are constructed in UK policy as 'European' enough to be welcome in the homes of British families, yet not worthy of equal rights with British or other European citizens. Like the Irish women working as domestics in the nineteenth century who are discussed by Walter (2001), their whiteness hides their difference and the discrimination against them.

From 1969 to 2008 the UK au pair scheme reflected the European Agreement on 'au pair' Placement, part of the Strasbourg Treaty,[3] and was formalized through the 'au pair visa.' Details of the scheme were set out by the Home Office as the authority that issued visas. Au pair visas were available only to people from Europe and, originally, only Western and Central Europe (see Cox 2006). The au pair visa specified that au pairs must be aged 17–27 years, unmarried and without dependent children; they could stay in the United Kingdom for up to two years but would have to leave the country within a week if they were not living with a 'host family.' In addition the Home Office stipulated that au pairs had to be engaged in 'cultural exchange' and improving their English. They could do twenty-five hours of 'light housework' or childcare per week plus an additional two evenings of babysitting, but should not be in sole charge of very young children. In exchange for this the au pair had their own bedroom, were provided with meals, and received 'pocket money.' For pocket money the Home Office advised £65 per week in 2008. It cautioned that if an au pair was given much above this amount this would suggest that the person was 'filling the position of domestic servant or similar, which would require a work permit' (Home Office website, quoted in Newcombe 2004: 16). The visa was not a work permit and the official construction of the au pair avoided other tropes associated with employment—the au pair received 'pocket money' not pay, and lived with a 'host family' rather than an employer.

As the EU expanded and treaties allowed EU and European Economic Area (EEA) nationals access to the UK labor market, the number of au pairs needing a visa declined. In November 2008 the au pair visa scheme was closed, as part of the United Kingdom's move to the Points Based Immigration System (PBS) that encompasses all visa and work permit categories. Despite the fact that a relatively small percentage of au pairs needed visas by 2008, the existence of the visa, and its subsequent abolition, have been important in delineating the au pair role and the rights of au pairs. The existence of the visa required the Home Office to define au pairing, to set expectations on host families and au pairs, to suggest pocket money rates and to delimit the hours an au pair should work. These guidelines had applied to all au pairs, not just those with visas. Official advice to au pairs and host families was provided by the Home Office through their website and in leaflets and it was a requirement that all au pairs entering the United Kingdom should be given a Home Office leaflet. The advice provided by the Home Office was recirculated by agencies and language schools as well as between au pairs and host families. Whilst there were still many abuses of the scheme and it is estimated that only a minority of au pairs worked within the boundaries set out by the Home Office (Cox 2006; Cox and Narula 2003), the guidelines had provided an official basis for delimiting the au pair role which, theoretically at least, provided some legal protection.

From Our Own Backyard? 259

Since November 2008, au pairs in the United Kingdom have officially been integrated into Tier 5 of the PBS. This is the tier that covers youth mobility and temporary workers. While au pairs are now mentioned in those roles covered by the Tier 5 Youth Mobility Scheme (YMS) (a category open only to nationals from a very small number of countries, most of them English speaking), there is no longer any detail given by the Home Office on what 'au pairing' does or does not involve; and no suggestion of pocket money, appropriate tasks or living conditions.

Despite the UK government no longer offering its own definition of or guidelines around au pairing, other legislation, including the National Minimum Wage (NMW), specifies that au pairs are not covered by their provisions. Guidance on holiday entitlement states that in order to have a right to holiday a person has to be considered a 'worker,' a status which au pairs do not clearly have. Au pairing is therefore still expected to exist but is now an unregulated and degraded role. The term 'au pair' can be applied to anyone from overseas who does domestic work within a private home and once this label has been given, au pairs are entirely unprotected by any form of employment legislation, as they are not considered to be employees and they are not monitored by any official body.

Importantly the government's own impact assessment for Tier 5 of the PBS concluded that *no one* was expected to enter the United Kingdom as an au pair through this route (UK Border Agency 2008: 5); it was imagined that instead au pairs would come from the new EU member states and would not need visas. The UK Government formally stated that its goal was that all 'low skilled' jobs would be taken by EU nationals (Home Office 2006) and this was clearly what was expected for au pairing. By opening UK labor markets to A8 nationals at the time of accession and closing almost all migration routes for 'low skilled' workers from outside the EU, the Government was attempting to meet demands for low-waged labor without increasing the numbers of visible (that is, non-white) migrants in the country. This approach treats Eastern Europe as the UK's backyard, an area that is close but not equal and which will supply workers to meet the UK's needs without those workers having the same rights as British citizens or other EU nationals.

Whilst this approach to A8 labor is not in any way restricted to au pairs, the example of the change in regulation of au pairing epitomizes the extremely strategic attitude of the UK government towards A8 workers and shows continuity with earlier schemes to supply domestic labor. Whereas a number of other European countries and the US have expanded the au pair scheme to include people from beyond Europe (see Macdonald 2010 on the US and Isaksen 2011 for the Nordic countries), the UK has attempted to exclude non-Europeans from au pairing, officially at least. In practice many people born outside Europe now live as au pairs and the deregulation of the sector has made this both easier and more socially acceptable. The increased supply of low-waged labor from the A8 countries combined with the deregulation of au pairing has created markets for au pairs and other domestic workers that did not previously exist. Families with much lower incomes are now taking on au pairs to perform a very wide range of tasks (see Busch 2011; Busch and Cox 2012). The landscape of au pairing has changed considerably in recent years with au pairs becoming much less distinct from domestic workers and less likely to be involved in any form of cultural exchange or language learning. UK migration policy has facilitated the employment of domestic workers and has constructed certain people as appropriate to provide cheap labor in denigrated work in private homes.

RACIALIZATION, COLONIAL HISTORY AND PAID DOMESTIC WORK

The employment of domestic workers within an advanced capitalist society creates a conundrum which the racialization of those workers seeks to resolve. Simply put, the conundrum is why one person should clean up after or wait upon another. In earlier societies the idea that some people were intrinsically better than others explained this; the wealthy deserved to be waited on by the poor simply because they were 'better.' Religious teaching reinforced such a view and class differences were portrayed as natural and desirable. In late modern societies there is an assumption that people are equal and take their roles in life due to merit or skill. Capitalism is, in theory at least, antithetical to the idea of 'god given' differences between people and uses instead the rhetoric of moral worth, education and initiative to explain class divides. When domestic workers are employed the fiction of social equality is made plain and employers of domestic workers and others (such as governments) who support the continuation of paid domestic work search around for an explanation to the question at its heart. As it is women who are the majority of employers as well as workers, gender norms cannot be invoked to explain the disparity, and it cannot be suggested that the maid is more able than her mistress, so explanations based on skill are unavailable. Some other 'natural' differences between workers and their employers are therefore looked to and differences in race, nationality or ethnicity are offered to explain why some people carry out domestic work for others. As an interviewee explained to Bridget Anderson:

> It's difficult having someone working for you from the same race because we have this idea of social class in our minds, don't we? And that would be uncomfortable in your house. Whereas when it's somebody from a different country, you don't have all that baggage. . . . There's none of that middle-class, working-class, upper-class thing . . . it's just a different race.
>
> (2007: 251–52)

Racialization, the 'othering' of one group based on a racial or ethnic characteristic, is therefore central to the organization of paid domestic work in many contemporary situations. Racialization makes natural a divide that is social, and offers a way to negotiate profound inequalities within the intimate space of the home. Racialization is also a dynamic process, producing categories of difference, whilst also responding to already existing axes of inequality (Anderson 2013).

The UK au pair policy can also be seen as part of a colonial legacy and that legacy is resonant in the organization of domestic work and the racialization of domestic workers. Anne McClintock (1995) argues that the British cult of domesticity, which underpinned the highest points of demand for domestic labor in Victorian times, was explicitly related to the colonial endeavor. British colonialism produced a particular imagining of 'home' which depended on domestic labor to produce and reproduce gender and class hierarchies. Home became a place of conspicuous idleness and consumption for middle-class women; a place to display objects—many of them the outputs and representations of imperialism—which had to be maintained and shown to others. In this period the home became a place to display class through gender difference. Women's idleness at home was *the* mark of men's wealth (see also Tosh 2007) but displays of middle-class femininity were based on the use of working-class women's labor, most obviously in the home but also, for example, in the 'sweated' trade of dressmaking. McClintock describes a 'doubling' of women (1995: 98) a looking-glass world in which the femininity and idleness of middle-class women depended upon the labor and degradation of working-class women.

In addition, racial difference was mapped on to class and gender difference in the homes of the British middle and upper classes. The physical closeness and social distance between the working and middle classes (in both homes and the new industrial cities) necessitated a profound and relentless 'othering.' Gender and class were both racialized in representations of working-class women. Working-class women were represented as dark skinned and simian and as masculine in build and facial features. Closeness to dirt literally produces blackness on the skin and this was used to connote a fundamental difference from those who are white and portrayed as both physically and morally 'clean.' Differences in race, class and gender, therefore, cannot be easily separated out from each other. Class difference was represented as gender and racial difference and women who were seen as 'less white' were also seen as 'less female.' The impact on the metropole was profound. As McClintock argues, 'In the urban metropolis some of the formative ambiguities of gender and class were managed and policed by the discourses on race, so that the iconography of imperialism entered white middle- and upper-middle class identity with fundamental if contradictory force' (1995: 77). Divisions of gender, class and race were negotiated through and within the middle-class home in the organization of domestic service. Inevitably, the colonial experience shaped the ways in which 'white' domestic service was managed and represented in Britain, and continues to reverberate today.

The British government took steps to ensure the supply of 'white' domestic workers during the nineteenth and twentieth centuries in ways which today's policy on A8 workers echoes. Bronwyn Walter (2001, 2004) has shown how Irish women were a small but significant part of the British servant workforce who were both racialized as 'different' and made invisible due to their whiteness. New analysis of the 1881 British census suggests that Irish women made up 3.4 percent of the servant workforce in London (more than numbers of Scottish and Welsh servants combined) and that numbers had grown since 1851. By the 1930s Irish servants would be viewed as indispensable to the English economy. A memo from the British Minister of Labour in 1932, written when the British government was considering the repatriation of Irish workers due to the Depression, stated that 'there is no doubt that under present conditions the total number of workers born in the Irish Free State *with the possible exception of those engaged in domestic service* could be replaced rapidly and without much difficulty by workers born in Britain' (quoted in Walter 2004: 479; emphasis added). As Walter states, echoing McClintock, 'In order that the "English" home could be clean, and the mother freed to devote her energies to her children's upbringing, working-class, including migrant, women provided invisible services. Their "whiteness" helped to produce this invisibility and obscure the dependence of constructions of Englishness on the labour of Irish women' (2004: 484).

In the second half of the twentieth century, other 'white' groups were looked to, to become domestic workers in British homes. One such group were Latvian 'European Volunteer Workers' (EVWs) who came to Britain at the end of the Second World War. They were recruited directly from labor camps where they had been taken by the Germans and were seen by the British government as a solution to labor shortages in 'female' jobs in hospitals, sanatoriums and private households. Between 1946 and 1950, 120,000 Latvians accepted assisted passages to the UK and France under economic migrant schemes (McDowell 2005: 95).

The UK developed the 'Baltic Cygnet' scheme to recruit women from the displaced persons camps to work in hospitals and private homes. British discourse around the development of this scheme focused on the attributes of women from various different countries and how appropriate their bodies would be as workers and citizens of the UK. Ministry of Labour officials traveled to the camps in 1946 to assess the suitability of women from Latvia, Lithuania and Estonia to be domestic workers in institutions and homes in the UK. The name 'Baltic Cygnet' conveys much about how the UK Government hoped the EVWs would be seen. As McDowell puts it, the name presents 'a vision of vulnerable yet attractive young swans, redolent of purity, sailing across the water to the UK and emerging from their drab protective colouring as cygnets into the full beauty of an adult swan under the guidance of the British state or public' (2005: 98). The whiteness and youth of the cygnet, both suggesting purity and vulnerability, cannot be overlooked. In its naming of the scheme the British state was clearly signaling the benign and acceptable whiteness of these workers. As 'cygnets' EVWs were also presented as innocent, and virginal and, therefore, as suitable wives for white, British men and potential mothers of future Britons. A memorandum from the Foreign Labour Committee after a visit to the camps in Germany recorded the advantages of Baltic women:

> The women are of good appearance, are scrupulously clean in their persons and habits. . . . There is little doubt that the specially selected who come to this country will be an exceptionally healthy and fit body . . . and would constitute a good and desirable element in our population.
>
> (quoted in McDowell 2005: 99)

It was whiteness that fitted Latvian women both to the work they were steered into and to the role as possible wives of British men and mothers of the next generation. The entry of European migrant workers and Irish migrants 'was regarded as less contentious than that of Caribbean migrants by both government officials responsible for immigration policy and by the UK public at large because "they passed an unwritten test of racial acceptability"' (Paul 1997: *xiii*; quoted in McDowell 2005: 93; see also Webster 1998).

This history cannot be overlooked in discussions of the organization of domestic labor today. An imagined temporal break in the employment of domestic workers in the UK during the 1960s and 70s makes it easy to discuss domestic work today as if it were shorn from historical context—a problem of the overworked 'career woman' rather than the middle-class home. This discontinuity never was as absolute as was imagined (Delap 2011) and the centuries of history do not disappear just because we overlook them. They shape immigration regulations as well as 'common sense' imaginings of exactly what sorts of bodies are welcome in the British home and the British nation.

Employing domestic workers is an exercise in managing ambiguity, in creating difference to justify inequality. The domestic worker makes possible the class, gender and racialized performances of her employers in part through her labor and in part through the contrast she provides (see Anderson 2000). Anderson (2007) unpacks the intertwining ways in which aspects of paid domestic labor combine to create a situation where employers favor migrant workers to work inside their homes. Immigration status, country of origin, and 'race' all interact and are used by employers in the management of their relationship of workers. Employing migrants can offer employers additional control over domestic workers, particularly when visa categories operate to limit the jobs open to a worker, but there are also more subtle effects of migrant status. Employers are able to recast class and income differences as racial differences in order to make themselves more comfortable, as in the case of Anderson's interviewee quoted above. Additionally, focusing on national differences allows employers to imagine themselves as providing opportunities to someone who would not have them at home. 'Working as a domestic worker or as an au pair in a private household can be transformed from a grim necessity to a golden opportunity when it is undertaken by a hard pressed migrant with limited opportunities' (Anderson 2007: 255). In turn the employer becomes a kindly person engaged in a relationship of mutual obligation and dependence, something that is much more comfortable in the private space of the home than the instrumentalist relations of the market would be (see also Anderson 2009).

There is now a large literature on contemporary domestic work which shows how in almost all situations it is structured along racial/ethnic lines. Not only are very large numbers of domestic workers migrants, or from minority ethnic groups in their home countries, but markets for domestic labor are segmented by ethnicity, with different groups of workers imagined as more or less appropriate to carry out particular tasks (see, for example, Pratt 1997 on the contrasting images of Filipina and European nannies in Vancouver; Stiell and England 1997 on the hierarchy of ethnicities of domestic workers in Toronto; and Cox 1999 on similar hierarchies in London). In a number of countries au pairs are important to this balancing of similarity and difference. By definition they must be migrants but are also construed as something other than labor migrants—somewhere between a student and a working holidaymaker (Newcombe 2004). For many employers the idea of engaging in a cultural exchange, however fictitious that might be, makes au pair employment morally more comfortable (Calleman 2010; Stenum 2010).

THE AU PAIR SOLUTION: A HISTORICAL OVERVIEW

The UK au pair scheme, both in its early form and its current incarnation, can be understood within this context of 'solving' the problem of finding (racially) acceptable domestic labor. Au pairs were originally young women from European countries who would move to live with a family in another country in order to learn about language and culture and to learn how to run a home. The idea of light household tasks undertaken by a young 'visitor' in exchange for language learning, plus room and board, had been popular in Europe since the 1890s (Delap 2011), but the au pair scheme really developed from the postwar movement of Swiss, German, Austrian and Danish women who traveled to the United Kingdom to take up domestic posts that British women would no longer fill (Liarou 2008).

Initially it was imagined that daughters would swap homes, each going to live for a period with the other's family, but this aspect of the scheme never caught on and the UK—or perhaps more precisely England—tended to host more au pairs than it sent abroad. The au pair would be an 'extra pair of hands,' an equal to her host family and not a servant, and she was imagined to come from a 'good' family and might employ domestic help herself in the future.

However, from the outset au pairs occupied a contradictory position, expected to do denigrated work that had previously been done by servants in the households they went to, but also imagined as relatively privileged and flighty (Liarou 2008). Au pairing was specifically portrayed as a solution to the class tensions of the servant problem. Lucy Delap (2011: 133) quotes the *Manchester Guardian* of 1958 which stated that it hoped the au pairs would solve 'a delicate social problem for the professional and middle classes who cannot quite afford a full time domestic and whose accommodation is limited so that it is easier for the housewife to have someone around her of her own standing. One does not apologise to social equals.'

Au pairing was formalized in 1969 through the *Treaty of Strasbourg*. The scheme then allowed young women (and it was specifically restricted to women at the start) to travel to another European country for a maximum of two years to provide 'help' to a family in return for room and board and a small amount of pocket money. On one hand, au pairing was seen as a way to travel and meet interesting people, but simultaneously there was evidence of au pairs being exploited and abused. Drawing on the British Vigilance Association's report on the 'Au Pair situation in Great Britain' (1958), Liarou comments:

> [By 1958] the 'Au Pair' system 'has become a means whereby girls under the age of 18 are employed to do almost exactly the same duties as regular domestic servants, with no insurance benefits or legal protection.' By the early 1970s this criticism amounted to what was called the 'Pink Slave Trade' as cases of economic and sexual exploitation of au pair girls were coming to light, and the government undertook to look at the arrangements for admitting them to Britain. On the other hand, au pair girls were accused of 'free-loading, laziness, arriving pregnant or ill to take advantage of free treatment on the National Health Service.'
>
> (2008: 221)

Despite increasing diversity in the British population in the late twentieth century, 'white' women from Europe and the 'old commonwealth' remained popular domestic workers in the UK. In the 1950s there were an estimated 17,000 au pairs coming to Britain each year (Delap 2011) and numbers increased in the 1960s and 70s. After the UK joined the European Union (then EEC) numbers were harder to gauge, as au pairs from member states did not need to apply for au pair visas and so were not counted in this category in immigration statistics. Extrapolations from official statistics and surveys of au pair agencies suggest that numbers continued to grow in the 1980s and 90s (Cox 2006).

The employment of other groups of domestic workers grew in the UK in the 1980s after having fallen for nearly fifty years. While some of the new domestic workers employed in the late 1980s were British women (see Gregson and Lowe 1994) migrants remained important to the sector, particularly within large cities such as London. Britain's colonial history directly shaped this labor market. Citizens of the 'old' (or white) Commonwealth continue to have preferential treatment in UK immigration schemes and until 2008 they were allowed to enter the UK for up to two years as working holidaymakers. This allowed young women from Australia and New Zealand to enter the UK to work as nannies and these women became particularly favored for these posts. They were seen by both employers and placement agencies as being 'like' British people, but with more enthusiasm and initiative. Domestic workers carrying out cleaning and housekeeping roles were more likely to come from Portugal and the Philippines. The UK had made work permits available for domestic servants until 1979 and women who entered the UK on these permits in the 1960s and 70s later moved out of full-time, live-in posts to become hourly paid cleaners. In the 1980s they were then joined by migrants from a range of other countries as the market for cleaning services grew (see Cox 1999). Au pairs were differentiated from these other groups. They were not as privileged as British, New Zealander and Australian nannies and would often be doing similar work for a fraction of the pay (Anderson, Ruhs, Rogaly and Spencer 2006; Busch 2011). Yet they were favored in comparison to Southern European, Asian and Latin American women, who were seen as appropriate to carry out cleaning, but not childcare.

There also were, and still are, differences amongst au pairs based on nationality, 'race' and religion. Anderson (2007), writing on the operation of the au pair scheme before the UK au pair visa was removed in 2008, describes both subtle and blatant ways in which prejudices for and against certain groups operated. Agencies she interviewed explained that they found it particularly difficult to place black au pairs (who were mostly French nationals[4]) and Muslim au pairs (mostly from Turkey). Host families were happy to express likes and dislikes for particular groups and to attribute 'national characteristics' such as being 'docile' or 'good with children' based on their previous experiences. My own research in the early 2000s found similar practices amongst host families in London. Agencies placing au pairs explained that certain nationalities were easier to place than others and could generally command better living and working conditions. Turkish au pairs (and male au pairs I was told) were those that were hardest to place and would be most likely to be offered placements in small flats or remote suburbs or where they were required to care for more than two children.

In the contemporary period, with continuing growth in the numbers of au pairs hosted in the UK, both immigration policies and host family practices continue to favor au pairs of particular nationalities and ethnicities. However, the racialization of migrants to the UK is dynamic, and there are subtle changes over relatively short periods of time in which groups or nationalities are favored. The UK has chosen to allow nationals of EU member states access to labor markets whilst hardening borders for third country nationals, particularly those perceived as 'unskilled.' As part of this process, (legal) access to au pair placements in the UK has been almost entirely restricted to EU passport holders. The policy of favoring 'Europeans' has not produced an undifferentiated experience common to all au pairs; rather, Eastern European 'A8' and 'A2' (Romania and Bulgaria) migrants have become racialized and there is some evidence that they are now disadvantaged within the au pair labor market. Research by Nicky Busch (2011), carried out after the A8 countries had joined the EU, suggested that au pairs could be divided into those from Western Europe who were primarily taking the role in order to perfect their English and enjoy some time abroad before returning home, and 'working' au pairs from Eastern Europe who stayed in the UK for much longer periods of time with no clear route out of au pairing. Members of the second group were generally working longer hours and their work was indistinguishable from that of nannies.

Recent interviews carried out with A2 nationals revealed that they felt particularly limited and poorly treated because of their position within the labor market. Au pairing was one of a small number of 'work' categories that did not require a work permit for this group but A2 au pairs were required to work for a named employer (UK Border Agency 2012). Bulgarian and Romanian nationals were therefore disadvantaged in terms of their choice of jobs and unable to easily leave or resist poor conditions once in an au pair placement. Interviewees explained how this affected them, putting them in a position where they will accept poorer conditions than other nationalities:

> Because for [a] Bulgarian here is very difficult to start a new job here because we have to wait for documents. Now I am with this family and I will receive one card, it's like permission card to stay with this family and it's only about this family. It's not for anyone else. You have to stay with this family one year after the issue of this card and you will get the documents, the rights to go and work somewhere else.[5]

> So I think we should make a difference between Western European au pairs and Eastern European also. . . . I'm seeing this from my Romanian perspective. I don't know, for a French—I mean you know for a French person, why would a French person accept this for the money? I would not accept it. You know I accept it because for me it was a way to get out of Romania and because I wanted to get out of there. I wanted to

learn English for me it was the driving force. I would accept a lot of things just to get out of there, you know?[6]

One result of this different positioning in the labor market was that A2 nationals felt that they were discriminated against and were more likely to be treated as domestic workers while Western Europeans were treated as 'real' au pairs. When asked if she thought her host family treated her differently than how they would treat a French or German au pair, a Bulgarian interviewee replied:

> Well, they will not stay French or German au pair because the French or German girl will not be like—will not agree to work the job I do. I work because I know how it's in my country and how difficult it's there to live. So, I do the job because I know that it's just a temporary job but I will change it and I will not be au pair. But the German people are like—they never used to work [while] they go to school. I used to work. I started to work with 14. So, they never—always their mum and dads give them money and they—it's like [real] life. They will come here just for the extra cultural exchange, not for the cleaning, or . . . I came here for the job, I didn't come just for the cultural exchange.[7]

Further, the same interviewee said: 'I know one German girl and the English family treat the Germans much better than us because we are so little country.'[8] These quotes suggest that immigration policies produce migrants with particular relationships to the labor market, to which employers then respond (Anderson 2010). In this case A2 nationals are constructed as available to do 'low skilled' domestic work in private homes but only in conditions which are less favorable than those of other 'Europeans.'

In the UK racial hierarchies have discriminated and still do discriminate against people of color in favor of those who are 'white.' However, whiteness is not essential, it is socially produced, neither is it undifferentiated but is mediated through age, class, religion and gender. Eastern European migrants to the UK may now be experiencing racism as they find themselves disadvantaged in labor markets relative to 'white' British people and facing hostility from coworkers and service users (McDowell 2009; Cook, Dwyer and Waite 2011; Stevens, Hussein and Manthorpe 2012).

CONCLUSION

Britain has a long history of trying to locate 'acceptable' servants to work in private homes. Acceptable servant bodies had to be different from those of their employers in order to justify and explain their different standings, but servants also needed to be similar enough to live in close proximity, to raise their employers' children and know their intimate lives. This negotiation of closeness and distance has meant that at particular times certain groups of women have been favored as domestic workers and constructed in lay and official discourses as particularly suited to this work. In contrast to areas colonized by Britain where the employment of non-white servants was often favored, since at least the mid-nineteenth century, within Britain different groups of white migrant women have been constructed as particularly suitable domestic workers. Migrant status positioned these women as both 'other' and needy, and therefore available to do this work which was being increasingly rejected by British women, while shared whiteness masked and silenced such difference allowing the gulf between masters and servants to continue to be seen as both natural and right.

In Britain the precise contours of domestic employment are fashioned by contemporary context, membership of the EU for example, and the colonial past. Britain's colonial history shapes both official policies, such as immigration regulations, and informal flows and relationships. Flows of knowledge, language, people and practices all inflect the domestic labor force and imaginings of it. The racialization of domestic work and domestic workers exists in conversation with government policies designed to ensure a supply of workers. That is only some people are considered to be appropriate for this intimately located work, but policy can also mold groups of migrants to make them available for certain jobs (Anderson 2010). In the past some groups of white women were molded to domestic work through conditions imposed when they migrated. Whilst current UK policy on au pairing appears to break with this approach—offering a free for all rather than regulation—it can be seen as in keeping with previous migration routes for domestic work. Rather than considering individual applicants for a visa to decide whether they are welcome in the country, the UK has now designated all A8 nationals as appropriate to carry out 'low skilled' (or rather low-waged) work.

Throughout this chapter I have argued that domestic work within the UK should be understood as shaped by colonial history. This history has shaped imaginings of domesticity which underpin demand for domestic labor, but employing 'others' within the home always brings its own contradictions. Colonialism offered a way of reframing these class and gender contradictions into racialized differences. The example of au pairing in the contemporary period illustrates how Britain's neocolonial relationship with its Eastern European neighbors reproduces earlier colonial structures of racialization to supply 'appropriate' workers to British homes.

NOTES

1. The 'A8,' short for 'Accession Eight' were eight Eastern European countries which acceded to EU membership at the same time in 2004: Estonia, Latvia, Lithuania, Poland, Czech Republic, Hungary and Slovenia.

2. A8 nationals were required to register under the Workers Registration Scheme (WRS) and could not access welfare benefits until they had been working for over 12 months. This restriction does not apply to nationals of the EU15. As au pairing is not classified as work, A8 nationals in au pair roles could not register with WRS and therefore could not establish any rights to welfare support including maternity benefits.
3. For details see http://conventions.coe.int/Treaty/en/Treaties/Html/068.htm.
4. Au pairs could come both from the French mainland and from the 'Overseas Departments' including French Guiana and islands in the Caribbean.
5. Lisa, Bulgarian au pair, interview by Nicky Busch, London, November 2012, transcript held by Nicky Busch.
6. Oscar, Romanian au pair, interview by Nicky Busch, Skype interview, November 2012, transcript held by Nicky Busch.
7. Lisa, Bulgarian au pair, interview.
8. Lisa, Bulgarian au pair, interview.

REFERENCES

Anderson, Bridget. 2000. *Doing the Dirty Work? The Global Politics of Domestic Labour*. London: Zed Books.

Anderson, Bridget. 2007. 'A Very Private Business Exploring the Demand for Migrant Domestic Workers.' *European Journal of Women's Studies* 14(3): 247–64.

Anderson, Bridget. 2009. 'What's in a Name? Immigration Controls and Subjectivities: The Case of Au Pairs and Domestic Worker Visa Holders in the UK.' *Subjectivity* 29(1): 407–24.

Anderson, Bridget. 2010. 'Migration, Immigration Controls and the Fashioning of Precarious Workers.' *Work, Employment & Society* 24(2): 300–17.

Anderson, Bridget. 2013. *Us and Them? The Dangerous Politics of Immigration Control*. Oxford: Oxford University Press.

Anderson, Bridget, Martin Ruhs, Ben Rogaly and Sarah Spencer. 2006. 'Fair Enough? Central and East European Migrants in Low-Wage Employment in the UK.' *Compas: Centre on Immigration, Policy and Society*. www.irr.org.uk/pdf/Fair_Enough.pdf. Accessed May 2012.

Busch, Nicole. 2011. 'A Migrant Division of Labour in the Global City? Commoditised In-Home Childcare in London 2004–2010.' PhD thesis, University of London, London.

Busch, Nicole, and Rosie Cox. 2012. 'Latin American Domestic Workers in London.' Paper presented at the Dimensiones del Empleo Doméstico Latinoamericano Conference, May 16–18, 2012, Monterrey, Mexico.

Calleman, Catharina. 2010. 'Cultural Exchange or Cheap Domestic Labour? Constructions of "Au Pair" in Four Nordic Countries.' In *Global Care Work: Gender and Migration in Nordic Societies*, edited by Lise Widding Isaksen, 69–96. Lund: Nordic Academic Press.

Cook, Joanne, Peter Dwyer and Louise Waite. 2011. 'The Experiences of Accession 8 Migrants in England: Motivations, Work and Agency.' *International Migration* 49(2): 54–79.

Cox, Rosie. 1999. 'The Role of Ethnicity in Shaping the Domestic Employment Sector in Britain.' In *Gender, Migration and Domestic Service*, edited by Janet Henshall Momsen, 134–47. London: Routledge.

Cox, Rosie. 2006. *The Servant Problem: Domestic Employment in a Global Economy*. London: I. B. Tauris.

Cox, Rosie, and Rekha Narula. 2003. 'Playing Happy Families: Rules and Relationships in Au Pair Employing Households in London, England.' *Gender, Place & Culture* 10(4): 333–44.
Delap, Lucy. 2011. *Knowing Their Place: Domestic Service in Twentieth-Century Britain*. Oxford: Oxford University Press.
Gregson, Nicky, and Michelle Lowe. 1994. *Servicing the Middle Classes: Class, Gender and Waged Domestic Labour in Contemporary Britain*. London: Routledge.
Home Office. 2006. 'A Points Based System: Making Migration Work for Britain: Cm 6741.' HMSO. www.official-documents.gov.uk/document/cm67/6741/6741.pdf. Accessed May 2012.
Isaksen, Lise Widding. 2011. *Global Care Work: Gender and Migration in Nordic Societies*. Lund: Nordic Academic Press.
Liarou, Eleni. 2008. 'The Cultural Politics of Identity: Film, Television and Immigration in Post-war Britain, 1951–1967.' PhD thesis, University of London, London.
MacDonald, Cameron Lynne. 2010. *Shadow Mothers: Nannies, Au Pairs, and the Micropolitics of Mothering*. Berkeley: University of California Press.
McClintock, Anne. 1995. *Imperial Leather: Race, Gender, and Sexuality in the Colonial Contest*. London: Routledge.
McDowell, Linda. 2005. *Hard Labour: The Forgotten Voices of Latvian Migrant Volunteer Workers*. London: Routledge.
McDowell, Linda. 2009. 'Old and New European Economic Migrants: Whiteness and Managed Migration Policies.' *Journal of Ethnic and Migration Studies* 35(1): 19–36.
Newcombe, Emma. 2004. 'Temporary Migration to the UK as an "Au Pair": Cultural Exchange or Reproductive Labour?' Working Paper 21. Falmer: Sussex Centre for Migration Research, University of Sussex. www.sussex.ac.uk/webteam/gateway/file.php?name=mwp21.pdf&site=252. Accessed November 4, 2014.
Pratt, Geraldine. 1997. 'Stereotypes and Ambivalence: The Construction of Domestic Workers in Vancouver, British Columbia.' *Gender, Place & Culture* 4(2): 159–78.
Stenum, Helle. 2010. 'Au-Pair Migration and New Inequalities: The Transnational Production of Corruption.' In *Global Care Work: Gender and Migration in Nordic Societies*, edited by Lise Widding Isaksen, 23–48. Lund: Nordic Academic Press.
Stevens, Martin, Shereen Hussein and Jill Manthorpe. 2012. 'Experiences of Racism and Discrimination among Migrant Care Workers in England: Findings from a Mixed-Methods Research Project.' *Ethnic and Racial Studies* 35(2): 259–80.
Stiell, Bernadette, and Kim England. 1997. 'Domestic Distinctions: Constructing Difference among Paid Domestic Workers in Toronto.' *Gender, Place & Culture* 4(3): 339–60.
Tosh, John. 2007. *A Man's Place: Masculinity and the Middle-Class Home in Victorian England*. New Haven: Yale University Press.
UK Border Agency. 2008. 'Impact Assessment of Tier 5 of the Point Based System for Immigration.' UK Border Agency. http://www.ialibrary.berr.gov.uk/uploaded/IA%20PBS%20Tier%205%20temporary%20workers.pdf. Accessed January 2010.
UK Border Agency. 2012. 'BR Guidance Notes 1: Guidance for Nationals of Bulgaria and Romania on Obtaining Permission to Work in the UK.' http://www.ukba.homeoffice.gov.uk/sitecontent/applicationforms/bulgariaromania/guidanceforbulgariaromania0408. Accessed August 2013.
Walter, Bronwen. 2001. *Outsiders Inside: Whiteness, Place, and Irish Women*. London: Routledge.

Walter, Bronwen. 2004. 'Irish Domestic Servants and English National Identity.' In *Domestic Service and the Formation of European Identity*, edited by A. Fauve-Chamoux, 428–45. Oxford: Peter Lang.

Webster, Wendy. 1998. *Imagining Home: Gender, 'Race' and National Identity, 1945–64*. London: Routledge.

15 Taking Colonialism Home
Cook Island 'Housegirls' in New Zealand, 1939–1948

Charlotte Macdonald

From 1941 to 1948 young women from the Cook Islands were recruited for positions in domestic service in New Zealand homes. The government administered scheme operated in a colonial context. The Cook Islands, annexed in 1901, were part of New Zealand's Pacific empire, along with Niue, the Tokelau Islands and Western Samoa. As a 'white settler dominion' New Zealand shared in the business of governing the wider British Empire through much of the twentieth century; it was itself a product of that empire's nineteenth-century formation. Following the outbreak of war in the Pacific in December 1941 colonial relations between New Zealand and its Pacific territories intensified. A new urgency on the part of the colonial administration was met by a growing resentment within island societies against the all-powerful authority exercised by resident commissioners. The domestic service scheme, which arose from New Zealand's pressing wartime labor shortage, was one place where contests in colonial power were played out. Instead of marking an end to domestic service, World War II enabled New Zealand to exploit its Pacific empire by taking colonialism home in the form of importing 'housegirls' from the Cook Islands to serve in well-to-do white New Zealand households (Taylor 1986; Macdonald 2000). At the same time, the domestic service scheme provided an opening for Cook Island people to push back against colonial power through establishing their status as citizens as well as subjects.[1]

Mobility, modernity and the decolonizing context provide important frameworks for considering this episode in the history of domestic service. Wartime exigencies provided the imperative for mobility, taking women from the Cook Islands to serve in New Zealand's economy, and men to work other parts of the Pacific. Such mobility, in the short term, provided new opportunities for work and for greater involvement in a cash economy. Young women who left Rarotonga, the most populous island within the Cook Islands, to take up positions in private households in Auckland and Wellington were part of this movement. While the colonial administration regarded the women's stay in New Zealand as a temporary measure, it proved instead to be a crucial catalyst to a longer term flow of people between the Cook Islands and New Zealand. A number of the women who were part of the 1940s domestic service scheme became key members of the diaspora community in New Zealand (Gilson 1980:192; Boyd 1990; Scott 1991; Denoon, Smith and Wyndham 2000: 398–408, 468–72; Morgan 2001; Salesa 2009; Mahina-Taui 2012).

The connection between migration and domestic service evident in this Pacific history is part of a broader global pattern from the mid-twentieth century identified by scholars such as Janet Henshall Momsen (1999). Her important collection draws together case studies including Filipina and Jamaican domestic workers in North America, Sri Lankan women working in the Middle East, African and East European women working as domestics in England and France. The pattern of Cook Island workers moving between societies of marked disparities in economic wealth, the importance of remittances in the economies of migrants' societies of origin, and the aspirations of migrant workers for education, freedom and independence are familiar. These features also point to the common tensions and possibilities of modernity within such movements. Among young adults who made up the majority of the Cook Island migrant group, there was a degree of impatience in their pursuit of greater autonomy, a desire to shake off the constraints of village elders and paternalistic colonial officials. Between those responsible for managing the migration in Rarotonga and Wellington, tensions came to the surface in arguments vying over the interests of island-based populations as against a growing Cook Island diaspora in New Zealand, between women as wage workers or as family members, and between daughters and parents. At the most general level, these conflicts underlay a struggle between political and economic autonomy in the islands as against access to a shared labor market and citizenship with New Zealand.

Yet there are also important distinctions to be made between the later twentieth-century migrations that Momsen focuses on and those of the immediate postwar years. Women from the Cook Islands coming to New Zealand in the 1940s form part of a distinctive history of migration from former colonial territories to metropolitan centers. New Zealand and Australia, like Britain and other European imperial powers, became settler destinations for people from 'their' colonial possessions in this period. While empires remained intact such mobility ran along the transport, labor and administrative lines connecting imperial and colonial spaces. Lines of connection between colonial metropoles and colonies were often retained in the postcolonial period. In New Zealand, discussions around decolonization, beginning in the 1940s, emerged alongside economic expansion and growing concerns about the shortage of unskilled labor. The movement of labor from the Pacific Islands to mainland New Zealand provided one solution (Scott, 1991: 227–31; Gilson 1980: 186–98, 217–20; Mahina-Taui 2012). With political independence marking the formal realization of decolonization in the Cook Islands in 1965, what had been mobility within an empire became migration across borders. The struggles over the terms for that postcolonial citizenship can be traced in the 1940s domestic service scheme.

Recent reconsiderations of the period from the 1940s to the 1960s as an era of contested rather than benign decolonization in the British Empire forms part of the broader setting of the relationship between New Zealand and the Pacific (Howe 2011; Lynn 2006; Elkins 2005; Darwin 1988, 1991). An historical view of the inevitable unraveling of ties of empire in the face of decolonization in the post-1945 years can no longer be sustained. New Zealand and the Pacific were characterized by complex colonial relationships within the British empire. Rarotonga, Wellington and London were linked constitutionally, politically and symbolically in a cascade of colonial relations. New Zealand occupied the status as a colonial power in the Pacific, what Damon Salesa has termed an 'empire state' (2009: 150) poised between old habits of colonial authority and modernizing imperatives of wartime. Yet it was also a former colony of Britain which had become a settler dominion and was moving towards greater independence from its own remaining ties to Britain from the 1940s onwards.

These decades were also ones of internal decolonization within New Zealand. Marginalized geographically, economically and politically by the violence and dispossession of colonization, for Indigenous Maori people World War II served as a powerful catalyst of mobilization and rapid urbanization. The mobilities of both Maori and Pacific Islander people which were accelerated during and after the Second World War were entwined with the modernizing policies pursued by the government of New Zealand towards Indigenous people both within New Zealand and its colonial territories in the Pacific. In formulating a modernizing social citizenship (social policies aimed at economic, educational and social as well as political equality), access to jobs in New Zealand's cities proved crucial for both Maori within New Zealand, and Cook Island peoples (Walker 1992; Harris 2007; Williams 2010). Both Maori and Indigenous Cook Islanders were Polynesian peoples who shared a common ancestry, and much common culture. The term 'Maori' was used to describe Indigenous people in both places though Maori from New Zealand and 'Cook Island Maori' were understood as referring to two distinct populations. But while there is much that is shared in the colonial and postcolonial histories of these two groups there are also crucial differences. These differences and the contradictions between the New Zealand government's old habits of colonial authority and pursuit of modernizing imperatives are highlighted in the domestic service scheme.

The detailed discussion which follows demonstrates the way in which domestic service provided a fulcrum for the playing out of colonial dynamics. Colonialism and domestic service have been linked by an emphasis on the intimate and familial space in which colonial relations have been formed; by the intense interest taken by colonial administrations in such relationships; through the use of domestic service as a tool of assimilation; and, most generally, on the ways in which colonial contexts intensify the already sharply hierarchical relation between workers and employers in domestic service. Yet at the same time domestic spaces could be places where the colonial relationship fractured, where ambiguities also existed (Stoler 2002: 8, 12, 206; Haskins 2001, 2009). Such ambiguities and limits to the exercise of state power can be seen in the experience of Cook Islanders in New Zealand in the 1940s. As British subjects the colonial law protected them against the repatriation which colonial administrators called for. In leaving domestic service positions once in New Zealand, a number subverted the colonial relationship by abandoning the work for which they were recruited to find more congenial employment.

'HOUSEGIRLS' FOR NEW ZEALAND FAMILIES

In June 1941 the Resident Commissioner in Rarotonga, Judge Hugh F. Ayson, was instructed to assist in the selection of young women deemed suitable for domestic positions in New Zealand households.[2] Over the next four years around two hundred young women sailed from Rarotonga to take up positions in domestic service. While the numbers may appear modest from a Pacific rim standpoint, from an island perspective they are highly significant, given the total Cook Islands population of just 14,000 in 1945 (Bertram and Watters 1984: 137).

The exceptional wartime circumstances enabled a privileged section of society to import to the mainland a set of hierarchical relations normally confined only to expatriate or colonial service beyond the shores of 'metropolitan' New Zealand. A portion of these employing households were ones in which the families had served in New Zealand's or the wider British imperial administration. The Cook Island domestic service scheme enabled such relations, normal in such settings, to be repatriated 'home' to mainland New Zealand. Official involvement in the scheme from mid-1941 brought a degree of formality and greater priority to what had been informally going on in very small scale in earlier years.

The terms in which householders wrote about their Cook Island employees, and which also appear in the official record, underlines the colonial and paternalistic character of these relationships. Cook Island domestics were commonly referred to as 'housegirls,' a title that was quite outside existing usage for domestic workers in New Zealand but common in Pacific colonies such as New Hebrides (Rodman, Kraemar, Bolton and Tarisesei 2007). Domestic servants leaving their positions were described as having 'absconded,' a term carrying punitive associations of illicit escape rather than a legitimate mobility. Possessives were freely used, as was the description of Cook Island girls as 'natives.' While the term 'native' was not unknown in New Zealand as a way to distinguish Maori, it was less commonly used to refer to individuals, and was taken out of official nomenclature in 1947 (Walker 2004: 196). A further deployment of a language of race to describe labor preferences is evident in some employers' correspondence. One wrote that she had been told it was 'an advantage' to get someone 'with Chinese blood.'³ Another sign of the way in which recruitment of domestic labor from the Pacific marked a departure from the metropolitan New Zealand pattern of domestic service is in requests specifying a 'houseboy' as well as a 'housegirl.' Domestic work's highly gendered character, as work for women and girls, was not seen to necessarily prevail when it came to 'native' recruitment, and elsewhere in the Pacific male domestic employment had been the norm (for the colonial pattern of employing male domestic workers in Papua New Guinea and the Asia Pacific more broadly, see Dickson-Waiko 2007, and in this volume Higman; Lowrie; and Nilan, Artini and Threadgold). Recruitment from the colonial Pacific mobilized a distinct language, marking a sharp departure from the existing character of domestic employment in New Zealand.

The contrast points to what can be thought of as a dual-tier structure to New Zealand's race relations in the period under analysis. Maori and *Pakeha* (white or European) relations were imagined within concepts of greater parity to those between 'New Zealanders' and peoples of the colonial Pacific. Considerable material disparities between Maori and Pakeha New Zealanders, and the legacies of colonialism made for marked inequalities. Yet Maori representation in Parliament, the prominent profile of professional and political leaders such as Sir Apirana Ngata, Te Puea Herangi, Sir Maui Pomare and Sir Peter Buck, and the central place occupied by Maori in national life (such as had been recently demonstrated at the 1940 Centennial Celebrations) all spoke to a respected and recognized complementarity rather than relations of sharp hierarchy or subordination. Crucially, household work had never been a place of any significant structuring of relations between Maori and Pakeha. There was no history of Maori women or men providing a domestic service labor force. Attempts had been made to recruit Maori girls and women into such work but all had failed (Macdonald 2000, forthcoming 2014; Pickles 2009).

For Cook Island people, waged employment in New Zealand brought the prospect of some remittance income to island families and communities. Work off the Islands appealed to some young people for its novelty; it carried the possibility of freedom and adventure. Interest in paid work beyond the Islands was also fed by considerable disappointment at the New Zealand Government's decision not to recruit Cook Islanders for military service. Whereas a number of Cook Island and Niue men had served in the Pioneer Battalion of the New Zealand Expeditionary Force in Europe in World War I, recruitment for overseas service was not repeated in World War II. By contrast, New Zealand Maori men served in World War II, largely in the famed 28 'Maori' Battalion (Soutar 2008). The service was on a voluntary basis but was hugely lauded during the war years and has been widely recognized subsequently. In the Pacific, military service was a privilege reserved to those designated of 'white' or 'British' race while civilian labor was designated for 'half bloods' and 'natives' (Gilson 1980: 192; Scott 1991: 224–25).⁴ Cook Islanders were deployed instead as a civilian labor force, along gender lines:

men were hired as laborers digging valuable phosphate (used in boosting agricultural production for wartime food supply on the island of Makatea from 1943 while young women were sought out for New Zealand's domestic labor force.

New Zealand householders eagerly took advantage of the new supply of domestic help. There was a crisis in the availability of paid household help with young women preferring the better paid and more congenial factory work which expanded with the outbreak of war (Taylor 1986: 1092–93; Martin 1996: 229). Letters flowed into the Wellington offices of the Cook Islands (later Island Territories) Department requesting Cook Island 'girls.' Prospective employers were largely drawn from the wealthier suburbs in the cities of Auckland and Wellington, with several sheep farmers on the North Island's East Coast also seeking workers through their stock and station agents, Dalgety's. In return for paying the passage fare, the costs of radio communication and signing a guarantee that they would pay for the worker's return fare should she wish to return home, the Department undertook to select and arrange for young women to be sent from Rarotonga to their workplace in New Zealand.

The Colonial Administration in Rarotonga was a reluctant party to the scheme, preferring instead to leave matters of employment in private hands. Resident Commissioner Ayson and his successor William Tailby, both complained about the time and trouble they had to expend selecting and arranging passages for girls for domestic service in New Zealand. Responsibility for fulfilling the demands flowing from New Zealand rested with them. Authority to issue permits for the young women to leave the islands lay with the Resident Commissioner.[5]

For New Zealand employers, Cook Island 'girls' were a cheap, available and compliant labor force. Starting incomes were approximately £1 a week, from which the cost of passage was deducted.[6] The minimum wage at the time for female employees in unskilled nonresidential jobs was £1.16s a week (Martin 1996: 199). Low wages were justified on the grounds of youth (most of the Cook Islanders were between fifteen to twenty years old), inexperience, or in some cases, on limited English language; and more generally on what some employers perceived as a more limited capacity than non-'native' labor. One employer wrote with some indignation about the abilities of the 'girl' he had been sent:

> The fact is that she cannot speak or understand English. She does not know how to tell the time. She cannot be sent out with the children as she does not understand when she is to come home. She cannot be sent messages, and the position is quite impossible.

At the same time he noted that 'any work which she is given to do she does very well. She is . . . very thorough and would be very useful to anybody who could speak Rarotongan.'[7]

GOING OR STAYING: REPATRIATION AND CITIZENSHIP

By the end of 1942 the fate of the scheme had become the subject of vigorous debate. The health and welfare of some women raised one set of concerns. Another was that several women who had come to positions in domestic service had left them to take up better paying jobs in factory work. Some employers, frustrated that the young women they had helped come to New Zealand had left their position, demanded that the Cook Islands Department officials direct them to return to their original positions. They were advised that the colonial administration in New Zealand had no powers to do so.[8] Who was responsible for the young women once they were in New Zealand, and on what terms they might stay, or return to Rarotonga, became a vexed and contentious question. That women were deciding on their own futures is also apparent. While the New Zealand government had been ready to look to the Cook Islands to secure an additional labor force, they were less prepared for the ongoing role of mediating relations between domestic workers and their employers after they arrived.

Illness, and in particular the scourge of tuberculosis, afflicted several of the Cook Island girls. Two died in New Zealand and it appears several others returned home after becoming ill. A different kind of danger to which Cook Island girls in New Zealand were being exposed was carried in rumors heard by Resident Commissioner Ayson in Rarotonga by August 1942. Allegations that several women in Auckland were living in 'a house of ill repute' and had been lured there under false pretenses were serious charges which demanded investigation. While the allegations were found to be entirely unfounded, the 'possibilities of moral disaster,' as an official perspective viewed put it, '[could not] be ignored.'[9] Also causing some concern was the handful of young women who gave birth after arriving in New Zealand or became pregnant while in positions in service. The circumstances in these instances remain only very partially represented in the official archive. In two of the cases there were suggestions that the young women were subject to unwanted attentions by male members of the household in which they were working.[10] In other cases the pregnancy appears to have been part of an ongoing relationship. Several young women married in New Zealand. The common spectrum of risk and danger, excitement and desire in which young single women, and domestic servants, are often situated, is a familiar one. A marked weighting towards the dangerous end of those possibilities was believed to have occurred by late 1942. From June, the first of around 20,000 US servicemen flowed into Auckland and Wellington, transforming the tenor of life in both major centers. Considering the situation of young and perhaps vulnerable women, it 'was soon felt, particularly while the cities contained large numbers of servicemen, that there was a risk of creating problems that might not lead to ultimate good.'[11]

Officials of the administration in Wellington looked first to 'solve' these various 'problems' by 'repatriating' those Cook Island women for whom life in New Zealand was, by their judgment, to have 'not gone well.' Officials clearly imagined that these young women could be persuaded to return 'home.' The evidence is sketchy, but there are indications that some young women were adamant in the face of officials' and parental entreaties: They did not, necessarily, wish to return to Rarotonga. Under what authority women who had been brought to New Zealand might be directed to return was unclear. It is a sign of the vagueness, if not outright ignorance, within which New Zealand's colonial administration operated, that this was unknown.

The advice given by the Crown Law Office left no room for doubt. There was no legal basis for repatriation. Any return to the Islands would have to be voluntary, on the basis of persuasion rather than coercion. The Crown Solicitor's advice, noting that he had been 'informed that there are certain natives of the Cook Islands in employment in New Zealand whose conduct, though they have not been guilty of any offences against the law, is so unsatisfactory that it is desired if possible to be in a position to send them back to the Cook Islands although they may wish to stay in New Zealand,' rehearsed all possible legal bases, finding them all wanting. The opinion underlined the ambiguous nature of Cook Islanders' status within the cascade of colonial relations. While they were 'British subjects under the general law,' they were not British subjects for the purposes of the *Immigration Restriction Act*. Once permitted to enter New Zealand, however, no section of that Act could be invoked against them. Considering freedom from unauthorized detention under the Aliens Emergency Regulations, the Crown Solicitor reminded his colleagues 'that the persons in question are not only British subjects, but are also citizens of New Zealand, since the Cook Islands are politically an integral part of the Dominion, and belong to a part of the Dominion which does not enjoy representation in Parliament. This may be a reason for expecting the courts of justice to be particularly vigilant in the protection of their civil rights.' Crown Solicitor Currie concluded his advice by noting that the only way to achieve repatriation would be for Parliament to act: 'It is very doubtful whether the desired end [repatriation] can be attained otherwise than by legislation enacted by the General Assembly.'[12]

The asymmetry of colonial relations between New Zealand and the Cook Islands was pronounced, but it was also one in which ambiguities flourished. While 'native' Cook Islanders required a permit to leave the Islands to work in New Zealand, there was no legal basis under which they could be directed to return. Domestic service tested the scope of citizenship not only in this legal question of 'repatriation' but also in relation to their status as workers in the wartime-controlled labor market. While the intention of the scheme had been to stem the crisis in domestic service, it was impossible to confine workers to such positions. Once in New Zealand Cook Island people were free to live and work where they chose.

The only effective tool that could be exercised over Cook Island women once in New Zealand was through the Manpower office which regulated conditions for all workers in the highly controlled wartime economy. On several occasions the Department of Island Territories and the Manpower Office worked together to keep Cook Island women in domestic employment. In one instance two sisters who had been working together in the same house left to take up a better paying work at a local factory. The Manpower office was quick to prohibit the factory from employing them, thereby cutting off their 'escape' and forcing the women back to their original positions. One consolation was that their original employer did agree to increase their wages.[13] Further complexities of citizenship were introduced when children were born to Cook Island women in New Zealand following liaisons with American servicemen.[14]

CONTROVERSY IN RAROTONGA AND NEW ZEALAND

In the face of these difficulties the recruitment of domestic servants from the Cook Islands was suspended in March 1943. While prospective employers in New Zealand were dismayed,[15] the Island Council in Rarotonga—a grouping of largely traditional leaders (including women)—supported the decision. Over the next two years the fate of the domestic service scheme became a prominent issue in the festering resentment against the colonial administration in the Islands. The Cook Islands Progressive Association, formed in 1943, was the most conspicuous evidence of this political restiveness. In 1944 and 1945 lifting the prohibition against women traveling to work in New Zealand had become one of the many points of tension between Cook Island people and the New Zealand administration. Cook Island leaders were not necessarily united about the benefits of young women working in New Zealand, but the absolute power exercised by the Resident Commissioner on this and other matters was increasingly resented. Conditions endured by men employed as contract laborers on the island of Makatea, and the lack of access to work resulting from the prohibition on young women traveling to New Zealand, caused the greatest offence. Discontent over these issues was aggravated by a rightful perception amongst Cook Island people that they were subject to greater restriction than were people in other parts of New Zealand's Pacific. Most, though not all, Cook Islanders wanted the domestic service scheme to resume. Debate between Cook Island leaders over the merits, or otherwise, of the scheme revolved around competing claims over the value of young women as members of local family and village communities or as wage earners sending funds from New Zealand, and whether it was right to allow young women to live outside the supervision of home and parents. Some leaders feared the scheme would draw the most eligible young women away from the Islands permanently, with detrimental effects on the future social and economic viability of small communities. Others regarded the prospect of their daughters, granddaughters and nieces sailing away from Rarotonga as tantamount to them disappearing off the moral horizon set by church and family. There was, in this sense, a degree of convergence between a section of Island leadership and the conservative tendencies of Resident Commissioner William Tailby.

Tailby was opposed to resuming the scheme because of what he saw as the dangerously destabilizing influences of mobility, urban living, wider experience, and distance from family, church and village. In Wellington, at the head office of what was now the Department of Island Territories, a different view prevailed. There was mounting political pressure to lift restrictions on Cook Islanders leaving the islands and to resume the domestic service scheme. Exchanges between Wellington and Rarotonga shifted from tense to acrimonious. Tailby was advised by his Wellington colleagues that it was becoming 'indefensible' for Cook Island men to be sent to Makatea in virtual indenture while women were prohibited from coming to New Zealand to work. There was a 'growing feeling against New Zealand treating its Islanders as foreigners.'[16]

At the same time, the Wellington officials admonished the resident commissioner for failing to pressure the Island Council into greater efforts to encourage young women already in New Zealand to return home. This was, in their view, the Council's responsibility. Reviewing the fates of the hundred women who could be traced in New Zealand (the numbers who remained in domestic service, those who had gone to factory work, had married, had died or returned to the Islands), it was noted that a 'Wastage of 21 girls out of 100 has already occurred and the position is certain to deteriorate with the passage of time.' 'Wastage' referred principally to those who had left to work in factories. But it also pointed to those women who had had children in New Zealand and others who had become ill. These 'risks,' as the Wellington administration labeled them, were ones which rested not in their hands, but with the Cook Island community in the Pacific. The message was plain: 'So long as the Island Council does nothing about the problem, it seems to me this risk is a responsibility which rests upon the Island Council.'[17]

In early 1945 the plight of Cook Island people as workers caused a public furor after the Auckland Trades Council took up the case of the Makatea workers, accusing the government of acquiescing in 'blackbirding' (a reference to the notorious nineteenth-century practice, of kidnapping and indenturing Pacific and South Sea Islanders for plantation labor). It was a sharp blow against a Labour administration whose senior figures were all former trade union activists. The New Zealand government, including its colonial arm in Rarotonga, was forced to act more justly. Better conditions and pay for the men contracted to work on Makatea resulted. The infamous episode and the ongoing labor agitation on the Rarotonga waterfront through the later 1940s has featured in histories of the Cook Islands and the Pacific more generally as important steps in shaping pressure for independence (Scott 1991: 234–37, 252–59; Gilson 1980). By comparison, little attention has been paid to the controversy surrounding the domestic service scheme.

In part this is due to the structure of the work and the workforce: domestic servants were not represented in a union or union movement; the domestic service workforce was by nature a dispersed and diverse one, and the workers entwined in personal and familial relations with their employers inhabiting the same working and social space. The people at the center of this scheme were also young women who were viewed by contemporaries in social as much as labor terms.

The lingering dispute over the fate of the domestic service scheme continued through March to July 1945. Nothing had been done to solve the impasse. In March William McBirney, a long-term resident of the Islands, threatened to embarrass the New Zealand government by 'going to the Press' if permission was not given for young women to be able to travel to New Zealand.[18] In May Tailby was strongly urged to lift the prohibition and operate a quota allowing a limited number of young women to leave the Islands. A local committee that could 'advise in the case of each applicant whether it would be both to her welfare and of no detriment to Rarotonga for her to be permitted to come to New Zealand' was suggested.[19]

By the time Tailby, reluctantly, took this proposal to the Island Council in early July, divisions had deepened. Those who spoke strongly against the resumption, including Makea Nui and W. H. Watson, did so on the grounds, as Tailby reported:

(1) That there is a surplus of males in all islands of the group.
(2) That only the brightest and most promising girls are selected to go to New Zealand and the others are left here.
(3) That the girls who go to New Zealand do not wish to return to Rarotongan conditions and that many of them marry in New Zealand.
(4) That it is to the detriment of the future race that the brightest and best girls should marry away from their home islands and thus lower the standard here.
(5) That under New Zealand climatic conditions many of our girls suffer ill health.
(6) That our girls are a continual source of trouble to all concerned with their well-being in New Zealand.
(7) That Maori committees are now making every endeavour to induce New Zealand Maori girls to leave the cities and return to their homes for their own good.
(8) That it is better to face a charge of being bureaucratic than one of not doing the best possible for our girls' welfare.[20]

The summary of arguments made by those in favor of resumption was terse, and highly abbreviated. They 'did not see why the girls should not proceed to New Zealand as the men are now permitted to do; they considered that the numbers should be strictly limited and they seemed to be impressed by the fact that New Zealand wants the girls there.' A motion opposing resumption was lost. After 'further rather bitter discussion' a motion proposing that ten girls be permitted to go was carried. Resident Commissioner Tailby, whose account of the debate is the one on which has survived in the archive, acceded to the Council's decision. But he could not refrain from ending his memo by reiterating his 'strong view that . . . it unwise to reopen permission for Cook Islands girls to come to New Zealand to employment.'[21]

In the end, the prohibition was lifted and Cook Islanders were able to travel to New Zealand for work, though permits were still required to leave the Islands. Of the two hundred or so women who had been part of the domestic service scheme, some returned to Rarotonga, others stayed in New Zealand, forming the core for a growing New Zealand-based Cook Islands community. Movement of people back and forth between Rarotonga and Auckland (and to a lesser extent Australia and the US west coast) continued through the 1950s and 1960s (Bertram and Watters 1984: 137; Bertram 2012). But domestic service did not survive much beyond the early 1950s. The poor wage rates and unattractive nature of the work could not compete in an employment market where workers were scarce. Labor migration would continue to underpin the relationship between New Zealand and the Cook Islands through to independence in 1965 and in subsequent years. Such movement, better thought of as instigating modern 'networks of mobility and exchange' than a linear migration, continued through the era leading up to and continuing after formal decolonization (Salesa 2009: 166; Morgan 2001).[22] The independence of the Cook Islands is based on a constitution of 'free association' with New Zealand in which Cook Islanders are also citizens of New Zealand.

CONCLUSION

The pattern of domestic service and colonialism that emerges from this study is one which runs against some of the prevailing narratives that sees World War II as marking an end to both domestic service and to old-style colonial relations. Wartime strategic and labor priorities enabled domestic service to continue in pockets rather than shrink away almost entirely. New Zealand's colonial populations in its Pacific empire provided a ready labor force that could, for a time, be employed as affordable live-in domestic servants in private households. In doing so a set of colonial service relationships that had previously been confined to 'off shore' settings was imported to metropolitan New Zealand. The Cook Island 'housegirl' was a new departure in the history of households and domestic work in New Zealand, and exists in stark contrast to a characterization of this period as one of the ubiquitous suburban 'housewife' (King 2003: 430; May 1992). The employment of Cook Island 'housegirls' in New Zealand occurred with the sanction, encouragement and substantial support of the state through the officials and resources of the colonial administration. Part of the business of New Zealand as an 'empire state' in this period proved to be the supply of domestic labor to a small but powerful section of New Zealand households.

The experience of wartime domestic service also served to push back against the asymmetries of colonial rule. In particular, the scheme exposed the ambiguous position occupied by Cook Islanders as colonial citizens. Subject to the Resident Commissioner's authority while in the Pacific, once in New Zealand Cook Island people were free to live and work where they chose, and to return to Rarotonga, or not. They had the freedom, if not representation, of 'British subjects.' But legal and constitutional status tells only part of the story. The social habits of colonial life lingered. In the early 1950s the widely read *Pacific Islands Monthly* magazine unselfconsciously carried prominent advertisements for Sydney-made domestic appliances under the banner: 'Your native servant will iron better with a Coleman's iron.' The small print promised an iron that would work equally well indoors and out (Brunt 2012: 351).

The nature of domestic service in the colonial context of the Pacific in the 1940s also tells us something of the tensions which exist between societies that are labor providers and those that are labor seekers, the sources of domestic servants and the locations of domestic servant employers. In this instance, small and geographically remote island communities debated and weighed up the benefits and costs of allowing young women to move away to take up domestic service and enter into modern urban wage earning society, whether temporarily or permanently. Control over the process and multiple perceptions of those involved in the scheme were issues for contemporaries and remain present in the varying histories that can be told. In the official archive it is the voices of the administrators, employers and island leaders that prevail rather than those of the women who traveled from Rarotonga to New Zealand. Restrictions on use of the archive also diminish the visibility of the individuals at the center of this history. In 2012 an exhibition at the Museum of New Zealand (*Te Papa Tongarewa*) featured Caroline Munokoa Tuteru Marsters, a woman who arrived in New Zealand from Rarotonga in 1942. Her story and that of her compatriots is only now beginning to be told.

NOTES

1. The principal official archive for the Cook Island Domestic Service Scheme is in IT1, 121/1/6 series, Archives New Zealand, Wellington. Some of the files within this series are under restriction. I am grateful to the Ministry of Foreign Affairs and Trade for granting permission to access these files. A condition of access is that the names of individuals cannot be revealed. The narratives of domestic service depicted here are, thus, ones which tell us more of the perspective of those who administered the work and workers than that of the workers themselves.

2. Tailby for Secretary, Cook Islands Department, Wellington to Resident Commissioner, Rarotonga, 24 June 1941: IT1, 664, 121/1/6 Part 1, Archives New Zealand, Wellington (ANZW).
3. C. B. to Ayson, Resident Commissioner, 6 November 1941: IT1, 664, 121/6 Part 1, ANZW.
4. Though Cook Island men made it very clear they were willing, and indeed, keen to serve. See petition to NZ Parliament, and report of same in *Evening Post*, 5 September 1941, 4; AD1, 312/2/623 Part 1, ANZW. Even after extensive petitioning from the Islands the New Zealand government was adamant. Some Cook Island men traveled to New Zealand and volunteered from there, but there was no Cook island contingent as such.
5. Resident Commissioner, Rarotonga to Secretary, Cook Islands Department, Wellington, May 24, 1941; Resident Commissioner, Rarotonga to Secretary, Cook Islands Department, 26 January 1942: IT1, 664, 121/6 Part 1, ANZW.
6. Resident Commissioner, Rarotonga to Secretary, Cook Islands Department, 26 January 1942: IT1, 664, 121/6 Part 1, ANZW.
7. J. N. to Secretary, Cook Islands Department, 4 August 1942: IT1, 664, 121/6, Part 1, ANZW. The story had a happy outcome; the servant employee was transferred to another household.
8. See, for example, H.B.W to Secretary, Cook Islands Department, 30 December 1942: IT1 665, 121/1/6 Part 3, ANZW; and other correspondence in IT1 665 121/1/6 Part A, ANZW.
9. Tailby for Secretary, Island Territories, Wellington to Resident Commissioner, 5 October 1942: IT1, 665, 121/1/6, Part 2, ANZW.
10. See IT1, 665, 121/1/6 Part A, ANZW; and Scott 1991, in which he refers to an interview alluding to informal knowledge about employers passed through the 'coconut wireless' (228).
11. Secretary (McKay), Department of Island Territories to Minister, Island Territories, 1 August 1945: IT1, 665, 121/1/6 Part 5, ANZW. US servicemen were also stationed on Aitutaki in the Cook Islands from 1942.
12. A. E. Currie, Crown Solicitor, Crown Law Office to Secretary, Cook Islands Department, 7 December 1942: IT1, 665, 121/1/6, ANZW.
13. T. P. and T. P., Bockett, Controller of Manpower to Secretary, Island Territories, 9 February 1945, and reply, 12 February 1945: IT1, 665, 121/1/6 Part 5, ANZW.
14. Judith Bennett, History, University of Otago is currently completing research on the children born to Pacific women and US servicemen during WW2 under the rubric of the 'Mothers' Darlings' project; see www.otago.ac.nz/usfathers/.
15. 'Island Domestics,' *Evening Post*, 20 April 1943, 3.
16. C. M. McKay, Acting Secretary, Island Territories to Resident Commissioner, 28 July 1944: IT1, 665, 121/1/6, Part 5, ANZW.
17. C. M. McKay, Acting Secretary, Island Territories to Resident Commissioner, 28 July 1944, IT1, 665, 121/1/6, Part 5, ANZW.
18. McBirney to Secretary, Department of Island Territories, 26 March 1945: IT1, 665, 121/1/6 Part 5, ANZW.
19. Secretary, Island Territories, Wellington to Resident Commissioner, Rarotonga, 18 May 1945: IT1, 665, 121/1/6 Part 5, ANZW.
20. Tailby, Resident Commissioner, Rarotonga to Secretary, Department of Island Territories, 11 July 1945: IT1, 665, 121/1/6 Part 5, ANZW
21. Tailby, Resident Commissioner, Rarotonga to Secretary, Department of Island Territories, 11 July 1945: IT1, 665, 121/1/6 Part 5, ANZW.
22. In 2004 around 19,200 people were living in the Cook Islands, of whom 13,500 counted as usual residents. A further 51,000 people identifying as 'Cook Islanders' were living in NZ and 15,000–30,000 in Australia (Walrond 2012).

REFERENCES

Bertram, Geoff. 2012. 'South Pacific Economic Relations—Pacific Neighbours.' *Te Ara—The Encyclopedia of New Zealand.* www.teara.govt.nz. Accessed April 15, 2012.

Bertram, I. G., and Ray Watters. 1984. *New Zealand and Its Small Island Neighbours.* Wellington: Institute of Policy Studies.

Boyd, Mary. 1990. 'New Zealand and Other Pacific Islands.' In *The Oxford Illustrated History of New Zealand,* edited by Keith Sinclair, 295–322. Auckland: Oxford University Press.

Brunt, Peter. 2012. 'Decolonization, Independence and Cultural Revival 1945–89.' In *Art in Oceania,* edited by Peter Brunt and Nicholas Thomas, 348–83. London: Thames & Hudson.

Darwin, John. 1988. *Britain and Decolonisation: The Retreat from Empire in the Post-war World.* Basingstoke: Macmillan.

Darwin, John. 1991. *The End of the British Empire: The Historical Debate.* Oxford: Oxford University Press.

Denoon, Donald, and Philippa Mein Smith, with Marivic Wyndham. 2000. *A History of Australia, New Zealand and the Pacific.* Oxford: Oxford University Press.

Dickson-Waiko, Anne. 2007. 'Colonial Enclaves and Domestic Spaces in British New Guinea.' In *Britishness Abroad: Transnational Movements and Imperial Cultures,* edited by Kate Darian-Smith, Patricia Grimshaw and Stuart Macintyre, 205–30. Melbourne: Melbourne University Press.

Elkins, Caroline. 2005. *Britain's Gulag: The Brutal End of Empire in Kenya.* London: Pimlico.

Gilson, Richard. 1980. *The Cook Islands 1820–1950,* edited by Ron Crocombe. Wellington: Victoria University Press in association with University of the South Pacific.

Harris, Aroha. 2007. 'Dancing with the State: Maori Creative Energy and Policies of Integration, 1945–67.' PhD thesis, University of Auckland, New Zealand.

Haskins, Victoria, 2001. 'On the Doorstep: Aboriginal Domestic Service as a "Contact Zone."' *Australian Feminist Studies* 16(34): 13–25.

Haskins, Victoria. 2009. 'From the Centre to the City: Modernity, Mobility and Mixed-Descent Aboriginal Domestic Workers from Central Australia.' *Women's History Review* 18(1): 155–75.

Howe, Stephen. 2011. 'Flakking the Mau Mau Catchers.' *Journal of Imperial and Commonwealth History* 39(5): 695–97.

King, Michael. 2003. *The Penguin History of New Zealand.* Auckland: Penguin.

Lynn, Martin. 2006. 'Introduction.' In *The British Empire in the 1950s. Retreat or Revival?* edited by Martin Lynn, 1–14. Basingstoke: Palgrave Macmillan.

Macdonald, Charlotte. 2000. 'Strangers at the Hearth: The Eclipse of Domestic Service in New Zealand Homes c.1830s–1940s.' In *At Home in New Zealand,* edited by Barbara Brookes, 41–56. Wellington: Bridget Williams Books.

Macdonald, Charlotte. Forthcoming 2014. 'Why Was There No Answer to "the Servant Problem"? Paid Domestic Work and the Making of a White New Zealand, 1840s–1950s.' In *History's Helpmeets,* edited by Caroline Daley and Deborah Montgomerie. Auckland: Auckland University Press.

Mahina-Tuai, Kolokesa. 2012. 'A Land of Milk and Honey? Education and Employment Migration Schemes in the Postwar Era.' In *Tangata O Le Moana. New Zealand and the People of the Pacific,* edited by Sean Mallon, Kolokesa Mahina-Tuai and Damon Salesa, 161–78. Wellington: Te Papa Press.

Martin, John E. 1996. *Holding the Balance. A History of New Zealand's Department of Labour 1891–1995.* Christchurch: University of Canterbury Press.

May, Helen. 1992. *Minding Children, Managing Men*. Wellington: Bridget Williams Books.
Momsen, Janet Henshall. 1999. 'Maids on the Move: Victim or Victor.' In *Gender, Migration and Domestic Service*, edited by Janet Henshall Momsen, 1–20. London: Routledge.
Morgan, Teupoko I. 2001. *Vainetini Kuki Airani. Cook Islands Women Pioneers. Early Experiences in Aotearoa—New Zealand*. Tokoroa: Anau Ako Pasifika.
Pickles, Katie. 2009. 'Colonisation, Empire and Gender.' In *The New Oxford History of New Zealand*, edited by Giselle Byrnes, 219–42. Melbourne: Oxford University Press.
Rodman, Margaret, Daniela Kraemer, Lissant Bolton and Jean Tarisesei. 2007. 'Introduction.' In *House-Girls Remember: Domestic Workers in Vanuatu*, edited by Margaret Rodman, Daniela Kraemer, Lissant Bolton and Jean Tarisesei, 1–26. Honolulu: University of Hawai'i Press.
Salesa, Damon. 2009. 'New Zealand's Pacific.' In *The New Oxford History of New Zealand*, edited by Giselle Byrnes, 149–72. Melbourne: Oxford University Press.
Scott, Dick. 1991. *Years of the Pooh-Bah. A Cook Islands History*. Rarotonga and Auckland: CITC.
Soutar, Monty. 2008. *Nga Tama Toa. The Price of Citizenship*. Auckland: David Bateman.
Stoler, Ann Laura. 2002. *Carnal Knowledge and Imperial Power: Race and the Intimate in Colonial Rule*. Berkeley: University of California Press.
Taylor, Nancy M. 1986. *The New Zealand People at War: The Home Front*. Wellington: Government Printer.
Walker, Ranginui. 1992. 'Maori People since 1950.' In *The Oxford History of New Zealand*, edited by G. W. Rice, 498–519. Auckland: Oxford University Press.
Walker, Ranginui. 2004. *Ka Whawhai Tonu Matou. Struggle Without End*. Auckland: Penguin.
Walrond Carl. 2012. 'Cook Islanders.' In *Te Ara—the Encyclopedia of New Zealand*. www.teara.govt.nz. Accessed April 15, 2012.
Williams, Melissa. 2010. '"Back home" and Home in the City: Maori Migrations from Panguru to Auckland, 1930–1970.' PhD thesis, University of Auckland, New Zealand.

16 British Caribbean Women Migrants and Domestic Service in Latin America, 1850–1950
Race, Gender and Colonial Legacies[1]

Nicola Foote

Between 1850 and 1950, large numbers of women from the British Caribbean migrated to Latin America to work as domestic servants in the economic enclaves created by US corporations. Rather than employing local labor in their homes, the US expatriate community preferred to bring in migrant labor to do their domestic work. The employment of these workers in white American homes in Latin America became a status symbol for local elites and middle classes. Thus, rather than the typical story of immigrants from Latin America working as domestic servants for elites within the United States, British Caribbean migrants traveled to Latin America to serve the same class in the same capacity. This example illustrates that the relationship between immigration, modernity and domestic service does not just hold for poor migrant women from the developing world coming to the metropolises. Even when there was a cheap local labor supply available, migrant domestic workers were sometimes preferred because of the prestige they brought through their association with British colonialism. The history of immigrant British Caribbean domestic servants in North American-dominated economic zones in Latin America thus provides an interesting preface to the patterns of global domestic work we see today (described in Ehrenreich and Hochschild 2004). In the economic enclaves created by American expansion in the Latin American tropics we see an early and important example of the use of female migrants for critical caring and household tasks; one that raises profound questions for understanding regional ideas of race, class and gender. Here too, we see how colonial legacies helped shape a preference in simultaneously postcolonial and neocolonial settings for certain non-white immigrant domestic workers, over women from other non-white local populations.

While there is a sizeable and growing literature on British Caribbean immigration to Latin America (Bourgois 1989; Chambers 2010; Chomsky 1996; Conniff 1985; Crawford 2011; Foote 2014; Harpelle 2001; Newton 1984; Opie 2009; Petras 1988; Purcell 1993; Putnam 2002; Putnam 2013), the role and experiences of women in these migratory currents has been largely neglected by historians (for exceptions see Foote 2004; Putnam 2002; Putnam 2013). Post-emancipation labor migration from the

Caribbean is typically gendered as male; and only in the case of post-World War Two migration to Britain, Canada and the United States has scholarly attention been paid to the experiences of women migrants (Bryon 1998; Calliste 1993; Chamberlain 2006; Foner 2001; Watkins-Owens 2001). Lara Putnam (2002) has drawn attention to the role played by women in the kinship and mutual aid networks that facilitated the movement of black immigrants through the enclave sectors of the Caribbean basin; yet few studies have sought to reconstruct the lived experiences of women in any detail. Franklin Knight (1985) provided brief biographies of two Jamaican women who had worked as domestic servants in Cuba in the 1920s and 30s based on interviews he conducted in Cuba in the summer of 1980; but virtually no sustained historical work has been undertaken on immigrant domestic workers, despite the fact that this represented one of the most common forms of labor for British Caribbean women in Latin America.

Leading migration scholar José Moya has argued that the feminization of domestic service is a key feature of modernity, and that this relationship was embedded in international migratory patterns. Moya documents a major shift in domestic service over the last two centuries, related to the abolition of slavery, which was characterized by a shift from bonded labor to contractual agreements and wages for domestic work, and from the paternalistic idea of domestic servants as members of the family to employees. Most importantly, domestic service shifted from serving as a signifier of aristocratic privilege—something just for the highest elites—to a 'bourgeois entitlement'; a symbol of middle-class status. As mass international population movements surged from the mid-nineteenth century, domestic service became a niche filled by immigrants: specifically, women immigrants (Moya 2007: 559–60). Moya argues that it was in Latin America that we see the earliest and most complete feminization of the domestic labor sector within the developing world (Moya 2007: 561, 569, 572). However, his focus is on European migrants to the Southern Cone (Argentina, Chile, Uruguay and Southern Brazil), and he does not assess Caribbean migrants in the Caribbean basin of Central and South America. But the presence of Caribbean migrant domestic workers was a central component of American-led modernization, and is essential to assessing the cultural impact of the American presence.

The absence of scholarly analysis of migrant domestic servants reflects not just the widespread omission of a gender perspective from the work on the West Indian diaspora in Latin America, but also the limited nature of historical work on domestic service in Latin America more broadly. Almost twenty-five years after Elsa M. Chaney and Mary Garcia Castro's (1989) seminal volume *Muchachas No More* underlined the pressing need for more research on Latin American domestic service, there remains a limited body of work on the topic relative to the prevalence of domestic service as an institution (see Blofield 2009; da Cunha 2008; Filet-Abreu de Souza 1980; Francois 2008; Graham 1988; Gill 1990; Pite 2011; Tinsman 1992). Pinho and Silva have argued that for social scientists the very ubiquity of maids in Latin American households fuels the shortage of academic analyses—the institution's commonness makes it seem unremarkable (when of course its ubiquity is precisely what makes attention to domestic service so important) (2010: 92). For historians the problem is less blindness to the significance of domestic service, and more a paucity of sources. Domestic workers are very difficult to find in archival records, while their isolation means that, as Chaney and Garcia Castro memorably phrased it, 'they are essentially invisible to themselves and others' (1989: 4).

This chapter uses British consular records as a source to challenge the invisibility of migrant domestic workers from the British Caribbean. One of the distinguishing features of West Indian migrants in Latin America was their status as British colonial subjects, which gave them access to consular protection. Most migrants had at least some level of education as a result of British colonial administration, and they were quick to appeal to British authorities when they felt their rights were being threatened, or when they needed help to return to their islands of origin. While colonial officials were generally dismissive of their concerns, their numerous petitions and letters—and the British reports and investigations that followed the most egregious accusations of abuse—provide a rich archival record of Caribbean immigration and have been one of the primary tools for historians seeking to examine the British Caribbean diaspora in Latin America. No one has previously used them to trace the experiences of domestic workers, who are less frequently represented in these records than other categories of migrants, for reasons to be discussed below. Yet their appearances in this archival record—however fragmentary and limited—can be used to reconstruct patterns of migration, and provide insight into some of the experiences and challenges faced by women workers. However, the voices of women domestic workers themselves are often muted and muffled in these top-down sources. As a counter to this, I seek to uncover women's direct experiences of domestic service through the use of the Costa Rican *Autobiografías Campesinas* (peasant autobiographies). Collected as part of a project by the National University of Costa Rica in the 1970s in which rural people from across the country were invited to submit written accounts of their lives, the Costa Rican peasant autobiographies are a unique source that represent the voices of large numbers of working-class men and women, who had the chance to describe their lives as they experienced them. Several of the life histories were submitted by second-generation West Indian women living in the province of Limón—the birthplace of the United Fruit Company and the center point of the Costa Rican banana industry in the early twentieth century—who had served as domestic servants during the 1930s and 1940s.[2] These women worked for Latin American nationals, rather than American elites, who had mostly left Limón for the Pacific coast of Costa Rica following the outbreak of disease among the banana crops in the 1920s. Their experiences underline how the employment of Afro-Caribbean domestic servants developed status and prestige among the Latin American upper and middle classes and provide insight into the long-term consequences of US neocolonialism in shaping racialized labor patterns.

The hidden histories of British Caribbean domestic workers illuminated in this chapter are significant for the ways in which they complicate our understanding of Latin American hierarchies of race and gender. The experiences of Afro-Caribbean women are in some ways a showcase for the pathologization of blackness in Latin America. Black immigrant women were characterized by elites as sexually profligate; as spreading disease and prostitution; as irresponsible mothers; and as having tendencies to criminality and lunacy. Yet in certain areas they were actively preferred for domestic service work—precisely because of their relationship to colonial and neocolonial powers—and this preference allowed them to carve out an ethnic niche that afforded them opportunities to earn reliable and significant sums of money. At least in enclave areas, these opportunities were not so readily available to lower-class Indigenous and *mestizo* women born in Latin America. Thus the presence of immigrant domestic workers subtly shifted Latin American racial hierarchies even as they built on familiar ideas about black women and servile labor in the home. These shifts also created a space for subaltern agency—albeit limited and constantly restrained—as black women migrants pushed to take control over their lives and improve their material circumstances. The experiences of immigrant domestic workers are thus deeply revealing about the relationship between race, sexuality and modernization in Latin American economic development, and underline the cultural power of American visions of domesticity in the region.

DOMESTIC SERVANTS AND LATIN AMERICAN MIGRATORY CIRCUITS

Immigration from the British Caribbean played an essential role in Latin American development and the spread of US power in the period 1850–1950. This was an era of massive US economic expansion in the region in which US companies worked with Liberal governments, which associated foreign capital with modernity and progress, to build railroads and highways and to develop agricultural projects in frontier regions. Political scientist Peter H. Smith (2008: 9) has argued that this period represented an 'Imperial Era' in US–Latin American relations, while historians and cultural theorists have highlighted the neocolonial economic and political relationships that characterized US dominance as an expansive commercial empire that was forged in the region (Joseph 1998; Grandin 2006).

US corporations showed a marked preference for British Caribbean labor. Racial ideas about the unique suitability of black workers for arduous physical work in the tropics intersected with the advantages accrued by the ability of West Indian workers to speak English and their relatively high level of education.[3] The English-speaking West Indian islands were still formal colonies of Great Britain until decolonization in the 1960s. Following the abolition of slavery in 1838 and the collapse of the sugar industry in the mid-nineteenth century, there were high levels of un- and under-employment among working-class blacks, leading to frequent riots and labor rebellions (Heuman 1995). Out-migration to Latin America was seized upon by British colonial authorities as a solution to labor unrest and unemployment, and became something of a rite of passage for young black men in particular, who sought out migration opportunities in a quest for higher wages, dignity and adventure (Richardson 1986; Chomsky 1996; Putnam 2013). As a result, Latin American modernization projects were intimately entwined with West Indian immigration. Almost every major infrastructural development across the continent relied on West Indian labor to connect agricultural regions to coastal ports and create international networks. British Caribbean laborers dug the Panama Canal, and chiseled roads and rail tracks through the Andes and the Amazon. West Indians became the major workforce in the booming agro-export sector, most notably in the United Fruit Company's banana plantations in Central America and in the booming sugar plantations of early twentieth-century Cuba. British Caribbean migrants were also essential to mining and mineral extraction, working in gold and tin mines across the continent and coming to play an especially critical role in the booming oil industry in Venezuela (Foote 2014; Putnam 2013). Historian Aline Helg has suggested that it is precisely this connection between the transnational migratory circuits of British Caribbean workers and the neocolonial power of American corporate interests that makes the history of West Indian migrants in Latin America of such critical importance (Helg 2006: 156).

Domestic servants were essential to the spread of US capital in Latin America throughout the nineteenth and early twentieth centuries. US corporations operating in the region employed a strict racial division of labor, in which managerial, clerical and technical positions were reserved for white Americans (Bourgois 1989; Conniff 1985; Chomsky 1996; Newton 1984). The result was the growth of a large expatriate population in US enclaves—many from the southern former slave states—as American male employees were encouraged to bring their wives and children with them to Latin America. This stood in marked contrast to policies towards immigrant laborers who were recruited typically as single men and housed in barracks. The North American display of race and class privilege and status was thus manifested in part through the social display of the family. A focus on leisure was central to this display. The families of white professional and administrative staff had busy social lives, with social schedules packed with lunches, dinners, sporting activities and dances (Donoghue 2006; Greene 2009). This meant that they needed expansive household staff who could attend to their domestic chores.

The same preferences for British Caribbean labor that held for infrastructural and agricultural work were also applied in the field of domestic service. The North American idea that West Indians represented a more skilled and educated labor force than the local Latin American population carried over into ideas about domestic service, and Afro-Caribbean migrant women were perceived by American expatriates as the most suitable providers of high quality domestic labor. In Cuba, for example, Jamaican women were preferred for domestic service jobs by US employers because they spoke English, and also because they were considered to be better trained and more highly skilled.[4] Such perceptions had some basis in reality. Marc McLeod (1998: 608) estimates that more than half of West Indian women migrants in Cuba had worked as seamstresses or domestic servants prior to their arrival, compared with less than five percent of Haitians—the other major immigrant stream.

But beyond their linguistic skills and practical training, British Caribbean domestics enjoyed a status that stemmed precisely from their association with British colonialism. Their familiarity with British standards of housekeeping and food preparation made them desirable to Americans keen to impose their vision of domesticity on the Latin American tropics. Rose Van Hardeveld, for example, an American woman from Nebraska who came to join her engineer husband in the Panama Canal Zone in 1906, relayed in her memoir the relief she felt at obtaining a Jamaican servant after several months in the Isthmus, specifically because the Jamaican had been trained by the British and therefore understood 'civilized ways'—in contrast to the servants she had previously worked with (1956: 91).

Racial codes rooted in slavery and colonial discourses were also a factor in shaping the preferential employment of British Caribbean domestics. For white Americans, the use of black domestics allowed the maintenance of the kinds of racial hierarchies that prevailed in the United States under Jim Crow, and served to underline their own racial power. American preferences in turn made the employment of British Caribbean women desirable for local elites and the aspirant middle classes as a status symbol, while also building on—yet subtly modernizing—colonial Iberian norms regarding the deployment of enslaved Africans and their descendants as domestic employees (see Andrews 2004; Graham 1988).

Thus black immigrant women came to have preferential access to domestic service jobs throughout the Caribbean basin of Central and South America and in the Hispanic Caribbean islands. In the Brazilian Amazon, Barbadian women were the domestic servants of choice for foreign merchants during the rubber boom, with the British Consul at Para noting that they were 'highly appreciated' and earned 'good wages.'[5] A similar pattern held in the Venezuelan oilfields, where domestic work became a niche enclave for women from Martinique, Curacao and Trinidad (Tinker-Salas 2009: 113–16; Wright 1990: 50).

Reliable figures on exactly how many women worked as domestics overseas are almost impossible to come by. Caribbean sending governments kept records only on the departures of male workers, since, as gender historian

Rhoda Reddock has argued, black migrant domestics 'were not accepted as real workers' (1984: 84). Latin American governments saw domestics as belonging to the informal economy, no matter their substantial numbers and economic contribution to their sending and host societies, and so they were not counted by census takers and are typically absent from official records. A rare estimate from British Consular officials in Cuba in 1930 suggested that 25,000 of the 60,000 Jamaican immigrants in the island were working as domestic servants, but such official efforts at calculation were infrequent, and I have not been able to find comparable consular figures for other Latin American territories.[6]

However, it is possible to make some general observations about migratory patterns. Women initially migrated for domestic work on an ad hoc basis. The earliest work programs for British West Indian migrants were infrastructure related, and American labor recruiters would work with British officials in the larger islands to bring over male workers in significant numbers to complete a specific project. Women were not typically recruited directly in the same way, but often followed husbands, boyfriends and brothers and found ad hoc work washing clothes and cooking meals (and sometimes offering sex) for migrants living in barracks. Occasionally British officials sought to formalize labor recruitment for women domestic workers by proposing schemes in which women would be recruited directly from the Caribbean islands for domestic service as part of an organized labor program akin to that of male workers on construction projects. These proposals, however, did not typically project Latin America as the migratory destination. In 1901 the governor of Barbados, in collaboration with local elite female philanthropists, sought to create a work program for 'women of good character' to move from Barbados to Canada and Bermuda, where they would undertake domestic labor in the homes of 'respectable' ladies. Ultimately this initiative floundered on the unwillingness of steamer companies to provide subsidized passage for the women in question, but the incident underlines the high levels of out-migration for domestic work, and the concern of British officials to mediate labor flows and ensure the safety and respectability of women migrants.[7] Women's migration from Barbados to the United States in the first decade of the twentieth century was also sponsored through a collaboration between the British government and the Barbadian philanthropy group The Victoria Society, an organization devoted to 'assist[ing] the emigration of poor women who are unable to make their living in Barbados.'[8] This project also collapsed as US immigration laws became more restrictive after 1907.[9]

However, Latin America was the major destination for autonomously migrating domestic workers, and as enclave economies developed throughout the Caribbean basin and populations of both American corporate officials and their families and British Caribbean migrants became more entrenched, West Indian women became the primary labor force in the domestic work sector in many parts of the region. Just like male workers, women domestics migrated from place to place within Latin America, and between Latin America and the United States, chasing the opportunities created by the flow of US capital.

By 1915, out-migration of women was creating a severe shortage of domestic servants in the British Caribbean islands. Sir H. Hesketh Bell, the Governor of the Leewards Islands, lamented that as a result of immigration opportunities 'young men and women of colour appear to be growing more and more restless in their dispositions' with the result that 'it is unusual to find a negro servant who is willing to spend more than a year or two in the same employment.' He proposed instituting a medal for long and faithful domestic service, in the hopes of providing an incentive for local women to stay and work for elites at home rather than away. While Bell recognized that 'domestic service carries with it few rewards and the wages are seldom attractive,' rather than address these structural flaws in the profession he posited that awarding medals would be an effective solution to the labor shortage because 'the coloured people of the West Indies are greatly affected and impressed by visible marks of appreciation.' He suggested that the medals would be especially effective if they had Queen Victoria's head on the back. The Colonial Office ridiculed Governor Bell's proposal. In handwritten notes on the front of his letter London officials suggested it was not even worthy of comment and that it was not clear why Governor Bell viewed the Queen as 'the proper personage to connect with long and faithful domestic service.' Bell's request to institute the medals was denied. The icy official response prompted Bell to defend himself by suggesting that he may have written his proposal in such a way 'which invested it with a degree of importance which was not intended.'[10] Despite its non-implementation and subsequent downplaying, the medal proposal remains significant for the light it sheds on how growing opportunities for emigrants impacted the realities of domestic work in the Caribbean islands. It also makes powerfully clear the disparagement of black subaltern aspirations for respect and fair remuneration.

Certainly, Bell's focus on the poor remuneration and lack of prestige of domestic service in the Caribbean underlines why domestic work overseas was viewed as such a positive opportunity by so many migrant women. Domestic service represented the first opportunity Afro-Caribbean migrant women had to earn a solid, reliable foreign-currency wage. Those who followed their husbands in the first stages of migration typically had ended up undertaking ad hoc labor in very poor conditions at labor camps. Thus even though female domestics still earned markedly less than men working in the oil or banana enclaves, they could pursue the same male strategies of saving money, remitting it home to families and nurture hope of going home to build a house, independent of access to a male wage. For second-generation immigrant women, domestic service provided the best hope of reliable, solid income—even if it was often fraught with problems.

ECONOMIC OPPORTUNITY, SEXUALITY, POWER AND RESISTANCE

Just like their male compatriots, female migrant workers were highly vulnerable to problems created by the boom-bust commodity cycle. While male migrants were more vulnerable to economic downturns than women, since they worked directly in the commodity sector, women also lost domestic jobs when the economy contracted. Events in Brazil during World War One provide a good example of some of the gendered dynamics of these vulnerabilities, and how economic problems were often refracted discursively through ideas of race and sexuality.

In the first decade of the twentieth century thousands of West Indian men migrated to Brazil to work on the Madeira-Mamoré Railway. Many stayed on after completion of the railway line and began work in the Amazonian rubber industry. When the rubber boom abruptly ended in 1914 as a result of competition from rubber plantations established in British-run Southeast Asia, these migrants found themselves unemployed and the subject of nativist agitation.[11]

A 1914 report by the British Consul in Para documented the problems created by the collapse of the rubber industry. The Consul noted that there were around 3,000 West Indians in Para and Mamore, and that a large percentage of them were women, who worked as higglers (informal roadside vendors), laundresses and domestic servants. According to the Consul, these women were mostly from Barbados, but a substantial number were also from Trinidad and British Guiana, and a smaller amount from St. Lucia and Grenada. As jobs for both male rubber gatherers and female domestics dried up with the movement of foreign rubber merchants out of the Amazon, British Caribbean migrants sought to return home. However, many lacked the financial capacity to be able to do so, and appealed to the British Consulate for help.

The Consul was sympathetic to their predicament, noting that many of the workers had sent money home to their families in Barbados and some had bought houses in their home islands. When the economy collapsed and they were unable to find continued employment they sought to return home before they exhausted all their savings. However, when they arrived at the Steamship Company that served the route to Barbados, they were charged a £5 deposit for their quarantine fee in Barbados in addition to their fare. Most simply did not have this money. The Consul argued the quarantine policy was unfair, and that if the colonial government in Barbados wished to quarantine returning migrants, it should pay for this itself, given the positive contribution the workers had made to the local economy through their remittances. He also noted that the only way to get back to any of the West Indian islands from Brazil was through Barbados, so other islanders had to pay the fee, even though they would not be staying in Barbados.

The Consul saw the vulnerability of the women who were trapped at the port as a particular problem. He wrote that many of the women unable to get home—those who had previously worked as domestic servants—ended up in prostitution out of desperation. As he put it: 'In a short time they are hopelessly stranded, the females being in an especially bad case, lapsing into prostitution and crime.'[12] This represents a clear appeal to the British government to act to preserve the honor and morals of women who were British subjects. However, the appeal was unsuccessful, and the Barbadian colonial government refused to waive the quarantine fee for repatriated workers, leaving many of them stranded.[13] While the British Consul in Brazil saw the morality of black Caribbean women as important to preserve, British colonial officials in London and Bridgetown were apparently less sympathetic.

Indeed, although the British Consul used the fear of migrant women falling into prostitution as an effort to engender sympathy on their behalf, this was not typical of how discourses about the sexuality of these domestic workers were projected in Latin America. Anti-immigration discourses represented the sexuality of Afro-Caribbean women as deviant and problematic, and women migrants were widely associated with prostitution and sexual promiscuity. Hortensia Lamar, the leader of an elite Cuban women's group, for example, lamented that with the rise in black migration, 'prostitution . . . increased considerably and with inconceivable loathsomeness' (1923: 134). Immigrant domestic workers were typically assumed to be prostitutes, with their domestic duties serving simply as a cover for these other activities. For example, when the US government brought 295 women migrants from Martinique and St. Kitts to Panama in 1905 under contract to serve as domestic servants and laundresses, many American observers were scandalized. US journalist Poultney Bigelow insisted that the women were all prostitutes and accused US authorities of importing the women specifically to staff brothels. The importation of the women caused such a scandal that it resulted in a US Senate investigation, ordered directly by President Roosevelt (Greene 2009: 258–59). Similarly, in Brazil, Barbadian and Martiniquean women migrants were consistently referred to as prostitutes in contemporary discussions, despite the fact most of them worked as laundresses or domestic servants.[14] Scholars have tended to uncritically follow suit, with historians writing about West Indian immigrants to Panama often referring to the arrival of the 'Martiniquean prostitutes' in passing (and for Brazil see Greenfield 1983: 51; Gauld 1964). Yet the US Senate investigation concluded that only three of the 295 Martiniquean women had engaged in prostitution, with 200 of them married and joining their husbands, and a further 50 living in stable common-law partnerships.[15] Similarly, my review of British consular sources did not reveal any evidence supporting the assertion that domestic workers in Brazil were actually sex workers. The contemporary reactions reveal more about fears of black female sexuality than about immigrant realities. But it is likely that these discourses translated into lived experience, as the imagined correlation between black women migrants and sexual availability factored into high levels of sexual abuse.

Certainly, sources that present women's experiences of domestic service from their own point of view show that sexual assault in the workplace was rife. The Costa Rican peasant autobiographies in particular offer often harrowing insights into the sexual abuse of West Indian domestic workers. One second-generation West Indian woman named Dalia recounted working as a domestic servant for two Costa Rican families during the 1940s. The experience of sexual abuse was a motivating factor for her to seek domestic work, but ended up being one of the defining elements of her work experience. She describes how she had been living in her aunt's house in the coastal town of Quepos as a teenager, but ran away because of sexual abuse by her aunt's husband. Domestic service offered Dalia an opportunity to support herself and to have a roof over her head. After she ran away from her aunt, her choices were to go and live with her mother in an isolated and impoverished rural community where she would have no access to cash currency, or to seek domestic service work in the capital city of San José. She chose to do domestic work, and found a woman in San José who took her in as a servant. Dalia was mainly charged with childcare, and she enjoyed a good relationship with her mistress. However, her vulnerability to sexual abuse ruined the situation. There was a neighbor whom she describes as having 'a filthy mouth' who was always making 'disgusting propositions' to her. One day when the mistress was not in the house the neighbor attempted to seduce her. He came to the upstairs floor when she was working and told her that he wanted a glass of water, but when she entered the room to bring it to him he was lying naked on the bed. She was so frightened she dropped the glass of water she was holding and went 'flying' down the stairs.[16] Interestingly, the neighbor was scared of what could happen if the mistress of the house found out, and he offered Dalia 500 *colones*—several months' wages—not to say anything. However, Dalia was so frightened she just wanted to leave, and when her employer returned home she told her she would have to find a new servant as she was quitting, but she did not explain why. The fact that Dalia did not feel able to tell her employer the truth about what had happened, despite reporting a positive work relationship with her, suggests that she was afraid she would be blamed for the incident. This was the second house in a row that Dalia had to leave because of sexual harassment.

After her resignation Dalia found another domestic service position through the classified advertisements in the newspaper, but she only lasted a month in her new job, due to overwork. She described how she had 'no life' because she had to be in the kitchen until 9 pm cooking for the teenage boys in her charge, who sometimes returned home even later and still expected to be fed. She had to wait around for them no matter how late they were. She also felt degraded by the accommodation—the mistress put an old mattress in the washroom and claimed this was her room. There was no bedding and so she shivered horribly at night. She described how she 'cried bitterly' every night from cold, exhaustion and frustration. She managed to escape the situation by taking refuge in a convent, where with many other young women who had no family she was taught how to cook, make bread and sew.[17]

Other women reported even more shocking abuses. Another second-generation Jamaican woman, who withheld her name, described how in fifth grade in the 1930s, she dropped out of school due to poverty and got work washing and ironing the clothes of the captains of the ships which came into Puerto Limón on Saturdays. They would drop the clothes off with her on Saturday and pick them up on Sundays. She couldn't afford proper cleaning supplies, so she describes how she developed a technique for cleaning the clothes using grains from ears of corn, which she used as a brush with which to rub the clothes. At the end of this all she earned was 1.5 colones for the weekend's work.

She thought she was going to be able to leave this difficult life when she became engaged to a young man, but then they found out that he was actually her half-brother (they shared the same Jamaican father but didn't know—she had never met her father because he had left Limón before she was born and then he died when she was five), so the marriage could not go through, and her suitor moved to Venezuela out of embarrassment. Still only thirteen years old, she found a job as a domestic servant in the town. Soon after, her mistress accused her of stealing $150 and she was sent to prison for seven months. She worked as a cook in the prison, and the prison commander was so impressed by her skills that he told the governor there was a 'little black girl who was innocent' and a lawyer worked to get her out. He then took her to live with him and work as a cook. However, he quickly became violent and abused her physically and sexually. When he was drunk he was violent and would attack her, smashing up her face and raping her. Twice 'the worst possible thing happened'—she got pregnant and was trapped. The first child died at birth. The second, a boy, lived to be five months 'before the normal calamity that would always happen when I was in that house struck again and the baby died.'

After her second baby died, she decided anything was better than what she was dealing with and she moved out, living with a string of men in succession, none of which she loved, but she 'looked simply for what I could use them for.' Happily this women's story had a positive ending, as at the age of twenty she moved to San José and met her husband, Erik, and got married, enjoying what she describes as a loving and supportive union in which she had a degree of financial security.[18] However, it is likely that many other women in her position were not so lucky.

Only one autobiography presents a more positive take on the experience of domestic service. A woman who gave her initials as L.R.A. describes how as a teenager in 1940 she left the family farm and went to San José to work as a domestic servant. She clearly found city life thrilling, and found that the work was so well paid in comparison to what she had been doing that she was able to buy presents and treats for her family. Significantly, she was working as a cleaner in a small shop rather than in a household per se, so while her tasks were largely the same—cleaning, washing clothes, childcare—she had a bit more autonomy as she was not always literally inside someone else's house, and her mistress would take her out into the city to run errands almost daily, so she had the excitement of lots of outings. She received 60 colones a month, in addition to room and board, and she considered this a good sum, and described how she loved having electric light, and being able to go to the theatre or to a restaurant once a month. Ultimately this woman only left San José because of the civil unrest of the mid-1940s that led up to the civil war.[19] Her more positive experience underlines how much women's experiences of domestic service depended on the individual character of the household in which they were working.[20]

However, the larger body of evidence suggests that vulnerability typified the experiences of migrant domestic workers, a situation that was often exacerbated by their age. As the Costa Rican peasant autobiographies make clear, many domestic servants were extremely young, beginning in their working life before they were even teenagers in some instances. The British government periodically became concerned about the migration of very young Caribbean girls overseas. In the 1880s the Colonial Office was scandalized by allegations of Jamaican children being sent to Haiti to do domestic work. Most of the girls making the trip in search of work appear to have been aged between 14 and 18, although some were as young as 11. The Colonial Office blamed poor parenting, and lamented the irresponsibility of parents who let themselves slip into such poor economic circumstances 'that they are only too glad to get rid of their children.'[21] Based on the British Consular sources it is not entirely clear how voluntary the migration was. The Jamaican governor and colonial office officials presented a picture in which Jamaican girls were sent to Haiti by their parents who could not afford to support them. As a result, a law was passed in Jamaica prohibiting 'the engagement of children below the age of 16 for service out of the colony.' Yet the racist discourses that underpin the idea of poor black parents callously sending their children overseas in order to 'get rid of them' are impossible to miss. It is possible that the girls in question saw migration as an opportunity to gain independence and to affirm an adult status, and without further research in Jamaican and Haitian archives such questions are impossible to answer. Regardless of whether migrating teenage domestics saw themselves as having been sent overseas by their parents unwillingly, or whether they saw themselves as mature economic actors making an independent decision to migrate, there can be little doubt that their youthfulness—with its connotations of enhanced sexual allure—and their lack of life experience would increase their vulnerability to abuses and control by their employers and other social actors.

As we saw in the Costa Rican peasant autobiographies, in addition to dealing with sexual and physical abuse, Afro-Caribbean domestic servants sometimes faced accusations of crime that led to their imprisonment. They were also vulnerable to accusations of insanity that could lead to them being detained in a lunatic asylum. In one particularly noteworthy example that took place in the Panama Canal Zone in 1926, Louise Walker, a 42-year-old Jamaican domestic 'who had been in the employ of a prominent woman for a number of years,' was arrested for insanity and taken forcibly to an asylum after she tried to commune with her dead father's spirit. Her employer, an American woman, told the English-language Panamanian press that 'her insanity . . . was brought about by the activities of a spiritist club' that told Louise that they would bring back the spirit of her departed father. Her employer related that 'Louise became quite fervent in the prayers and incantations she offered each day' at an altar she had set up in the employer's home. The biggest problem seemed to stem from the fact that she lit candles at the altar to help in these prayers, and the employer alleged that 'she handled them in such a careless manner' that she 'came to fear a conflagration.' This fear of a fire was apparently enough for the employer to be able to have her arrested for insanity, with the fact that Louise had told her employer that her father had indeed returned to her used as proof of the insanity.[22] Aline Helg (1995: 16–17) has argued that along with sexuality, black religion was one of the 'icons of fear' surrounding blackness in early twentieth-century Latin America, and certainly it seems that in this instance spiritism was being used as a shorthand to convey a broader set of racialized imageries. But this example reveals the special vulnerabilities of these particular domestic workers to the lived consequences of such discourses. It was only because Walker lived in the same house as her employer that her nighttime activities and her personal quest to find solace and grieve by speaking to her dead father in prayer came to her employer's attention, and gave the employer the opportunity and the rationale to have her detained—and most likely deported, the typical course of action with immigrant 'lunatics' (Harpelle 2001: 101).

Certainly, employers had immense control over the most intimate activities of their black domestic workers. The experience of Sebastiana Veragua, a second-generation Jamaican woman who was born in the Panamanian city of Colón and taken to Limón, Costa Rica, by her grandma in the late 1920s, is deeply revealing in this regard. Historian Lara Putnam discovered the story of Sebastiana in legal records in the Costa Rican National Archives, and describes how at the age of fourteen Sebastiana was placed as a domestic servant in the home of a Colombian lawyer named Salomón Zacarías Aguilera, where she cleaned and cared for his children. A few years later, aged seventeen, Sebastiana met a young man named Leandro Chacón in the park. They fell in love. One weekend she stayed with Chacón, and the couple decided to move in together in a common-law marriage which was the typical form of union for working-class people in the banana-growing zone in this era. When she went back to collect her belongings from her employer's house, the lawyer had Chacón charged with rape—the official charge was 'deflowering his ward'—and demanded that Sebastiana be returned to his house. An investigation was opened, and a doctor was brought in to conduct a vaginal examination on Sebastiana to prove that her virginity been taken. The doctor wrote a report arguing that the loss of her virginity had been consummated without resistance and Sebastiana concurred that she had indeed consented to the sexual intercourse. As a result, the charges were dropped and she was able to return to her lover (Putnam 2002: 3–4). However, the case is deeply revealing about the sexual control to which domestic workers were subject. Afro-Caribbean women had to contend with discourses that represented them as sexually promiscuous and available, and their employers and other more powerful males with whom they came into contact often acted upon these ideas in frequently violent sexual overtures. Yet at the same time, women's true sexual agency—their human desire to seek their own romantic partners and to form reciprocal unions—were often viewed by employers as problematic and disruptive, and efforts were made to subvert and control these desires.

In some areas the state formally stepped in to regulate the intimate lives of migrant domestic servants. In 1940s Aruba, for example, extremely strict regulation of migrant women's bodies was legally enforced. Immigrant domestic servants were not allowed to cohabit with male partners, become pregnant or be joined by their dependents.[23] Female domestics were legally required to reside directly in their employer's houses and living even in a separate building adjoining the residence was not allowed. Migrant women were subject to spot-checks by immigration authorities to make sure they were not breaking the law. Any woman found to be pregnant would be deported (Aymer 1997: 59–61). This policy was based on the assumption that their children would be burdensome both for the employing family and for the state, and the collusion of these interests impacted the most intimate spheres of domestic workers' lives. The ability of the state to regulate domestic worker's sexuality in such an intense manner underlines the power of race and gender ideologies which presented migrant domestics as a potential threat to the social body: the same dynamics that made migrant women so vulnerable to sexual abuse.

CONCLUSION: DOMESTIC SERVICE, RACE AND NEOCOLONIALISM

The recruitment of domestic servants was essential to the projection of power and modernity by elite white American enclave households, and those local elites who aspired to be like them. Domestic servants conveyed wealth, status and leisure. Their employment was critical to efforts to project American civilization through a particular vision of the home. Legacies of British colonialism allowed West Indian domestics to be viewed by Americans as more highly skilled, and thus endowed them with special prestige and desirability as employees. American preferences helped identify Afro-Caribbean female labor in the home as a signifier of the modern; and as a result, the Latin American upper and middle classes in enclave areas used the employment of black migrant domestics to project their own claims to whiteness and modernity.

These relationships highlight the profound ways in which American economic penetration impacted the Latin American domestic sphere, and underline that even when explicitly articulated family-based morality discourses were absent; neocolonialist discourses of cultural modernization were implicitly deployed through the models presented by the practices of elite American families.

The race of migrant domestic workers seems to have been a central component of the social meaning with which their recruitment was imbued. As US implementation of racial segregation intensified the meaning and operation of racial hierarchies, employing black domestics was prestigious precisely because it highlighted the non-blackness of the employer. However, the presence of Afro-Caribbean domestics did not simply reconstitute racial hierarchies stemming from regional histories of slavery; it also shifted them in subtle ways. The racial discourses surrounding migrant domestics were complex and contradictory. On the one hand elite discourse stigmatized them as sexually promiscuous, lowly and mentally unstable, invoking deep-rooted colonial racial stereotypes. Yet at the same time migrant domestics were elevated by the social prestige assigned to their employment. Certainly, the development of an economic niche for black immigrant domestics created meaningful opportunities for Afro-Caribbean women to enhance their material circumstances. While working conditions were challenging, and migrant domestics faced the ongoing specter of sexual abuse, some black women did appear to have successfully used domestic service as a strategy for family support and upward mobility. The prestige associated with black immigrant domestic labor provided Afro-Caribbean women with opportunities that complicate ideas about the positioning of blackness within regional hierarchies and underlines the importance of neocolonial discourses and practices in shaping Latin American race formation.

Much more work remains to be done to fully uncover the experiences of immigrant domestic workers in Latin America. The preliminary overview provided in this chapter underlines the importance of these hidden histories in providing a window into the domestic dimensions of US neo-imperialism and assessing the impact of US penetration at the level of the household. It also highlights the complexity of the colonial legacies through which migrant women navigated, as discourses and practices shaped by histories of British colonialism in the West Indies and Spanish colonialism in Latin America segued with neocolonial realities to shape the spaces in which Afro-Caribbean domestics negotiated their quest for social mobility, autonomy and an independent income.

NOTES

1. The author would like to thank Erin O'Connor, Joanna Crow, John Cox and Fae Dussart for their comments on an earlier version of this paper, as well as Victoria Haskins and Claire Lowrie for outstandingly helpful editorial suggestions.
2. The full collection of original manuscripts is housed in the library of the National University of Costa Rica in Heredia.
3. This chapter uses the term 'British Caribbean' to refer to migrants who originated from the British West Indian islands and British Guiana. Migrants from this region often identified themselves as 'West Indian'—a classification that has more typically been used in the scholarly literature—and so this term is also employed here as a descriptor.
4. Jamaican men were also widely employed by American families in Cuba in tasks such as chauffeuring and gardening; they also formed a large proportion of hotel servants and doormen (McLeod 1998: 609). However, they are not considered in this essay, which focuses primarily on domestic labor inside the home.
5. Geo. B. Mitchell, HM Consul at Para, 'Memorandum on Distressed British West Indians in the Amazon States of Brazil,' January 19, 1914, CO 295/490/59, National Archives of the United Kingdom (hereafter NAUK).
6. Mr. Ewen, Secretary for Immigration, to Chargé, Santiago, July 31, 1930, FO 371/14221/2177, NAUK.
7. See Hodgson to Chamberlain, September 23, 1901, in CO 28/255/35328, NAUK; Hodgson to Colonial Office, January 21, 1902, CO 28/256/6371, NAUK.
8. Cecil Spring-Wright to British Embassy, Washington D.C., August 15, 1913, CO 28/282/41102, NAUK.
9. Changes to US immigration laws meant that the Victoria Society's subsidization of women's passages was deemed illegal, as US officials argued that the subsidization gave a false picture of the economic status of the would-be migrants, and the British government stepped in to halt the program. See discussion in Ernest Scott to the Colonial Office, September 29, 1913, and Moore to Springer-Wright, November 6, 1913, CO 28/282/41102, NAUK; and enclosures in 'Emigrants to USA from Barbados' in CO 28/286/45299, NAUK.
10. Sir H. Hesketh Bell to the Secretary of State for the Colonies, February 25, 1915, CO 152/345/13909, NAUK; Hesketh Bell to the Secretary of State for the Colonies, December 27, 1915, CO 152/348/3771, NAUK.
11. Despite its size and significance, migration of Barbadians to Brazil has been almost completely neglected by scholars and the only comprehensive article on the topic was written in the early 1980s (Greenfield 1983).
12. Geo. B. Mitchell, HM Consul at Para, 'Memorandum on Distressed British West Indians in the Amazon States of Brazil,' January 19, 1914, CO 295/490/59, NAUK.
13. 'Repatriation of Distressed West Indians in Brazil,' September 7, 1915, CO 28/286/62, NAUK.
14. See for example, Julio Nogueira, 'A Madeira-Mamoré: A Bacia do Mamoré,' *Jornal do Commercio*, January 31, 1913, 15.
15. *The Daily Gleaner*, December 28, 1905.
16. All translations from the original Spanish made by the author.
17. Dalia, *Autobiografías Campesinas*, Vol. XXIII, Universidad Nacional de Costa Rica, Heredia, Costa Rica, 272–74.
18. Anonymous, *Autobiografías Campesinas*, Vol. XXIII, Universidad Nacional de Costa Rica, Heredia, Costa Rica, 361–63.

19. L.R.A. *Autobiografías Campesinas*, Vol. XXIII, Universidad Nacional de Costa Rica, Heredia, Costa Rica, 394–95.
20. The two women Franklin Knight interviewed in 1980 in Cuba do not reflect negatively on their time spent in domestic service, although the biographies Knight sketches are brief and do not provide much detail on work life. Notably, however, both women expressed regrets at staying in Cuba, suggesting their experiences had not been wholly positive (Knight 1985: 107–108).
21. 'Importation of Jamaican Children at Haiti for Domestic Service,' December 3, 1884, CO 137/519/20717, NAUK.
22. 'Jamaican Woman Crazy Over Spirits,' *The Daily Gleaner*, April 9, 1926.
23. While Aruba—a Dutch colony off the coast of Venezuela—is not technically part of 'Latin America,' it merits inclusion here, as it was the major processing site for oil extracted from the Venezuelan Amazon by Royal Dutch Shell, and formed part of the same migratory circuits through which British Caribbean migrants moved. Many of the Trinidadian, Grenadian and St. Vincentian workers in Aruba had previously spent time in Venezuela, and there was ongoing interregional migration between these sites and the other Dutch island of Curacao.

REFERENCES

Andrews, George Reid. 2004. *Afro-Latin America*. New York: Oxford University Press.

Aymer, Paula L. 1997. *Uprooted Women: Migrant Domestics in the Caribbean*. Westport: Praeger.

Blofield, Merike. 2009. 'Feudal Enclaves and Political Reforms: Domestic Workers in Latin America.' *Latin American Research Review* 44(1): 158–90.

Bourgois, Philippe. 1989. *Ethnicity at Work: Divided Labor on a Central American Banana Plantation*. Baltimore: Johns Hopkins University Press.

Byron, Margaret. 1998. 'Migration, Work and Gender: The Case of Post-war Labour Migration from the Caribbean to Britain.' In *Caribbean Migration: Globalized Identities*, edited by Mary Chamberlain, 217–35. London: Routledge.

Calliste, Agnes. 1993. 'Women of Exceptional Merit: Immigration of Caribbean Nurses to Canada.' *Canadian Journal of Women and the Law* 6(1): 83–102.

Chamberlain, Mary. 2006. *Family Love in the Diaspora: Migration and the Anglo-Caribbean Experience*. London: Transaction Publishers.

Chambers, Anthony. 2010. *Race, Nation and West Indian Immigration to Honduras*. Baton Rouge: Louisiana State University Press.

Chaney, Elsa M., and Mary Garcia Castro. 1989. 'Introduction: A New Field for Research and Action.' In *Muchachas No More: Household Workers in Latin America and the Caribbean*, edited by Elsa M. Chaney and Mary Garcia Castro, 3–16. Philadelphia: Temple University Press.

Chomsky, Aviva. 1996. *West Indian Workers and the United Fruit Company in Costa Rica, 1870–1940*. Baton Rouge: Louisiana State University Press.

Conniff, Michael Jr. 1985. *Black Labor on a White Canal: Panama, 1904–1981*. Pittsburgh: University of Pittsburgh Press.

Crawford, Sharika. 2011. 'A Transnational World Fractured but Not Forgotten: British West Indian Migration to the Colombian Islands of San Andres and Providence.' *New West Indian Guide* 85(1–2): 31–52.

da Cunha, Olivia Maria Gomes. 2008. 'Learning to Serve: Intimacy, Morality, and Violence.' *Hispanic American Historical Review* 88(3): 455–91.

Donoghue, Michael E. 2006. 'Imperial Sunset: Race, Identity and Gender in the Panama Canal Zone, 1939–1979.' PhD thesis, University of Connecticut, Storrs, United States.
Ehrenreich, Barbara, and Arlie Russel Hochschild. 2004. *Global Women: Nannies, Maids and Sex Workers in the New Economy*. New York: Macmillan.
Filet-Abreu de Souza, Julia. 1980. 'Paid Domestic Service in Brazil.' *Latin American Perspectives* 7(1): 35–63.
Foner, Nancy. 2001. 'Introduction: West Indian Migration to New York—An Overview.' In *Islands in the City: West Indian Migration to New York*, edited by Nancy Foner, 1–22. Berkley: University of California Press.
Foote, Nicola. 2004. 'Rethinking Race, Gender and Citizenship: Black West Indian Women in Costa Rica, 1920–1940.' *Bulletin of Latin American Research* 23(2): 198–212.
Foote, Nicola. Forthcoming 2014. 'British Caribbean Migration and the Racialization of Latin American Nationalisms.' In *Immigration and National Identities in Latin America*, edited by Nicola Foote and Michael Goebel. Gainesville: University Press of Florida.
Francois, Marie Eileen. 2008. 'The Products of Consumption: Housework in Latin American Political Economies and Cultures.' *History Compass* 6(1): 207–42.
Gauld, Charles Anderson. 1964. *The Last Titan: Percival Farquhar, American Entrepreneur in Latin America*. Stanford: Stanford University Press.
Gill, Lesley. 1990. 'Painted Faces: Conflict and Ambiguity in Domestic Servant-Employer Relations in La Paz, 1930–1988.' *Latin American Research Review* 25(1): 119–35.
Graham, Sandra Lauderdale. 1988. *House and Street: The Domestic World of Servants and Masters in Nineteenth Century Rio de Janeiro*. Austin: University of Texas Press.
Grandin, Greg. 2006. *Empire's Workshop: Latin America, the United States, and the Rise of the New Imperialism*. New York: Henry Holt and Company.
Greene, Julie. 2009. *The Canal Builders: Making America's Empire at the Panama Canal*. London: Penguin.
Greenfield, Sidney M. 1983. 'Barbadians in the Brazilian Amazon.' *Luso-Brazilian Review* 20(1): 44–64.
Harpelle, Ronald N. 2001. *The West Indians of Costa Rica: Race, Class and the Integration of an Ethnic Community*. Montreal: McGill University Press.
Helg, Aline. 1995. *Our Rightful Share: The Afro-Cuban Struggle for Equality, 1886–1912*. Chapel Hill: University of North Carolina Press.
Helg, Aline. 2006. 'The Aftermath of Slavery in the Spanish-Speaking Caribbean: Historiography and Methodology.' In *Beyond Fragmentation: Perspectives on Caribbean History*, edited by Juanita de Barros, Audree Diptee and David V. Trotman, 141–62. Kingston: Markus Weiner.
Heuman, Gad. 1995. 'Post-emancipation Resistance in the Caribbean: An Overview.' In *Small Islands, Large Questions: Society, Culture and Resistance in the Post-emancipation Caribbean*, edited by Karen Fog Olwig, 123–34. London: Frank Cass.
Joseph, Gilbert. 1998. In *Close Encounters of Empire: Writing the Cultural History of U.S.–Latin American Relations*, edited by Gilbert Joseph, Catherine LeGrand and Ricardo Salvatore, 3–46. Durham: Duke University Press.
Knight, Franklin W. 1985. 'Jamaican Migrants and the Cuban Sugar Industry, 1900–1934.' In *Between Slavery and Free Labor: The Spanish-Speaking Caribbean in the Nineteenth Century*, edited by Manuel Moreno Fraginals, 94–114. Baltimore: Johns Hopkins University Press.
Lamar, Hortensia. 1923. 'La lucha contra la prostitución y la trata de blancas.' *Revista Bimestre Cubana* 18:132–35.

McLeod, Marc C. 1998. 'Undesirable Aliens: Race, Ethnicity, and Nationalism in the Comparison of Haitian and British West Indian Immigrant Workers in Cuba, 1912–1939.' *Journal of Social History* 31(3): 599–623.

Moya, José. 2007. 'Domestic Service in a Global Perspective: Gender, Migration and Ethnic Niches.' *Journal of Ethnic and Migration Studies* 33(4): 559–79.

Newton, Velma. 1984. *The Silver Men: West Indian Labour Migration to Panama, 1850–1914*. Kingston: Institute of Social and Economic Research, University of the West Indies.

Opie, Frederick Douglass. 2009. *Black Labor Migration in Caribbean Guatemala, 1882–1923*. Gainesville: University Press of Florida.

Petras, Elizabeth MacLean. 1988. *Jamaican Labor Migration: White Capital and Black Labor, 1850–1930*. Boulder: Westview Press.

Pinho, Patricia de Santana, and Elizabeth B. Silva. 2010. 'Domestic Relations in Brazil: Legacies and Horizons.' *Latin American Research Review* 45(2): 90–113.

Pite, Rebekah E. 2011. 'Entertaining Inequalities: Doña Petrona, Juanita Bordoy and Domestic Work in Mid-Twentieth Century Argentina.' *Hispanic American Historical Review* 91(1): 96–128.

Purcell, Trevor W. 1993. *Banana Fallout: Class, Color and Culture among West Indians in Costa Rica*. Los Angeles: University of California Press.

Putnam, Lara. 2002. *The Company They Kept: Migrants and the Politics of Gender in Caribbean Costa Rica, 1870–1960*. Chapel Hill: University of North Carolina Press.

Putnam, Lara. 2013. *Radical Moves: Caribbean Migrants and the Politics of Race in the Jazz Age*. Chapel Hill: University of North Carolina Press.

Reddock, Rhoda. 1984. *Women, Labour and Struggle in Twentieth Century Trinidad and Tobago*. London: Zed Books.

Richardson, Bonham C. 1986. *Panama Money in Barbados, 1900–1920*. Knoxville: University of Tennessee Press.

Smith, Peter H. 2008. *Talons of the Eagle: Latin America, the United States and the World*. Oxford: Oxford University Press.

Tinker-Salas, Miguel. 2009. *The Enduring Legacy: Oil, Culture and Society in Venezuela*. Durham: Duke University Press.

Tinsman, Heidi. 1992. 'The Indispensible Services of Sisters: Considering Domestic Service in the United States and Latin American Studies.' *Journal of Women's History* 4(1): 37–59.

Van Hardeveld, Rose. 1956. *Make the Dirt Fly!* London: Pan Press.

Watkin-Owens, Irma. 2001. 'Early Twentieth-Century Caribbean Women: Migration and Social Networks in New York City.' In *Islands in the City: West Indian Migration to New York*, edited by Nancy Foner, 25–51. Berkeley: University of California Press.

Wright, Winthrop. 1990. *Café con Leche: Race, Class, and National Image in Venezuela*. Austin: University of Texas Press.

17 Contemporary Balinese Cruise Ship Workers, Passengers and Employers
Colonial Patterns of Domestic Service

Pamela Nilan, Luh Putu Artini and Steven Threadgold

This chapter considers Balinese service staff on transnational cruise ships. We propose that racially-targeted service staff recruitment and cruise passenger advertising point to a touristic re-creation of colonial nostalgia expressed in personalized domestic service. The luxury colonial aura attracts the white working-class to cruises, especially retirees and honeymooners. The first section of this chapter considers resonances of colonialism and the triangular relationship of power between passengers, Southeast Asian service workers and transnational cruise companies. The second section focuses on the experiences of Balinese cruise ship workers, presenting the voices of the workers themselves.

Mass cruising has greatly expanded in the last twenty years (Larsen, Marnburg and Øgaard 2012), in large part because costs remain affordable. The cruise company Carnival Australia's website (2012) reported that cruising is the standout success of Australian tourism.[1] More than 690,000 Australians took a cruise holiday in 2012 compared with just 116,000 in 2002 (Allen 2013). Elsewhere on the Carnival website, the assurance is given that 'You are the Boss' on our ships.[2] The service corollary to this promised position of authority is exemplified by another transnational cruise site, Holland America. Passengers are assured that the Indonesian service staff can be relied on because, 'trained at our very own school in Jakarta, Indonesia, *they pride themselves in exceeding your every wish*' (quoted in Wood 2002: 425; our emphasis). In his study of heritage hotels in Southeast Asia, Maurizio Peleggi stresses that 'global consumer culture that references colonial imagery [is] especially conspicuous in tourism' (2005: 255), and cruise tourism is no exception. Promises of personalized service by foreign workers are central to cruise advertising (Carrigan 2007: 148).

There is a profit benefit in the arrangement. Working-class passengers from developed countries can afford to cruise because costs are kept within their budget. To create the patina of luxury experiences, transnational cruise lines have to employ 'an enormous number of shipboard service workers' (Weaver 2005: 180), with an estimated 85 percent of the crew in hospitality (Wu 2005: 35). But while luxury and indulgence are promised, labor costs must remain low, so suitable workers from selected developing countries, especially Southeast Asia, are eagerly sought.

The selling point of the nostalgic master/servant travel fantasy glimpsed above is strengthened by employing Southeast Asian service staff (Wood 2002; Seal 1998). In his study of cruise lines, William Terry found that cruise lines prefer service workers to be the right 'color'; not too dark but not too light either (2011: 663). According to an online cruise ship recruitment firm, the ideal Southeast Asian employee is a young man or woman with good grades, of average height and pleasing appearance. The website emphasizes that the prospective employee should possess good manners, self-confidence and be able to speak English well. He or she should not be too religious and must be willing to do whatever is asked (Cruiseshipjobs 2010). The description supports John Urry's (1998) argument that labor itself is a component of the tourist product and therefore every aspect of the worker's demeanor matters to the employer, including appearance, the way they speak and representation of personality. This is especially so for tourism enterprises that promise colonial-era luxury.

An experienced cruise ship worker in our study observed that fellow crew members were usually from '[the] Philippines, Indonesia and India.' He added, 'Nobody from Malaysia or Singapore because they have good money there, they don't need to go.'[3] This comment confirms Terry's (2011: 663) finding that 'the majority (70%) of the people that work on cruise ships come from low-wage countries.' Indonesia has had a long history of temporary overseas migration for work and this trend has greatly increased and diversified since the late twentieth century (Ford 2001). Cruise ship work is part of this new trend, and has become ever more popular, especially with well-educated young men. The Indonesian province of Bali has an excellent reputation for both education and tourism, yet wages are not very high, and only the urban middle-class lead prosperous lives. Bali is therefore a target for agents that train and recruit cruise ship service staff. As a cruise ship trainer called Betty explained in our interview with her in 2012, 'They want to recruit from Bali, because the English is much better. And also they have the history of serving guests.'[4]

However, we avoid the inference that colonial relations, or conditions, or inequalities, are directly comparable with the contemporary situation of transnational cruising. Rather we show how resonances with the past are embedded in the colonial aura that is needed to produce unchallenged white privilege in the cruising experience, and thereby deliver profits to cruise lines.

COLONIALISM AND SERVICE

In an essay reviewing various themes in studies of colonialism, Ann Laura Stoler and Frederick Cooper (1997) identify two relevant approaches. The first locates colonies as a preeminent site for identification of the 'Other' against whom the ideal of Europeaness was expressed (for example, Said 1979). The second offers a definition of colonies as a 'domain of exploitation where European powers could extract land, labor and produce' (Stoler and Cooper 1997: 4). The first of these approaches finds expression in our analysis of how the colonial aura is conveyed in budget cruising for twenty-first-century passengers. The second finds expression in analysis of the labor conditions of Balinese workers, who form an integral part of the persuasive colonial aura. The two are closely linked due to the triangular relationship of power between the passengers, Southeast Asian service workers and transnational cruise line companies.

Passengers

In the popular imagination, early twentieth century luxury cruising is associated with cinema images of the Titanic. Yet this was not a cruise but a transatlantic crossing. The first official cruise took place in 1922, 'on a ship built specifically for the purpose of traveling from port to port with on-board luxury and leisure' (Morgan and Power 2011: 277). The billion dollar transnational cruise lines of today evolved from steam cargo ship companies that transported passengers as a sideline. At first, passengers were given only basic facilities on board. Later, much more was expected. A passenger hierarchy lasted right up until the mid-twentieth century:

> Millions of people crossed the Atlantic aboard ocean liners. The market was partitioned into distinct passenger types, members of which were accustomed to unique social atmospheres, particular styles of accommodation, and varying modes of service . . . immigrants in steerage, third-class tourists, second-class, and first-class passenger types.
> (Coye and Murphy 2007: 174–75)

Steerage passengers were provided with bedding, food and hygiene amenities. First-class passengers however enjoyed all the services and comforts of first-class resort hotel accommodation, including not only spacious rooms, haute cuisine, sumptuous decoration (Coye and Murphy 2007) but also a 'high-servant ratio' (Maxton-Grahame 1972). Fifty years later, transnational cruises evoke this first-class ocean liner experience in advertising to attract what we have elsewhere described as the 'white working class on holiday' (Artini, Nilan and Threadgold 2011), who might well have been consigned to steerage class in the golden days of steamship travel.

In North America, 18 percent of economy cruise passengers in the new millennium were found to be 'luxury seekers' (Teye and Leclerc 2003: 231–37). Their highest motivations were 'uninhibited pursuits' and 'special treatment.' The following offers an example of the promises of privilege, personal service, luxury, opulence, choice and the exotic orient made by cruise ship companies:

> Lucky guests on MSC Magnifica are expertly looked after by a 1,000-strong crew, enjoying the best of modern Italian style. At the heart of MSC Magnifica is a lush haven of tranquillity, the luxurious MSC Aurea Spa. This sumptuous wellness centre offers a myriad of relaxation options from saunas and Turkish baths to a fitness centre, beauty salon, Thalassotherapy room, relaxation area and massage rooms. Why not give in to the magic of an authentic Balinese massage?
> (MSC Cruises 2010)

The example shows how budget cruising passengers of today are lured by the promise of a luxury experience beyond their everyday existence. It is clear that the expectation of being 'the boss' and enjoying service from staff who 'pride themselves in exceeding your every wish' (quoted in Wood 2002: 425) is an integral part of the anticipated cruise pleasure. Southeast Asian tourism has been re-creating the exotic (and nostalgic) colonial service encounter in the name of heritage over at least three decades (Sofield 2001: 112).

In the face of a growing democratization of tourism and a corresponding decline of tourism in itself as a marker of social status (Peleggi 2005: 263), cruise lines have sought to answer the perceived need of the mass cruising passenger to feel special. Cruise lines peddle the promise of a luxury, hedonistic experience, and dedicated service from a 'colored' roomboy or waiter lies at the heart of the anticipated experience. As Peleggi points out, not only is the 'colonial-era traveller' evoked in room and lobby fittings, but 'South-East Asians continue to serve (with a smile) a largely foreign clientele, making colonial nostalgia appear to be something more substantial than a figment of the imagination' (Peleggi 2005: 263). By evoking the settings and labor relations of the colonial era, Asian heritage tourism 're-solidifies the former colonial construction' while actually standing 'bereft of all its historical ties' (Winter 2007: 97).

Southeast Asian Service Staff

Service staff on the liners of a bygone era were not from foreign countries, although crews were. Balachandran (2011: 290) describes the Asian maritime 'coolie' as a 'product of a political and social project to mobilize colonial labour for a global labour force.' Maritime workers from European colonies in Asia in the nineteenth century were central to building the shipping trade (Ewald 2000: 72). British shipowners began to employ foreign workers in increasing numbers from about the middle of the nineteenth century. As wages fell behind what American and European seamen could earn ashore, an increasing proportion of crews came to be recruited not only from Africa and the Caribbean, but also from Asia. They were contracted under restrictive 'Asiatic articles' to distinguish them from European sailors, setting wages at one-fifth to one-third of European wages. They typically worked seventy to eighty-four hours a week and shared cramped quarters. Unlike European crew members, their contracts were short and they had to return to their home port. Such a racialized onboard work hierarchy was an expression of colonial difference in employment (Balachandran 2011: 281). Shipowners and masters regarded Asian crew members as much 'easier to recruit and discipline' (Ewald 2000: 76). The goal for many was to 'return to their homelands, using profits from their work to establish households' (Ewald 2000: 86), and this is still the case today for Southeast Asian maritime workers, including those on cruise ships. In fact it is remarkable how little has substantially changed for them since the nineteenth century in terms of restrictive contracts, the wage differential and arduous onboard conditions.

Use of foreign service workers on ships began in the first half of the twentieth century as a means for shipping companies to increase profits by upgrading amenable foreign crew members to work as waiters and room-boys. They could be paid far less than their European or North American counterparts (Toh, Rivers and Ling 2005: 123), while providing an attractively 'exotic' experience for passengers (Wood 2002: 425). It is at this point that resonances of an imagined colonial past of dedicated personal service became part of cruise advertising. These resonances 'paint the cruise industry in a light highly reminiscent of colonialism' (Terry 2011: 663).

Europeans in Southeast Asian colonies imagined themselves and constructed communities built on 'asymmetries of race, class and gender.' Colonial authority depended on racial distinctions linked 'with a racist and class-specific core' of reasoning (Stoler 1989: 634, 636). The colonizer carried out the 'discursive work of "othering" the colonized' (Go 2009: 7). This 'othering' was strongly evident in encounters between colonial masters and mistresses and their Southeast Asian servants. In the Dutch East Indies, the domestic service relationship formed one of the most frequent encounters between Indonesians and their Dutch *belanda* colonial rulers (Stoler 2002: 168).[5] It is this kind of experience of mastery over 'native' 'others,' fictionalized in films and novels, that injects nostalgic attraction into the onboard mass cruising experience of being 'the boss' over 'colored' service staff. Indeed 'on several major lines, employees wear name tags with their nationality prominently displayed' (Wood 2002: 432). Labeling serves as a forcible reminder of the race and class difference between the server and the (unlabeled) served. It also echoes the maritime history of 'Asiatic articles' where Asian seamen 'traversed an often vast and open seascape, yet lived in the tightly bounded confines of ships where life was, to varying degrees, hierarchical and regimented' (Ewald 2000: 70) according to boundaries of race and class.

Cruise ship service staff are trained to be particularly attentive and obliging (Testa and Mueller 2009). Some colleges encourage trainees to never say no. Ex-cruise line chef Ketut C. in Bali admitted a major challenge is to teach young recruits to smile. 'You have to smile all the time,' he said, 'and a real smile, as if you mean it.'[6] As trainer Betty indicates above, Balinese are perceived as highly suitable for cruise ship service work. Yet while cruise ship work represents choice, it is a labor decision made in coercive conditions (see Balachandran 2012: 10). As Weaver (2005: 178) points out, 'Individuals from these [Southeast Asian] countries can usually earn more money on board cruise ships than they ever would in their respective home countries as civil servants or school teachers.' Youth unemployment in Bali is high, with many high school graduates and even university graduates looking for work. In Indonesia a standing joke goes, 'the higher one's education the smaller the chance one will get a job' (Jardine 2008: 3). Headlines to this effect feature in the Indonesian media at graduation time in June each year, and undoubtedly affect the post-senior high school choices of poorer young Balinese and their families. Cruise ship work is appealing because it pays more than local tourist work, so training colleges are 'swamped with applications.'[7]

Balinese cruise ship service workers are predominantly male. Roomboy training in the history of the Southeast Asian region emphasized male service workers as 'feminised and submissive' (Martinez and Lowrie 2009: 305; see also Lowrie in this volume). Some cruise ship researchers claim this is still the case (Chin 2008: 2). Apparently the job of cruise ship service worker has a poor reputation among seafarers. Dennett, Cameron, Jenkins and Bamford argue that this 'could be caused by the perceived *master/servant identity* historically and operationally created' (2010: 5; emphasis in original).

The Transnational Cruise Industry

It can be argued that low-paid Southeast Asian workers on cruise ships represent an extension of the temporary labor migration that goes on worldwide. For example Indonesia sends migrant labor to Malaysia and Saudi Arabia (Ford 2001). These receiving countries reap significant economic benefits from the cheap labor of Indonesian workers, but the benefits at home are not so great. Adams and Cuecuecha (2010) found that households receiving international remittances in Indonesia were much poorer than for many other labor-exporting countries and remittances were spent primarily on fuel and food. The fact is that cruise lines do not recruit from all Southeast Asian countries. Filipinos and Indonesians are preferred, perhaps because both countries have a high level of education but a relatively low Human Development Index, which means migrant workers will accept lower salaries.

Transnational cruise lines take advantage of legal loopholes and weak regulation to pay Southeast Asian workers—crew and service staff—low wages for very long hours and shifts. They can do so because cruise ships sail under 'flags of convenience' from nations outside international labor agreements. Cruise workers are therefore 'subject neither to the labor laws of their countries of origin nor to those of the country of their employer; rather, their contracts specifically state that they are subject to the laws of the country in which the ship is tagged,' usually Panama, Liberia and the Bahamas (Wood 2000: 351). Thus, 'cruise lines can hire cheap foreign labor from less developed countries like the Philippines and Indonesia, and then charge low fares to create a mass market for cruising' (Toh, Rivers and Ling 2005: 131). Racialized recruitment is openly practiced. In fact, 'the deeper you go in the belly of the ship, the darker the crew' (union worker quoted in Terry 2011: 663).

Although more comfortable than the steam ships of the nineteenth century, the closed work environment of a cruise ship still represents a domain of exploitation where a transnational company owned by investors from developed countries can extract value from the labor of low-paid Southeast Asian maritime workers in an unfettered work environment (see Balachandran 2011: 290). Due to the flag of convenience convention, there is no external vigilance over the enforcement of safety or shift regulations, such as would normally prevail in land-based hospitality work, even in Bali. It is a minimally regulated work environment, demanding a much greater level of personal service because of the advertising expectation and the overwhelming need to get tips. Land-based tourism in Bali does not formally involve tipping.

Those working in the ship's kitchen, laundry or similar, earn a base salary of less than US$1000 per month with no tips. This is the base level of service work on board. At the highest service skill level of chefs, assistant chefs and head waiters, salaries are much higher. Between these two status levels of service work are waiters, assistant waiters, bar staff, bartenders, roomboys and so on. They earn a base salary of as little as US$74 per month but because they are in direct contact with passengers, they can get tips of more than US$35 per day, so their income can reach US$2500 per month or more. It is the lure of these kinds of jobs that attracts young Balinese to sign up for cruise ship work. Yet while US$2500 per month might seem a considerable amount of money back home in Bali, it disappears rapidly in repaying the loan for training (up to US$3000), agent percentages and cost of travel to and from the departure port. Cruise lines demand contract employees buy a one-way ticket and pay a return-trip deposit. If the worker is fired or leaves the job, the deposit is forfeited. There are also costs on board. Made D. told us that a fresh uniform must be worn each day, but workers themselves must pay for uniform laundering from their salary.[8] Conditions can be harsh. The shifts are around 12 hours a day, for an average of 6.5 days a week, for up to 9 months at a time (Brownell 2008: 204). The warning is given on one recruitment website that workers must be prepared to sleep in a crowded, windowless cabin (Cruiseshipjobs 2010).

The cruise ship works according to Erving Goffman's (1961: 1) concept of the 'total institution,' where the person is isolated from family and friends for long periods. So another way in which cruise ship service labor differs from standard hotel labor is that workers 'can't go home, see their family or separate themselves from the place of work' at all (Dennett, Cameron, Jenkins and Bamford 2010: 3). This means that if working conditions are intolerable they cannot leave until the next port, where they will be stranded far from home and penniless. Worker Internet and phone access is limited and unreliable. There is literally no escape from humiliation or harassment should it occur (Chin 2008). It is this custodial aspect that resonates with past conditions of colonial domestic service.

The emotional labor required of staff on a typical cruise ship also differs from that of staff in land-based mass tourism resorts and hotels in Asia. A service encounter onboard is likely to be an intense personal engagement quite unlike the usual hotel service encounter, even in Bali. For example, the average hotel roomboy and the cruise ship roomboy provide a different level of emotional labor, despite similarity of functional tasks. The former knows nothing about the guests in a room and that knowledge does not form part of the hotel service or supplement his wage. However, a cruise ship roomboy must know his passengers by name and their preferences. He does not just come in twice a day to clean, but is on constant call for all kinds of requests, usually fulfilled in the intimate space of the cabin, like a domestic servant. Because his company salary is low, he depends on tips, so he must do what he can to gain favor with guests, including anticipating their needs. This level of attention is not always to the liking of cruise ship passengers. Australian Passenger J. recalled with frustration that whenever he left his cabin the roomboy appeared like magic to straighten the room, replenish the bathroom and replace chocolates on the pillow, then was always waiting to welcome him back with a smile. Passenger J. said he tipped the roomboy high to get him stop but it had the opposite effect.[9] In the training colleges provided by cruise lines in Southeast Asia, applicants are schooled in the development of 'expressive dimensions to satisfy guests (i.e. courtesy, friendliness, empathy, etc.)' (Testa and Mueller 2009: 196). They do not merely carry out tasks. They are required to manage 'their emotional expressions so as to generate in customers an appropriate feeling state' (Sallaz 2010: 301). Through such self-management they can maximize tips to supplement the low wages they are paid.

The triangular relationship of power between the passengers, Southeast Asian service workers and transnational cruise line companies can be summarized as follows. Cruise companies offer a highly profitable leisure product carefully crafted for an apparently luxurious onboard holiday, at a low running cost, to a mass tourism market. To achieve this, companies register ships under flags of convenience so their labor costs are low. Many polite workers are needed to construct the luxury cruising experience. However, to make profits, wages must kept low while hours of work remain high. Well-educated Southeast Asian service workers fit this worker profile and make it possible for companies to shape their advertising to match a nostalgic ideal of upper-class cruising during the colonial era.

Budget cruise passengers are promised not only luxury accommodation and food, but control of on-call foreign service staff who will do whatever is asked of them. This promise is premised upon behavior driven by payment of low service wages and forced dependence on tips. In his study of Angkor Wat, Tim Winter recommends understanding tourism in terms of performativity, so that the production and consumption of the leisure experience can be seen as 'contingent and mutually constitutive processes' (2007: 16). Applying that insight here, 'white' passengers are encouraged to exercise the privilege of authority over Southeast Asian service staff, while staff are under financial pressure to behave like a personal servant rather than a tourism service provider.

THE WORKERS' EXPERIENCES: NEOCOLONIALISM?

The second section of this chapter focuses on the experiences of Balinese cruise ship trainees and workers. Here the voices of the workers themselves are represented. The authors interviewed thirty-five informants in Bali between 2010 and 2012. The informants included ready-to-depart, experienced or retired cruise ship workers, representing about one-third of those interviewed, the remainder being trainees still attending college. Interview transcripts were analyzed using a thematic coding technique (Ryan and Bernard 2000). Some secondary data in the form of online comments is also included. These are from a blog site used by Indonesian cruise ship workers at sea, and give an immediate sense of life on board.[10]

Building on the background provided above, we find the comments of cruise ship workers convey the extent to which cruise tourism is a kind of colonial encounter. Dennison Nash (1989: 45) argued that tourism itself is inherently located within the broad context of imperialism because 'others must serve while the tourist plays, rests, cures or mentally enriches himself.' Where those serving are strongly distinguished by race and socioeconomic status from those they serve, then Nash's thesis that tourism is a form of imperialism seems even stronger. The quite similar claim by Hal Rothman (1998: 11) that 'tourism is the most colonial of colonial economies,' is also enhanced when we consider the situation of service workers from Southeast Asia providing personalized service to cruise ship passengers from the global North. In view of the fact that Southeast Asian cruise ship workers are from developing nations previously colonized by European powers, we define the cruise ship service encounter as neocolonial because it reproduces some of the original colonialist relations of power.

Motivation: Money

All interviewees in this study were from poor families. The great motivation was building wealth. As Gede, one of our respondents, put it: 'I want a better life for my family, for my future. Because you know, work in Bali—you can't get a lot of money.'[11] Obligations to family are strong in Balinese culture. Nyoman B. relinquished a career as a mathematics teacher to work as a waiter for MSC Cruises in order to assist his younger siblings and parents:

> Working in the cruise ship is because of the money. Yeah at that time honestly, my family was very bad economically. My younger brother couldn't continue his study and my parents had to borrow a lot of money from many people, including from the bank. So I had a responsibility: how to help my family. Actually I didn't have knowledge of tourism since I graduated in mathematics. I was supposed to be a teacher of maths.[12]

The sometimes harsh choices made by cruise ship workers is also illustrated in the story of recent training college graduate Agus. Agus tried hospitality work in Dubai but finding the wages were too low, turned to laundry work on a cruise ship:

> I worked in a hotel in Dubai but the salary is only enough for myself. I could not help my brother go to school in Indonesia, nor my parents. That's why I applied, to get the better salary from the cruise ship.[13]

In addition to providing financial assistance to their family, new recruits explained that a secondary motivation was acquiring the money to build a business. As Wawan, a newly appointed barman on MSC Cruises put it in an interview in 2012: 'The first thing is, I want to get more salary to make my family happy. Then I want to develop a small automotive business. I want to make a small garage in my home.'[14]

Yet realizing these goals can take up to ten years of repeated contracts, due to the high debts incurred in beginning cruise ship work, and subsequent years taken up by loan repayments. Indeed, cruise ship workers often find themselves unable to afford a vacation between contracts, let alone realize broader financial goals. Normally each contract is around nine months, followed by a three-month break. From our observations, back in Bali they take short-term casual jobs in the break.

Debt Burden

A twenty-first-century echo of indentured work in the colonies is observable in the debt cycle of Balinese cruise ship service staff. As one blogger put it on the blog site *Kerja di Kapal Pesiar* in 2010, 'Although cruise ship work builds up money, when you get back to the village you are still poor, basically going backwards.'[15] Significant debt is incurred to even enter employment. Local agents representing cruise lines control the whole process of training, registration, applying for positions, visa applications, travel and so on. Like all migrant labor agencies they set high premiums on the 'packages' they offer. With very poor cruise ship applicants who cannot obtain a bank loan they make special 'deals,' with even higher interest to be repaid over the years.

The burden of debt repayment was a regular theme in interviews. For example, Nengah, a 37-year-old cook, had worked for ten years in a hotel but wanted more money. He applied through the Bali Paradiso agency. He was shocked at the cost of the application form (US$10). He gained an interview and was offered a cruise contract, but first had to pay US$3200 for a 14-day training program in the city of Surabaya. Travel to Surabaya, accommodation, food, passport, visa, travel to the point of departure and so on, cost a further US$1000. All this money was borrowed from a bank. Nengah was paid US$1001 per month and 50 percent of his first month's salary went to the agent. On return loan repayments were waiting, leaving just a few hundred dollars. For the next contract he paid US$1200 to the agent, who once again took 50 percent of a month's salary. On return, Nengah had a few thousand US dollars left after the loan repayment. He enrolled his wife in a master's degree program and then took a third contract. This time he paid US$800 to the agent and 50 percent of the first month's salary. Nengah said that after two more contracts he would finally buy a used car. His long-term goal to start a small agribusiness will take more than five further contracts.[16] Nengah's friend Komang worked on cruise ships for eleven years until he finally saved enough to open a small karaoke restaurant.[17] Ten years or more was the typical amount of time needed to save enough for a small business. When the second author interviewed Ketut W. in 2010 he had been working on cruise ships for ten years, up to twelve hours every day. There was nothing he liked about the work except exploring different ports on half-day shore leave. He had still not saved enough to create a business.[18] These examples show the cycle of incurred debt and how it binds workers into contract after contract.

Expectations and Reality

In seeking work on cruise ships new recruits expressed excitement at the possibility of seeing the world and having an adventure. At the time of our interview Agus had just gained a contract with an international cruise ship company. He was optimistic and enthusiastic, imagining a wonderful future. He relished the prospect of traveling 'around the world by sea.'[19] New training college graduate Wawan explained, 'I want to work on a cruise ship to have an overseas experience, to learn about everything in the world.'[20] Postings on the cruise ship worker blog site *Kerja di Kapal Pesiar* demonstrated the same kind of imaginings. For example, this comment from a female blogger: 'Hey hey, I want to travel around the world saving up money and getting rich working on a cruise ship.'[21]

Comparing the comments of new and aspiring cruise ship workers with responses from experienced cruise ship service workers demonstrates the gap between expectations and reality. *Kerja di Kapal Pesiar* in 2010 carried the following warning, 'For ordinary people [Indonesians], working on a cruise ship seems exciting, full of promise. But the reality is quite the opposite. Living on the ship for months is like living in hell.' Another male blogger on the same site advised his fellow countrymen to 'say NO to joining a cruise ship crew.'[22]

Once on board the ships several young new recruits reported feeling desperate, lonely and homesick. As Gede, an assistant waiter put it in an interview in 2012:

> First time on board I always get homesick. It's around one month or two months. I always want to go home because there's a lot of jobs and a lot of pressure and we are far from families, far from friends. That's why my workmates on the ship gave me advice. They said just be quiet, everybody gets feelings like that.[23]

Many of our respondents with basic service skills had aspirations of rapid promotion to positions where they could get tips or a higher salary. However, there were no guarantees that this would eventuate. For example, Carik worked as a cook's assistant in the kitchens. He hoped for a promotion but was finding the work difficult: 'I help the cook in the kitchen. First time on the ship I worked in the fish station, after that I worked in the hot appetizers and then the last, the sauces . . . it's hard work.'[24] He may not progress upward unless he puts in a special effort. Another interviewee, Ketut C., had risen from cook's assistant to Head Chef, but only by dedicating himself to improving his skills. From the beginning of his career he saved money to complete specialist cuisine courses during each break.[25] Agus was a laundry worker on a base salary but he too had higher ambitions: 'For the cruise ship, first I will be a laundry attendant. After three years or four years I should be an assistant and then a laundry master.'[26] There might well be a gap between expectation and outcome here too.

Working Conditions

A typical voyage lasts one week. As Gede, an assistant waiter on MSC Cruises, explained in an interview: 'For the first week they're sailing from Miami to the Caribbean, and then the next week they're sailing to the Bahamas or wherever.'[27] Each trip requires thorough cleaning tasks and replenishment of supplies on return to port, so the work never stops. A normal working week entails an early start each day and a 12-hour shift. There is usually a half-day off per week at sea, and a day off in port. Gede described his working day:

> I start at 7 o'clock. I go there and then prepare: set up the tables, arrange the cups, arrange the glasses, everything. Because the system is self-service. So when the guest asks for something I come over to them. May I help you? Something like that. I clear up the dirty glasses and dirty cups. At night, I start from 6 o'clock in the evening. I work in the dining room as an assistant waiter. The waiter takes orders from the guests, I pick up the food for them. It's 12 hours [a day].[28]

In other words, Gede serves at breakfast, lunch and dinner. He listed confidence and politeness as important job skills. Polite phrases in English and some European languages as well as proper body deportment are rehearsed daily in cruise training programs.

Other waiters also mentioned hard work and pressure. As Nyoman B. put it: '12 hours a day, everyday, 7 days a week with break, and if we have a midnight buffet, we can work 14, 16 hours a day. It is very hard. And then so we get too much pressure, not only from our supervisor or our bosses, but from our guests, because we often have very demanding guests, very demanding guests.'[29] Echoing the theme of hard labor in the interviews, one young woman wrote on the *Kerja di Kapal Pesiar* blog in 2010: 'My feet are falling off. I'm at sea again, once again on a cruise ship. It is all bad! Sigh.' Another wrote ruefully: 'So much work. We are required to work so fast. No time off except when the contract ends.'[30]

In addition to fulfilling the requirements of the job, some workers try and develop extra skills to impress even the most discerning guests, thereby increasing tips. Deta, a barman, had taken a bartender course to learn to juggle bottles of alcohol so that, as he put it, he could 'really serve the guests.'[31] As this implies, those who deal directly with tipping passengers develop different kinds of strategies to charm and entertain them, so as to increase their income.

Gede summed up the benefits and the downside of cruise ship work: 'The good thing is, we can get more money. We can enjoy it when we are on board, so sometimes we are overnight in Venice, so we go out. But the bad thing is we need to work hard . . . so maybe sleep for only 3 or 4 hours, and then we have to work again.'[32] In addition to the intense demands of the job, living conditions on board can be trying. Carik said that on the Happy cruise line, he shared a very small cabin (no windows) with three others.[33] Gede said that on the Carnivale ship he shared a 2-meter by 2-meter cabin with another crew member. He added, 'It's only fit for sleeping.'[34]

All of our interviewees complained about crew food. International cruise ship regulations require nutritious food to be separately provided to the crew. However, as mentioned previously, not all cruise lines are bound by labor regulations. Some cruise ship workers reported eating passenger leftovers. Gede explained: 'For the crew it's not such good food, because the cook is for the passengers. Food is served for passengers today, and if it's not finished, if there is still some remaining, they give it to the crew.'[35] Gede also described a crew member paying a cook out of his own wages to prepare food. Obviously this would cut into the monthly salary, like the forced laundry bills.[36]

Interactions with Passengers

As glimpsed above, cruise ship workers agreed that at times they had to deal with 'very demanding guests.'[37] Yet they had to be very careful not to displease them. In an interview conducted in 2012, Made D., a waiter, explained that: 'If you make one mistake, you have one guest complain, you can go home. You can get fired. Yeah, it's very bad.'[38] A blog comment indicates that under the polite mask of deference, service workers may resent the passengers they serve:

> I'm very tired here today. My section is full of Europeans: stupid, lazy and arrogant. I might add that their dinner menu is far away from the word enjoyable so they're emotional right now. 'Hey we made personal sacrifices to travel on this boat' and so on.[39]

Unpacking this account, we are reminded that the transnational company pursuit of profit through cost-cutting may not deliver to mass cruising passengers the luxury and indulgence they anticipate, nor, implicitly, the salary that service workers expect. One imagines the (presumed) assistant waiter here is not going to be highly tipped because his diners are not happy with their food. This example points to the triangular power relationship described earlier in the chapter.

Many stories were told about the provision of personalized services to passengers, but perhaps none are as telling as the following. Semi-retired cruise worker Made D. said that as a waiter on Carnival cruises in Europe, he was responsible for a section of the dining room. Over the course of two dinner sittings (7 pm and 8.15 pm), Made D. waited on thirty people at a time. He had to memorize each person's name, nationality, and food and beverage preferences on the first night he met them, so that the next evening he could greet each one by name and supply their preferences without asking. On each new cruise there were new sets of passenger names to remember, and as cruise trips are normally a week or two weeks, this meant a challenging feat of memory for him with such a high turnover. Made D. said that when he came back to Bali in the break he always made it a point not to remember anyone's name, or anything else either. On another occasion a European passenger in a wheelchair requested that Made D. carry him, and then the wheelchair, up a narrow stairway to the rear entrance of the dining room. There was a lift at the other end of the corridor, but the passenger was adamant. Made D. obliged and was tipped. But he added, his back was hurt [*sakit*].[40]

With his savings Made D. had started a small business, which was doing well. However, he had reluctantly emerged from retirement for yet another contract with Carnival Lines. A family member had incurred debts and he thought he could pay them off with just one more cruise. He was not looking forward to it. It was also informative that when we asked Gede and Carik if they would like their younger brothers to work on cruise ships they simultaneously exclaimed: 'No!!'[41] Gede said firmly: 'I would never recommend my younger brother work on a cruise ship. I do not want [him] to have experiences like me. He will get more education and become a bank teller.'[42]

Gede implies that those Balinese from poorer families who have done cruise ship service work experienced it as exploitive and demeaning. We are reminded of the conclusion reached by Dennett, Cameron, Jenkins and Bamford (2010) that the job of cruise ship service worker has a poor reputation among seafarers because of the master/servant identity that it operationalizes. While Gede's nominated occupation of bank teller may not, in the end, deliver to his younger brother a very different total salary over an entire working life—indeed it might be less—but bank work carries a far higher status, connoting regular working hours, a pleasant working environment, and a measure of autonomy in the workplace, as well as daily contact with family. Such conditions are a world away from the demanding personal service encounter so vividly depicted in Made D.'s account above.

Summing up the themes above in relation to our argument that the contemporary cruise ship service encounter is neocolonial in nature, we find that the reported conditions of work and service do seem to encode power relations between the dominating and the dominated; perhaps showing some colonial legacy in how both sides perceive the relationship between them. Recruits are hired on the basis of their race, socioeconomic status and level of education. They come from situations of privation. They perceive the privileged cruise tourists as a source of high income, but the price they pay to enter the cruise ship service industry and demands from home mean that capital builds only very slowly, so they are bound into repeated cycles of hard labor in trying conditions. Workers in direct contact with passengers serve them in every way and adjust their behavior to maximize tips and avoid the threat of a complaint. Passengers are promised and expect a luxury cruising experience flavored by colonial nostalgia in the level of personalized service provided and the type of workers who provide it.

CONCLUSION

So who gains and who loses in the triangular relationship of power between passengers, Southeast Asian service workers and transnational cruise line companies? We found Balinese cruise ship workers eventually did save up enough money to start up a small business at home, often one premised on hospitality or entertainment skills acquired through cruise ship service work. Yet they did not have good memories of the arduous ship-board work, and did not want their children or younger relatives to follow in their footsteps. Budget cruise passengers are promised, and presumably receive, a luxury colonial-era style experience of privilege and authority for a brief holiday period in their otherwise non-luxurious lives. Yet annoyingly over-attentive roomboy service and poor food may also be their experience. The international cruise corporations gain most, taking value and profit from passengers and Southeast Asian service staff alike. In advertising and in onboard ambience, they mine the rich seam of class and race that harks back both to the golden age of first-class steamship cruising, and to colonial relations between white masters and 'colored' servants.

Urry (1998: 76) argued that in tourist labor, every aspect of the worker's demeanor matters to the employer, including appearance, way of speaking and personality. This is particularly true for tourism enterprises that promise luxury and privilege, such as cruise lines. They recruit service staff from Southeast Asian countries not only to keep labor costs low, but because the recruits are expected carry out tasks of emotional labor in service to support the colonial-era cruising aura that builds profits. Temporarily privileged passengers exercise authority over deliberately recruited Balinese service staff, who are under pressure to behave like a personal servant because of low company wages and dependence on tips. The debt burden and obligations to family bind them into years of back-to-back contracts. The voices of the workers themselves tell of homesickness, hard work, long shifts, cramped quarters, leftover food, self-paid expenses and inability to save. They also talk about demanding passengers and the fear of displeasing them lest they be fired and sent home. We conclude there is a reflexive relationship of domination and exploitation between the reconstruction of colonial-style service in mass cruising, and the fact that cruise line profits are made by employing Southeast Asian workers on very low rates of pay, in hard working conditions.

NOTES

1. Carnival Australia website. www.carnivalaustralia.com. Accessed July 7, 2012.
2. Carnival Australia website. www.carnivalaustralia.com. Accessed July 7, 2012.
3. Ketut C., M, 46, Chef, interviewed by the authors, Lovina, July 14, 2012.
4. Betty, 32, cruise ship trainer, interviewed by the authors, Bangli, July 13, 2012.
5. For a discussion of status-reinforcing practices of Indonesian domestic service in the colonial and postcolonial periods, see Elmhirst 1999.
6. Ketut C. interview.
7. Betty interview.
8. Made D., 45, waiter, interviewed by the authors, Lovina, July 14, 2012.

9. Pam Nilan, personal communication with Passenger J., June 7, 2012.
10. The blosgspot is part of the *Kerja di Kapal Pesiar* [Cruise Ship Work] website. http://cerita-kerja-kapalpesiar.blogspot.com.au. The comments were collected from the blog site in June 2010. All translations to English are by the first and second authors.
11. Gede, 23, assistant waiter, interviewed by the authors, Singaraja, July 14, 2012.
12. Nyoman B., 48, waiter, interviewed by the authors, Lovina, July 14, 2012.
13. Agus, 21, laundry attendant, interviewed by the authors, Bangli, July 13, 2012.
14. Wawan, 20, barman, interviewed by the authors, Bangli, July 13, 2012.
15. *Kerja di Kapal Pesiar* blog site. A decision was made by the authors not to use the names of bloggers, since they did not give permission for their comments to be translated and used for research purposes.
16. Nengah, 37, cook, interviewed by the second author, Singaraja, April 2010.
17. Komang, 45, waiter, interviewed by the second author, Singaraja, April 2010.
18. Ketut W., 47, waiter, interviewed by the second author, Denpasar, April 2010.
19. Agus interview.
20. Wawan interview.
21. *Kerja di Kapal Pesiar* blog site.
22. *Kerja di Kapal Pesiar* blog site.
23. Gede interview.
24. Carik, 34, cook's assistant, interviewed by the authors, July 14, 2012.
25. Ketut C. interview.
26. Agus interview.
27. Gede interview.
28. Gede interview.
29. Nyoman B. interview.
30. *Kerja di Kapal Pesiar* blog site.
31. Deta, 21, barman, interviewed by the authors, Bangli, July 13, 2012.
32. Gede interview.
33. Carik interview.
34. Gede interview.
35. Gede interview.
36. Gede interview.
37. Nyoman B. interview.
38. Made D. interview.
39. *Kerja di Kapal Pesiar* blog site.
40. Made D. interview.
41. Gede and Carik, at the end of their interviews, when talking with the authors.
42. Gede interview.

REFERENCES

Adams, Richard, and Alfredo Cuecuecha. 2010. *The Economic Impact of International Remittances on Poverty and Household Consumption and Investment in Indonesia*. Washington: The World Bank, East Asia and Pacific Region.

Allen, Lisa. 2013. 'Full Steam Ahead for Booming Cruise Industry.' *The Australian*, April 30. www.theaustralian.com.au/business/economics/full-steam-ahead-for-booming-cruise-industry/story-e6frg926–122663186318. Accessed May 10, 2013.

Artini, Luh Putu, Pamela Nilan and Steven Threadgold. 2011. 'Young Indonesian Cruise Workers, Symbolic Violence and International Class Relations.' *Asian Social Science* 7(6): 3–14.

Balachandran, Gopalan. 2011. 'Making Coolies, (Un)making Workers: "Globalizing" Labour in the Late-19th and Early-20th Centuries.' *Journal of Historical Sociology* 24(3): 266–96.
Balachandran, Gopalan. 2012. *Globalising Labour? Indian Seafarers and World Shipping, 1870–1945*. New Delhi: Oxford University Press.
Brownell, Judi. 2008. 'Leading on Land and Sea: Competencies and Context.' *International Journal of Hospitality Management* 27(2): 137–50.
Carrigan, Anthony. 2007. 'Preening with Privilege, Bubbling with Bilge: Representations of Cruise Tourism.' *ISLE* 14(1): 143–59.
Chin, Christine. 2008. *Cruising in the Global Economy: Profits, Pleasure and Work at Sea*. Aldershot: Ashgate.
Coye, Ray, and Patrick J. Murphy. 2007. 'The Golden Age: Service Management on Transatlantic Ocean Liners.' *Journal of Management History* 13(2): 172–91.
Cruiseshipjobs. 2010. 'Life on Board & Tips from a Recruiter.' www.cruiselinesjobs.com. Accessed December 2, 2010.
Dennett, Adam, Derek Cameron, Andrew Kevin Jenkins and Colin Bamford. 2010. 'The Social Identity of Waiters Onboard UK Cruise Ships: "Quasiprofessionals" Forming Occupational Communities.' 19th CHME Annual Hospitality Research Conference, May 5–7, 2010, University of Surrey. http://eprints.hud.ac.uk/8526/. Accessed June 3, 2012.
Elmhirst, Rebecca. 1999. 'Learning the Ways of the Priyayi: Domestic Servants and the Mediation of Modernity in Jakarta, Indonesia.' In *Gender, Migration and Domestic Service*, edited by Janet Henshall Momsen, 242–62. London: Routledge.
Ewald, Janet. 2000. 'Crossers of the Sea: Slaves, Freedmen, and Other Migrants in the Northwestern Indian Ocean, c. 1750–1914.' *American Historical Review* 105(1): 69–91.
Ford, Michele. 2001. 'Indonesian Women as Export Commodity: Notes from Tanjung Pinang.' *Labour and Management in Development Journal* 2(5): 1–9.
Go, Julian. 2009. 'The "New" Sociology of Empire and Colonialism.' *Sociology Compass* 3(1): 1–14.
Goffman, Erving. 1961. *Asylums*. London: Penguin.
Jardine, David. 2008. 'Indonesia: High Graduate Unemployment.' *University World News*. www.universityworldnews.com. Accessed November 7, 2010.
Larsen, Svein, Einer Marnburg and Torvald Øgaard. 2012. 'Working Onboard: Job Perception, Organizational Commitment and Job Satisfaction in the Cruise Sector.' *Tourism Management* 33(3): 592–97.
Martinez, Julia, and Claire Lowrie. 2009. 'Colonial Constructions of Masculinity: Transforming Aboriginal Australian Men into "Houseboys."' *Gender and History* 21(2): 305–23.
Maxtone-Graham, John. 1972. *The Only Way to Cross*. New York: MacMillan.
Morgan, Patsy, and Lisa Power. 2011. 'Cruise Tourism and the Cruise Industry.' In *Research Themes for Tourism*, edited by Peter Robinson, Sine Heitmann and Peter Dieke, 276–88. Cambridge: CAB International.
MSC Cruises. 2010. 'Our Ships.' www.msccruises.com/gl_en/homepage.aspx. Accessed December 2, 2010.
Nash, Dennison. 1989. 'Tourism as a Form of Imperialism.' In *Hosts and Guests: The Anthropology of Tourism*, 2nd ed., edited by Valene Smith, 37–52. Philadelphia: University of Pennsylvania Press.
Peleggi, Maurizio. 2005. 'Consuming Colonial Nostalgia: The Monumentalism of Historic Hotels in Urban South-East Asia.' *Asia Pacific Viewpoint* 46(3): 255–65.
Rothman, Hal. 1998. *Devil's Bargains: Tourism in the Twentieth Century American West*. Lawrence: University of Kansas Press.

Ryan, Gery W., and H. Russell Bernard. 2000. 'Data Management and Analysis Methods.' In *Handbook of Qualitative Research*, 2nd ed., edited by Norman K. Denzin and Yvonna S. Lincoln, 769–802. Thousand Oaks: Sage Publications.
Said, Edward. 1979. *Orientalism*. New York: Vintage.
Sallaz, Jeffrey. 2010. 'Service Labor and Symbolic Power: On Putting Bourdieu to Work.' *Work and Occupations* 37(3): 295–319.
Seal, Kathy. 1998. 'Cruise Ships Draw New Crews.' *Hotel & Motel Management Magazine* 213(4): 9.
Sofield, Trevor. 2001. 'Globalisation, Tourism and Culture in Southeast Asia.' In *Interconnected Worlds: Tourism in Southeast Asia*, edited by Peggy Teo, T. C. Chang and K. C. Ho, 103–20. London: Pergamon.
Stoler, Ann Laura. 1989. 'Making Empire Respectable: The Politics of Race and Sexual Morality in 20th-Century Colonial Cultures.' *American Ethnologist* 16(4): 634–60.
Stoler, Ann Laura. 2002. *Carnal Knowledge and Imperial Power*. Berkeley: University of California Press.
Stoler, Ann Laura, and Frederick Cooper. 1997. 'Between Metropole and Colony: Rethinking a Research Agenda.' In *Tensions of Empire: Colonial Cultures in a Bourgeois World*, edited by Frederick Cooper and Ann Laura Stoler, 1–58. Berkeley: University of California Press.
Terry, William C. 2011. 'Geographic Limits to Global Labor Market Flexibility: The Human Resources Paradox of the Cruise Industry.' *Geoforum* 42(6): 660–70.
Testa, Mark R., and Stephen L. Mueller. 2009. 'Managing Service Quality: Demographic and Cultural Predictors of International Service Worker Job Satisfaction.' *Managing Service Quality* 19(2): 195–210.
Teye, Victor, and Denis Leclerc. 2003. 'The White Caucasian and Ethnic Minority Cruise Markets: Some Motivational Perspectives.' *Journal of Vacation Marketing* 9(3): 227–42.
Toh, Rex, Mary Rivers and Teresa Ling. 2005. 'Room Occupancies: Cruise Lines Out-Do the Hotels.' *Hospitality Management* 24(1): 121–35.
Urry, John. 1998. *The Tourist Gaze*. London: Sage.
Weaver, Adam. 2005. 'Spaces of Containment and Revenue Capture: "Super-sized" Cruise Ships as Mobile Tourism Enclaves.' *Tourism Geographies* 7(2): 165–84.
Winter, Tim. 2007. *Post-conflict Heritage, Postcolonial Tourism: Culture, Politics and Development at Angkor*. London: Routledge.
Wood, Robert E. 2000. 'Caribbean Cruise Tourism: Globalization at Sea.' *Annals of Tourism Research* 27(2): 345–70.
Wood, Robert E. 2002. 'Caribbean of the East? The Southeast Asian Cruise Industry.' *Asian Journal of Social Science* 30(2): 420–40.
Wu, Bin. 2005. *The World Cruise Industry: A Profile of the Global Labour Market*. Cardiff: Seafarers International Research Centre (SIRC).

18 A Contemporary Perspective
'Picking the Fruit from the Tree': From Colonial Legacy to Global Protections in Transnational Domestic Worker Activism

Jennifer N. Fish

> Today we celebrate a great victory for domestic workers. Until now we have been treated as 'invisible', not respected for the huge contribution we make in society and the economy and denied our rights as workers. It is an injustice that has lasted too long. After five years of organizing domestic workers through the world, the International Domestic Workers Network (IDWN) became the driving force behind this massive campaign to finally recognize domestic work as real work, worthy of the recognition and protection of all other sectors.
>
> —Myrtle Witbooi
> President, International Domestic Workers Network[1]

The United Nations' 2011 establishment of the first international set of standards for paid household labor signified a pivotal moment in the history of labor organizing and gender justice.[2] At the 100th annual conference of the International Labour Organization (ILO), 96 percent of the votes cast from Member State governments, employer bodies and national labor unions supported the establishment of Convention 189 on 'Decent Work for Domestic Workers'[3]—setting in place the first global standards for paid work performed in private households. For the first time, domestic workers around the world would be protected by an international instrument that assures the right to collective bargaining, minimum wage standards, protections against abuse, harassment and discrimination, regulated hours of work, occupational safety, social security and maternity benefits. By assuring that domestic workers enjoy 'conditions that are no less favorable than those applicable to workers generally,' Convention 189 provides the most comprehensive measure to date that standardizes, mainstreams and formalizes household labor.[4]

Beyond the material protections and concrete standards defined in Convention 189 and its accompanying recommendations, the adoption of this international framework shifts historical perspectives on domestic labor from a colonial institution to a vital sector of the existing global economy. Myrtle Witbooi, Chair of the International Domestic Workers Network (IDWN) proclaimed that with the adoption of this international instrument '[o]ur dream became a reality, and we are free—slaves no more, but *workers*.'[5] The inclusion of domestic work in the ILO's standards signifies a historic moment in terms of recognizing women's labor, the household as a viable employment context worthy of protections and a larger movement to formalize the informal economy. While these global standards mark tangible recognition of the formerly invisible work performed in the household, their impact will be measured through the Convention's implementation at the member state level. In order to guarantee domestic workers the protections set forth in Convention 189, states must ratify the instrument and assure that their legislation falls in line with the principles of its standards. Since it passed on June 16, 2011, eight countries have ratified this Convention by securing national laws and protections that specifically address domestic workers and align UN policies with state practices.[6] The realization of the first international Convention on domestic labor therefore allows us to examine the dialectic relationships among the household, state and international levels, as perceptions and practices surrounding this historic profession shift with the introduction of international and national policies, as well as the influence of global activism.

Beyond the victory of attaining the first standard-setting Convention for household labor, the ILO's attention to this sector also facilitated a transnational activist agenda that aligned domestic worker organizations worldwide. The first transnational network of domestic workers, the IDWN, defined a common objective to play a major role in the annual conferences of the ILO so that domestic workers themselves would have a voice in the setting of global standards surrounding their profession. The opportunity to gain international recognition for the value of household labor strengthened long-standing national movements and shared struggles to improve working conditions. Across differences in geographic location, race, ethnicity and language, the emergent global network of domestic workers established a unifying campaign tool that drew upon the history of colonial relations of servitude to problematize the lingering injustices in this occupation. The common historical dimensions of paid household labor actually became a strategic tool for the IDWN to assert a more powerful voice within the institutional dialogue on global standards. This active involvement of domestic worker leaders from around the world within the ILO negotiations of the first global standards allows us to examine how reference to historical inequality and oppression was used as a strategic campaign tool, thus bringing the historical to the contemporary. Furthermore, by analyzing the discursive and strategic practices enacted through the process of crafting the first international policy for this sector, we may reconsider how domestic workers have historically accessed and demonstrated agency at the individual and collective levels.

The presence and involvement of domestic workers themselves throughout the ILO standard-setting tripartite processes established a landmark model of collective activism *within* international institutions. Throughout the 2010 and 2011 International Labour Conferences (at which the ILO's broad policies are set), as well as the global organizing surrounding these UN meetings, the 'subjects' of neocolonial power relations demonstrated individual and collective agency within traditional institutional power structures. Marcelina Bautista, General Secretary of the regional Confederation of Domestic Workers in Latin America and the Caribbean (CONLACTRAHO), addressed the ILO working group on Decent Work for Domestic Workers in her 2010 opening statement by asserting, 'Informal workers and domestic workers are treated as slaves. They are treated as nothing. In the Convention, we must emphasize the value of domestic workers because they have skills and they should be rewarded.' Domestic worker organizations, advocacy groups, global unions and policy-research networks repeatedly pointed to contemporary conditions of servitude as one of the main arguments for demanding recognition and protection through the ILO. This active presence of domestic workers appealed to a moral obligation to assure protections that redress colonial conditions of servitude and slavery by legitimizing, regulating and professionalizing domestic labor. This use of historical symbolism played a substantive role in the eventual adoption of ILO Convention 189.

The transnational activism that emerged from this process demonstrates a distinct model of utilizing international institutions as a central means to promote changes in this historical and deeply embedded global institution of labor. Even though feminist politics of struggle have identified UN institutions as laden with heavily bureaucratic structures and male dominated, as the first transnational network of domestic worker organizations and unions, the IDWN engaged with this complex structure and approached participation within it as a new site for transformative politics. By strategically identifying the historically feminized, racialized and class-based nature of this labor institution across geographic contexts, domestic worker organizations and their allies effectively called upon governments' and United Nations' moral and social obligations to redress the severe inequalities that continue to define this occupation. The contributions domestic workers have made to social reproduction, as well as the global economy, continually served as a rationale for the 'long-overdue' need for international standards of protection for those historically considered outside of the purview of labor regulations. As the IDWN Platform of Demands states, 'Our work frees up others for their economic, educational and social activities. We are the "oil in the wheels" and, without us, many societies and economies would not function.'[7] Throughout the ILO campaigns and conference discussions, this global domestic labor movement positioned women workers as the voice of a larger demand to recognize the substantive changes in the world of work by formalizing rights for those historically excluded from international protections.

Such symbolic uses of slavery and colonial servitude became an effective discursive strategy for domestic workers in their demands for the first international set of standards through this UN institution. By examining the active reference to colonial conditions of domestic labor in contemporary ILO discussions of global standards, this chapter explores how the historical nature of this institution informs the present-day call for rights, equality and justice. I draw from direct observations of the IDWN's participation in the 2010 and 2011 ILO conferences, along with a series of interviews with leaders of the organization, ILO officials, government delegates and representatives in a range of human rights organizations, policy networks and global unions.[8]

POSTCOLONIAL ACTIVISM: BUILDING A GLOBAL DOMESTIC WORKERS MOVEMENT

As several chapters in this collection point out, the relationship between 'servants' and employers during colonial and postcolonial periods encapsulates and simultaneously reproduces macro power relations of occupation and dominance. In contemporary forms of household employment, race, class, gender and social status divides reflect the lingering colonial qualities of this social institution, where everyday power relations most often override legal and social protections, even in the countries with established policies for domestic workers. In the existing postcolonial context, domestic worker activists used the pervasive historical exclusion of paid household workers from legal protections as a foundational argument in their demand to recognize the contemporary value of this transnational institution. To redress this historic inequality embedded in the institution of household labor worldwide, they sought protections and standards through the ILO. At the same time, domestic workers demanded and realized symbolic recognition for the value of household labor.

Activism within the ILO drew upon the strength of existing national movements for domestic worker rights, while strategically utilizing this UN institution to set international standards that would encourage a greater accountability for states without labor and social protections for domestic workers. The struggle to realize rights through the formalization of domestic work has seen several victories at the national level, where states have implemented a series of legislative and social policy protections to recognize domestic work as 'real work' and to redress former colonial relations of power through efforts to adopt standards for this labor sector. For example, in its immediate post-apartheid process of rebuilding a new nation, South Africa instituted a series of legislative measures to provide basic conditions of employment, social security and maternity coverage for domestic workers (see Ally 2009 and this volume; Fish 2006). These efforts reflected national measures to assure democracy through formalizing protections for this embedded colonial labor institution. In New York and California, domestic workers' organizing to realize a state-level Bill of Rights based a national campaign on the call to 'end slavery' through assuring legal protections for domestic workers (Poo 2010; see also Glaser in this volume). The success of these victories provided the foundation for a transnational domestic workers' organization that facilitated a larger global movement to establish international standards by tearing away associations of domestic work from historical colonialism.

FOUNDING THE IDWN

In 2006, sixty leaders from the most established domestic worker organizations and unions throughout the world took part in the first and largest international meeting during the 'Respect and Rights: Protection for Domestic Workers!' conference in Amsterdam. Approximately sixty domestic worker member organizations, representing six world regions and delegations from twenty-one countries, met together under the facilitation of the International Restructuring Education Network Europe (IRENE) network.[9] The goals of this gathering focused on identifying a common agenda for the new organization, beginning a process of setting global standards, and linking domestic worker rights to wider gender and labor movements. As they looked forward, conference representatives expressed the specific goal of founding a longer-term organization in pursuit of the topics discussed at this initial gathering. For their first step, leaders elected a steering committee of domestic workers' organizational representatives in 2008, the same year the International Labour Organization announced that the 'Decent Work for Domestic Workers' agenda item would be included in the 2010 conference. The merger of the establishment of a transnational network of domestic workers and the inclusion of domestic labor within the ILO discussions solidified the IDWN's primary goal and its working agenda for the next three years: to establish a presence within the International Labour Conference (ILC) discussions in order to realize the first global policy on domestic work.

As the largest international institution focused on setting and maintaining global standards of labor, the ILO held promise for the establishment of not only an international Convention on domestic work, but also a moral recognition of the value and contributions domestic workers make to the livelihoods of households, as well national and global economies. Within the new emphasis on 'fair globalization' and 'decent work' under the leadership of Juan Somavia, the ILO embraced the possibility of formalizing the informal by setting standards for the domestic labor sector. This inclusion of domestic labor occurred nearly a half a century after the ILO last held preliminary discussions on the particularities of the household labor sector in 1948, followed by a second call for standard-setting action in 1965. The lack of action on setting standards for domestic work can be attributed to a number of factors including the struggle for gender justice within the

UN system, internal politics and prevailing assumptions that questioned the need for policies to regulate household labor. Eileen Boris explores how considerations of domestic worker protections exposed substantive tensions between feminists over 'women-only labor legislation,' as well as the competing agendas of the ILO and the UN's Commission on the Status of Women (CSW). Within this larger institutional political framework, consideration of domestic work had been postponed because the UN requested that the ILO take up equal pay (Boris 2013).

Discussions also debated the role of the ILO in regulating the private household, fueled by some employers' perceptions that domestic work would not become a source of international competition (Boris and Fish forthcoming). Over the past sixty years, however, as numerous studies have shown, global capitalism, globalization and its consequential neoliberal economic policies have created structures of transnational exchange relations that hinge upon a racialized, feminized, class-based international care chain in order to reproduce families and societies (for example, see Parreñas 2001; Chang 2001; Hondagneu-Sotelo 2001; Gamburd 2000; Anderson 2000; Chin 1998). This global commodification of women's service, care and 'love labor' became central to the contemporary demands for the protection through the ILO.

As the network of domestic workers pointed out in the 2010 and 2011 ILC discussions, this globalization of domestic labor stores the residue of colonial labor and servitude. According to the network's Platform of Demands:

> Our economic contribution is not taken seriously, often merely described as 'helping out.' We are called 'maids' or 'servants,' barely worthy of attention or to be ordered around or even abused. Added to this, many of us are from communities and regions that have been disadvantaged over history. Many are migrants, living isolated from our host community, and far away from our own families and even our own children.[10]

Many individual domestic worker testimonials echoed these sentiments and called on the ILO to redress the insufficient considerations of household labor in the organization's history and to honor their moral obligation to establish a standard-setting process for domestic work.

While drawing from historical references to strengthen the ILO's obligation to set standards, domestic workers simultaneously utilized the contemporary technological dimensions of globalization as new avenues for building solidarity through international networking and virtual transnational activism (see Naples and Desai 2002). They built a movement surrounding the ILO Convention process through the use of social media, cell phone messaging and Internet communication. As a result, over forty domestic workers from Africa, Asia, South America, North America and the Middle East came to the ILC discussion with a strengthened platform of connections, based upon the cohesion, network building and shared identity they had developed through use of technology. Their ability to forge, strengthen and maintain networks with global union leaders and gender and labor rights organizations through the means of technology also fostered a wider representation of the IDWN within the ILO negotiations, which ultimately fortified the worker position in building a case for the Convention.

This global network of domestic workers formed through an established history of ideological and resource support from two central organizations: Women in Informal Employment: Globalizing and Organizing (WIEGO) network and the International Union of Food, Agricultural, Hotel, Restaurant, Catering, Tobacco and Allied Workers' Association (IUF). As the first global union to provide a 'home base' for workers in the informal economy, the IUF shared its existing resources and provided vital conduits for workers to communicate across geographic regions. At the same time WIEGO's substantial international resource base and vital ties to policy-making processes supplied material and ideological support to 'organize the unorganized.' Both the WIEGO and IUF structures provided domestic workers with a larger umbrella network otherwise unavailable because of the lack of representation and inclusion of the sector within national trade unions. Within national labor structures, the unionization of domestic workers is often considered 'nonviable' because of the challenges in collecting dues from individual workers, the informal nature of the sector and its location in the private household.[11] The support available through these partner organizations allowed domestic workers to establish vital ties with both the labor movement and the global gender justice movement.

On a pragmatic level, the resource base and political ties held by both organizations provided avenues for the IDWN to access the formal structures of the ILC. The central tripartite framework of the ILO allows for sanctioned and equal participation among employers, governments and labor delegates. At the annual conference of the ILO, designated observer spaces are also available on a limited basis for nongovernment and civil society organizations. In order to assure the presence of domestic workers within the 2010 and 2011 conferences, WIEGO and the IUF held two of the thirty-five places available to observer civil society/nongovernmental organizational representatives. This allowed IDWN members to access the formal ILC proceedings, including the inner discussions on domestic worker protections, as a result of the observation status they acquired as members of the NGO delegations. Without ties to WIEGO and the IUF, domestic worker organizations' access to the ILC would have depended upon national unions' willingness to appoint a domestic worker to one of the few representative positions within national labor delegations.[12]

With their presence at the table of the negotiations, however, domestic workers gained a stronger position through their integration in the formal institution and the recognition they received from government delegates. By the second year meetings in 2011, domestic workers had gained more than twenty official seats as voting members of the labor delegations from their respective countries. Domestic workers' formal representation in national labor delegations in the ILC meetings paled in comparison to the collective presence and the subsequent persuasive capacities exerted by the larger network. By drawing upon a collective history of struggle against neocolonial power structures, the global network of domestic workers established a common voice and tangible presence that challenged the formal structural boundaries of the ILO. This collective activism clearly influenced the outcome of the final near unanimous vote in favor of Convention 189. By utilizing transnational networks to infuse the boundaries of formal power in global institutions, domestic workers' use of activist strategies—along with the allied social and political capital of larger global union and nongovernmental organizations—provided new models of realizing rights at the international level.

The victory of Convention 189 represented a critical step in moving representations of domestic labor away from the traditional associations with colonial servitude, to framing it as a professional, competitive resource, central to the growth of the global economy and the regeneration of societies. Louise McDonough, the government representative for Australia at the 2011 ILC, captured this victory in her closing remarks:

> We pay tribute to every one of the 100 million domestic workers across the world, including those who have attended these proceedings. We recognize domestic workers for the professional workers that they are, and we commend them for having the courage to stand up and seek this recognition as legitimate workers, often against all odds.

Many other government and labor delegates in favor of the Convention echoed this notion of the professionalism of household labor. By positioning household labor as a professional occupation, domestic workers purposefully reconstructed their work as a valuable commodity on an international market, where predominantly female migrant workers supplied a much greater demand for service labor across regional contexts. To this end, the IDWN made intentional efforts to define contemporary domestic labor in sharp contrast to its historical conditions of family servitude, embedded within larger systems of colonial power relations. This strategic reframing of the institution strengthened domestic workers' platform of demands for ILO rights and protections.

In fighting for international standards through the ILO, activists repeatedly referenced the residue of colonial labor as a central dimension of their strategy to highlight contemporary injustices and call for global rights and protections. By illustrating how exploitative forms of employment are anchored in the colonial period, domestic workers and ally organizations built a strong and persuasive case for the establishment of international labor standards and policies that would distinguish the contemporary global climate's emphasis on human rights, decent work and fair globalization. The transnational mobilization of domestic workers provided a means to establish a collective presence within the ILO, as an organized network of subaltern voices. Despite the serious structural barriers present in this institution, national and global networks afforded the opportunity to strengthen domestic workers' demands for rights and global protections. Throughout this process, severing the connection with historical colonialism served as a vital discursive strategy for the contemporary movement's identity, as well as an applied approach to demanding particular rights through the ILO.

ACTIVIST STRATEGIES WITHIN BUREAUCRACIES

The two-year negotiations for a Convention on domestic labor fostered a climate for this largest participation of 'actual workers' to utilize distinct strategies within the ILO standard-setting process. Members of the IDWN participated in every aspect of policy formation surrounding the Decent Work for Domestic Workers standard-setting process. Through the support of WIEGO, the IUF and the wider network of ally organizations, the IDWN organized speeches, assured that domestic worker testimonials got to the agenda for key moments in the public discussions, met with the Director General of the ILO to present domestic workers' Platform of Demands and fed into policy negotiations at each stage in the process of crafting Convention 189. While they followed the governing rules of the organization that limited spaces available for observers to speak within the social dialogue process, members of the IDWN infused a collective voice by working with formal delegates who attained authorization to speak on the floor. By providing concrete lived experiences, domestic workers bolstered the positions of aligned labor and government delegates as a way of strengthening government statements made in support of a global Convention. By working through the wide range of human rights NGOs, migrant education groups, women's rights advocates and faith-based parties present at the ILC meetings to support the Convention, domestic workers' perspectives fortified the labor position and to a certain extent tipped the balance of power within the tripartite dialogue.

Members of the IDWN asserted that a central component of the organization's strategy within the ILC meetings focused on assuring that decision-makers 'could not ignore domestic workers' when deciding upon a global Convention. Because of the historical marginalization of this sector, coupled with its underrepresentation in union and ILO labor delegations, the participation of workers in this standard-setting process became a vital means to demarcate the particular needs of domestic workers, while setting new processes in place that allowed 'actual workers' to access the ILO through larger ally NGO and policy organizations. In reflecting upon the infusion of domestic worker activists throughout this process, ILO government delegates and organizational leaders repeatedly assessed this standard-setting process as distinct from any other because it required the institution to confront the 'actual workers' who would be most impacted by the policies established within the tripartite negotiations. To this end, the face-to-face interaction with domestic workers infused a living historical dimension within the ILO process through the presence of both individual stories as well as the wider collective representation of longstanding social struggles and activist movements for labor, gender and economic justice. The domestic workers network capitalized on the strengthened potential to build their case by presenting vivid accounts of the impact of their historical circumstances of struggle to government and employer delegates who would decide on the scope and terms of any ILO standards. At the same time, national representatives of domestic worker organizations continually referenced histories of slavery and servitude as a moral call to reparations through the establishment of global policies that would validate and recognize centuries of contributions made by labor performed in private households throughout the world.

FACING DOMESTIC WORKERS

The physical and symbolic presence of domestic workers conveyed an obligation to consider the impact of historical exclusion from social protections, a common feature of this institution across national contexts since the colonial period. For their part, domestic workers used creative forms of agency to establish a persuasive voice within the governing UN labor organization. Their participation within the ILO created a space for the marginalized and silenced domestic worker to speak through policy formation processes within international institutions. The direct involvement of domestic worker representatives within the ILO decision-making processes merited frequent recognition by leaders of labor, employer and executive bodies. In his 2010 ILC opening remarks, Chair of the overarching ILO Workers Group, Sir Leroy Trotman, stated that because domestic workers were 'present in the room' the deliberations would assuredly reflect a certain 'reality on the ground.' Similarly, Secretary of the Workers Group, Raquel Gonzales, in her first statements on the public floor, conveyed, 'We are happy that there will be a representatives from the domestic workers to bring their experiences. I think it will be a very lively dynamic.' These sentiments conveyed a wider recognition that the ILO process would open in new ways to afford space for the voices of workers, yet positioned domestic workers outside of the mainstream and historical processes of social dialogue so central to the ILO's governing framework. From these earliest statements, the discourse within the formal Convention negotiations reflected a parallel embracing of 'actual workers' in the ILO and a frequent uncertainty about how to cope with their expanding presence and 'disruption' in the standard institutional process of tripartite social dialogue.

Domestic workers echoed their enthusiasm about the opportunity to take part in the ILO negotiations, publicly affirming the timing of this Convention as 'right, just and long overdue.' Throughout their interactions, IDWN members enacted norms central to the organization, such as the use of formal names and statements of gratitude for being given 'the floor' during public statements. Based on WIEGO/IUF trainings on the complexities of the ILO process, they demonstrated knowledge of the formal procedures and made sure to follow the rules of order in each meeting. Most central to these guiding procedures is adherence to formal standards about when to speak. While domestic workers embodied activist norms of bringing voice to negotiations and public participation processes, the formal ILC rules of governance restricted their rights to speak. According to ILC procedures, only one representative speaks on behalf of the entire labor delegation of the tripartite representation. In this sense, in order to comply with ILC regulations, activists were told to 'keep quiet' verbally during the formal sessions of social dialogue among labor, employers and government delegations. Yet, throughout the process, IDWN representatives made sure that all members of the tripartite bodies recognized their presence. They sang, danced, wore campaign clothing to align their cause and spoke through the formal delegations that would hear and echo their demands. In doing so, IDWN members embodied the face of domestic workers' historical conditions of struggle and contemporary realities in ways that made denying their rights at an international level seemingly immoral. At the same time, they refuted constructions of docile servitude by consistently interjecting creative use of voice, resistance strategies and a unified stance.

In the preparatory workshop meetings, IDWN leaders strategized on how to represent collectively the international face of domestic labor, in order to strengthen the case for global standards. The network established a shared goal of demonstrating that domestic workers face similar experiences of oppression within their daily work lives, regardless of the diversity of labor contexts across world regions. Representatives of the IDWN aligned their messages accordingly to present a unified message within the ILO venues that allowed observer civil society organizations to make public statements. In both years' conferences, at the opening statements, the workers group meetings, the gender meetings and the closing statements, domestic worker voices continually echoed three main points: 1) the historical nature of the institution of domestic worker as one rooted in severe inequalities stemming from the colonial period; 2) that the ILO had a moral obligation and emotional appeal to redress the continued exclusion of this sector from national laws; and 3) a demand to adopt a Convention that would be ratified by all Member States.

Through these aligned strategies, domestic worker representatives conveyed a particular and consistent emotional appeal by referring to the historic *exclusion* of domestic workers from labor protections across contexts. As Ernestina Ochoa, IDWN Vice Chair from Peru, expressed:

> I am a domestic worker. I *work*. Up to this day, I have worked. I am here because I want to be re-vindicated of all of the mistreatment of our ancestors. We are asking you governments. We do not want nice speeches; we want *actions*. We want you to hear us. We need your support. . . . We don't want you to say this is what we have done for women. We want you to open the doors, sit down with us and listen to our voices.
>
> (Fish, Crockett and Ormiston 2012)

This appeal to decision-makers to consider the years that domestic workers had awaited protections formed a consistent message and an emotional appeal throughout the negotiations. Speaking on behalf of the IDWN in her opening public statement at the 2010 ILC, Myrtle Witbooi professed:

> We want to say to you the ILO delegates: We have been waiting for 65 *years* for this to happen and we cannot lose this opportunity to appeal to you to please secure the minimum labor standards for the millions of domestic workers that are still unprotected in their respective countries, in order to create an international instrument that will not only protect domestic workers, but will also give us back our dignity and allow us to walk tall as workers, just as any other worker in the world![13]

These individual narratives, stories of lifelong struggle and highly personalized appeals provided core content in each public statement on behalf of the IDWN. By drawing upon the long-standing exclusion of domestic workers and the impact of the lack of protections in the household labor context, leaders of the IDWN enacted an emotional appeal within the traditionally masculine space of the ILO. This particular strategy held a very prominent role within the deliberations on domestic work throughout the two years of ILC discussions.

Members of the IDWN also enacted a collective voice beyond the limitations of the prescribed formal channels for (often pre-approved) public statements within the ILC rules. Drawing upon a wider shared identity in the labor movement, IDWN members often broke into song immediately after formal meetings were called to conclusion: 'My mother was a kitchen girl, my father was a garden boy, that's why I'm a unionist, I'm a unionist, I'm a unionist.' Such practices of song, dance and physical gestures of solidarity ensured that employers and governments could not ignore the presence of domestic workers, and the singing, in particular, fortified the strength of the network by drawing upon a wider collective history of social struggle and union activism. As the chamber filled with the echoes of 'Solidarity Forever' and 'La Lucha Continua,' historical movements to realize rights became active forces within this transnational institution (Fish, Crockett and Ormiston 2012).

Throughout the ILO proceedings, the performance of song accompanied visual rhetorical statements of solidarity through shared dress, T-shirt messages, persuasive buttons, and campaign colors. In many instances, domestic workers and allies used their physical bodies to convey antislavery messages through dress and politicized accessories such as buttons, hats and mini campaign banners. One organization chose a message, 'Slaves no more' as a bold statement worn throughout both years of the ILO meetings. To position the case for equal rights, other domestic worker organizations used the phrase 'domestic work is work!' across their clothing, campaign material and verbal appeals. In this sense, the physical bodies of domestic workers became a rhetorical tool to strengthen the position of labor within formal physical spaces hosting the ILC negotiations. Furthermore, such collective actions and statements provided modes for IDWN members to express voice and agency, even when formal ILO procedures formally restricted their opportunities to speak from the floor. To this end, activist strategies worked at the borders of this rule-driven UN institution to overcome the historical silencing and exclusion of domestic workers. Through collective voice, strategic inputs in the public statements, repeated emotional appeals, and use of visual rhetoric, the overwhelming presence of domestic worker organizations shifted the tripartite power relations in ways that carved a wider space for the civil society/observer designation within the tripartite process. In the case of this first negotiation of domestic workers' standards, this mobilized presence of 'actual workers' ultimately influenced the final vote in favor of Convention 189.

COLONIAL HISTORIES IN CONTEMPORARY DEMANDS FOR RIGHTS

Throughout the two years of policy deliberations within the ILO, the historical marginalization of domestic workers formed a persuasive position as a moral imperative for recognition and rights. In the formal ILC discourse, statements by IDWN members, labor representatives and UN officials continually integrated the defining colonial conditions of service labor as a rationale for the need to establish ILO protections. By connecting the 2010–2011 campaign to histories of struggle and social exclusions, the IDWN established a moral ground for recognizing 'domestic work as decent work' that is 'eligible for the same protections as all other workers.' This call to action echoed an expectation that the ILO's policies could redress historic inequalities through the scale of international recognition afforded in UN agencies. At the same time, the inclusion of domestic work within the ILO represented a substantial step toward formalizing the informal, while integrating global standards within the private employment sphere.

A Contemporary Perspective 341

In the larger ILO discourse on the meaning of Convention 189, discussions repeatedly referenced the 'historic significance' of gaining protections for domestic workers. Juan Somavia, Director General of the ILO, described his emotional experience in reflecting upon the historic and symbolic meaning of Convention 189, at the 2011 ILC. 'It is not too often that you have the opportunity of feeling that you are part of history being made.' Bob Shepard, US government representative to the ILO, echoed the significance of the historic moment in his opening 2011 address: 'I would hope that two weeks from now we can depart for home knowing that we have taken part in a great and historic breakthrough, a moment when the three social partners, working together, determined that the time had come to afford domestic workers effective protections no less favorable than those provided for workers generally.' The IDWN also referred to the historic significance of Convention 189 throughout their public statements. Indeed, the passing of Convention 189 represented the substantial shift in the perception of household labor from a symbol of colonized servitude to a significant sector of the global economy.

Throughout the ILO negotiations, as well as the activism that surrounded the meetings to build a global movement, the use of the term 'slavery' emerged often to illustrate some of the most severe forms of exploitation that continue to exist in neocolonial private household labor relations. In the IDWN's overarching demand to count domestic work as 'real work,' 'just like any other profession,' constructions of slavery became an effective rhetorical, emotional and visual tool to promote the core changes necessary to attain fair labor standards and recognition of 'domestic work as decent work' within the ILO. Hong Kong activist and Regional Coordinator of the Asian Domestic Workers Network Ip Pui Yu explained:

> People don't really feel domestic workers are workers. So the use of this term, 'slavery,' together with 'servant' is on the other side of 'workers.' I feel that we use the term 'modern slavery' to arouse people's concern about something that should be something in the past and should not be acceptable. It also reminds people that slavery still exists.[14]

Other activists confirmed that this discursive use of slavery became a powerful tool to arouse emotion and gain support in national and global campaigns. Yet members of the IDWN also intentionally promoted the positive contributions of domestic workers as central to the global economy, empowered by an extensive skill set and emboldened with individual and collective agency through the growing movement of domestic workers worldwide. Thus Ip Pui Yu elaborated, that domestic workers exercised caution with this use of imagery surrounding slavery, in order to avoid the representation of domestic workers as poor, victimized and 'vulnerable' women. The IDWN sought alternatively to promote domestic worker activists as women whose strength emerged throughout a history of slavery and servitude. Rather than such historical conditions defining them, the IDWN strategically wove in concepts of slavery to demonstrate the sharp contrast to the recognition they sought through ILO protections, recognition and global rights for 'decent work.' This strategic use of historical imagery proved an effective and persuasive dimension of domestic workers' rhetorical and emotional influence within the formal ILO negotiations, as well as the surrounding public relations campaigns during the 2010–2011 meetings.

As a collective representation, members of the IDWN continually illustrated how their public presence within the ILO standard-setting arena distinctly contrasted the pronounced isolation of labor in the private household across historical periods. By organizing, forming unions and resisting the lingering structures of oppression, domestic workers presented a face of global activism, agency and mobilization within the ILO proceedings. This presentation of domestic workers' collective strength provides a distinct alternative from historical imagery surrounding servitude, oppression and victimhood. In contrast to historical working conditions of slavery, the overarching platform of demands put forth by the IDWN framed domestic labor as a professional institution, worthy of the same rights as other sectors and the protections of global and national standards. The strength of this intentional construction of the IDWN as an organized front within the ILO expanded beyond the campaigns surrounding Convention 189 to enliven a transnational activist movement that has effectively linked domestic workers rights with wider sustained labor, human rights, migrant and gender justice campaigns.

CONTEMPORARY REPRESENTATION OF DOMESTIC WORKERS IN GLOBAL CAMPAIGNS

The ILO's inclusion of the Decent Work for Domestic Workers agenda item formed the foundation for a global activist movement surrounding the moral imperative to establish rights for this sector through an international institution. In many respects, the opportunity to align domestic worker organizations, unions and allied networks through the ILO process may be equally, if not more important than the actual achievement of a global policy on domestic labor. The space provided to mobilize national domestic worker organizations around Convention 189 has since expanded to strengthen a global movement that has drawn together labor, gender, migrant and human rights organizations. Furthermore, from the victory of establishing the world's first international standard on domestic work, we see a series of transnational organizations taking up the cause of domestic labor as a result of the publicity surrounding the ILO. In efforts to promote the implementation of a global policy 'with teeth,' global unions, international NGOs and national campaigns have focused on the promotion of state ratification since the passing of Convention 189. These campaigns illustrate the expansion of collective activism from the ILO policy-forming process to the priorities of international organizations, as well as national and local movements. Through Convention 189, the interconnected levels of local, national and transnational organizing have strengthened with the call for specific actions stemming from the ILO. Yet the transference of the 'domestic worker cause' across these levels reveals how the use of imagery and rhetoric engages with historical notions of servitude and essentialized constructions of vulnerability as a recurring theme in the call for ratification and domestic workers' rights.

The use of a familiar face of women's oppression serves as an affective technique to garner support for domestic worker rights throughout the ILO discussions on domestic labor. While Convention 189 represents a clear victory, the emotional rhetorical appeal that emerged in this standard-setting process drew upon notions of victimhood, constructions of modern slavery, and the oppression of women of color from the Global South. In many cases, throughout the ILC proceedings, government delegates, employers and even representatives of labor referred to domestic workers as the 'most vulnerable' sector of the working population.[15] By drawing from representations of domestic workers as 'poor, migrant women,' advocates for the Convention employed essentialized notions of women and girls as persuasive tools in calling for standards of protection. At times, domestic workers themselves played into this strategy in efforts to bring an emotional appeal to the formal tripartite conversations. Shirley Pryce, President of the Jamaican Domestic Workers Union, spoke to the media about her experiences of 'living in a dog house' as a way to demonstrate the severe exploitation potential in household labor, as well as the capacity to overcome such obstacles through the model of individual and collective activism she modeled. Such visual and textual images of domestic labor reify women's vulnerability, thereby reproducing historical servitude constructions in contemporary demands for rights.

This imagery stands in sharp contradistinction to the models of domestic worker leadership seen throughout the ILO process. For example, Hester Stephens, President of the South African Domestic Service and Allied Workers Union, began her union activism in a garage under the apartheid system of governance. After over thirty years of union activism, she spoke from the floor of the ILO as a leader of the global network of domestic workers. And Shirley Pryce moved from an extremely exploitative job to work for the Prime Minister of Jamaica and eventually form the nation's first domestic worker union in 2013. Like Hester and Shirley, the women present at the ILO represented models of activism that contradicted the repeated associations to vulnerability throughout the national and international campaigns that emerged from Convention 189.

In assessing the ILO process, we must also ask feminist political questions about how allied organizations with increased access to social, political and economic capital represent the voices of domestic workers throughout these international campaigns. In many respects, the ILO process reified notions of domestic workers' vulnerability and dependency. The ILO's attention to domestic worker rights resulted in many organizations taking up this cause also, and in the process crafting imagery for an international campaign based upon familiar historical images of poor marginal women in need of protection. Furthermore, such organizations used their own power to speak for domestic workers in ways that would seem to invoke the postcolonial feminist challenges to questions of standpoint and representation. This designing of a 'typical domestic worker' within the global movement surrounding Convention 189 reinforces power-laden West–Other binary imagery reminiscent of Chandra Mohanty's (1991) postcolonial feminist analysis of the 'typical third world woman.' Although these dynamics of representation have allowed domestic worker organizations to gain access to and influence within the larger ILO system, we must be cautious about how these processes reinforce a hierarchy within the social justice, women's rights and labor movements. In many cases, such advocacy campaigns build upon the same dimensions of colonial servitude that arose as the central inequalities within the domestic work labor relationship: race/class gender divides, social status differentials and migration.

CONCLUSION

The historical context of domestic labor became a powerful lobbying tool to evoke emotion and shared empathy for the contemporary demands for global protections for domestic workers. Colonial foundations of migration, race, class and gender divides and the reproduction of social inequalities formed pivotal reference points in the collective activism of the IDWN. In many cases, domestic workers used this history of inequality to build powerful demands for protections through the ILO. As this chapter highlights, rather than assuming passive positions as victims of structural oppression, domestic workers navigated the ILO process, while working to transcend it as agents of individual and collective activism. In this sense, they continually pushed the boundaries of this traditional institution by utilizing the strength of the histories of union activist practices to advocate for the attainment of global policies that recognized this historically marginalized sector of labor. Strategically, the conditions of labor established in the colonial period served as lobbying tools to evoke both an emotional and moral response to the need to establish protections. As Hester Stephens (a founding leader of the domestic workers' initial international meetings in Amsterdam in 2006) stated in her reaction to the Convention 189 victory, 'This conference, it is such a history, it will be a history worldwide, that we picked the fruit from the tree that we planted over the years.'[16]

Along with the activism of the IDWN, a collection of NGOs, research policy institutes and global unions took active roles to realize Convention

189. While the resource bases of larger organizations have pushed an agenda and strengthened a larger domestic worker movement, real change to redress historical circumstances must require sustained commitment beyond the 'flavor of the day' approach to this particular cause. Similarly, ratification and implantation efforts will provide the next measure of the effectiveness of this movement in terms of implementing Convention 189. Only with ratification and enforcement will the activists within the IDWN be assured that national and global policies on domestic labor 'have teeth.' As Michelle Bachelet, then Director General of UN Women, pronounced in the closing session of the Decent Work for Domestic Workers discussions in 2011, a global Convention's 'flip side is resilience, determination.' Convention 189 symbolized a 'lifeline to families at home and abroad' through its promises of recognition and tangible protections. Yet beyond the global standards that define domestic work, Bachelet declared that an international Convention 'provides parameters within which to act as committed governments.' It is critical that national governments take up the responsibility to act on this global agenda, and indeed, in the words of the Australian government representative assessed in both the opening and closing statements of the 2011 ILC, 'There is no doubt that the measure of our success is in terms of the impact the Convention will have in the real world.' Without such determination to make changes at the local level, the legacies of past oppression will continue to burden the present. Yet, domestic worker organizing continues to center around the notion of picking the 'fruits from the tree' through assuring that Convention 189's universality is accessible across localities and meaningful in terms of promoting rights in national legislative frameworks. As the IDWN banner read when it dropped from the General Assembly Hall of the United Nations on June 16, 2011:

C189 CONGRATULATIONS! NOW THE DOMESTIC WORK FOR GOVERNMENTS. RATIFY. IMPLEMENT.

NOTES

1. Delivered after the passing of Convention 189 at the 2011 ILC.
2. An international Convention sets global standards of practice through the UN system. In this case, Convention 189 refers to the International Labour Organization's two-year discussion of the proposed set of standards on 'Decent Work for Domestic Workers.' Possible international Conventions and accompanying recommendations are discussed during a two-year process within the annual International Labour Conference (ILC) meetings, comprised of delegates from 183 governments, employers and labor representatives. For fuller discussions of the legal dimensions of Convention 189, see Blackett 2011.
3. The Convention on Domestic Workers won by a vote of 396 to 16, with 63 abstentions. The accompanying set of Recommendations also earned overwhelming support with a vote of 434 to 8, with 42 abstentions. As stated

in the organizational press release on June 16, 2011, 'The ILO is the only tripartite organization of the UN, and each of its 183 Member States is represented by two government delegates, and one employer and one worker delegate, with an independent vote.' ILO Website, 'Press Release: 100th ILO annual Conference decides to bring an estimated 53 to 100 million domestic workers worldwide under the realm of labour standards,' www.ilo.org/ilc/ILCSessions/100thSession/media-centre/press-releases/WCMS_157891/lang—en/index.htm. Accessed July 6, 2013.
4. Article 14 of Convention 189. A full reference to the Domestic Workers Convention is available through the ILO website at www.ilo.org/dyn/normlex/en/f?p=1000:12100:0::NO::P12100_ILO_CODE:C189. Accessed July 6, 2013.
5. International Domestic Workers Network. 'A Message from Myrtle Witbooi, IDWN Chair,' *IDWN News*, October 2011. www.idwn.info/sites/default/files/publications/IDWN_Newsletter_2011.pdf. Accessed July 6, 2013.
6. As of June 2013, the order of ratification of Convention 189 is as follows: Uruguay, Philippines, Mauritius, Nicaragua, Paraguay, Bolivia, Italy and South Africa.
7. International Domestic Workers Network. 'Platform of Demands.' www.idwn.info/publication/platform-demands. Accessed June 20, 1913.
8. I draw from direct observational data collected from the 2010 and 2011 ILC meetings in Geneva, Switzerland, interviews with members of the International Domestic Workers Network (IDWN), and key informants within the ILO. Unless otherwise attributed, all quotations come from this data. In particular, I thank members of the IDWN, the Women in Informal Employment: Globalizing and Organizing (WIEGO) network, and the International Union of Food Workers (IUF) and the International Trade Union Confederation for affording my observational access to the ILC meetings. In addition, I am grateful for my colleagues in the South African Domestic Service and Allied Workers Union (SADSAWU), the National Domestic Workers Alliance (NDWA) in the United States, the Social Law Project (SLP) at the University of the Western Cape in South Africa, the Center for the Study of Work, Labor and Democracy at the University of California, Santa Barbara, and the Workers Bureau of the International Labour Organization for their continued support and collaborative contributions to this research project. In particular, I thank Mary Romero, Eileen Boris, Jennifer Rothchild, Mona Danner and Lauren Eastwood for their repeated contributions to my overall analysis of domestic labor within the ILO.
9. For more information on the International Restructuring Education Network Europe and its work with the informal economy, see IRENE, www.irene-network.nl/index.html. Accessed July 6, 2013.
10. International Domestic Workers Network. 'Platform of Demands.' www.idwn.info/publication/platform-demands. Accessed June 20, 2013.
11. In South Africa, the national COSATU union leaders repeatedly referred to domestic work as a 'nonviable' union (Fish 2006). Within the ILC deliberations, this same sentiment surfaced surrounding the challenges to regulating international standards within national contexts. International Labour Conference Fieldnotes, 2010, 2011.
12. Most global unions and international organizations are considered NGOs in the ILO structure. Therefore, their access to the ILC discussions is limited to observer status. Observer delegates may take part in conversations among the worker groups on particular subcommittees. All formal tripartite discussions and voting procedures, however, limit verbal participation to government

representatives from the 183 member states and one representative from both the employer and worker groups.
13. Delivered at the Plenary Panel of the Decent Work for Domestic Workers committee, International Labour Conference, June 16, 2010.
14. Personal communication with author, July 2013.
15. Shireen Ally discusses the state's use of vulnerability in South Africa as a guiding paradigm that reinforced structures of power in the post-apartheid rights-centered democracy. See Ally 2009, also her chapter in this volume.
16. Interview with author, immediately after the vote on Convention 189, June 16, 2011.

REFERENCES

Ally, Shireen. 2009. *From Servants to Workers: South African Domestic Workers and the Democratic State*. Ithaca: Cornell University Press.
Anderson, Bridget. 2000. *Doing the Dirty Work? The Global Politics of Domestic Labor*. London: Zed Books.
Blackett, Adelle, ed. 2011. *Special Issue of the Canadian Journal of Women and the Law: Regulating Decent Work for Domestic Workers* 23(1).
Boris, Eileen. 2013. 'Slaves No More: Making Global Labor Standards for Domestic Workers.' Unpublished presentation at the Global Workers' Rights: Patterns of Exclusion, Possibilities for Change. A Symposium at The Pennsylvania State University, Center for Global Workers' Rights, March 20–23.
Boris, Eileen, and Jennifer N. Fish. Forthcoming. '"Slaves No More": Making Global Labor Standards for Domestic Workers.' *Feminist Studies*.
Chang, Grace. 2001. *Disposable Domestics. Immigrant Women in the Global Economy*. Cambridge: Cambridge University Press.
Chin, Christine. 1998. *In Service and Servitude. Foreign Female Domestic Workers and the Malaysian 'Modernity' Project*. New York: Columbia University Press.
Fish, Jennifer N. 2006. *Domestic Democracy: At Home in South Africa*. New York: Routledge.
Fish, Jennifer N., Rachel Crockett and Robin Ormiston, directors. 2012. *C189: Conventional Wisdom*. DVD. Norfolk: Sisi Sojourner Productions.
Gamburd, Michele Ruth. 2000. *The Kitchen Spoon's Handle. Transnationalism and Sri Lanka's Migrant Housemaids*. Ithaca: Cornell University Press.
Hondagneu-Sotelo, Pierrette. 2001. *Doméstica: Immigrant Workers Cleaning and Caring in the Shadows of Affluence*. Berkeley: University of California Press.
Mohanty, Chandra Talpade. 1991. 'Cartographies of Struggle: Third World Women and the Politics of Feminism.' In *Third World Women and the Politics of Feminism*, edited by Chandra T. Mohanty, Ann Russo and Lourdes Torres, 2–47. Bloomington: Indiana University Press.
Naples, Nancy, and Manisha Desai. 2002. *Women's Activism and Globalization: Linking Local Struggles and Transnational Politics*. New York: Routledge.
Parreñas, Rhacel Salazar. 2001. *Servants of Globalization: Women, Migration and Domestic Work*. Stanford: Stanford University Press.
Poo, Ai-Jen, for Domestic Workers United. 2010. 'Organizing with Love: Lessons from the New York Domestic Workers Bill of Rights Campaign.' Center for Education of Women, University of Michigan. www.cew.umich.edu/sites/default/files/Organizingwithlove—FullReport-Cover.pdf. Accessed July 9, 2013.

Conclusion
Agency, Representation, and Subalternity: Some Concluding Thoughts

Victoria K. Haskins and Claire Lowrie

It was the intention of this collective research project to initiate and develop a truly meaningful conversation between scholars from a whole range of backgrounds, on the connections between colonization and domestic service, or domestic work, in both historical and contemporary contexts. As these essays demonstrate, there is indeed fertile ground for cross-disciplinary and interdisciplinary research and study, where diverse sources, methodologies, and approaches can be usefully brought to bear to generate new insights within a larger discussion. As histories of domestic service in colonial contexts inform and shape the present-day position of domestic workers at local and global levels, so the present-day situation, whether postcolonial or neocolonial, helps us to make sense of these past histories, and to see their significance more clearly. Large-scale overviews, small-scale case studies, comparative and transnational explorations, all and any of these can be deployed to better understand—and potentially to change—our world. We make no revolutionary claims for our collection, but we do see it as opening a door for further, engaged studies of colonization and domestic work, and for a continued interdisciplinary discussion that will deepen awareness and understanding of the position of domestic workers today.

Many of the chapters in this book intersect and overlap with each other, both within the thematic sections and across them, and as such are open to multiple comparative readings. But if we were to identify and draw out one theme in particular that has emerged across our discussions and conversations in the process of bringing this collection together, it would be the idea of representation and agency: of domestic workers as colonized people, and colonized people as domestic workers, struggling to control the conditions in which they live by negotiating the ways in which they are represented, and the ways in which they can represent themselves. The theme of representation underpins all the thematic essays to varying degrees, as well as the two 'global' perspectives offered by B. W. Higman and Jennifer N. Fish. We see it in Shireen Ally's meditation on the anxieties produced by conflicting representations of domestic workers in postcolonial South Africa, Caribbean domestic workers asserting their mothering skills in the chapters by Michele Johnson and Alana Glaser, Michael Aird's photo-essay on

Aboriginal Australian domestic workers' photographs, and Pamela Nilan, Lu Puh Artini, and Steven Threadgold's study of Balinese cruise workers, to single out just a few. Inextricably linked to this struggle over representation is the focus within many of the chapters on recuperating the voices of domestic workers themselves. They speak to us relatively directly in those studies based on interviews, but also, we 'hear' fragments of their distant voices indirectly through some of the more historical chapters.

Historically, the colonized domestic worker was arguably the most subaltern of the subalterns. The condition of subalternity, a concept developed in the work of Antonio Gramsci, Ranajit Guha, Gayatri Chakravorty Spivak, and others (see Green 2010), is defined by exclusion from the structures of hegemonic power, and of a socialized difference that intensely constrains any kind of social mobility and the ability to 'speak' back to those in positions of power. Pressed into the closest relationship with the colonizer, colonized domestic servants, like other servants, were and are reduced to silence simply by the nature of their occupation. Yet the wider conditions of colonialism further compelled their subjection and silence, their silencing compounded by the employers' urge to represent domestic workers in such a way as 'to establish hegemony over the subaltern population,' as Swapna Banerjee has asserted (2004: 162). In postcolonial and neocolonial contexts today, both the domestic workers who serve the rising middle classes within formerly colonized countries (see for example Ray 2000), and the far-flung global migrant domestic workers working in conditions of racialized difference, isolation and exclusion from the political and social institutions of their host countries can be considered 'the truly subaltern' (Parreñas 2001: 78). We see in the various studies brought together in this collection the continuity of representations that work to reinforce the employers' power, and the power of the wider state authorities, over colonized domestic workers' lives, whether that be as servile and inferior people, vulnerable and feminized (Ally; Lowrie; Nilan, Artini, and Threadgold), sexually promiscuous (Platt), or basically incompetent and in need of training and education in 'civilized' behavior, to be made 'useful' (McCabe; Robinson; McCallum; Macdonald). They continue to be represented in ways which enable their control and subjection, and they continue to struggle to 'speak back' in order to resist such subjection, utilizing what opportunities there are to do so—as Jennifer N. Fish's closing chapter makes brilliantly clear. That this collection allows us to hear some of these voices from both the past and the present is, we believe, one of the strengths of this collection.

All of these chapters, in different ways, allow us to consider the condition of colonized domestic workers. The extent and nature of such agency that domestic workers may have been and are able to exercise over their own lives will inevitably remain a bone of contention while conditions of severe inequality and oppression persist (see Aguilar 2000). Nevertheless, any movement towards a decolonizing agenda requires recognizing not only the structures of oppression that confined and continue to confine domestic workers, but also recognizing domestic workers past and present as human beings with the capacity to shape their own lives and the ability to make whatever efforts possible, on their own terms as far as possible, to realize that potential. It is clear from the essays here, that representation and self-representation—and particularly representations of domestic workers' agency and power—are critical to any project that aims at empowering domestic workers. Read together and in conversation with each other, these diverse historical and contemporary perspectives on the relationship between colonization and domestic service may hopefully go some way towards decolonizing domestic service, both historically and in the contemporary world we live in.

REFERENCES

Aguilar, Delia D. 2000. 'Questionable Claims: Colonialism *Redux*, Feminist Style.' *Race & Class* 41(1): 1–12.

Banerjee, Swapna M. 2004. *Men, Women, and Domestics: Articulating Middle-Class Identity in Colonial Bengal*. Oxford: Oxford University Press.

Green, Marcus. 2010. 'Gramsci Cannot Speak: Presentations and Interpretations of Gransci's Concept of the Subaltern.' *Rethinking Marxism: A Journal of Economics, Culture & Society* 14(3): 1–24.

Parreñas, Rhacel Salazar. 2001. *Servants of Globalization: Women, Migration and Domestic Work*. Stanford: Stanford University Press.

Ray, Raka. 2000. 'Masculinity, Femininity, and Servitude: Domestic Workers in Calcutta in the Late Twentieth Century.' *Feminist Studies* 26(3): 691–718.

Contributors

Michael Aird has worked in the area of Aboriginal cultural heritage in Australia since 1985. He has curated over 20 exhibitions, published several academic articles and has been involved in numerous research projects. In 1996 he established Keeaira Press, an independent publishing house, and has produced over 25 books.

Shireen Ally teaches in the Department of Sociology at the University of the Witwatersrand in Johannesburg, South Africa. She is the author of *From Servants to Workers: South African Domestic Workers and the Democratic State* (Cornell University Press 2009).

Luh Putu Artini is a Senior Lecturer in English language education at *Universitas Pendidikan Ganesha* in Singaraja, Bali, Indonesia. She holds a PhD in Education from the University of Newcastle, Australia. Artini has published widely (in Indonesian) on the learning contexts of English in high schools, training colleges and universities in Bali.

Swapna M. Banerjee is an Associate Professor of History at Brooklyn College, The City University of New York (CUNY), US. She is the author of *Men, Women, and Domestics: Articulating Middle-Class Identity in Colonial Bengal* (Oxford University Press 2004), a groundbreaking history of employer–servant relationships in colonial Bengal, India.

Fida Bizri is an Assistant Professor of Sinhala and South Asian Linguistics at the Institut National des Langues et Civilisations Orientales, Paris, France. She has written on Sinhala, Lebanese Arabic, language use in Lebanon and migrant pidgins across the Middle East.

Rosie Cox is a Reader of Geography at Birkbeck, University of London, UK. She has been researching paid domestic work for over 20 years and has published widely on the topic, including *The Servant Problem: Domestic Employment in a Global Economy* (I. B. Tauris 2006).

Contributors

Fae Dussart is a Lecturer in Human Geography at the University of Sussex. She has recently completed work on a book, coauthored with Alan Lester and published by Cambridge University Press, entitled *Colonization and the Origins of Humanitarian Governance. Protecting Aborigines across the Nineteenth-Century British Empire.*

Jennifer N. Fish is Chair of the Department of Women's Studies at Old Dominion University in Virginia, US. For the past fifteen years, she has worked with the South African Domestic Service and Allied Workers Union to promote domestic workers' rights and collective organization capacity. She is the author of *Domestic Democracy: At Home in South Africa* (Routledge 2006).

Nicola Foote is Associate Professor of Latin American and Caribbean History at Florida Gulf Coast University. She is the editor of *The Caribbean History Reader* (Routledge 2012) and coeditor of *Immigration and National Identities in Latin America* (University Press of Florida 2014) and *Military Struggle and Identity Formation in Latin America* (University Press of Florida 2010).

Alana Lee Glaser is completing her dissertation, 'A New Day for Domestic Workers: Migrant, Race-minority Women's Caregiving Labor and Cross-Race Activism in New York City,' in the Anthropology Department at Northwestern University in the United States. Her research for the chapter in this volume was supported by Wenner-Gren, Kellogg School of Management, and Northwestern University's Program of African Studies.

Victoria K. Haskins is an Associate Professor of History at the University of Newcastle, Australia. She has published widely on histories of gender, colonization and domestic service, including two books, *One Bright Spot* (Palgrave 2005) and *Matrons and Maids: Regulating Indian Domestic Service in Tucson, 1914–1934* (University of Arizona Press 2012).

B. W. Higman is Emeritus Professor of the Australian National University and Emeritus Professor of the University of the West Indies. He has published a number of chapters and articles on the history of domestic service in Australia and Jamaica and is the author of *Domestic Service in Australia* (Melbourne 2002).

Michele A. Johnson is an Associate Professor in the Department of History, York University in Canada. Her publications include a number of articles and book chapters as well as *Neither Led nor Driven: Contesting British Cultural Imperialism in Jamaica 1865–1920* (University of the West Indies Press 2004) and *'They do as they please': The Jamaican Struggle* *for Cultural Freedom after Morant Bay* (University of the West Indies Press 2011) with Brian L. Moore.

Claire Lowrie is a Lecturer in History at the University of Wollongong, Australia. She has published a number of articles and chapters on the history of domestic service and is currently working on a book manuscript, titled *Masters and Servants: Cultures of Empire in the Tropics, 1880–1930*, under contract with Manchester University Press.

Charlotte Macdonald is Professor of History at Victoria University of Wellington, New Zealand-Aotearoa. She is author of *A Woman of Good Character: Single Women as Immigrant Settlers in Nineteenth Century New Zealand* (Allen and Unwin1990), and *Strong, Beautiful and Modern* (UBC Press 2011).

Jane McCabe is a Teaching Fellow with the Department of History and Art History at the University of Otago in Dunedin, New Zealand. She recently completed her doctoral dissertation examining the lives and labors of 130 Anglo-Indian adolescents raised at St. Andrew's Colonial Homes in Kalimpong in India and resettled in New Zealand.

Mary Jane Logan McCallum is an Associate Professor in the Department of History at the University of Winnipeg in Canada and a member of the Munsee-Delaware Nation. Her book *Indigenous Women, Work and History 1940–1980* is forthcoming with the University of Manitoba Press.

Pamela Nilan is Professor of Sociology at the University of Newcastle, Australia. Professor Nilan has published widely on youth and school-to-work transitions in Indonesia, Australia, Vietnam and Fiji. Her most recent book is *Adolescents in Contemporary Indonesia* (Routledge 2013), with Lyn Parker.

Maria Platt is a Research Fellow at the Asia Research Institute, National University of Singapore. Her work focuses on issues relating to gender, sexuality and religion within the Southeast Asian region, with a particular focus on Indonesia, and has appeared in *Ethnos: Journal of Anthropology*, *The Asia Pacific Journal of Anthropology* and *Intersections: Gender, History and Culture in the Asian Context*.

Shirleene Robinson is a Vice Chancellor's Innovation Fellow in the Department of Modern History at Macquarie University, Australia. Her major publications include *Something Like Slavery? Queensland's Aboriginal Child Workers, 1842–1945* and the edited collection, *Homophobia: An Australian History*.

Steven Threadgold is a Senior Lecturer in Sociology at the University of Newcastle, Australia. His research interests focus on inequality and youth, especially the interplay between class, risks and governmental discourses. His most recent work is on young people's construction of 'DIY Careers' and on the ways figures such as 'hipster' and 'bogan' are invoked to perform distinction whilst eschewing the very notion of class.

Index

Note: Page numbers with *f* indicate figures; those with *t* indicate tables.

Aboriginal child domestic servants, in Australia 97–108; assimilation policies and 100–1; civilization through labor ideology and 98–9; colonization and 99–104; domestic service impact on 104–7; educational reform and 100; good demand for 97, 104; laws involving 100; missions and reserves for training of 103; overview of 97–8; protective legislation for 100, 183; reformatory convictions and 99–100; reforming, by separation 100; sexual abuse of 106–7

Aboriginal missions: as labor reserves 100–1; training of domestic servants and 103; underfunding of 100

Aboriginal Protection Act 184, 187

Aborigines: assimilation and 100–1; as domestic workers 97–108, 182–90; employment of 102, 103, 104–7; eugenic theories 101; removal to missions and reserve 103

abuse: of Aboriginal adults in occupation 107; of Aboriginal children in occupation 104–5, 106–7; of Afro-Caribbean women 301–2, 304; of au pairs 265; sexual, of Aboriginal child domestic servants, in Australia 106–7

Accession Eight (A8) workers 256–7, 259–60

activism: colonial histories and 340–2; contemporary representation and 342–4; domestic workers and 337–40; global protections and 328–31; International Domestic Workers Network, founding 332–6; postcolonial, building workers movement 331–2; strategies within bureaucracies 336–7; transnational 329, 330, 333, 342

An Act to Amend and Consolidate the Laws Respecting Indians 195

An Act to Repeal the Masters and Servants Law 79

advice manuals 157, 158

Afro-Caribbean women: abuse of 301–2, 304; American expatriates and 294, 303–4; domestic service opportunities for 296; experiences of, in Latin America 291–2; imprisonment of 301–2; sexuality of 298–9, 303

Afrocentric ideology of motherhood 84–5

Afro-Creole culture 79

age of discharge, Indian Act 195–6

agriculture, colonies and 30, 33

Aliens Emergency Regulations, New Zealand 280

amahs 133, 219

ambivalence, of racialized intimacy 53–7, 58

Andolan 173

Anglo-Indian (mixed-descent): children in New Zealand 67–70; immigration restrictions 64; infectious accent of 64; "lady-help" 63–76; women, as servants 64

Anglo-Indian (European), employers of servants 1559, 1614, 167
anti-white woman rhetoric 222
anxiety, of racialized intimacy 53–7
apartheid 49, 50, 56–7, 59
Apprentices and Servants Act of 1851 158
Arabic diglossia 115
Arabic language 115
art/aesthetics, in South African cities 45, 58, 59
Aruba 303
aspiration, Queen Sophie and 45, 59
assault 153; by Anglo-Indian (European) employers 156; bringing cases of 158; reporting, in India and Britain 159–66; servant freedom from, rights 158–9; sexual 299–300
assimilation 192, 275; Aborigines and 100–1; Australia policies 100–1; cultural, Canadian Indian residential schools and 192
A2 migrants 267–8
Auckland 273, 278, 279, 284
au pair policy, UK 256–69; applications of 258–9; colonial history and 261; domestic workers and 263–4; overview of 256–7; Points Based Immigration Scheme (PBS) and 257–60; racialization and 260–4; solution to 264–8; as solution to servant problem 265
au pairs: abuse of 265; defined 256; differences amongst 266; feelings of discrimination against 267–8; regulation of 259–60; women as 265
au pair visa 258, 266
Australia: female Aboriginal domestic labor in 8–9; Indigenous peoples as domestic workers in 8
Australia, domestic workers in 97112, 18290, 21031
Australia Aboriginal assimilation policies 100–1
Australian Workers Union (AWU) 225
authority 19–20
ayah 58, 64, 65–6, 74

Babies Cottage 64
Baby Halder 239–52; life history of 242–3; see also *A Life Less Ordinary* (Baby Halder)

Bali 310, 314, 315–16, 319
Balinese cruise ship workers 309–24; colonialism and service 310–17; neocolonialism 317–23; overview of 309–10; salaries 315
'Baltic Cygnet' scheme 262–3
Barambah reserve 97
Barbados 295, 297
Bengal: cult of domesticity in 8; female authors from 245–6; feminization of domestic service in 8, 240–2; upper castes/class women in 240, 241; Western modernity in 239; women reforms in 239–40
Bermuda 295
bhadramahila 240
blackness, in Latin America 292, 302, 304
Black Peril scares 56–7
black settler colony 22
bondage 34
Brazil 297–8
Bringing Them Home (study) 97
Britain: au pairs in 265–6; cult of domesticity in 261; domestic workers in 153–61, 256–72, domestic worker preference in 256; Latvian European Volunteer Workers (EVWs) in 262; white domestic workers and 261–2
Britain servant-employer relationships 153–68; capitalism/colonialism and 155–7; court cases and 153–4; laws governing 158–9; overview of 153–5; servant assault, reporting 159–66; violence against servants and 157–9
British Caribbean *see* Latin America, British Caribbean women migrants in
British Empire 273, 275
British Guiana 297
British North America Act at Confederation 191

Canada, domestic workers in 191–209
Canadian First Nations 150
Canadian Indian residential schools 191–206; age of discharge disputes at 194–5; correspondence 193–204; cultural assimilation and 192;

funding of 192; gender and division of labor at 192–3; gender disparity in discharge practices at 199–200; half-day system 192–3; history of 191–2; maintaining, female students and 199–200; other voices 204–5; overview of 191–3
capitalism 34–5, 260; servant-employer relationships and 155–7
care-chains 34
Carnival Australia 309
caste: issues, in India 67–8; potter 242; upper, Bengal women 240, 241
CCMA *see* Commission for Conciliation Mediation and Arbitration (CCMA)
Cherbourg Aboriginal Settlement 186
childcare, au pairs and 258, 266; domestic service in Jamaica and 81–6; age of nursemaids 82–3; classified newspaper advertisements 81, 82; as employers concern 82; importance of 90–1; length of time for 85–6
child dispersal 82
child saving ideology 97, 98, 108
child shifting 82
China, socialism and 34
Chinese houseboys *see* houseboys
Chinese Revolution 211
Chinese servants 210–11
City (suburb of Johannesburg) 46–7
civilization through labor ideology 98–9; problem populations and 98–9
class: coolie 214; difference 261; domestic service and 7; England categories of 156–7; in India, and disciplining servants 158; issues in India 67–8; racialization and 261; upper, women in Bengal 240, 241; white working, on holiday 311
collective bargaining 176
Collingham, Elizabeth 157–8
colonial India: culture 250–1; domestic workers in 240; Indian citizens in post- 246; modernization process in 240
colonialism: domestic service in Jamaica and 80–1; servant-employer relationships and 155–7

colonialism, cruise ship service and 310–17; overview of 310–11; passengers and 311–12; Southeast Asian staff 312–14; transnational cruise industry 314–17
colonial nostalgia 309, 312, 323
colonial powers 25*t*
colonial relations 273, 275–6, 280
colonies: characteristics of 19–20; classifying 20–2, 23–6*t*; definition of 311; dependencies and 19–20, 21; settler 21–2, 23*t*; status of 34; types of 21–2
colonization 28; Aboriginal child removal and 99–104; authority and 19–20; definition of 2, 20–1; domestic service and 19–20; domestic service patterns and 32–3; hierarchy and 20, 21; historical outline of 3–4; impact of, through domestic service in Australia 104–7; present-day forms of 2
colony servant-employer relationships 153–68; capitalism/colonialism and 155–7; court cases and 153–4; laws governing 158–9; overview of 153–5; servant assault, reporting 159–66; violence against servants and 157–9
coloured race 225
Commission for Conciliation Mediation and Arbitration (CCMA) 47, 50
Commission on the Status of Women (CSW) 333
Committee Against Asian-American Violence 173
communism 211
community unionism, legal exclusion and 175–6
compulsory schooling 196
Confederation of Domestic Workers in Latin America and the Caribbean (CONLACTRAHO) 330
Contagious Disease Ordinance 133–4
continuity, domestic servants and 33–5
Convention 189 328–9, 330, 335, 336, 341, 342–3, 345
Cook Islands: housegirls from 276–8; waged employment in New Zealand and 277–8
Cook Islands Progressive Association 281

358 *Index*

coolie class 214
Costa Rica 291, 299, 301–2
critical feminist practice 239, 249, 252
Crown Law Office, New Zealand 280
cruise ship workers *see* Balinese cruise ship workers
Cuba 290, 294
Cullwick, Hannah 236, 243–4
cult of domesticity 7–8, 261
cultural exchange 258, 260, 264, 268
Curacao 294

Darwin 210–26; Australian Federation and 212; domestic work hierarchy in 213–14; houseboys and 214–17, 215–16*f*; master-servant relationship 214–17; mistress-servant relationship 220–3; overview of 210–12; politics and 223–5; servants per household in 212–13; as settler colony 212; trade unionism and 225; transcolonial traditions of 212–14; white mistresses and 217–20
decent work conditions, in South Africa 49
Decent Work for Domestic Workers 328, 330, 332, 336, 340, 342, 345
decolonization 2, 4, 19, 22, 174, 235, 273–5
decolonizing 273, 274–5
demography 31–3
the Department *see* Department of Indian Affairs (DIA)
Department of Indian Affairs (DIA) 193–4; domestic service placement and 201; domestic training and 191, 193, 204, 205; young Native adults and 202; *see also* Canadian Indian residential schools
Department of Island Territories 278, 281, 282
dependencies 19–20, 21
desire, education of 55
dialectal fragmentation 117
difference: au pairs and balancing of 264; class 261; natural, between workers and employers 264; racialization and 263–4, 266, 269; between Western and Eastern European au pairs 267–8

dirty work 48
displacement, Baby Halder and 246–9
distancing, intimacy and 51
domestic colonialism 55
domesticity, colonial 54, 55, 56, 57
domestic labor: Canadian Indian residential schools and 191–206; male 7
domestic servants *see* domestic workers
domestic service: abuse of Aboriginal adults in occupation 107; abuse of Aboriginal children in occupation 104–5, 106–7; Anglo-Indian lady-help and 63–76; apartheid 56–7, 59; authority and 19–20; in British India 64; Chinese categories of 133; class and 7; colonization and 32–3; decolonizing and 2, 4; defined 1; empires and 19, 21, 22, 29; employment relation and 19–20, 26–7; feminization of 8, 32, 214, 240–2, 290; gender and 6–7; global patterns of 19, 34; historical outline of 3–4, 19–20; impact on Aboriginal children 104–7; in India 239; Indigenous labor studies of 8; in Latin America 289–304; mothering discourses in Jamaican 79–91; in New Zealand 273–85; patterns of 27–31; race and 7; re-masculinization of 4; scale of Aboriginal workforce 97, 98; sexuality and 6–7, 54–5, 131–45, 297–303; tasks 102, 105; technology and 102; *see also* domestic service, intimacies and anxieties of
domestic service, intimacies and anxieties of: in Australia 97–108; colonial aspect of 3, 41; Jamaica, mothering in 79–81; in Johannesburg, South Africa 45–60; in New Zealand 63–76; overview of 41–3; in Singapore 131–44; Sri Lankan housemaids in Lebanon 113–27; *see also individual headings*
domestic service placement 201
domestic service scheme 273–4, 276
domestic training 191, 193, 204, 205
domestic work: defined 27; in Zambia 6–7; *see also* domestic service

Index 359

domestic workers: Aboriginal children, in Australia 97–108; Aboriginal women, in Australia 182–90, 214; Aboriginal men, in Australia 217, 214; Anglo-Indian (mixed-descent) women and girls, in New Zealand 63–78; Black American 5; British women, in the U.K. 153–71; Canadian Indian, in Canada 191–209; Carribean women 79–96, 172–81, 289–308; characteristics of 19–20; Chicana, in United States 5; Chinese men, in Australia 210–31; communications technology and 141–2; contemporary proportion of, per colony 29; continuity and 33–5; Cook Island women, in New Zealand 273–88; defined 26–7; dependencies of 19–20; Eastern European, in the U.K. 256–72; female percentage of 23–6t, 31–2; Filipina 114–5, 125, 131–45, 176, 264, 274; fiscal surveillance of 141; foreign, in Singapore 131–44; gender and 23–6t, 31–2; income and 30–1; Indian men in British India 153–71; Indian women in India 239–55; Indonesian, in Singapore 131–45; Irish women 258, 262; othering of 137; Latina, in the U.S. 89, 172–81, Native American 5; occupations of 31–2; per thousand population 23–6t, 28; physical and social mobility concerns 140; protection of 134–5; religion and 32–3; servant-employer relationships, England and India 153–68; South African women, in South Africa 31, 45–62, 322; Sri Lankan, in Lebanon 113–30; status of 34; transnational migrations of 9; West African, in New York City 172–81; see also domestic service
Domestic Workers Bill of Rights 173
Domestic Workers Convention 13
Domestic Workers United (DWU) 150, 172; formation of 173–5; members of 173
domination, in mass cruising 324
domination and resistance: Canadian Indian residential schools 191–206; Darwin domestic politics 210–26; domestic worker organizing, postcolonial New York City 172–80; overview of 149–51; servant-employer relationships, Metropole and Colony 153–68; survival tactics, Aboriginal women 182–90
doomed race theory 100–1
Dutch East Indies, colonial domestic service in 7–8

economic development: servant growth and 19, 34; stages of 19
educational reform, in Australia 100
empires, domestic service and 19, 21, 22, 29
employer control, lack of 131
employer-maid relationship in Singapore 137–43
employment relation 19–20, 26–7
enclaves, economic 289, 293, 296
England: class categories 156–7; domestic service, gender dynamics of 157; servant-employer relationships 153–68; violence against servants 157–9
Englishness 157
EU 15 256
European Economic Area (EEA) 258
European Union (EU) 256, 265
European Volunteer Workers (EVWs) 262
exploitation, in mass cruising 324
exploitation colony, Singapore as 212

factory work, New Zealand 278, 279, 282
fair globalization 332, 336
fantasy, Queen Sophie and 45, 58–9
female education 192–3
female percentage of domestic workers 23–6t, 31–2
feminism 47–8; domestic workers and 248–9
feminization: of domestic service in Britian and Europe 214; of domestic service in India 8, 240–2; of domestic service in Latin America 290; of migration 32

Index

feudalism 34
First Nations 191, 193, 203
foreigner talk 118
Foreign Maid Scheme 135
Foreign-Workers Dutch language 117
Foucauldian concept of power 149
free association 284
free labor systems 29
frontier: colonial 47, 58; fantasy and 58–60

gender: domestic servants and 23–6t, 31–2; racialization and 261; violence against servants and 154, 155, 159
gendered judgments 176–8
genocidal practices 3
global care-chains 34
globalization: 2, 175–6, 332–3; of domestic service 34, 179, 251
Graham, John 63–76; church involvement and 68–9; colonial servanthood and 67–8; domestic service scheme of 64; female emigrants to New Zealand and 65; Kalimpong community and 74–5; pupil number growth and 68–9; race and miscegenation attitude of 66; servant-free policy and 66–7; Sinclair, Aileen and 63; St. Andrew's Colonial Homes and 63–4; *see also* New Zealand, Anglo-Indian lady-help in
guest-worker German language 117
Guomindang (National Party) 223

Haiti 301
half-day system 192–3
hierarchy 20, 21
host family 256, 258, 265, 267
houseboys 214–17, 215–16f; alleged sexual perversion of 217; decline in numbers of 225; female migrants and 219; Hainanese *kongsi* role 215; Malayan communist party and 224
housegirls, Cook Island 276–8; illness and 279; moral disaster and 279; as natives 276–7; New Zealand citizen status of 273–4
household technologies 31
housemaids *see* Sri Lankan housemaids in Lebanon
Human Development Index 314

ideological linkages 174
Ilbert Bill 159
ILO *see* International labor Organization (ILO)
immigration: domestic service as a vehicle of, 76; regulation 257, 263; restriction 64, 68, 219, 221, 224, 295; to Australia, 220; to Latin America 289–90, 292–6; to Singapore, 133, 219;
Immigration Restriction Act 219, 220, 280
Immigration Restriction Amendment Act 72
imperialism 211
imperialism-without-colonies 2
imperial metropoles 22, 33
imprisonment, of Afro-Caribbean women 301–2
income, domestic workers and 30–1
indentured labor systems 29
India: Anglo-Indian (European) life in 157; Anglo-Indian (mixed-descent) population in, as problem 63–4; British, beginnings in 65–7; class and caste issues in 67–8; domestic service in 64; domestic workers in 153–71, 239–55; immigration restrictions against 64; institutional training in 64; servant-employer relationships 153–68; violence against servants 157–9; *see also* Graham, John; New Zealand, Anglo-Indian lady-help in
Indian Act 194–5; age of discharge in 195–6; education clauses in 195
Indian idiom 157
Indian Penal Code 159
Indian residential school system *see* Canadian Indian residential schools
Indigenous parents and guardians, letters by 193–204
Indigenous women, importance of 194, 196–7, 202
individualism 244–5
Indonesia 309, 310, 314; as migrant worker sending-country 4
Industrial Schools Act 100
inequality 30, 31, 33–4
institutional training, of Anglo-Indians 64

International Domestic Workers Network (IDWN) 328, 332–6
International labor Conferences (ILC) 330, 332
International labor Organization (ILO) 13, 328–32; Convention Concerning Decent Work for Domestic Workers 27; domestic work definition by 27; domestic worker definition by 27; *see also* activism
International Restructuring Education Network Europe (IRENE) 332
International Union of Food Workers (IUF) 334, 336
interracial sex, racial violence and 211, 226
intimacy: anxieties of 47; dialectic of 51; in domestic service 41–3, 121–2; and estrangement 58; labor of, in South Africa 50–3; personalized 53; politics of 137–43; racialized categories and 132; racialized 47, 53–7, 58; sexualized 56
intimate work 51, 54
Island Council in Rarotonga 281
IUF (International Union of Food Workers) 334, 336

Jamaica 301
Jamaica, mothering discourses in 79–91; childcare, domestic service and 81–6; domestic workers in 79–96; colonialism, slavery and 80–1; exploitation, resistance and 86–91; overview of 79–80
Jamaicans 290, 294–5, 300–1
Jim Crow-era race relations 176, 294
Johannesburg, South Africa, domestic service in 5–6, 45–60; conclusions 58–60; labor of intimacy 50–3; maid as politically obstinate 47–50; as most vulnerable workers 46–7; Queen Sophie tale 45–6; racialized intimacy, anxieties of 53–7

Kahlin Compound 103
Kalimpong: homes in 65–6; legacies 74–5

labor: bonded 26, 34; free 29; indentured 26, 29; slave 21, 29, 30
labor migration 114, 175, 289–90; 310, 314
Labor Relations Act 176
labor shortage: Britain 70; New Zealand 69, 72, 76
lady-help *see* New Zealand, Anglo-Indian (mixed-descent) lady-help in
language: acquisition of 118; of domination 118, 126; of subordination 113, 118
Latin America, British Caribbean women migrants in 289–304; domestic servants and 292–6; economic opportunity for 297–303; neocolonialism and 303–4; overview of 289–92; race and 303–4; sexuality and 298–9
Latin America, domestic service in 289–304
law, domestic workers 46–7, 49–50
Lebanese Arabic (LAR) language 115, 119–20
Lebanon, Sri Lankan domestic workers in 113–30
legacies and dreams: activism, transnational domestic worker 328–45; au pair policy in UK 256–69; Balinese service staff, cruise ship 309–24; Cook Island housegirls in New Zealand 273–85; domestic service in Latin America 289–304; *A Life Less Ordinary* (Baby Halder) 239–52; overview of 235–7; *see also individual headings*
leisure, focus on 293, 303
A Life Less Ordinary (Baby Halder) 239–52; displacement and 246–9; feminization in India 240–2; history of Baby 242–3; motherhood and 249–51; originality of Baby as author of 243–6; overview of 239–40
like one of the family ideology 51, 70–1, 86–7, 106
lunacy, black immigrant women and 292
luxury seekers 311

maid, as politically obstinate 47–50
'maids and madams' (Cock study) 57
maids in Singapore, managing 135–7
Makatea island 278, 281, 282
Makea Nui 283
males, as domestic servants 31–2, 157, 210–31
mandates 22, 24t
Manpower office 280–1
Maori people 275
Martinique 294, 298
master/mistress/servant relationship 155; 210–31; 244
Masters and Servants Act 79, 81
maternalism 90–1
mem, memsahib, mems 217–22, 243
metropole *see* servant-employer relationships, England and India
Middle East: foreign maids in 113, 115, 126; migration to 114, 116; Sri Lankan domestic workers in 121, 123–4
migrants: A2 267–8; British Caribbean, in Latin America 289–304; houseboys and female 219
migration: cheapness/speed of travel and 34; of domestic workers 28, 31, 32, 64–5, 67, 81, 114, 116, 126, 174, 246–7, 257, 259, 260, 274, 284, 289, 290, 291, 293, 295, 296, 298, 301, 344 *see also* immigration
military bases, as colony classification 21
Miscellaneous Offences Act 135
mistresses 211, 217–20
mixed type, of colony classification 21
mobility, domestic service and 273–4, 276, 284
modernity 289, 290, 292, 303; domestic service and 273, 274
modernization 19, 240; Latin American 290, 292, 293
Modern Standard Arabic (MSA) 115
motherhood, Baby Halder and 249–51
mother surrogates 85
motherwork, explained 79
Mui Tsai Ordinance 134
multiple-voiced subjectivity 245

nanny 48, 53–4, 58
the nanny bill 173
Nanyang General labor Union 223–4

National Domestic Workers Movement 252
nationalism 156, 168, 211
National Minimum Wage (NMW) 259
natives, as Cook Island girls description 276–7
neocolonialism 2, 175, 235–6, 303–4
neocolonialism, cruise ship workers and 317–23; debt burden and 318–19; expectations and reality of 319–20; money as motivation and 318; overview of 317; passenger interactions and 322–3; working conditions and 320–2
New Hebrides 276
newspapers, as sources 150, 154–5, 156
New York City, domestic workers in 172–81; domestic worker organizing in postcolonial 172–80; community unionism and 175–6; Domestic Workers United, formation of 173–5; gendered judgments and 176–8; overview of 172–3
New Zealand: colonial power status of 275; decolonization within 275; domestic service scheme 273–4, 276; domestic workers in 63–78, 273–88, dual-tier structure of race in 277; wartime labor shortage 273; as white settler dominion 273
New Zealand, Anglo-Indian lady-help in 63–76; Anglo-Indian children and 67–70; British India and 65–7; Kalimpong legacies 74–5; labor shortage and 69, 72, 76; New Zealand context of 70–2; overview of 63–5; settling in by 72–4; *see also* Graham, John
New Zealand, domestic service in 273–85; housegirls from Cook Island 276–8; overview of 273–6; Rarotonga Island Council controversy 281–4; repatriation and 279–81
New Zealand Expeditionary Force 277
non-colonies 25–6t
Northern Australian Workers Union (NAWU) 225
nostalgia 309, 312, 323

Index   363

occupation, colonial 21, 22, 24–5t
Occupation Colonies 11
occupations, of domestic servants 31–2
occupied colony 21, 22, 24–5t
oil industry, Venezuelan 293, 294, 296
oil states 28, 34
othering 132, 137, 261
otherness 257, 311
outing system 200

Pacific territories 273–4, 275, 276–7
Pakeha (white New Zealander) 277
Panama 293, 298
Panama Canal Zone 294, 302
Parramatta Native Institution 99
passengers, cruise ship 311–12
pass laws, apartheid 56
pastoral economies 30
paupers 156, 165–6
peasant agriculture 30
permit system, Aboriginal workers and 106
persistent poverty 30
personalism 91
Philippines, as migrant worker sending-country 4
Pidgin Madam language: context-sensitive grammar of 118–21; development and practicality of 121–4; emergence of 114–18; explained 113, 116; grammar examples of 119
pidgins 116–17; Arabic-based 117, 126; grammar of 118–21; industrial labor 117
plantation economy 21, 30
plantations 30
Platform of Demands 330, 333, 336
Points Based Immigration Scheme (PBS) 257–60; Tier 5 259
policing of sex 134
political independence 274–5
politics 223–5
postcolonial Singapore, regulating sexuality in 132–5
potter caste 242
primary hybridization language contact 117
problem populations, reforming 98–9
prostitution, black immigrant women and 292, 298; claims relating to Canadian Indians 203; in Britain and India 153; in Singapore 134, 136
Protection of Women Against Sexual Harassment at Workplace 252
protective legislation, Australia Indigenous people 100
protectorates 22, 24t
Protectors of Aboriginals 103, 104, 105, 106

Queen Sophie tale 45–6

race 154, 155
race/ethnicity, domestic worker as one 237, 247, 260
racial classifications 41
racial codes 294
racialization 291–2, 302; au pair policy and 260–4; defined 261; difference and 263–4, 266, 269; gender and class 261
racialized categories 132
racialized intimacy, anxieties of 53–7
racial recruitment 309, 310, 315
racial segregation 304
racial stereotypes, colonial 304
Rarotonga Island Council controversy 281–4
regulation, cruise line 314, 315, 321
religion: domestic servants and 32–3; Sri Lankan housemaids in Lebanon and 124–5
repatriation, of Cook Island women 279–81
Reserve 195
Resident Commissioner 276, 278, 279, 281, 282, 285
rest day 133
resumption 283–4
rubber industry, Amazonian 294, 297
rule, as colony classification 21

SADSAWU *see* South African Domestic Service and Allied Workers Union (SADSAWU)
St. Kitts 298
St. Lucia 297
secondary hybridization language contact 117
self-writing 239, 244, 245
servant assault, reporting 159–66

servant-employer relationships, England and India 153–68; capitalism/colonialism and 155–7; court cases and 153–4; laws governing 158–9; overview of 153–5; servant assault, reporting 159–66; violence against servants and 157–9

servant problem 131, 156; Anglo-Indian (mixed-descent) population as 63–4, 68–9; British women migrants as 69; racial issues as 67, 72

servant resistance 223–5
service, defined 1–2
service workers 317–23
settlement colony 11, 21, 22, 23–4*t*
settler colonialism 22, 202, 273
settler colony 21–2, 23*t*; Darwin as 212
sexual abuse, of domestic workers 28, 105–7, 299, 303
sexual control, of domestic workers 303
sexuality: of Afro-Caribbean women 298–9, 303; of British Caribbean women migrants 298–9; Chinese men's 217; domestic service and 6–7; of maids in Singapore 135–7; regulating, in Singapore 132–5
sexual violence, Afro-Caribbean women and 301–2, 304
Shepard, Bob 341
Sibande, Mary 45, 59
Sinclair, Aileen 63
Singapore 210–26; domestic workers in 131–45, 210–32; domestic work hierarchy in 213–14; as exploitation colony 212; houseboys and 214–17, 215–16*f*; master-servant relationship 214–17; mistress-servant relationship 220–3; overview of 210–12; politics and 223–5; servants per household in 212–13; transcolonial traditions of 212–14; white mistresses and 217–20
Singapore, foreign domestic workers in 131–44; employment conditions of 134; maids and sexuality of 135–7; overview of 131–2; politics of intimacy and 137–43; regulating sexuality and protecting 132–5

Slavery, 30, colonialism and 21; domestic service and 30–4; domestic service in Jamaica and 80–1; domestic service in Latin America 293–4; rhetoric of 330, 332, 337, 340–3

slave societies 29
social inequality 48
socialism, China and 34
social mobility 65, 69, 71, 76
social regulation 132–5
South Africa, domestic workers in 45–62
South African Domestic Service and Allied Workers Union (SADSAWU) 47
Southeast Asia 309–10, 316
Southeast Asian cruise ship service staff 312–14
Sri Lanka, as migrant worker sending-country 4
Sri Lankan housemaids in Lebanon 113–27; Arabic language and 115; colonization framework for 113; context-sensitive grammar and 118–21; as intimate intruder 121–4; overview of 113–14; Pidgin Madam, emergence of 114–18; religion and 124–5; value system ranking of 124–5
St Andrew's Colonial Homes 63–4; Babies Cottage at 64
state, domestic service and 42–3, 46–7, 49, 52–3
state children 106
statistics, ILO, of domestic workers 27
status: of domestic servants 20; of domestic service workers 34; legal or illegal 27; of male servants *vs.* female 31–2
Status Indian 195
stolen generations policies 100
Structural Adjustment Program 175
student labor 192–3
sugar plantations, Cuba 293

tactics of survival: Aboriginal women 182–90; defined 183
tea-planters 42, 63, 65, 66, 68
technocratic rationality, Singaporean 136

technological change 31
technologies, household 31
tertiary hybridization language contact 117
theories: of plantation economy 30; of servant growth 19; of settler colonialism 22
Third World Women 176, 179
Tier 5 Youth Mobility Scheme (YMS) 259
total institution concept 316
tourism 309, 310, 312, 315, 316–17
trade unionism 156, 211, 225
trading posts, as colony classification 21
transnational activism 330
transnational cruise industry 309, 311, 314–17
Treaty of Strasbourg 265
Trinidad 294, 297
tropics, white women in 217–20
tuberculosis 279
Turner v. Mason 158

Unfinished Business: Indigenous Stolen Wages (SSCLCA report) 97
uniform (dress) 45, 53
United Fruit Company 291, 293
U.S. corporations, British Caribbean labor and 292–3
U.S. imperialism 304
urbanization 19, 31, 34

Venezuela 293, 294, 300
victimhood 45, 47, 58, 59
Victoria Society 295
violence, against servants 54, 157–9; *see also* assault
vulnerability 43, 58, 59
vulnerable workers 49, 53, 57, 58

Wagner Act 176
wealth, domestic service and 19, 21, 30–1, 34
Wellington 273, 278, 279, 284
West Indians 293, 294, 297
white mistresses 211, 217–20
white women (British and Australian): Chinese houseboys and 211, 216; household management in Singapore and Darwin 210, 212–13; power in home and 217
whiteness 257, 262–3; Latvian women and 263
white settler colony 21–2
white working class on holiday 311
WIEGO (Women in Informal Employment: Globalizing and Organizing) 334, 336, 338
women: doubling of 261; feminization of domestic workforce 241–2; modernization process and 240; reform in India 239–40; upper castes/classes of 240, 241
Women and Child Development ministry 252
Women in Informal Employment: Globalizing and Organizing (WIEGO) 334, 336, 338
worker status 259
working holidaymaker 264, 266
World War I, New Zealand Expeditionary Force 277
World War II: domestic service/colonialism and 284; Maori men and 275, 277; modernizing policies and 275; New Zealand and 273

Zambia, domestic work in 6–7